The Gaza Strip
The Political Economy of De-development

Sara Roy

The Gaza Strip
The Political Economy of De-development

Sara Roy

Institute for Palestine Studies
Washington, DC

The Institute for Palestine Studies, founded in Beirut in 1963, is an independent nonprofit Arab research and publication center, not affiliated with any political organization of government. The opinions expressed in its publications do not necessarily reflect those of the Institute.

Library of Congress Cataloging-in-Publication Data

Roy, Sara M.
    The Gaza Strip : the political economy of de-development / Sara Roy.
            p.   cm.
    Includes bibliographical references (p.) and index.
    ISBN 0-88728-260-1. -- ISBN 0-88728-261-X (pbk.)
    1. Gaza Strip--Economic conditions. 2. Gaza Strip--Economic policy. 3. Israel--Economic policy. 4. Palestinian Arabs--Government policy.--Israel.
I. Title.
HC415.25.Z7G397   1995
330.9531--dc20   95-12112

Printed in the United States of America

To the camp people

Our territory is inhabited by a number of races speaking different languages and living on different historic levels. . . . A variety of epochs live side by side in the same areas or a very few miles apart, ignoring or devouring one another. . . . Past epochs never vanish completely, and blood still drips from all their wounds, even the most ancient.

> Octavio Paz
> *Labyrinth of Solitude*

The Jewish state cannot exist without a special ideological content. We cannot exist for long like any other state whose main interest is to insure the welfare of its citizens.

> Yitzhak Shamir
> *New York Times*
> 14 July 1992

There is no primitive. There are other men living other lives.

> Paul Rabinow
> *Reflections on Fieldwork*
> *in Morocco*

Table of Contents

Acknowledgments   xi

Preface   xiii

Part I: **History**

Introduction: The Gaza Strip and the Question of Development   3

Chapter 1:   The Gaza Strip Today: An Overview   13

Chapter 2:   The Development of the Gaza Economy during the British Mandate—The Peripheralization of the Arab Economy in Palestine   31

Chapter 3:   Gaza under Egyptian Military Administration (1948–1967)—Defining the Structure of the Gaza Strip Economy   65

Chapter 4:   The Gaza Strip under Israeli Military Occupation (1967-1987)—A Political History   103

Part II: **Israeli Occupation and De-development**

Chapter 5:   Theories of Development and Underdevelopment: The Particularity of Palestinian Dependence   117

Chapter 6:   The Policy Roots of De-development   135

Chapter 7:   Expropriation and Dispossession   161

Chapter 8:   Integration and Externalization   209

Chapter 9:   Deinstitutionalization   263

Part III: **Continued Economic Dislocations**

Chapter 10: The Intifada—Economic Consequences of a Changing Political Order   291

Chapter 11: The War in the Gulf and the March 1993 Closure—Gaza's Economic Dismemberment   309

Part IV: **The Face of the Future**

Conclusion: The Gaza–Jericho Agreement: An End to De-development?   323

Bibliography   335

Index   365

Maps   373

ACKNOWLEDGEMENTS

I am indebted to literally hundreds of people, without whose assistance this book could not have been written. Many if not most of these individuals, both Palestinian and Israeli, risked a great deal to help me. The people of Gaza's refugee camps, to whom this book is dedicated, deserve special mention. On occasions too numerous to count, they willingly endangered themselves and their families by allowing me to live with them and by escorting me surreptitiously throughout the camps so that I could do my work. No one ever refused me, and no request was ever too great. I cannot name all or even most of them, for they fear retribution. But they know who they are, and I shall never forget what they did for me.

I would like to thank the following people for the roles each played in the writing of this book: Alya Shawa; Talal Abu Rahme; Haidar and Huda Abd al-Shafi; Martha Myers; Meron Benvenisti; Henry Selz; Sharhabeel Alzaeem; Kassem Ali; Abu Abed; Mohammed Abu Shawish; Abu Mahmood; Itaf and her parents; Raba; Halima; Hatem and Aida Abu Ghazaleh; Oun Shawa; the late Assad Saftawi; Mohammed Najah; the men and women of the popular committees; Yassir; Fatma; Salah; Mohammed Zenadine; Abdel Latif Abu Middain; Salah El Ryashi; Mary Khass; Hisham Awartani; Salah Sakka; Hatim Abu Shaban; Samir Badri; Khaled and Salah Abd al-Shafi; Fawaz Abu Sitta; the "bad boys"; Ahmad Abdullah; Rhona Davies; Peter Johnson; Rick Larson; Douglas Ross; Michael Daum; Jake Walles; Agneta Bohman; Jorgen and Carmen Rosendal; Dean and Donna Fitzgerald; Leila Richards; Ulrike Krammer; Klaus

Worm; Rick Hooper; John Viste; Chris George; Lance Matteson; Peter Gubser; Harold Dueck; Lynn Failing; Terry Lacey; Roger Hurwitz; Maxim Ghilan; the teachers and pupils of the Sun Day Care Center; the doctors and nurses of the Ahli Arab Hospital; Munir Fasheh; Salim Tamari; Suad Ameri; Samir Hulayleh; Ibrahim Dakkak; Yusif Sayigh; Charles Shammas; Raja Shehadeh; Afif Safieh; Crist'l Le Clerq Safieh; Avigdor Feldman; Yossi Amitay; Yitzhak Zaccai; Avraham Lavine; the staff of the Truman Center library at Hebrew University and the Dayan Center library at Tel-Aviv University; Yael at the Central Bureau of Statistics in Jerusalem; Frania Freilich; Jean-Luc Porte; Emmanual Marx and his daughter, Dina; Russell Davis; Herbert and Rose Kelman; Elaine Hagopian; Donald Warwick; Bassam Tibi; Judith Kipper; Gail Pressberg; Bill Kirby; Landrum Bolling; Philip Khoury; Philip Mattar; Linda Butler; Mark Mechler; Myron Weiner; Lois Malone; William Graham; Roy Mottahedeh; Susan Miller; Tom Mullins; Theresa Clark; Jeffrey Rubin; Tom McCready; Father Tom Stransky; Father Vincent Martin; Nada Salaam; David Benchetrit; and Bob Simon. I would also like to acknowledge the assistance of the late Merle Thorpe, Jr.

I am most grateful to Walid Khalidi for his unfailing support and patience. He has played a critical role in the preparation of this manuscript.

My heartfelt thanks to the Diana Tamari Sabbagh Foundation, the Institute for Palestine Studies, the Center for International Studies at the Massachusetts Institute of Technology (MIT), the Center for Middle Eastern Studies at Harvard University, and the Center for Contemporary Arab Studies at Georgetown University for making this work possible.

Kate Rouhana deserves honorable mention for her superb editorial work on the manuscript.

I also thank my close friends who have always given freely and generously of their support and encouragement. They include Jill Costa-Jevtic; Leticia Pena; Sharry Floyd; Kim Burnham; Souad Dajani; Clifflyn Bromling; Deena Hurwitz; Steve and Angela Bader; Ellen Greenberg; Gitte Schulz; Bill Hansen; Hilda Silverman; Ellen Siegel; and Gary Taubes.

I especially want to thank my husband Jay, who interrupted his professional training and accompanied me to a place completely unknown to him. Jay worked as a general surgeon in the Ahli Arab hospital in Gaza City and earned the respect and admiration of all who knew him. I love him and treasure him. Most importantly, I thank my mother Taube, a Holocaust survivor, who taught me the importance of truth and the unacceptability of silence. Being apart for so long was difficult for both of us. Her support is something I shall cherish always. A special note of gratitude to my father Abraham, also a survivor of the Holocaust, who believed tenaciously in the power of the written word and who always encouraged me to use it.

PREFACE

R esearch for this book began in the summer of 1985, when I first traveled to the Gaza Strip and West Bank to conduct fieldwork for my doctoral dissertation, which dealt with U.S. development assistance to the occupied territories. This venture was supported by a grant from the Foundation for Middle East Peace in Washington, D.C. During that time, Dr. Meron Benvenisti asked me to prepare a report on conditions in the Gaza Strip under the auspices of the West Bank Data Base Project in Jerusalem, which he headed. I returned to the occupied territories for five weeks in 1986 with funding from the Project, and *The Gaza Strip Survey* was published by the Jerusalem Post Press in May 1986. It was my work on that book more than anything else that educated me to the unique and critical problems confronting the Gaza Strip, and the potential costs to both Palestinians and Israelis of allowing these problems to remain unaddressed. For that and for much more, I shall always be grateful to Dr. Benvenisti.

After publication of the report and a much-needed rest, I returned to my dissertation research, which provided me with an extended avenue for pursuing my interests in the Gaza territory. After receiving my doctorate from Harvard University in June 1988, I returned to the Gaza Strip for ten months between 1988 and 1989 as the intifada was entering its second year. My work was funded by a grant from the Diana Tamari Sabbagh Foundation and a Constantine Zurayk Fellowship from the Institute for Palestine Studies. Gaza had changed in some significant ways under the impact of the Palestinian uprising, and any research effort demanded a study of these changes.

Methodologically, my research consisted of several parts. Interviews were an extremely important component of my work and were conducted on a formal and informal basis with Palestinians, Israelis, Jordanians, Americans, and Europeans. By the end of my stay, I had carried out several hundred interviews with Palestinians from a range of political and socioeconomic backgrounds, in Gaza, the West Bank, and Jordan; Israeli government officials, academics, and political activists; Jordanian government officials, especially those directly responsible for the West Bank and Gaza Strip; American government officials and staff of U.S. private voluntary organizations; officials of UN specialized agencies in Gaza and the West Bank; officials and staff of the United Nations Relief and Works Agency (UNRWA); and European Economic Community officials and European diplomats posted in Israel and Egypt.

Another critical part of my research was based on primary source documentation prepared by the Israeli military government, Palestinian institutions, and UNRWA, and by other international and foreign institutions that asked to remain unidentified. In addition, secondary source materials provided needed supplementary data and were obtained from Israeli, Palestinian, and American universities; Israel's Central Bureau of Statistics; the PLO Bureau of Statistics in Damascus, Syria; and other institutions on both sides of the green line engaged in research on the occupied territories. Those I can identify include *Al-Haq*/Law in the Service of Man, the Arab Thought Forum, the Economic Development Group, the Data Base Project for Palestinian Human Rights, the Jerusalem Media and Communications Center, the Gaza Center on Rights and Law, the West Bank Data Base Project, *B'tselem*/the Israeli Information Center for Human Rights in the Occupied Territories, Yad Ben Zvi Library, the Dayan Center for Middle Eastern Studies and the Jaffee Center for Strategic Studies at Tel Aviv University, the Truman Center for International Studies at Hebrew University, the Dewey Library for the Social Sciences at MIT, the Library of the Center for Middle Eastern Studies and the Center for International Affairs at Harvard University, the Widener Library and the Government Documents Section of the Lamont Library (both of Harvard University), the Central Bank of Israel, the Jerusalem Post Archives, USAID, AMIDEAST, and American Near East Refugee Aid (ANERA).

In addition, I traveled extensively throughout the Gaza Strip and spent a considerable amount of time in the refugee camps where the majority of Gaza's inhabitants live. Experiencing the patterns of daily life together with the people of Gaza—living in their homes, shopping with them in local markets, visiting their injured or sick relatives in hospital, attending the funerals of children and fathers, being confined with them during curfew—was, without question, the most valuable and meaningful aspect of my research.

This study was completed in 1994 after three additional trips to the territory in 1990 and 1993. This volume is a record of my fieldwork, analysis, and conclusions.

PART I:

History

INTRODUCTION

The Gaza Strip and the Question of Development

I n the forty-five years since it became an internationally recognized entity, the Gaza Strip has been called "the forgotten man of the Middle East," "the stepchild of the West Bank," "the black hole of the Arab world," and "Israel's collective punishment." Since its creation, this tiny, artificial entity has known only one political reality—occupation—and two occupiers—Egypt and Israel. The Gaza Strip is the only part of Mandatory Palestine that was never incorporated into a sovereign state, and no Arab nation has ever claimed it as its own. Yet Gaza has remained a critical part of the Palestinian-Israeli conflict: Gaza was where the All-Palestine Government was established in 1948, where the Palestinian uprising (intifada) began in 1987, and where limited self-rule for the occupied territories began in 1994.

Despite its contentious and distinctive history, Gaza has consistently been neglected by Middle East scholars, both Arab and non-Arab. The reasons for this neglect have to do with Gaza's tiny size, weak political culture, and modern historical obscurity. Instead, scholars have treated Gaza as an analytical appendage of the much larger and more widely studied West Bank. However, it is important to examine the Gaza Strip as a separate entity because the Strip, perhaps more than any of the territories occupied by Israel, provides a stark clarification of the intentions as well as the consequences of Israeli policy. Gaza reveals poignantly the lineament and the texture of Israel's occupation, its harsh exterior and banal underside, its unique form and particularistic substance. Gaza dispels the myriad myths and illusions consistently invoked to legitimize Jew-

3

ish control and depicts the bleakness of a future in which that control is allowed to persist. Given the latest breakthrough in Palestinian-Israeli relations, the signing of the Gaza–Jericho Agreement, in which Israel and the PLO agreed to implement partial autonomy in the Gaza Strip and in the West Bank town of Jericho, the need to understand Gaza has never been greater.

Gaza's Economy since 1967

The objective of this study is to analyze systematically the impact of Israeli occupation policy on economic development in the Gaza Strip. As background to the study of Gaza's post-1967 development, the study also traces the political and economic history of the Gaza region. The study explores why, after a decade of rapid economic growth, marked improvements in the standard of living, and substantial international assistance, the Gaza Strip remains one of the most impoverished, underdeveloped regions in the world.

In this study, development is defined as a process of widespread structural change and transformation at all levels of society: economic, social, cultural, and political. It is as much about enhancing the productive performance of the economy to satisfy basic human needs as it is about increasing political freedom and the range of human choice through the elimination of servitude and dependency. However, given the profound economic content of Israel's occupation policy as well as the availability of longitudinal data, development, as measured by the degree of structural change, will be viewed largely through an economic lens. Where applicable, social, cultural, and political factors will be discussed as well.

The central argument of the book is that the relationship between Israel and Gaza is unusual and lies outside existing development paradigms. Instead, this relationship is characterized by an economic process specific to Israeli rule, a process that could be characterized as *de-development*. De-development, it is here asserted, is the deliberate, systematic deconstruction of an indigenous economy by a dominant power. It is qualitatively different from underdevelopment, which by contrast allows for some form, albeit distorted, of economic development. De-development is an economic policy designed to ensure that there will be no economic base, even one that is malformed, to support an independent indigenous existence.

The distinction between underdevelopment and de-development, a distinction that underlies many of the arguments in this study, turns on the specific goals and objectives of the colonizing power. Israel, which meets the four main criteria for settler states (as described in chapter 5), is nonetheless different in one key respect: For better or worse, Israel never sought to promote the interaction of Palestinian society with its own, and through such interaction, to educate and "enlighten" Palestinians. It did not even seek to exploit the Palestinians for economic gain, although that did occur. Rather, it sought primarily to dispossess the Arabs of their economic and political resources with the ultimate aim of removing them from the land, making possible the realization of the ideological goal of building a strong, exclusively Jewish state. The State of Israel was never interested in immediate economic gain from the Palestinians or in keeping the Palestinians in an easily exploitable economic role. Indeed, although Israel built infrastructures relevant to its own economic and political interests, it did not allow the Arab population to interact with these structures or create a token Palestinian business class.

Israel's particular form of settler colonialism has not treated the occupied Gaza Strip and West Bank as separate colonial areas to exploit in the usual settler fashion (i.e., by creating structures that relate to and generate profit for the home state), but has integrated Palestinian resources and labor into Israel as a mechanism to hasten the full incorporation of the land and other economic resources into the Jewish state. In this sense, the economic exploitation of the Palestinians did occur but for goals that were principally political, not economic. Moreover, Israel's ideological and political goals have proven more exploitative than those of other settler regimes, because they rob the native population of its most important economic resources—land, water, and labor—as well as the internal capacity and potential for developing those resources. Thus, not only is the native population exploited economically, it is deprived of its means of livelihood and potential, its national identity, and its sovereignty. This, of course, has had pronounced implications for the indigenous development of the Gaza Strip and West Bank. In the Gaza Strip, it has resulted in de-development.

The study will answer the following questions: How much economic damage has Israeli policy actually caused, and how much good has it done? What has Gaza lost as a result of Israeli rule, and how has it benefited? What was Gaza never allowed to have? How developed or underdeveloped was the Gaza District before Israel assumed control? Is the underdevelopment of the Palestinian economy attributable to the "natural poverty" of the Arab people and the regressive policies of previous Arab occupiers, as Israel has argued? Or was the Gaza region so debilitated and backward that even the most advanced Israeli measures would have failed to promote any substantive economic change or meaningful economic development?

The literature on development theory fails to explain the lack of economic development in the Gaza Strip, let alone describe or even allow for a process of de-development.[1] Existing theories largely relate to former colonies that have gained or will gain majority control and offer some ideas on the difficulties of achieving economic development even within the context of political independence. Chapter 5 provides a brief overview of the general conceptual weaknesses of some of these theories and the reasons they fail to explain the economic situation in Gaza.

The study argues that despite the economic benefits that have accrued to the Gaza Strip as a result of its interaction with Israel, Israeli policy in the Strip has been guided by political concerns that not only hindered but deliberately blocked internal economic development and the structural reform upon which it is based. This study maintains that Israeli control in the occupied territories is motivated not by labor integration, market dependency, or physical infrastructure per se, but by the political imperatives of Jewish sovereignty and the military force needed to achieve them. (Arguably, the establishment of limited self-rule in the Gaza Strip may represent an extension of this policy, albeit in a different form.) That is why, for example, the government of Israel has never articulated a development plan for the Gaza Strip or the West Bank, or why official Israeli investment in Palestinian industry and agriculture has consistently been negligible. Rather, through its policy, the government of Israel has structurally and institutionally dismantled the Palestinian economy as well as undermined the fabric of Palestinian society and the expression of cultural and political identity. The economy is but one (critical) reflection of this phenomenon.

The primacy of political ideology over economic rationality in Israeli policy (an approach that has its roots in the development of the Jewish economy during the British Mandate) has not only precluded the development of the Palestinian economy but those attempts, both indigenous and foreign, to promote such development. This reality is most acute in the Gaza Strip, where the extent of Israeli control has always been greater and the impact of Israeli policy more extreme than it was in the West Bank. The implications of this for the promotion of economic development under conditions of partial autonomy are discussed in the concluding chapter.

Although Israel is the dominant power in Gaza, it has not been and is by no means the only actor influencing the nature of development activity. The Palestine Liberation Organization (PLO) and other Arab regimes also have had a marked impact on the character of economic activity inside the occupied territories, as have other foreign assistance donors, including the European Economic Community (EEC). Their policies are briefly examined in this study.

The subordination of economic factors to ideological and political imperatives in official approaches to the Gaza Strip has posed some quixotic dilemmas for Palestinian development under Israeli occupation: What, if anything, can Palestinians do to resist Israeli policies, particularly when they have little or no control over their own resources, and where appeals on the basis of economic rationality do not hold much strategic weight? What kind of change is possible in a context where, for largely political reasons, Israel is unwilling to allow, let alone promote, those economic activities that would not only benefit the Palestinian economy, but its own economy as well? Can indigenous development ever be initiated in the Gaza Strip? If so, what are its pitfalls? Does the Gaza–Jericho Agreement with its promise of self-rule represent a real departure from past trends, or is it merely a new guise for a fundamentally unchanged structure of occupation?

The question of whether Palestinian economic development is attainable or should even be pursued under Israeli occupation is an extremely sensitive one for both Palestinians and Israelis. Perhaps that is why only a handful of studies deal with this question. Even raising the question incurs political risks for both sides. For Palestinians, it runs the risk of acknowledging the political status quo, normalizing relations with the occupier, and admitting that a political solution other than an independent Palestinian state might be acceptable, though on a temporary basis. For Israelis, it risks acknowledging the legitimate right of the Palestinian people to their own economic development apart from their role as auxiliaries to the Israeli economy. Hence, Israel would have to acknowledge the possibility of an independent Palestinian economy, and most objectionable of all, an independent Palestinian state. Even Israel's acceptance of limited self-rule in the Gaza Strip and Jericho does not as yet represent such an acknowledgement.

Over the course of the occupation, Palestinian literature (and in particular the writings of the PLO) dealt with the West Bank and Gaza as a political question in need of a political solution. Palestinians have not addressed the importance of development and its critical relationship to political change, let alone the articulation of development strategies. Indeed, the Palestinians do not have a coherent development strategy toward the occupied territories.[2] The possibilities created by the Gaza–Jericho Agreement may lead to the articulation of a coherent development strategy for the occupied territories; at present, however, no such strategy is apparent.

Similarly, Israeli political and academic literature has viewed the West Bank and Gaza Strip through the political lens of the Palestinian national movement, as state security concerns or as appendages of the dominant Israeli economy. Economic development inside the occupied territories has been addressed rarely (if ever).[3] A small body of international work has dealt with economic conditions inside the West Bank and Gaza Strip and, to a lesser degree, with the economic viability of a Palestinian state. However, this literature has been restricted largely to formal economic studies of the Palestinian economy (with little if any discussion of external economic relations), much of it devoid of political or nationalist considerations, and to studies that primarily (and often exclusively) describe the impact of Israeli policy on the West Bank economy.[4] Again, the question of development under prolonged occupation has not been seriously considered in any of these studies. By examining the impact of Israeli, Palestinian, and Arab policies on the economic development of the Gaza Strip and the unique dynamics and constraints that characterize this particular environment, this study defines a new variation of development, that is, de-development.

This book is divided into three parts: a political and economic history of the Gaza region and Gaza Strip; Israeli occupation and de-development; and Gaza's future. Part I is divided as follows: Chapter 1 introduces the Gaza Strip and provides an overview of key sectors. Chapters 2–3 discuss the historical antecedents of Palestine's economic development in general and Gaza's economic development in particular. In these chapters the argument is made that the current state of the Gaza Strip economy can be traced back to its economic past and must therefore be understood in relationship to that past. Chapter 2 looks at political and economic developments in Palestine and Gaza during the British Mandate, and argues that the conditions of underdevelopment, commonly attributed to the "natural poverty" of Palestinians and to the regressive policies of occupying Arab governments, are in fact deeply rooted in the complementary policies of the British Mandate and the Zionist national movement. The relationship between the Arab and Jewish communities that evolved during this period provided a political, economic, and philosophical template for Israeli occupation policy. Chapter 3 details the Gaza economy during the Egyptian period and describes the defining contextual features of this period for local economic development. Chapter 4 provides a political history of Israeli occupation as a context within which to view economic developments.

Part II is divided as follows: Chapter 5 discusses the conceptual framework of this study by reviewing different theories and paradigms of development to illustrate the ways in which Palestinian development is unique. In this chapter it is argued that under Israeli rule a new process, de-development, emerged. De-development and its components are defined, and it is distinguished from the process of underdevelopment. Chapter 6 discusses Israel's policy framework for economic growth in the Gaza Strip. Chapters 7 to 9 provide the structural context for economic de-development in the Gaza Strip and analyze the impact of Israeli policy on the indigenous economy. Chapter 7 focuses on the first component of de-development, expropriation and dispossession, and those sectors where this policy has been applied. Chapter 8 discusses de-development's second component, integration and externalization and its sectoral illustrations. Chapter 9 looks at the process of deinstitutionalization, the last component of de-development. Critical constraints to the development process are analyzed, and the context for economic growth and development is defined. The impact of Palestinian and Arab strategies on local development is discussed, and the role of foreign assistance is examined in terms of its ability to overcome the structural and institutional inequities created under occupation and to foster local development.

Part III consists of two chapters: Chapter 10 provides a political context and analyzes the economic impact of the Palestinian uprising on the Gaza Strip. The intifada is analyzed both as a response to and a departure from previous socioeconomic and political patterns. Its contributions to the formulation of an indigenous development strategy are also discussed. Chapter 11 assesses the economic and developmental impact of the Gulf War and the March 1993 closure on the Gaza Strip.

Part IV, the conclusion, looks to the future and discusses the Gaza–Jericho Agreement. The chapter analyzes whether the implementation of limited self-rule in the Gaza Strip as defined in the Declaration of Principles can arrest de-development.

Research in and on the Gaza Strip: Some Methodological Notes

There are many methodological difficulties in conducting research on the Gaza Strip. Some of these problems should be identified so that the reader can determine the strengths and weaknesses of the data being presented.

First, the Israeli government prohibits the disclosure of information dealing with the occupied territories. Employees of Israeli governmental and nongovernmental offices, are unable and often unwilling to release information on the Gaza Strip and West Bank, and numerous requests by the author to obtain information were denied. In particular, data relevant to the study of economic development, such as sector surveys and master plans, are simply impossible to obtain. Official procedures do exist for securing the release of some kinds of information, but such procedures, which require permission from the appropriate government ministry, can drag on for months or years with no guarantee of approval. With the onset of the intifada, reliable data became even more difficult to obtain, particularly from official sources.

Second, the data that are available are often unreliable. For example, the last official census of the Gaza Strip and West Bank was conducted in 1967. Official population statistics and demographic predictions are based on 1967 figures, which makes them questionable at best. Israel's Central Bureau of Statistics (CBS) publishes what is probably the most comprehensive compendium of statistics on the occupied territories. Although most of the CBS data are economic, information about other sectors is also available. One problem with the CBS data is that they are based on a national accounting system for the territories that has no territorial basis. Consequently, economic interaction between two adjacent localities—an Israeli settlement and a neighboring Palestinian town—is considered international trade. The lack of monitoring and control of daily economic exchanges between Israel and the territories further underlines the unreliability of statistical data.[5]

Officials have also indicated that with the outbreak of the intifada, field studies in the territories virtually ceased for one to two years. In 1990, one official at the Bureau openly admitted, "I wouldn't trust much of the data we have, particularly since the intifada. Our researchers are too scared to go into the field."[6] Those same officials warned this author to treat the published data with extreme caution.

Third, official data critical to the study of economic development—for example, an up-to-date population census or planning (e.g., manpower) data—simply do not exist even among Palestinian researchers. Accurate and systematic Palestinian statistics are often impossible to acquire. Even PLO sources on the occupied territories rely heavily on Israeli statistics. The lack of a substantive database on the Gaza Strip is due to several factors, including military orders restricting Palestinians from engaging in many forms of research and a weak institutional infrastructure incapable of supporting research. Given the political constraints on the exchange of information, those Palestinian studies and data that do exist on Gaza are often difficult to obtain, particularly from municipalities, unions, and other local economic institutions, because many are vulnerable to retribution by government authorities.

A fourth problem regards the underuse and inaccessibility of data produced by international (e.g., United Nations Relief and Works Agency [UNRWA], International Committee of the Red Cross) and foreign agencies such as nongovernmental agencies (NGOs) and private voluntary organizations (PVOs) that work in the occupied territories. These agencies do not share information. To the contrary, they are extremely territorial about their information and reluctant to release it.

A fifth problem is data interpretation. On a subject as contentious as Palestinian-Israeli relations, conclusions are often a function of the researcher's biases. The charge of political bias persistently confronts the researcher working in the Middle East. There is no such thing as a totally objective researcher; there is, however, research that attempts to be objective. This book falls into that category.

In conclusion, there may be no absolutely reliable set of statistics on the Gaza Strip. How does this problem affect any attempt, including the present one, to write about the territory? It demands that the author seek information from as many different and opposing sources as possible, seek disconfirming information as a means of testing the validity of different facts and assumptions, and triangulate as much data as possible. All these methods were used in this study.

Notes to Introduction:

1.   It should be mentioned that although the focus of this study is on the Gaza Strip, many points apply to the West Bank as well.

2.   Just prior to the initiation of the October 1991 Middle East peace talks, the Economic Department of the PLO and the United Nations Conference on Trade and Development (UNCTAD) each undertook studies planning for the future Palestinian economy across sectors and under different political scenarios. In addition, several smaller studies were prepared by various organizations in the occupied territories during the last two to three years.

3.   A notable exception has been the work of Meron Benvenisti and the West Bank Data Base Project. For example, see his study entitled *U.S. Government Funded Projects in the West Bank and Gaza (1977–1983) (Palestinian Sector) Working Paper #13* (Jerusalem: The West Bank Data Base Project, 1984).

4.   For example, see Brian Van Arkadie, *Benefits and Burdens: A Report on the West Bank and Gaza Strip Economies since 1967* (New York: Carnegie Endowment for International Peace, 1977); Elias Tuma and Haim Darin-Drabkin, *The Economic Case for Palestine* (London: Croom-Helm, 1978); and Vivian A. Bull, *The West Bank: Is It Viable?* (Lexington, MA: Lexington Books, 1975).

5.   Meron Benvenisti, *1986 Report: Demographic, Economic, Legal, Social and Political Development in the West Bank* (Jerusalem: West Bank Data Base Project, 1986), p. 5. Sarah Graham-Brown also discusses the problems of conducting research in the occupied territories in *Occupation: Israel Over Palestine*, ed. by Nasser Aruri (Belmont, MA: Association of Arab-American University Graduates, 1989), pp. 298–300. Also see the preface in Van Arkadie, *Benefits and Burdens*.

6.   Author's conversation with an official in the Central Bureau of Statistics, Jerusalem, 1990.

1

The Gaza Strip Today: An Overview

The tiny Gaza Strip is an area of extreme, almost impenetrable complexity—geographic, demographic, economic, social, political, and legal. Geographically, it lies wedged between two larger, more powerful countries, Egypt and Israel, both of which have ruled over it in turn. Demographically, it is an area with one of the highest population densities in the world. Two-thirds of the residents are refugees, and nearly half are younger than fourteen years of age. Economically, Gaza remains weak and underdeveloped and at present has virtually no economic base. Socially, the residents of the Gaza Strip consist of three historic groups: urban, peasant, and bedouin. In 1948, the influx of 250,000 refugees irrevocably altered the social structure of the area. Politically and legally, the territory has been under Israeli military occupation since 1967 and was under Egyptian occupation before that. All forms of political activity are prohibited, and the law is defined by more than 1,000 military orders; no one in the Strip carries a passport; everyone is stateless; and no one can leave the territory without permission from the Israeli military authorities.

This chapter introduces the reader to the variations and complexities that characterize the Gaza Strip.

Geography

The Gaza Strip is a roughly rectangular coastal area on the eastern Mediterranean, 28 miles long, 4.3 miles wide at its northern end, 7.8 miles wide at its southern end, and 3.4 miles wide at its narrowest point. It encompasses a total area of approximately 140 square miles. Bordered by Israel on the north and east, Egypt on the south, and the Mediterranean Sea on the west, the Strip's geographical boundaries have remained virtually unchanged since its creation in 1948.

At first, the visitor to Gaza is struck by the dramatic juxtaposition of a serene Mediterranean coastline with teeming poverty and squalor. The Strip appears to be sand rather than soil; however, the aridity of Gaza's sprawling gray desert is punctuated throughout by pockets of lush, green vegetation. The area's seeming barrenness belies remarkable fecundity.

Gaza's considerable topographic variation starts in the northern third of the Strip, a part of the territory belonging to the red sands of the Philistian Plain, and ends in the southern two-thirds, an area (south of Gaza's main watercourse, the Wadi Gaza) considered to form a part of the more fertile sandy loess of the northern Negev coast. Gaza has three narrow, distinct bands of land that extend the length of the territory: a wide belt of loose sands in the west, running from the shoreline to a sand dune ridge 120 feet above sea level; a central depression with highly fertile alluvial soils; and a sandstone ridge in the east extending into the northern Negev.[1] These bands have long shaped agricultural activity and settlement patterns in the Strip.

Gaza City, the largest in the territory, is situated at 31°31' latitude and 34°26' longitude. It rises 132 feet above sea level and belongs to the Coastal Plain, one of four climatological regions in the country. Stretching from Gaza to Acre along the coast and southeast to the Plain of Esdraelon, the Coastal Plain is distinguished by its proximity to the sea, its hot and humid summers (mean summer temperatures of 24–27 degrees Centigrade), and damp and chill winters (mean winter temperatures of 13–18 degrees Centigrade).[2]

History

In the earliest available reference to Gaza, it is described as a Canaanite city-state dating from 3200 B.C., making it one of the oldest cities in the world.[3] Gaza's present debilitation seems antithetic and paradoxical when viewed against its remarkable history of resilience and growth. The city of Gaza (and its environs) experienced a continuous succession of conquerors and occupiers beginning with the Egyptian pharaohs and ending with the Israeli army. From its ancient beginnings down to the present day, the city of Gaza has been attacked and destroyed, and its population enslaved and expelled, by a succession of invaders—Israelites, Egyptians, Assyrians, Scythians, Babylonians, Persians, Romans, Muslims, Crusaders, Mamelukes, Ottomans, British, and Israelis—struggling for its control.

Gaza's contentious history has clearly been shaped by its geographic position. Gaza was of crucial importance to the ancient conqueror attempting to invade Egypt from the north or Palestine from the south. Situated on the *Via*

Maris,[4] a road that ran from Egypt along the coast of Palestine and Phoenicia (with a branch leading eastward to Damascus and Mesopotamia), Gaza also served as a critical commercial link between Egypt and other ancient empires and was considered the southern counterpart of Damascus. Gaza was the key commercial outpost and provisioning center for caravans traveling between Asia and Africa. Whoever controlled Gaza, therefore, could shape the nature of interregional trade at the time.[5] A noted historian, Martin A. Meyer, wrote "...as long as the center of history remained in the Mediterranean world, the fate of nations was mirrored in that of this solitary city."[6]

Prior to 1948, the Strip had no territorial demarcations but was part of the southern district of Mandatory Palestine. The declaration of Israeli statehood in May 1948 precipitated not only the birth of the Gaza Strip, but also its defining social and economic feature, the Palestinian refugee problem. Within days of its geographic delineation, the territory was besieged by 250,000 refugees fleeing the war in Palestine. The Strip's population tripled almost overnight, and the internal dynamics of the territory were altered forever (see chapters 2–3).

Demography

The Gaza Strip is one of the most densely populated regions in the world. By 1993, it was home to about 830,000 people, the overwhelming majority of whom (99 percent) are Sunni Muslim Arabs. There is also a tiny minority of Arab Christians, mostly Greek Orthodox. About 70 percent of Gazans—583,000 people—are refugees of the 1948 war and their descendants. Over half of the refugees still live in camps; the remainder reside in local villages and towns.[7] The annual population growth rate in Gaza is 4 percent, one of the highest in the developing world.

When calculated on the basis of Arab-owned land alone, Gaza's population density exceeds 12,000 people per square mile, which surpasses the density levels of many major American cities. The density levels in the refugee camps are far higher: Jabalya, the largest camp, has a population density equivalent to 133,400 people per square mile, over twice that of Manhattan Island. Population density in Israel, by contrast, is 80 people per square mile.[8]

Gazans live in 13 cities and towns. The five largest and most populous centers are Gaza City, Khan Younis, Rafah, Jabalya, and Deir el-Balah.[9] Population figures for these cities (cited below) include residents of adjoining refugee camps that are located within municipal boundaries.

Gaza City (population 292,999[10]) is by far the largest urban area in the Strip. Indeed, Gaza has retained the largest Arab population of any city in the former Mandate since 1948. Established as a municipality in 1893, Gaza City today encompasses several different quarters, sections, and communities once entered through seven different gates.[11] The city's population explosion and shrinking land resources have placed poverty literally next door to privilege. For example, since 1948, Rimal, a comparatively plush suburb, and the Shati refugee camp have grown incongruously close to each other. In more recent times, Gaza City has also spread to include previously separate communities and housing developments.

Khan Younis (population 160,463) is the Strip's second largest city, a status it has retained since its founding in the fourteenth century by Younis, a Mameluke governor.[12] Situated in the southern half of the Strip, Khan Younis, like Gaza, historically served as an important trade and communications center. It received municipal status in 1912. Since 1945, the population of the city has grown almost eightfold and it has become the second subdistrict capital.

Rafah (population 101,926), south of Khan Younis on the desert's edge, is the third largest city in the Gaza Strip. Nearly as old as Gaza itself, Rafah suffered total physical destruction at the hands of a foreign power on more than one occasion, including the invasion of the Crusaders in the twelfth century. Thereafter, population dwindled until the beginning of this century. It picked up again in earnest during the Mandate period and rose dramatically after 1948.

The fourth largest population cluster in the Gaza Strip is Jabalya, whose popular constituency of 94,710 people also includes the once separate locality of Nazla as well as the Jabalya refugee camp. Located in the lower northwest corner of the territory, Jabalya (which the Israeli authorities still classify as a "village") is an extremely overcrowded town whose population density is exceeded only by that of the neighboring refugee camp. The camp population of 66,710 has spilled into the town, and the municipal services provided by the local village council are increasingly inadequate. The influx of refugees in 1948 also had a dramatic impact on local population growth. In 1945, the town of Jabalya/Nazla alone had only 5,000 residents.

Deir el-Balah, or "the monastery of the dates," is the Strip's fifth largest area, with 38,000 residents. Its location just a few miles south of Gaza City gave it a strategic significance that was not lost on an array of foreign conquerors. During the Muslim conquest of southern Palestine, Deir el-Balah became the site of a fortress, and later, during the Crusades, an important military post.

In addition to these large urban centers, there are eight smaller towns and villages (listed in Table 1.1).

Table 1.1.   Estimated Population of Villages and Refugee Camps in the Gaza Strip, 1992

Village	Population	Refugee Camp	Population
Beit Hanoun	17,000	Jabalya	67,000
Beit Lahiya	20,000	Rafah	62,000
Bani Suhalia	20,000	Beach	52,000
Abasan el-Kabira	9,000	Khan Younis	43,000
Abasan el-Saghira	3,000	Nuseirat	35,500
Khuza'a	4,500	el-Bureij	22,500
Qarara	15,000	el-Maghazi	15,000
Zawaida	10,000	Deir el-Balah	12,400

Of UNRWA's eight refugee camps only Nuseirat, el-Bureij, and el-Maghazi have been allowed to form their own local committees, a category designed to recognize United Nations jurisdiction over refugee housing. These three camps, also known as the middle camps because of their geographic location in the center of the Gaza Strip, are the only ones that are not next to or conjoined with a "major" urban locality (e.g., Shati camp in Gaza, and refugee camps in or near Jabalya, Deir el-Balah, Khan Younis, and Rafah). Table 1.1 provides a population breakdown by camp.

The Gaza Strip is also home to 4,000–5,000 Israeli settlers. Competition over land and water has created considerable hostility between the Palestinian population and the Jewish settlers.

Settlement Patterns

Population centers have always clustered in the central band where the fertile alluvial soils confer clear agricultural advantage. This settlement pattern arose in part due to the linear axis of the ancient Via Maris, the territory's main communications highway, which passed through the central depression and stimulated commerce and employment. Furthermore, settlement in these plains was not as problematic as elsewhere in the country, because there were no swamps.[13]

Since 1967, settlement patterns have been shaped to a far greater degree by Israeli government policy than by any natural resources or commercial trends. The Israeli government has directly confiscated or otherwise assumed control of at least 50 percent of Gaza's land, large portions of which are allocated to the establishment of sixteen Jewish settlements spread across the entire length of Gaza's coastline. Although they comprised one-half of 1 percent of the territory's total population in 1993, Israeli settlers were allotted, per capita, 84 times the amount of land allotted to Palestinians, and they consumed nearly 16 times the amount of water.[14]

To support this massive land confiscation, the government placed myriad restrictions on Arab land acquisition and water use. The combination of declining land resources, escalating land prices, and massive population growth has resulted, in the past decade, in a new phenomenon: the emergence of the outlying community.

At least forty-one outlying communities have already been established. They comprise 10 percent of the Strip's population and lie on 37 percent of its total land area. Small and completely unplanned, these communities are located outside municipal and village boundaries. Many receive no basic services at all, not even water. The typical community consists solely of one family or clan that left a refugee camp or found survival too difficult in a city. Residents engage in simple agriculture and live on a subsistence basis. For many, life is quite harsh and even primitive. Housing may consist of canvas tents or multiroomed cement structures. The population of these small communities ranges from 300 to 6,000. Average family size, however, is quite large, with the smallest consisting of eight people and the largest of fifteen. The number of families living in each of these communities ranges from 20 to 500.[15]

Future settlement in the Gaza Strip will likely occur in the rural areas in the form of these unchecked and unplanned communities. Indigenous development efforts have long neglected these areas but can no longer afford to do so, especially as they expand to encompass over 40 percent of Gaza's territory.

Economy

Prior to 1967, Gaza's economy was weak and underdeveloped despite some limited growth and sectoral expansion. Highly dependent on external sources of income, the economic infrastructure was rudimentary and markets were not integrated. The service sector accounted for the largest share of gross domestic product (GDP) (55.2 percent), followed by agriculture (34.0 percent), construction (6.2 percent), and industry (4.2 percent). Gaza's balance of trade was marked by a huge deficit, where imports exceeded exports almost 3 to 1. In 1966, the total gross national product (GNP) of the Gaza Strip and West Bank combined equalled only 2.6 percent of Israel's GNP. Gaza's GNP, moreover, totalled just 20 percent of the West Bank GNP, and per capita income stood at less than half the West Bank's. On the eve of Israeli occupation, the economy of the Gaza Strip was characterized by a preponderance of services, an agricultural sector devoted almost exclusively to citrus, an industrial sector of marginal importance, a high level of private consumption, and a low level of investment in resources. Per capita GNP ranged from $78 to $106 per annum (see chapter 3).

The occupation of the Gaza Strip brought the Strip's small and unorganized economy into direct contact with Israel's highly industrialized one. Since 1967, the Gazan economy has undergone specific changes, the most significant of which is the employment of Gaza labor inside Israel. Between 1970 and 1987, the number of Gazans crossing the green line, the border between Israel and the occupied territories, grew from 10 percent of the total labor force to at least 60 percent.[16] Wage income earned in Israel did a great deal to stimulate domestic economic growth, especially in the first decade of occupation, by increasing demand in the domestic economy. However, increases in GNP, which were largely attributable to external payments in the form of salaries earned in Israel and foreign remittances, fostered extreme economic dependency at the cost of internal economic development. Contributing only 2 percent to GNP in 1968, external payments increased to 42 percent of GNP in 1987, revealing the weakness of Gaza's internal economy and the lack of structural growth. By 1987, Gaza's economy equalled only 1.6 percent of Israel's GNP (dropping to 1.0 percent by 1992), wheras the combined GNP of the occupied territories had reached only 6.7 percent of Israel's GNP.[17] (See chapters 7–9.)

Social and Political Structure

The residents of the Gaza Strip fall into a variety of crosscutting, seemingly maze-like categories that confound as much as they clarify. Foremost is the social division between groups of different origin: refugees,[18] indigenous Gazans, and bedouin.

The majority of Gaza's refugees live in eight squalid and overflowing camps on sites first claimed by their forefathers in 1948. The remainder live elsewhere in the Strip. The organizational and social basis of camp life is the pre-1948 village of origin. When the refugees left their homes and fled to Gaza in 1948, whole villages, particularly from the coastal areas north of Gaza, were uprooted and transplanted to the Strip.[19] Refugees remained with their relatives and townsmen. As a result, even today, the camps are divided into district quarters, each with its own *mukhtar*, or leader, which preserve the original village framework. Refugees in the camps, even the youngest among them, identify themselves as members of villages that they have never seen, but that they nonetheless can describe in meticulous detail. Even those who live outside the camps feel little allegiance to or identification with the Gaza Strip, despite a steady though incomplete process of interaction and integration. To be a refugee, therefore, is much more than an expression of political status; it is an intimate and indivisible expression of self.

Alongside the refugee community, there are the indigenous Gazans. This social class is distinguished by its lineage, the majority being direct descendents of the territory's pre-1948 residents, and by its power, which, to limited degrees, expressed itself politically. The most prominent are Gaza's small but wealthy elite, composed primarily of landowning families who have traditionally depended on export trade for their income. Other indigenous residents are Gaza's tiny middle class and peasants. The relationship between indigenous inhabitants, especially the rich, and the refugee community has often been strained, even hostile. Disparate social backgrounds and economic conditions and conflicting political agendas have historically fuelled tensions.

Perhaps least understood is Gaza's small bedouin minority. Two tribal confederations with historical ties to the Gaza region still reside inside the territory: the *Hanajreh* and the *Tarabin*. The *Hanajreh* is the largest grouping in the central part of the Gaza Strip and includes five tribes known as Abu Middain, Nuseirat, Sumeiri, Abu Hajaj, and Abu Daher. Traditionally, these tribes planted barley and wheat and grazed their animals on tribal lands located in the central plains of Palestine. During the winter, they settled in the Gaza Strip, where each tribe cultivated additional areas. In 1948, many of the traditional lands belonging to the Abu Middain, Nuseirat, and Sumeiri tribes were incorporated into the Gaza Strip, which allowed them to live on their lands. Lands belonging to the Abu Hajaj and Abu Daher tribes, however, located east of the territory, were lost to Israel, forcing many to settle as refugees in Gaza. The Tarabin tribes were historically concentrated in the southern Strip, near Rafah, where they engaged in trade and wage labor in addition to agriculture. After 1948, many settled on lands in the Rafah area. However, these lands were sorely inadequate for their needs, so those bedouin became refugees and settled in Rafah camp.[20]

Whereas group of origin is a major dividing line in Gazan society, social class is less significant. The reason is that the economic dislocations created in 1948 and 1967 wrought social dislocations that affected all Gazans, although the poor suffered much more than the wealthy. Moreover, the distortion of Gaza's economy—particularly after Israeli occupation, when droves of Gazans were heading to Israel to work—prevented the emergence and delineation of well-defined social classes.[21] Nonetheless, certain class divisions do exist: the upper class—Gaza's landed aristocracy, capitalist farmers, and large merchants; small and tenant farmers or peasants producing for profit and subsistence; the petite bourgeoisie—professionals (such as academics, engineers, teachers, and UNRWA administrative staff) and entrepreneurs; and a working class drawn mainly from the marginalized refugee population.[22] These four classes have been markedly transformed under Israeli rule but have remained, to varying degrees, economically isolated from each other.

Perhaps the most dramatic development in the social structure of the Gaza Strip since 1967 has been the formation of distinct (though loose) political alliances across classes that were totally isolated from each other before 1967. Throughout the occupied territories, Israel's occupation forged alliances that were based almost exclusively on nationalist politics, in a common stand against the political and economic consequences of the occupation.[23] In Gaza, however, these alliances, which contributed to a kind of social cohesiveness among people, were largely unable to breach the economic isolation of social classes, because the occupation affected these groups differently.

The intifada, however, introduced changes that for the first time blurred class distinctions on a socioeconomic level. The political imperatives of the uprising, as well as the mass-based nature of its organization, devalued class-based distinctions and institutionally submerged them. Without question, two of the most important achievements of the intifada were the consolidation and unification of social classes and political factions around common national objectives, and the creation of an institutional structure designed to support and sustain popular unity. Opprobrious economic pressures, which in the early years of the uprising served to unite the population against Israeli policy, combined with the consistent absence of political progress, have taken their toll in the form of new social divisions, increased political factionalism, and interfactional violence. As Gazans become more and more impoverished, class divisions are reemerging along lines that no longer differentiate between upper, middle, and lower income levels, but between those who have some income and those who have none at all.

The confluence of forces inside Gaza has, for the most part, not produced disorder as one might expect, but a peculiar combination of social cohesiveness and political divisiveness. Social cohesiveness derives from a shared set of norms and values, which serve an important integrative function. However, social cohesiveness breaks down in the face of political affiliation, an even more important form of organization in the Gaza Strip. Political divisions are perhaps the most pronounced and deeply felt. They cut across social class distinctions in surprising ways.

Everyone in the Gaza Strip is a political being. Politics directly and immediately influence daily life. Every action, no matter how banal, has political significance. Consequently, politics far transcends party membership or ideological conviction; rather, it assumes a deeply personal, almost primordial dimension that molds individual philosophy and shapes individual action in a profoundly intimate way. Thus, the divisions that characterize the political domain in the Gaza Strip represent much more than a simple difference of opinion; they differentiate one human being from another. One cannot understand Gaza without understanding its politics—not only what is said, but what is meant.

In the early 1990s, at least seven political factions and subfactions claimed the allegiance of Gaza's highly politicized population. Almost every Palestinian in the Strip claims membership in one or more of these categories, and this membership manifestly shapes the individual's worldview. These factions are Fateh, the Popular Front for the Liberation of Palestine (PFLP), the Democratic Front for the Liberation of Palestine (DFLP), the Palestine Democratic Union (FIDA), the Communists (now known as the People's Party), Hamas (otherwise known as the Islamic Resistance Movement), and *al-Jihad al-Islami* (the Islamic Jihad). The primary definitional distinction between these seven factions is their position on the Israeli occupation. The first five espouse a secular, democratic ideology, and fall under the umbrella of the Palestine Liberation Organization (PLO). The last two are based on religious belief and remain distinctly outside the structure of the PLO. The division between these two blocs is fraught with tension and conflict and is most clearly expressed in the conflicts between Fateh and Hamas. Of the PLO factions, Fateh, Gaza's largest party, is the more centrist and moderate, and appears to have remained the most popular, despite considerable ebbs and flows. To the left of Fateh is the socialist PFLP, and then further to the left is the DFLP, a splinter of the Popular Front, and FIDA, a splinter of the DFLP.

Fateh first articulated its support for a two-state solution in 1973, and despite a long-held commitment to armed struggle as a means of attaining national self-determination, has clearly advocated political struggle as well. Despite its small size, the Popular Front has a strong and well-organized following inside Gaza, particularly in the more isolated, southern part of the Strip. The DFLP, FIDA, and the People's Party have tiny constituencies.

Of the two parties of the religious right, Hamas is the largest and most popular. Both Hamas and the Islamic Jihad espouse the same objective—the creation of an Islamic state in all of pre-1948 Palestine. However, they disagree on how to achieve it. Hamas believes that an Islamic state will emerge when

Palestinian society is de-secularized; to that end, it has emphasized internal and societal reform, not military struggle against Israel. The Islamic Jihad, on the other hand, rejects Hamas's reformist approach and holds that an Islamic state can only be created as a result of armed confrontation with Israel. *Hamas*, an acronym derived from the consonants of *Hakarat al-Muqawamah al-Islamiya* (Islamic Resistance Movement), is the strongest Islamist force in Gaza, in part because the Israeli authorities destroyed many Jihad cells and deported Jihad leaders during the 1980s and 1990s. In local elections held in 1992 and 1993, Hamas won control of several organizations and unions, including the Gaza Association of Engineers, one of the most prominent and influential.

The Islamic movement is far stronger in Gaza than in the West Bank. By combining religion with a clear political agenda, Hamas and the Islamic Jihad provide an increasingly attractive and compelling alternative to secular nationalism. Their strength undoubtedly will grow in the 1990s, a pattern that can be found in other parts of the Arab world for many of the same reasons. The strength of Islamism is rooted in the territory's extreme poverty, isolation, and traditional social structure, and its growth has been nourished by a profound sense of popular despair over the steady disintegration of daily life and the consistent failure of the nationalist movement to achieve any political resolution to the Palestinian-Israeli conflict and to end the occupation.

In the aftermath of the Gulf war, as repression heightened in Gaza, Hamas assumed a more militant tactical style. This change in Hamas strategy, if not policy, represented not only an attempt to increase popular support for the organization in its ongoing leadership struggle with the nationalist forces, but a response to the growing influence of the more militant and violent Jihad. With the inception of the Middle East peace process in October 1991, factional violence between Hamas (which opposed the initiative) and Fateh increased markedly. The signing of the Israeli-PLO Declaration of Principles in September 1993, which Hamas fiercely opposes, intensified existing divisions with Fateh and led to greater violence. Also significant is the opposition of the PFLP and DFLP to the agreement, which has caused serious and possibly irreversible fractures within the PLO.

Legal System

The growth of political violence in Gaza occurs, in part, because under occupation there is no legal system to which individuals and groups can appeal. Despite the implementation of limited self-rule in Gaza, the law of the land remains Israeli military law, which is completely separate from and independent of Israeli civil law. According to the terms of the agreement, all legal authority ultimately rests with the Israeli military government. Since 1967, nearly 1,000 military orders have been issued in the Gaza Strip. These orders, which have the weight of laws, regulate all activity in all areas of Palestinian life. In Gaza, only 70 military orders will be abrogated by the self-rule agreement.

The Israeli system of military law in Gaza is self-contained and is not accountable or subject to review by any Israeli governmental body. Palestinians have little effective recourse and the new Palestinian Authority has no power to challenge Israeli legislation in the Gaza Strip.[24] Israeli Jewish settlers, however, are not subject to this military legal system but are governed by Israeli civil law. Thus, settlers continue to enjoy all the rights, privileges, and protections of Israeli law, whereas Gazans enjoy none at all.

The foregoing discussion illustrates some of the complexities of the Gaza Strip, complexities that are invariably overlooked by scholars who fuse Gaza into the West Bank. However, the Gaza Strip is very different and should be examined separately.

Gaza Versus the West Bank

Most studies on the occupied territories focus on the West Bank because of its greater historical, political, religious, and geographical significance. The smaller, poorer, and far more isolated Gaza Strip is often appended to discussions of the West Bank simply by virtue of having been occupied by Israel at the same time. In fact, the differences between the two territories, though commonly overlooked, are significant.

The most obvious distinction is geographic. Gaza is small, circumscribed, and isolated; the West Bank is fifteen times larger, contiguous with another Arab state, Jordan, and exposed to external influence. Gaza's size and location make it easier to control than the West Bank. Gaza's borders are rarely crossed except by its own laborers; the West Bank's borders are far more open. Prior to the intifada, the West Bank received thousands of visitors annually, the Gaza Strip no more than 35.[25]

Socially, Gazans are far more traditional than West Bankers, whose continuous exposure to foreign visitors has bestowed a sophistication and worldview not often found in Gaza.

Demographically, the West Bank has about 700,000 more residents than Gaza.[26] However, given Gaza's substantially smaller size, higher fertility and lower mortality rates, lower rates of emigration, and larger refugee population, population density per square mile is at least fifteen times that of the West Bank.

The differences between the two territories go beyond geography and demography to the very fabric of social structure and political culture. In the Gaza Strip, the decisive majority are refugees and their descendants. In 1948, 250,000 men, women, and children flooded the Strip. They were completely severed from their previous lives in Palestine and alienated from their unfamiliar and grossly insecure surroundings. As a result, class realignments in the post-1948 period were superimposed almost instantly and with traumatic effect. The small size of the territory and its sharply limited resources precluded the refugees' economic absorption or integration. In response to their profound dislocation, the refugees turned inward. They clung to traditional forms of so-cial organization and authority relations, which has given camp life in Gaza a homogeneity that it does not have in the West Bank.

The persistence of traditional structures also prevented the emergence of an effective leadership structure capable of articulating the refugees' needs and interfacing with the indigenous population. Thus, it is no surprise that almost five decades after the loss of their original homes, the majority of Gaza's refu-gees continue to live in camps that are generally much larger than those in the West Bank. By 1993, the average refugee camp in the Gaza Strip held 40,058 people; in the West Bank, 6,542. In fact, some of Gaza's camps are as large or larger than some West Bank towns.

In the West Bank, by contrast, a majority of residents are indigenous. Many Palestinians who escaped to the West Bank in 1948 later left for other Arab countries, notably Jordan, where they were socially and economically integrated. Most of those refugees who remained in the West Bank were ab-sorbed into the cities and towns of the West Bank; the remainder settled in camps. Unlike Gaza's refugees, whose familial and all other ties were severed in 1948, West Bank refugees and residents were able to maintain longstanding ties in Amman and beyond, because the West Bank was formally incorporated into the Kingdom of Jordan. Clearly, the economic and social integration expe-rienced in the West Bank could not have happened in Gaza.

Differences in social structure between the Gaza Strip and West Bank were sustained and deepened by widely divergent political realities until 1967. The former was occupied by Egypt and the latter by Jordan, two countries that at the time were not only politically opposed but pursuing very different poli-cies of political development in the territories under their control. In Gaza, for example, the Egyptian government never made any attempt to incorporate or annex the territory. The Egyptians viewed Gaza as distinctly Palestinian and did little to foster an alternative national identity. The government regularly emphasized the temporary political status of the Gaza Strip, a status it felt could only be resolved through the total liberation of Palestine.

Despite this policy, Egypt spared no pains to suppress most political ac-tivity. Consequently, the Gaza Strip never developed a distinct and well-de-fined political sector. The Egyptian authorities prohibited both the develop-ment of an independent Palestinian political movement and the kinds of institu-tions needed to sustain it. The government also refused most forms of participa-tory politics; all Palestinian officials were appointed. Thus, although political sentiment in the Strip ran high, Gazans were unable to develop their own politi-cal culture and leadership. Moreover, the combination of weak exposure to institutional development and a majority refugee population that was rural, un-educated, poor, and dependent, shaped a political culture that saw violence, not debate, as its primary form of mediation and political action. Gaza's political culture has not changed significantly under Israeli occupation. Indeed, one com-munity activist described Gaza's lack of political development as "a flock in search of a shepherd."

The West Bank's political development under Jordan was quite different. Jordan annexed the West Bank, due to King Abdullah's expansionist objectives and desire to carry the mantle of Palestinian nationalism. Although Jordan placed many political restrictions on the Palestinian community, it did allow West Bankers to participate in national and local government. West Bankers held administrative positions in the government bureaucracy and even in the Jordanian parliament.[27]

Jordanian policy allowed the growth of a differentiated political sector and class structure whose leadership base was not restricted to one class (as it was in Gaza) and where a variety of political, economic, and social interests were represented.[28] By 1967, two classes contended for political and economic power in the West Bank: the traditional landed elite and a new class of urban merchants and traders. In Gaza, only the old landed families had real power, and they had no popular base of support among the majority refugee community. Power was based on economic strength, not political votes.

Thus, the political socialization of West Bank Palestinians diverged sharply from that of Gazans. West Bankers were exposed to institutionalized political forms of participation, where, political constraints aside, disagreements were mediated through organized structures that recognized and valued the role of discussion and debate in resolving disputes and provided an alternative to violence. In this sense, West Bankers received a range of political skills and institutional mechanisms that Gazans never did.

Israeli policy in each of the occupied territories has consistently reflected the fundamental differences between them. The Israeli authorities have always viewed the Gaza Strip with far greater suspicion and mistrust than the West Bank. They have considered Gaza to be angry, restless, and malcontent. As a result, they have exercised much tighter control in Gaza than in the West Bank. For example, Israelis have often relied on brute military repression, particularly against Gaza's refugees, whereas in the West Bank, more indirect forms of cooptation (of "notables" with ties to Jordan and urban middle class merchants with economic interests in maintaining the status quo) have been the mainstay, although by no means the only forms, of control.[29]

The social and political distinctions described have had a pronounced impact on the economic development of the two territories. Not surprisingly, their economies have evolved differently. Some of these economic distinctions are highlighted in later chapters, but in light of the present discussion, give rise to three important questions:

1) Can a common Palestinian economy be created out of two separate and distinct entities that differ economically, socially, politically, and demographically?

2) Given the fundamental differences between Gaza and the West Bank and consistent political pressures not to distinguish between them in any form, can development in the Gaza Strip mean something different from develop-

ment in the West Bank? More importantly, should it?

3) Will the Gaza–Jericho Agreement, with its initial economic and political focus on the Gaza Strip, widen existing differences and antagonisms between the two areas, and decrease rather than increase the possibility of creating a unified political and economic entity?

It is the contention of this study that if in fact a common "Palestinian" economy is to be created in the occupied territories, then development in the Gaza Strip must, in part, be treated as unique and distinct, an approach that Israel has historically rejected and that Palestinians have historically resisted. The imperatives of economic development, unlike those of politics, dictate the acknowledgement of difference, for without such acknowledgement, complementarity, let alone unity, cannot be achieved.

Notes to Chapter 1:

1.   Efraim Orni and Elisha Efrat, *Geography of Israel*, 4th rev. ed. (Jerusalem: Israel Universities Press, 1980), pp. 44–45, cited in Thomas J. Neu, "Employment, Labor Migration and Economic Development in the Gaza Strip: A Case Study of Rafah" (Ph.D. diss., Fletcher School of Law and Diplomacy, Tufts University, 1987), p. 27. See also Elisha Efrat, "Settlement Pattern and Economic Changes of the Gaza Strip, 1947–1977," *Middle East Journal* 31, no.2 (Summer 1977): p. 351.

2.   Government of Palestine, *Statistical Abstract of Palestine 1944–45* (Jerusalem: Government Printer, 1946), p. 5.

3.   Genesis 10:19 indicates that the southern border of Canaan extended as far as Gaza.

4.   The Via Maris was the Latin term for what the Bible (Isaiah 9:1) referred to as "the way of the sea." See Carol A.M. Glucker, *The City of Gaza in the Roman and Byzantine Periods* (Oxford, England: B.A.R. International, 1987), p. 8.

5.   Mordechai Gichon, "The History of the Gaza Strip: A Geo-Political and Geo-Strategic Perspective," in Lee I. Levine (ed.), *The Jerusalem Cathedra* (Jerusalem: Yad Izhak Ben-Zvi, 1982), pp. 291–92.

6.   Martin A. Meyer, *History of the City of Gaza From the Earliest Times to the Present Day* (New York: Columbia University Press, 1907), p. 4. Gaston Maspero, *The Struggle of Nations: Egypt, Syria and Assyria* (London: Society for Promoting Christian Knowledge, 1896), p. 135, makes the same argument. There are only two other books written on the history of Gaza: K.B. Stark, *Gaza und die philistaische Kuste: Eine Monographie* (Jena: Druck und Verlag von Friedrich Mauke, 1852); and Glanville Downey, *Gaza in the Early Sixth Century* (Norman, OK: University of Oklahoma, 1963). A few articles and studies deal with the ancient history of Gaza, notably, A. Guillou, "Prise de Gaza par les Arabes au VII Siecle," *Bulletin de Correspondance Hellenique* 81 (1957): pp. 396-404; Uriel Rappaport, "Gaza and Ascalon in the Persian and Hellenistic Periods in Relation to their Coins," *Israel Exploration Journal* 20 (1970): pp. 75–80; Aryeh Kasher, "Gaza during the Greco-Roman Era," in Levine (ed.), *The Jerusalem Cathedra*; pp. 63–78; and R.W. Hamilton, "Two Churches at Gaza as Described by Choricius Of Gaza," *Palestine Exploration Fund* (January 1930): pp. 178–91.

7.   UNRWA, *Registration Statistical Bulletin For The Fourth Quarter 1992* (Vienna: Relief Services Division, UNRWA HQ, January 1993), p. 7; and UNRWA, *UNRWA General Information Sheet* (Vienna: Programme Planning and Evaluation Office, UNRWA HQ, January 1993). Population figures for any given time vary even within the same agency.

8.   This is when accounting for total land area; when accounting for agricultural lands only, the figure rises to 868.

9.   See Neu, pp. 38–46; and Arab Thought Forum, *Statistics*, Gaza City, 1991.

10.   Figures are taken from The Planning and Research Centre, "Population Break-down" in *Jerusalem Media and Communications Center (JMCC) Weekly Report 9*, Jerusalem, 15 May 1993, p. 7; UNRWA, *Population Data For Camps And Communities Surveyed* (Gaza Strip: UNRWA-Water and Sanitation Department, 1992); Mahmoud Okasha, *Population and Labour Force in the Gaza Strip: Statistical Survey* (Gaza City: Arab Thought Forum, 1990), p. 24. See also Neu, pp. 38–45.

11.   Meyer, p. 109.

12.   Neu, p. 40.

13.   Neu, p. 37; Efrat, p. 351.

14.   See Peace Now, *The Real Map: A Demographic and Geographic Analysis of the Population of the West Bank and Gaza Strip, Report No. 5* (Jerusalem: Peace Now, 1992). The water consumption ratios are based on 1986 figures given the unavailability of 1993 figures. However, it is safe to assume that 1986 estimates have not changed significantly and may even be conservative given the growth of the Arab population and the depletion of water. (The growth of the settler population between 1986 and 1993 was not large enough to alter appreciably 1986 ratios.)

15.   Salah S. Sakkah, *Survey of the Infrastructure Needs of the Outlying Communities in the Gaza Strip* (Jerusalem: Save the Children Federation, 1988).

16.   The Israeli government regards this as a benefit of its rule. See, for example, State of Israel, *Judea-Samaria And The Gaza District—A Sixteen Year Survey (1967–1983)* (Tel Aviv: Coordinator of Government Operations in Judea-Samaria and the Gaza District, Ministry of Defense, November 1983); and State of Israel, *An Eighteen Year Survey (1967–1985)* (Tel Aviv: Coordinator of Government Operations in Judea-Samaria and Gaza District, Ministry of Defense, July 1986).

17.   Gaza's extreme economic weakness is indicated by the assessment of Yad Tabenkin, an Israeli research institute, that the 1988 economy of the occupied territories would have to grow by an estimated 250 percent by the year 2000 if the standard of living in the Gaza Strip was to reach that of the West Bank. See David Rosenberg, "The territories: economic scenario," *The Jerusalem Post*, 23 November 1988.

18.   The word *refugee* in this context is somewhat of a misnomer. A refugee usually refers to someone fleeing to another country. In the Palestinian case, however, individuals fled to areas within their own country, making them displaced persons.

19.   For example, of the forty-six Arab villages belonging to the Gaza subdistrict before 1948, but not incorporated into the Gaza Strip, none remain; all were destroyed by the State of Israel. See Bashir K. Nijim (ed.), *Toward the De-Arabization of Palestine/Israel 1945–1977* (Dubuque, IA: Kendal/Hunt, 1984), pp. 70–73.

20.   Neu, pp. 46–47.

21.   Ziad Abu-Amr, "Class Structure and the Political Elite in the Gaza Strip: 1948–1988," in Aruri (ed.), pp. 77–78.

22.   See Sara Roy, *The Gaza Strip Survey* (Boulder, CO: Westview Press, 1986), pp. 84–86. For an excellent discussion of social class structure in the Gaza Strip, see Abu-Amr, "Class Structure," in Aruri (ed.), pp. 77–98. For a similar discussion of the West Bank, see Sarah Graham-Brown, "Impact on the Social Structure of Palestinian Society," in Aruri (ed.), pp. 361–97.

23.   Jeffrey Paige, *Agrarian Revolution: Social Movements and Export Agriculture in the Underdeveloped World* (New York: Free Press, 1975), underscores the powerful role of nationalist ideology as opposed to class in uniting disparate social groups against a common enemy, the settler class. Cited in Joost R. Hiltermann, *Behind The Intifada* (Princeton, NJ: Princeton University Press, 1991), p. 6.

24.   For a more detailed treatment of the legal system in the occupied territories, see Meir Shamgar (ed.), *Military Government in the Territories Administered by Israel 1967–1980: The Legal Aspects* (Jerusalem: Hebrew University, Faculty of Law, Harry Sacher Institute for Leigislature Research and Comparative Law, 1982); Raja Shehadeh, *Occupier's Law* (Washington, DC: Institute for Palestine Studies, 1988); and Eyal Benvenisti, *Legal Dualism: The Absorption of the Occupied Territories into Israel* (Boulder, CO: Westview Press, 1990). For a study of the impact of military and international law on economics specifically, see Richard T. Drury and Robert C. Winn, *The Economics of Occupation in the West Bank* (Boston: Beacon Press, 1992). See also Raja Shehadeh, "Questions of Jurisdiction: A Legal Analysis of the Gaza–Jericho Agreement," *Journal of Palestine Studies* 23, no. 4 (Summer 1994): 18–25.

25.   This number was calculated by an UNRWA official in Gaza and does not include foreign personnel working in the Gaza Strip.

26.   Census figures are at best reasonable guesstimates. The last census conducted by the Israeli government was in 1967.

27.   Before the intifada, a small pro-Hashemite camp also existed in Gaza, led by Mayor Rashad Shawa, the head of one of Gaza's wealthiest families. Shawa's dislike of Egypt was well known and his tilt toward Jordan was in no small part a function of economic opportunity. As one of Gaza's largest citrus growers, Shawa had a vested interest in expanding Arab trade in and through Jordan.

28.   Amnon Cohen, "The West Bank-Gaza connection," *The Jerusalem Post*, 17 February 1978, discusses some of these differences and their ramifications for the Camp David agreements.

29. Israeli policy consistently met with failure because the government had very little to offer these groups in return for their cooperation and was unable to mute those indigenous forces (e.g., mass-based groups, university students) rising to oppose it. The example of the village leagues, rural-based groups organized and funded by Israel to serve as instruments of local control, is indicative of official approaches and illustrative of

their failures. See Graham-Brown, "Impact on the Social Structure," in Aruri (ed.), pp. 366–71, for a more detailed discussion.

2

The Development of the Gaza Economy during the British Mandate—The Peripheralization of the Arab Economy in Palestine

T he course of economic and political development in the Gaza region has been shaped by three major political events: the conquest of the area by the British, the creation of the state of Israel and beginning of Egyptian control, and Israel's military occupation. Each event had a pronounced effect on economic and social organization in Palestine generally and Gaza specifically, and introduced significant, and in some cases irrevocable, changes into the character of economic life. This chapter and the two that follow deal with each of these historical periods in turn.

The economic history of Gaza is directly tied to that of Palestine, and both were shaped by the political developments of the time. During the Ottoman period, important changes occurred that laid the foundation for Gaza's later economic development. Prior to the nineteenth century internal instability had a pronounced impact on economic activity, particularly in the drastic decline of the agrarian sector in the Gaza region. Beginning in the mid-nineteenth century, however, European interest in Palestine and the restoration of internal order resulted in expanding commerce and the emergence of an export trade that encouraged a shift from subsistence to market production in agriculture. By the end of the nineteenth century, Gaza, with its predominantly agricultural economy, had become a center of local and regional trade, particularly in the export of wheat and barley. Industrial activity was primitive and focused on the production of pottery, woven textiles, and soap.

During this period, Gaza's economic growth, like that of Palestine's, was based primarily on the extension of cultivable land and new and improved market forces. It was not spurred by the introduction of new land reforms, new product lines, or new production methods, nor did it result in any internal economic restructuring. To the contrary, economic change only occurred within the existing social and economic structure. However, the traditional character of economic organization underwent certain changes that included the emergence of large landed estates and a commercial bourgeoisie.[1] Although these changes did not result in the penetration of the capitalist mode of production into the rural economy, they laid the foundation for the subsequent transformation of the Palestinian economy along capitalist lines and the domination of the Palestinian economy by foreign powers under the British Mandate.

The socioeconomic transformation of Palestine began in earnest with the beginning of British colonial rule in 1917. Many of the features that have characterized the Palestinian economy since 1967 originated under the Mandate. Although successive regimes have had their own defining impact on the indigenous economies in the Gaza Strip and West Bank, the policies of the British Mandate, particularly with regard to the creation of a Jewish national home in Palestine and the public sector, set into motion new dynamics that would forever shape the context and structural parameters for Jewish development and Arab underdevelopment in the land both peoples claimed as their own. The complexity of the Mandate period is rooted in the implantation in the Arab Middle East of a European colonial state that was militarily powerful, politically committed to a Jewish national presence in Palestine, and economically committed to the development of capitalism within a precapitalist (or noncapitalist) social formation. Then, as now, economic change was directly tied to political objectives and intentions.

This chapter aims to describe the defining impact of the Mandate period on the economic development of Palestine in general and Gaza in particular. The chapter briefly examines the political history of the period and those Mandate and Zionist policies most critical to Palestine's economic transformation, particularly with regard to the impact of capitalist penetration on the agrarian sector and the dualistic economic development of the Arab and Jewish communities. The Gaza economy is then examined in light of these transformative changes.

Political Background to the British Mandate Period (1917–48)

By the end of World War I the British were in control of Palestine and had established a military government. In 1920, the military government was replaced by a civilian administration; in 1922 the League of Nations formally approved the British Mandate.[2] The twenty-five years leading up to the establishment of the Mandate and of a Jewish state in Arab Palestine were a politically volatile and complex period characterized by profound societal disunity. The defining political features of the Mandate period were the government's official support for the establishment of a Jewish homeland in Palestine and the rise of Jewish and Arab nationalism that inevitably resulted. Palestine was far from being a binational society at this time, but instead existed as a society of two nationalisms.

Jewish aspirations for a homeland gained political expression in the Zionist program articulated at Basel, Switzerland in 1897. Between 1882 and 1922, the number of Jewish immigrants in Palestine grew from 500 in 5 agricultural settlements to 14,140 in 159 settlements, including parts of the southern coastal plain.[3] In 1917, the British government issued the Balfour Declaration, a document authored by British Foreign Secretary Arthur James Balfour, that would change the course of regional history. By declaring its support for "the establishment in Palestine of a national home for the Jewish people" and for policies "that would facilitate the achievement of this object,"[4] the British government sanctioned the Zionist colonization of Palestine and placed the future destiny of Palestine primarily in hands that were not Palestinian. That this was to be done in a way that would not "prejudice the civil and religious rights of existing non-Jewish communities in Palestine" (who constituted 92 percent of the population) presented an inherent contradiction that plagued the Mandate administration throughout its tenure. The government's promise of independence for its Jewish subjects created profound hostility among Palestine's Arab population, which the British failed to see but were soon forced to confront.

In the period following the Balfour Declaration, Jewish immigration flowed into Palestine at an accelerated rate, rising from 9,149 immigrants in 1921 to 33,801 in 1925. By the end of the Mandate, Palestine's Jewish community nearly tripled and comprised one-third of the country's total population. During this time, the *yishuv*, as the Jewish community was known, purchased land from anyone willing to sell, including resident Palestinians, Palestinian absentee and non-Palestinian absentee landowners, and foreign agencies and governments.[5]

The Arab community became increasingly alarmed as the danger to Palestine's national existence grew. The steady consolidation of the *yishuv* with its own national goals also had a clear and defining impact on the development of the Palestinian economic sector. By the time of the second major surge in Jewish immigration following Hitler's rise to power in 1933, the Arab community openly began to pressure the Mandatory government to limit Jewish immigration and land purchases. From 1936 to 1939, the period of the Arab Revolt, it resorted to violent means to do so.[6]

Faced with the acute political reality of Arab rejectionism and rising intercommunal tension, the government appointed a royal commission under Lord Peel to recommend a solution. In May 1937, the Peel Commission recommended the partition of Palestine into three autonomous states or cantons: a Jewish state covering 40 percent of the country's most fertile regions (Jews owned only 5.6 percent of the land at the time); an Arab state (under the control of Emir Abdullah); and a canton under Mandatory administration that would include the holy places of Jerusalem and Bethlehem in addition to the Haifa port.[7]

Grossly offended by any notion of dividing Palestine, especially among three external authorities, the Arab Higher Committee rejected the proposal, whereas the Jewish leadership agreed to support the principle of partition only.[8] The "cantonization" of Palestine was as doomed to failure in 1937 as it was in 1948 for reasons that the Peel Royal Commission itself enunciated:

> [Our recommendations] will not...'remove' the grievances nor 'prevent their recurrence'. They are the best palliatives we can devise for the disease from which Palestine is suffering, but they are only palliatives. They might reduce the inflammation and bring down the temperature, but they cannot cure the trouble. The disease is so deep-rooted that, in our firm conviction, the only hope of a cure lies in a surgical operation.[9]

With war in Europe imminent, the British labored to appease Jewish and Arab demands. In May 1939, the government issued its second official White Paper, which it considered to be a reasonable, if not acceptable, compromise calling for a final fixed quota on Jewish immigration, restrictions on Jewish land purchases, and the establishment of an independent Palestine over a ten-year period. This time, the emphatic rejection came from the Jews and the qualified acceptance from the Arabs. The White Paper intensified the divisions between the two peoples. In so doing, it discredited the government as a legitimate institutional authority and invited popular defiance of its laws.

The final months of the Mandate were chaotic. On 29 November 1947, the United Nations Special Commission on Palestine proposed a partition of the country into two independent states: one Jewish and one Arab. According to this plan, the Jewish state would comprise 56.5 percent of Mandatory Palestine (Eastern Galilee, central Coastal Plain, and most of the Negev), an area in which Jews owned less than 9.4 percent of the land. The population of this state would have included 498,000 Jews and 497,000 Arabs. The Arab state, which included 10,000 Jews, was to be established on 42.9 percent of 1947 Palestine (Western Galilee, central hill region, Jaffa enclave, and the southern Coastal Plain), a territory where Jewish land ownership equalled 0.84 percent. In addition the plan proposed that an international zone be established in Jerusalem on close to 0.6 percent of the land.[10] The Gaza District was to provide a central part of the Arab state in the Mandate territory of Palestine. The UN resolution calling for partition, however, was unanimously rejected by the Arab Higher Committee, as it was by the people of Gaza, who vehemently condemned it because it would lead to the division of their agricultural lands. On 13 May 1948, the Mandate ended; one day later the State of Israel officially came into existence, and the first Arab-Israeli war began.

The Economic Transformation of Palestine: Key British and Zionist Policies

British rule in Palestine intensified and institutionalized many of the economic patterns that had begun to evolve under the Ottomans. However, the Mandate period represented an important structural break with Palestine's Ottoman past. Whereas the Ottoman administration had remained the "organ of a noncapitalist state,"[11] of which the indigenous Arab and Jewish communities were integral and similar parts, the British Mandate established the preconditions for the growth and development of a capitalist sector in Palestine, increasingly segregating the two communities into distinct spheres. British policies also facilitated the integration of the Palestinian economy into the world market.

During the Mandate, the determining features of Palestine's economic development were implanted and institutionalized, features that would be expressed in Israeli occupation policy after 1967. This section looks at (a) the policies of the British Mandatory government, which promoted the social dislocation and proletarianization of the Arab peasant and "insured the long-term growth of the capitalist mode of production [Jewish] at the expense of the noncapitalist mode [Arab]"[12]; and (b) the political-economic imperatives of Zionist colonization, which aimed at creating a system that was not only politically separate but economically autarkic. The policies of the Arab community, although not as critical in shaping Palestine's changing economic reality, no doubt intensified the emerging distinctions between Jews and Arabs through measures that sought to restrain the political development of the Zionist movement but in fact contributed to the economic decline of the Arab sector.[13]

British Government Policies

The context for British policy in Palestine was the Balfour Declaration which regarded a Jewish home in Palestine as small but just compensation to be demanded of the Arab people for the gift of independence they had achieved elsewhere in the region (Syria, Transjordan, Iraq).[14] The British regarded Palestine as a distinct and separate entity within the Arab world. A member of the House of Lords explained why:

> Palestine can never be regarded as a country on the same footing as other Arab countries. You cannot ignore all history and tradition in the matter ... and the future of Palestine cannot possibly be left to be determined by the temporary impressions and feelings of the Arab majority in the country of the present day.[15]

The delegitimization of the indigenous Arab population is explained in part by the racist outlook of the colonial government and by the mutual interests of British colonialism and Zionism. Initially, the granting of the Jewish National Home was an attempt to secure the political support of world Jewry for the Allies during World War I. The British government also believed that with the establishment of such a home, the large capital reserves assumed to be at the disposal of world Jewry would be invested in Palestine, and, through capitalist development, would serve Britain's debt and imperial interests. Palestine was not a typical British colony; it offered few exploitable economic resources. Rather, Palestine's importance lay in its strategic geographic position between Africa and the Middle East.

The economic development of Palestine was therefore shaped by political objectives that reflected Britain's imperial interests—to secure military and political control over the country—and local imperatives—to implement the Jewish National Home and to appease resultant Arab nationalist tensions. Britain's economic policy in Palestine fostered the socioeconomic development of the Jewish sector at the expense of the Arab, through government policies that facilitated Jewish immigration, land purchase, settlement, and capitalist development, and by giving the Zionists time to establish the institutional foundation of a pre-state structure. British policies also encouraged a process of incipient proletarianization among the Arab peasantry that continued long after the Mandate had ended.

The economic transformation of Palestine at both its aggregate and ethnic levels was rooted in the changes taking place within the agrarian sector where the majority of the population worked. For most of the Mandate period, the Palestinian economy remained largely agricultural, especially when measured in terms of national income. By 1938, close to 7.6 million dunums were under cultivation, about 60 percent (4–5 million dunums) of which was devoted to the production of wheat and barley.[16] Much of the cereals produced were for subsistence consumption, and only one-third was marketed.[17] By 1944, 51.4 percent of the population lived in rural areas, although a certain percentage of the rural population engaged in nonagricultural activities. Despite the large number of people living in the agrarian sector, Palestine was not self-sufficient in a range of foodstuffs[18] (much of which were imported) except for citrus, its leading export.

The Arab economy dominated agricultural activity in Palestine, and the overwhelming majority of Arab land was devoted to the cultivation and production of grains—wheat, barley, and dura.[19] These crops, however, were less lucrative than others because they depended on irregular rainfall patterns and inefficient production methods (extensive vs. intensive farming) that yielded the lowest productivity ratio for wheat and barley among the leading agricultural countries of the time. Jewish agriculture also produced grains but was more evenly distributed among other crops—fodder, fruits, and vegetables— and productivity was considerably greater than it was in Arab agriculture. Consequently, only 20–25 percent of Arab agriculture (excluding citrus) was marketed, compared to 75 percent of Jewish agricultural production.[20]

By 1936, more than 60 percent of Arabs were working in agriculture, compared to 21 percent of Jews. The relative contribution of agriculture to national income was more than twice as high in the Arab than in the Jewish sector.[21] The heavier reliance on agricultural employment among Arabs combined with lower output per worker, the incomplete use of labor, the relatively small share of invested capital in agriculture, the oppressive structure of peasant farming, and the competitive disadvantages created by a well-organized, capital-rich, and highly subsidized Jewish economy, contributed to growing Arab rural unemployment (and a per capita national income in the Arab economy that was 40 percent of its Jewish counterpart in 1936).[22]

As the problem of rural unemployment among Arabs increased, the colonial government sought to stem the social disorder and political unrest that accompanied it. It therefore devised policies designed to provide employment for the village worker, who could be employed at a lower wage rate than his urban counterpart. These policies also aimed to preserve the basic mode of production in the Arab agricultural sector and prevent a situation in which large numbers of Arab peasants became separated from their means of production, forcing them into urban areas that could not absorb them.[23] The British government used two modes of recruitment. Before World War II, it created jobs in the rural sector through the Department of Public Works. These jobs were generally within the laborer's area of residence. The government, however, was not seeking to create a rural labor force dependent on the state for its livelihood. The British feared the creation of a rural *lumpenproletariat* and avidly resisted the introduction of any significant change into the prevailing social structure and relations of production. "In fact their main hope of containing and controlling the Arab population was through the preservation and even ossification of the existing patterns of domination."[24] For recruitment, therefore, the government relied on village *mukhtar*s, a class already allied with the government for the purpose of maintaining rural security. By assigning the village notable the role of recruiter, the authorities reinforced the linkage between seasonal wage labor and traditional village organization,[25] and with it, insured a stable peasantry and protected the political, economic, and social status quo against any radical change.

Consequently, the peasant-worker remained economically and culturally tied to his land and to his village. This not only allowed the traditional elite continued powers of control and accountability, but also depressed the wages of those (urban) workers who had no land to which to return. Moreover, the nature of the agrarian regime at this time, characterized by dry farming and acute peasant indebtedness, not only encouraged proletarianization, but precluded total urbanization, because the peasant-worker would return to his land despite his lessened dependence on it.[26] The peasant-worker became a migrant worker. Thus, the state-generated demand for wage labor was an important force behind the exodus of village labor and a critical factor in the transformation of the rural sector. It is important to note, furthermore, that the occupational transformation of village structure did not occur as a result of indigenous economic growth, but as a result of forces external to the local Arab economy. The status of the peasant and the worker were the same.[27]

During World War II, the second mode of labor recruitment emerged. The wartime boom heightened the demand for labor. Increasing numbers of rural workers left the agrarian sector for a variety of occupations in urban labor markets that physically separated the worker from his village. By 1945, 33 percent of the male Arab workforce were employed in wage labor in cities and towns. Despite strong occupational ties to agriculture, the Arab economy enjoyed considerable occupational diversification.[28]

With greater employment opportunities and improved access to them, the peasant found his status as a casual laborer significantly enhanced. This, in turn, weakened his relationship to his village. An even more critical change occurred within the village, where the traditional elite, now deprived of its recruitment function, lost much of its political power and were less able to serve the reactionary interests of the colonial authorities.[29] The traditional nature of village organization, its social structure, and relations of production were beginning to weaken, with no viable alternative available.

Employment opportunities in the public or colonial sector were often temporary and seasonal, and working conditions were appalling. Unlike Jews, Arabs had no government protections such as social security, employment benefits, trade union protection, job security, and few opportunities for training. Furthermore, they were paid one-third the Jewish wage for the same work by the same employer. Nor did the proletarianization of the Arab worker lead to class solidarity and a change in the social order. Arab wage labor never really developed into an identifiable urban proletariat that could challenge Jewish labor or the power of the Arab landowning classes. The small-scale nature of the Arab urban economy,[30] coupled with the fragmented and seasonal nature of the migrant labor force, and the commitment of the Jewish community and British government alike to provide employment for Jewish immigrants, militated against the emergence of a cohesive and well-organized Arab proletariat or working class.[31] Instead, the proletarianization of the Arab workforce fostered continued exploitation by the Arab effendi and Jewish employer, and greater social dislocation. In this way, the village gave way to the shantytown, creating the social and political base for continued violent opposition to Zionist colonization.

The Mandate administration further exacerbated the problems of the Arab producer by pursuing fiscal policies that, in effect, promoted the development of the Jewish capitalist sector at the expense of the Arab noncapitalist sector. First, government expenditure in the five years between 1933 and 1937 was greatest for two single sectors: development and economic services, and defense.[32] The former referred to the development of infrastructural services and public works—the improvement and construction of railways, roads, bridges, communications, telegraphs, harbors, and airports[33]—which were far more important for capitalist (as opposed to noncapitalist) production, largely the domain of the Jewish sector. Outlays for defense supported the maintenance of a security apparatus "continuously and primarily directed against the Arab producing masses."[34] More critical, however, was the system of taxation to which both Arabs and Jews were equally subject, but which exacted greater absolute and relative costs from the Arab than from the Jewish population. Asad, a Palestinian historian, cites three kinds of taxes that had particular significance for the Arab sector: indirect, direct (rural property), and urban property.

Indirect taxation provided the Mandate government with its most important annual source of revenue (50 percent to 60 percent of the total). These taxes were levied primarily on necessities (sugar, butter, fruit, fish, flour, cigarettes, rice, coffee beans) and included custom duties; excise taxes on matches, salt, tobacco, and alcohol; and stamp duties.[35] As the largest source of indirect taxation contributing an average of 46.4 percent between 1933 and 1938, custom duties played an important fiscal role in the Mandate government but one that proved discriminatory in its impact. Custom duties were levied primarily to protect local industry, a predominantly Jewish domain, against the importation of foreign goods, most of them necessities. Consequently, these taxes proved especially regressive because they exacted greater relative costs from the Arab consumer, the poorest and least able to afford a "duty often out of proportion to the value of the goods he consumes."[36] Inflation also had a disproportionately greater impact on Arab consumers.[37] It should be noted that the taxes paid by the nonproductive Arab classes (landowners, urban elites) were a form of indirect taxation on Arab rural labor, because it was the exploitation of the rural producer that provided the landowner with his surplus (some of which was also transferred to the Jewish capitalist sector).[38]

Direct taxes were imposed on land and its products, not on income. As such, direct taxes had greater significance for the agricultural sector, which predominated the Arab economy.[39] The rural property tax was a direct tax paid largely by the Arab peasant. Although it was not an important source of government revenue, it imposed a financial burden on the rural producer. The rural property tax was linked to the *net* annual income earned from the use of land (or industrial buildings in village areas). Land was taxed according to a fixed rate per dunum on the basis of the estimated net annual yield after production costs had been subtracted. Although the taxation of net rather than gross yield eased the cultivator's financial burden, the presumed net return from cultivation did not account for the net return, actual or assessed, to the owner-cultivator.[40]

The direct tax became especially burdensome in times of poor harvests when the cultivator had no money to buy his seed, let alone pay his taxes, forcing him to seek credit or short-term loans at higher interest rates from usurious moneylenders, the government, and commercial banks. In the end, such credit, which for the most part was not linked to finance capital, would only worsen the peasant's debt, increase his vulnerability, and preserve the structural status quo within the rural economy. Clearly, rural indebtedness was not a problem borne of Mandate policy; however, it was most certainly a problem made more acute by that policy.[41]

In industry, where the urban property tax was levied, the outcomes of government taxation policies were no different. Even though the weight of taxation was shifted to large-scale industries that were centralized in the Jewish economy, Arab industry was too small and undercapitalized to compete, despite some expansion at the aggregate level and increased share of total Arab economic output achieved during the wartime expansion.[42] By 1942, the Arab economy employed 8,800 industrial workers; the Jewish economy employed 37,800. Capital investment in Arab industry was only 10 percent of total industrial investment, and gross output accounted for only 15 percent of the total.[43] Moreover, the growth of a modern industrial sector accelerated the dissolution of traditional Arab home industries, which had supplemented the peasant producer's income.

Hence, as structured, the fiscal system not only hindered the development of Arab industry but encouraged and sustained the difference in Arab and Jewish wage rates. In the end, the government did not alleviate unemployment and landlessness among the Arab agricultural population by creating alternative employment or establishing a more progressive system of taxation. Rather, it opted to continue to extract surplus from that same population and preserve those social agents within the Arab economy—providers of rural credit, landowners, and merchants—who made extraction possible. In this way, the rapid expansion of the Jewish sector rested in part on the extraction of surplus from the Arab population, either from farmers or wage laborers. Stated differently, the traditional precapitalist sector of the economy was preserved to serve the process of capital accumulation in the modern, predominantly Jewish sector, ensuring a flow of surplus from the Arab peasantry to the emerging Jewish capitalist mode of production.[44]

Finally, the Mandate facilitated the evolving dualism of the economy by recognizing the legitimacy and institutional autonomy of the quasi-governmental structure developed by the *yishuv* since the earliest days of Jewish immigration. This structure, comprised of several Jewish national institutions[45] (for which the Arab community had no counterpart), served as a parallel government to that of the Mandate and possessed the authority to act in areas of importance to the Jewish community. Most significantly, these institutions were external in origin and thus represented not just the interests of the local community in Palestine, but those of Jews everywhere. As such, they were able to orchestrate the flow of people and money into Palestine on a scale vastly disproportionate to the size of the resident population and served as the locus of economic control for the Jewish community.[46] Between October 1917 and September 1944, for example, the income of the Jewish National Fund equalled 35,633,060 Palestinian pounds (£P), of which 83.9 percent was contributions. The Fund's expenditure during this period totalled £P 35,753,004. The largest single source of expenditure (40 percent) was on agricultural settlements, followed by education and culture (18.5 percent).[47]

British support for the establishment of a Jewish National Home in Palestine defined the political and economic parameters for the dualistic economic development of the Jewish and Arab sectors. Government policies were critical in catalyzing a process of proletarianization among the Arab peasantry. These policies tried to preserve traditional village structure, on one hand, and undermine it on another, leaving the peasant with few viable alternatives. The government's political commitment to the Jewish community was supported by policies that not only facilitated the institutionalization of the *yishuv* but encouraged the penetration of the capitalist mode of production into a largely precapitalist Arab economy that was ill-equipped to deal with it. Thus, the British created structural parameters to which Arab economic growth was strictly confined. Zionist policies, which aimed to achieve a form of economic autarky, reinforced the limitations to which the Arab economy was subject.

Zionist Policies

The political objectives of the Zionist movement in Palestine, which always superceded economic interests, were to establish rapidly as large a Jewish presence as possible, and to create a new kind of Jewish society rooted in the land and productive labor that would reverse the diaspora structure of Jewish life.[48] These objectives, in turn, were based on three fundamental assumptions: (1) Arab opposition to the Jewish National Home was not and could not be based on nationalism, which was not seen to exist among Arabs[49]; (2) the only way to generate Arab acceptance of Zionism was to force it, by establishing "a great Jewish fact in [Palestine]"[50] through heightened immigration and rapid economic growth; and (3) the clear economic benefits arising from the Zionist enterprise would, over time, dissolve all opposition to its presence.[51]

An important component of the Zionist economic platform was that Jewish advances, no matter how disproportionate to those of Arabs, were justifiable as long as the economic position of the Arab community did not worsen.[52] This position clearly implied that economic conditions in the Arab sector should not be compared with those obtained in the Jewish sector, but with the position of Palestinian Arabs prior to Jewish colonization, or with the standard of living obtained by Arabs in neighboring Arab states.[53]

A critical component of the Zionist platform was the call for the exclusive employment of Jewish labor, *avodah ivrit*. This consumed the Zionist labor movement throughout the Mandate period, and "contributed more than any other factor to the crystallisation of the concept of territorial, economic and social separation between Jews and Arabs."[54] In 1947, the United Nations Special Commission on Palestine, writing on the features of the Palestinian economy, observed:

> Apart from a small number of experts, no Jewish workers are employed in Arab undertakings and apart from citrus groves, very few Arabs are employed in Jewish enterprises...Government service, the Potash Company and the oil refinery are almost the only places where Arabs and Jews meet as co-workers in the same organizations....There are considerable differences between the rates of wage for Arab and Jewish workers in similar occupations, differences in the size of investments and differences in productivity and labour costs which can only be explained by the lack of direct competition between the two groups....The occupational structure of

the Jewish population is similar to that of some homogenous industrial countries, while that of the Arabs corresponds more nearly to a subsistence type of agricultural society.[55]

The distinctive features of what could be termed a "bi-national Jewish-Arab dualism,"[56] were clearly evident in Zionist policies on labor.[57] The elimination of the Arab worker from the Jewish sector of the Palestinian economy was a struggle that met with repeated failure, because many settlers considered the use of cheap Arab labor extremely profitable. Later immigrants, imbued with socialist and Zionist ideals, attempted to eradicate what they perceived as the moral decay of Zionism and pursued a policy of "100 percent Jewish labor." It was against the failures of the first Zionist settlements

> that new concepts of colonization took shape: the concept of *the Jewish economy as a closed circuit, in which Jews would fulfill all the functions and which would become independent of Arab labor and food supplies*; the concept of national funds and nationalized land as a basis for colonisation and a guarantee against land speculation and exploitation of Arab labour; the concept of co-operative settlements based on self-labour and motivated by Zionist ideals ....Along with these concepts developed also the strategy of settlement in contiguous areas where *the danger of interaction with Arab population would be minimized and where Jews would rapidly become a majority....*[58]

This feature of Zionist ideology critically distinguishes it from other forms of colonialism. By restricting capitalist relations to Jewish owners and workers, the Zionists did not fulfill "the historically progressive function of colonialism—the generalisation of the capitalist mode of production."[59] Moreover, the Zionist interest in Arab *land* rather than in Arab *people*, of which labor exclusivism was a critical expression, is perhaps the most important factor distinguishing Israeli colonialism from its European counterparts.

Economic separatism was reinforced when, in an attempt to insure a continued Arab majority, the Arab leadership instigated the 1936 revolt. Lasting three years, the revolt was violent in nature and began with an economic boycott of Jewish goods and services. Ben-Gurion understood that the conflict between Arab and Jew was political, not economic:

> Arab leaders see no value in the economic dimension of the country's development, and while they will concede that our immigration has brought material blessing to Palestine, they nonetheless contend—and from the Arab point of view, they are right—that they want neither the honey nor the bee sting.[60]

Ironically, the Arab strike solidified the physical separation of the two communities and underscored the many Zionist invocations of the preceding two decades.[61] All economic contacts between Jews and Arabs ended. For the Jews, the political advantages, in particular, were clear. For the Arabs, short-term political success was achieved at the price of long-term economic decline. In response to these events, the Peel Commission recommended partition instead of integration, which again fueled the separatist interests of the Jewish sector. When the Arab strike ended in 1939, the Jewish community refused any resumption or normalization of relations with the Arab population, staking everything it had on partition.

Policy Effects

British and Zionist policies created a profound crisis in the agricultural sector, where the majority of the Arab population lived and worked. This crisis was precipitated by the rapid penetration of capitalism into a predominantly noncapitalist agrarian society, itself characterized by primitive subsistence and a system of land ownership that was regressive and unproductive.

During the Mandate period, the structure of land tenure and the social relations of production underlying it remained largely unchanged. The overwhelming majority of the land was owned by 250 Palestinian families, whereas 35 percent of the peasantry did not have enough land for subsistence. The ratio of indebtedness to the value of annual production was 1:1 for the Palestinian peasant, compared to a far more favorable ratio of 1:6 for the American farmer and 1:20 for the English cultivator.[62] The famous Johnson-Crosbie Report, commissioned by the government in response to the economic crisis affecting Arab agriculture in the early 1930s, surveyed 25 percent of Palestine's villages in 1930 and found that less than one-third were economically solvent. The survey also found that the average level of indebtedness was £ 27 per family, compared with an average income of £ 25–£ 30, meaning that the cultivator was trapped by his situation, unable to pay his rent and meet other externally imposed financial demands.[63] Under this system, investment in agricultural development simply did not occur, and land reform was an abstract concept. The cultivator was too impoverished, and the landowner, enriched by the rents, had no incentive to invest in measures that would improve production and change the structure of productive relations. In this way, the Johnson-Crosbie survey revealed the response of the productive unit to market forces.[64]

Although the land tenure system was exploitative, the Palestinian village had remained self-sufficient. Indeed, it was the primary social unit that offered the peasant security and protection. During the Mandate, however, this protective village function was increasingly undermined. The weakening of traditional support systems constituted a significant change in the peasant's socioeconomic reality. The introduction of capitalist relations in Palestine dissolved the social structure of village life by creating a new context for the organization of economic exchange in which the *fellah* became increasingly dependent on and vulnerable to external economic forces that ultimately contributed to his total dispossession.

As the self-supporting and highly insulated system of the village began to dissolve and was drawn into national and international markets with which it could not possibly compete, the village economy was converted into an exchange or cash economy, where taxes and debts could no longer be collected in tithes of crops. Small proprietors therefore sold their land to pay their debt,[65] became dependent on wage labor wherever they could find it, and in some cases, became landless as well. Others who had no alternative sources of employment were subject to harsher forms of exploitation by the Arab effendi. Land acquired in this way was sometimes resold to Jewish buyers in order to raise capital for the expansion of Arab citriculture. Thus, land purchases by the Jewish community contributed directly to the commoditization of land in Palestine. Contrary to Zionist claims, however, little of this money reached the tenant farmer. Similarly, the expansion of Arab agriculture, itself a response to the market demands created by the influx of Jewish immigrants, produced benefits that accrued only to the small minority of privileged landowners, whereas unemployment and economic displacement accrued to at least 35 percent of the peasantry.[66]

The Gaza Economy During the Mandate Period

Economic dualism and the resultant disparities between the Jewish and Arab populations were highly visible in the Gaza region. Table 2.1 indicates that in 1944, 95.5 percent of the Gaza subdistrict was owned by Arabs and 4.5 percent by Jews. Indeed, Gaza is a good example of the economic segregation of Jews and Arabs into their own distinct spheres of action. In the aftermath of the 1929 Arab riots, for example, which occurred in several cities including Gaza, Jews had physically disappeared from the southern half of the country, a reality that was secured by official British policy, which prohibited the use of state lands in the Gaza District for purposes of Jewish settlement.[67] In 1930, Jewish land purchases in the Gaza region were less than one percent of total land purchases for that year and only 5.7 percent of total land purchases by Jews between 1930 and April 1935.[68] The Jewish National Fund had purchased only 65,000 dunums in the entire Gaza District; in the Galilee and in Haifa, by contrast, its land holdings totalled 451,700 and 206,400 dunums, respectively.[69] As such, the economic development of this region (which included the future Gaza Strip) illustrates the nature of economic activity in the Arab sector during the Mandate.

Table 2.1.   Land Ownership in the Gaza Region, 1944

(Sub)District/Ownership	Area (in dunums)	% of total
Gaza Subdistrict		
Arab-Owned	1,062,896	95.5
rural	1,033,158[a]	
(cultivable)	(853,984)	(76.7)
urban	6,155	
roads, railways, etc.	23,583	
Jewish-Owned	49,566[b]	4.5
Total	1,112,462	100.0
Beersheba Subdistrict		
Arab-Owned	12,511,769	99.5
(cultivable)	(1,938,659)	(15.4)
Jewish-Owned	65,231[c]	0.5
Total	12,577,000	100.0
Gaza District		
Arab-Owned	13,574,665	99.1
Jewish-Owned	114,797	0.9
Total	13,689,462	100.0

Source: Calculated from: Government of Palestine, *Statistical Abstract of Palestine 1944–45* (Jerusalem: Government Printer, 1946), 273; and Sami Hadawi, *Palestinian Rights and Losses in 1948* (London: Saqi Books, 1988), 254, 232. All calculations are approximations because they derive from different sources. 1 dunum = 1/4 acre.
[a] Hadawi places this at 900,483.
[b] Jews owned land in the following villages: Barqa, Batani, Sharqi, Beer Tuvya, Nir 'Am (Beit Hanun), Beit Jirja, Bi'lin and Ard el-Ishra, Bureir, Deir Suneid, Gan Yavne, Kefar Bitsaron, Gaza (rural), Hamama, Hirbiya, Dorot (Huj), Gat ('Iraq el-Manshiya), Isdud, Kefar Warburg, Masmiya el-Kabira, Najd, Negba, Qastina, Sawafir esh-Shamaliya, Sawafir esh-Sharqiya, Summei Sumsum, Tell et-Turmos, and Yasur.
[c] Jewish-owned land consisted of Tel Tsofim and Ruhama.

It is important to note that during Mandate rule, the term *Gaza* was variously used to describe a town/municipality, a subdistrict, and a district. The Gaza District, one of six administrative units in Mandate Palestine, comprised two subdistricts: Gaza and Beersheba. The Gaza District was the largest in Palestine, accounting for just over 50 percent of the country's total land area. It spanned 13,813 square kilometers (5,333 square miles), of which 13,689 square kilometers (5,285 square miles) were land.[70] The Gaza subdistrict occupied 8 percent of the district area (1,113 square kilometers) and contained 1,112,462 dunums (278,115 acres). (Before 1948, the 360-square kilometer area that is today the Gaza Strip did not constitute an independent economic unit and was not very productive. Rather, it was integrated into the economy of southern Palestine and existed primarily as an export and marketing center for its hinterland.)

One policy objective of the British Mandatory government was the improvement of economic conditions in Palestine, specifically in Gaza. Gaza town, which by then had its own municipal council, was made capital of the Gaza District by the British. The town had been shaken and reduced in size by the two-year battle (1915–1917) for its control between the British and the Turks. The majority of Gaza's 42,000 people fled or were killed. It was not until 1931 that the population reached 17,480. The emphasis on this former Philistine stronghold was in large part the result of its proximity to Egypt, now politically independent but economically a continued part of Britain's sphere of influence.

Although detailed information on the economy of the Gaza region during the Mandate is scarce, available data suggest that it exhibited specific patterns and changes similar to those of the larger Arab economy. These patterns include a predominantly agricultural economy with low productivity, limited employment diversification, the lack of structural transformation, and the preservation of a productive regime that was, to a large degree, precapitalist in character.

Throughout most of the Mandate period, the Gaza subdistrict remained largely agricultural. One-third of Gaza's dunums were cultivable; indeed, Gaza had the highest proportion of cultivated arable land of all subdistricts in Palestine.[71] Although agricultural data vary among sources, a general picture does emerge that suggests that the Gaza District and Gaza town continued to play a marked role in the production and marketing of some of Palestine's key agricultural and export crops, particularly wheat and barley, but also dura, vegetables,[72] citrus, grapes, melons, figs, and other fruits.[73] Of all the land under wheat and barley cultivation in the Arab sector in 1936, for example, 65 percent was located in the Gaza District and 10 percent in the Gaza subdistrict, indicating the region's pivotal role in Arab agriculture and trade. The British promoted a variety of commercial exchanges across the Sinai, and trade continued to form the primary basis of Gaza's economic growth.

In 1936, the Gaza District accounted for at least 36 percent of the total area under cultivation in Palestine, and the Gaza subdistrict accounted for at least 8 percent. Approximately 70 percent of the Gaza subdistrict's arable land was under cultivation. By 1945 Gaza town boasted wholesale and retail markets that played an important role in the country's agricultural marketing system. By the end of the Mandate, according to one observer, Gaza had evolved into

> a rather prosperous market town functioning as a collecting and forwarding center for the citrus, wheat, barley, and dura crops of the Gaza and Beersheva districts. About one-fifth of the whole Palestinian citrus crop and 150,000 tons of cereals were annually collected here and sent north, partly for export to Jaffa. There were small local industries and....[t]he popu-

lation of what is now known as the Gaza Strip [enjoyed good] communications with the outside world. Both a tarmac road and the standard gauge railway line from Egypt to Haifa and Beirut ran through Gaza.[74]

However, although the Gaza and Beersheba subdistricts jointly accounted for a huge share of the area under cultivation in Mandatory Palestine, they had among the lowest productivity ratios for key crops, especially wheat, barley, and dura.[75] In 1935, for example, the Gaza District accounted for 70 percent of the total area under barley cultivation but 30 percent of crop yield.[76] One year later, barley production in the Gaza District fell by 50 percent. Fluctuating output ratios in the Gaza region were primarily due to irregular rainfall patterns, particularly in the desert climate of the Beersheba subdistrict. Declining yields in the mid-1930s also reduced the amount of production available for export, and to a lesser degree, the commercial importance of the Gaza market.

By 1944, the relative levels of production improved slightly for both the Gaza District and subdistrict.[77] Among all districts, the Gaza District produced the largest share of barley and dura, between 20 percent and 24 percent of wheat and melons (despite lower levels of productivity per dunum) and 20 percent of all citrus. In fact, one year before the end of World War II, the Gaza District produced close to 19 percent of total agricultural output (making it second among all districts), whereas the Gaza subdistrict produced close to 15 percent of Palestine's total (making it third among all subdistricts).[78]

Although the Gaza region was largely agricultural, it underwent certain changes in economic activity due in part to the wartime mobilization. Employment patterns in Gaza exhibited a similar diversity to national patterns among Arabs. Although the area that would become the Gaza Strip did not have an independent economic existence at this time, an occupational breakdown of the population living within the area of the Strip by 1947 reveals six occupational groups: (1) landowners who lost most of their holdings in 1948; (2) agricultural workers who lived in the Gaza Strip area; (3) individuals who were employed in the export or manufacture of agricultural products that originated in the Gaza District; (4) individuals who engaged in agriculture within the area that would become the Gaza Strip and exported their products domestically (approximately 20 percent of the population); (5) skilled workers employed by the Mandate authority; and (6) skilled workers employed by companies located outside the Gaza Strip boundaries.[79]

Clearly, agriculture dominated the economy and provided the basis for industrial activities linked to citrus processing and packaging. However, Gaza's important administrative status increased the number of clerical jobs, and the many military bases in the area employed numerous Gazans in construction and services. The discovery of sulphur deposits just south of Gaza in the late 1930s provided many additional, albeit temporary, jobs in mining.[80] However, despite some occupational diversification in the local economy, economic change occurred within a decidedly traditional framework. Indeed, the rising importance of the local Gazan service sector reflected the limited impact of industry and agriculture on employment generation and occupational change, itself indicative of the structural limitations on local economic development. Hence, the changes in Gaza's economy were confined to a social, economic, and political framework that in certain ways had not changed since Ottoman times. Market growth, for example, was not accompanied by changes in economic organization or social relations of production. Palestinians living in Gaza town and the larger Gaza region, like the majority of the Arab population, remained tied to precapitalist agriculture. Although industry had experienced limited growth and diversification, which was linked in large part to agriculture, the development of a modern sector was all but precluded, particularly by the emphasis on trade. In his multivolume history of Gaza, Palestinian historian Arif al-Arif states that by the end of World War II, the city had only eight physicians, eight lawyers, and two engineers. The only resident with a doctorate in chemistry had left for Iraq.[81]

The lack of structural transformation within the Gaza subdistrict economy did not preclude certain improvements in the standard of living, as reflected by specific indicators. However, when compared to changes in the Jewish sector, these same indicators reveal the gross disparities between the Arab and Jewish populations and the existence of two divergent economic realities, and underscore the lack of development in the Gaza area.

The rising standard of living in the Gaza region is supported by indicators such as population growth and declining infant mortality rates. Gaza subdistrict enjoyed considerable population growth during the Mandate period. Table 2.2 indicates that between 1922 and 1945, the population of Gaza town alone virtually doubled, whereas that of Khan Younis almost tripled. Together, they accounted for 33 percent of the population of the Gaza subdistrict in 1944 and were considered among Palestine's twelve principal towns. Table 2.2 also reveals the considerable population growth in the Strip's ten most populous localities (for which data are available).[82]

Table 2.2.   Population of Individual Towns and Villages in the Gaza Strip (selected years)

Locality	1922	1931	1938	1944-45	% Increase 1931-45
Abasan		1,114	1,314	2,230	>100.0
Abu Middein		0	0	2,000	2000.0
Bani Suheila		2,063	2,730	3,220	56.1
Beit Hanoun		849	976	1,730	>100.0
Beit Lahiya		1,133	1,302	1,700	50.0
Deir el-Balah		1,587	1,823	2,560	61.3
Gaza	17,480	21,643	25,782	34,250	58.2
Jabalya		2,425	2,786	3,520	45.1
Khan Yunis	3,890	7,251	8,832	11,220	54.7
Khuza'a*		0	0	990	990.0
Nazla		944	1,085	1,330	40.8
Nuseirat		0	0	1,500	1500.0
Rafah		1,423	1,635	2,220	56.0
Sumeiri		0	0	1,000	1000.0
Total		40,432	48,265	69,470	71.8
Gaza Subdistrict	73,885	94,634	100,250	137,180	44.9
Gaza District	147,349	145,716	n/a	190,880	31.0
All Palestine	757,182	1,035,821	n/a	1,764,520	70.3

Source: 1922—David Gurevich, *Statistical Abstract of Palestine 1929* (Jerusalem: Keren Hayesod), 1930, pp. 25–28; Anglo-American Committee of Inquiry, *A Survey of Palestine, Vol. 1* (Jerusalem: Government Printer, 1946), pp. 147–51.

1931—E. Mills, *Census of Palestine 1931* (Jerusalem: Greek Convent and Goldberg Presses, 1932), 2–6; and *A Survey of Palestine*, pp. 147–51.

1938—Government of Palestine, Office of Village Statistics, *Statistical Abstract of Palestine* (Jerusalem: Government Printer, 1938); and Neu, p. 52.

1945—Government of Palestine, Office of Village Statistics, *Statistical Abstract of Palestine* (Jerusalem: Government Printer, 1945); Neu, pp. 52, 54; and Government of Palestine, Office of Village Statistics, *Statistical Abstract of Palestine 1944–45* (Jerusalem: Government Printer, 1946).

These figures do not reflect the many modifications in community structure that occurred after 1948 and 1967.

* The original name as it appeared in the 1945 census was Khirbet Ikhza'a.

As the Gaza subdistrict population grew, infant mortality declined, an important indicator of economic development. Aggregate figures for the subdistrict are not available. However, figures for subdistrict areas reveal a declining infant mortality rate. Between 1925 and 1944, for example, the infant mortality rate in Gaza town decreased by 10 percent to 158 per 1,000, whereas in surrounding villages, the rate declined by a dramatic 30 percent from 222 to 156. However, the growth of the Gaza region and Gaza town appears less impressive when seen in the context of Jewish growth. For example, from 1927 to 1944, infant mortality rates among the country's Jewish population declined from 100 per 1,000 to 48 per 1,000. The national Muslim infant mortality rate, by contrast, stood at 121 per 1,000 in 1944, which also indicates Gaza's relatively weaker position among Muslims elsewhere in the country.[83]

Gaza's disadvantaged position was clear vis-à-vis towns with Jewish or mixed Jewish-Arab populations, such as Jerusalem, Haifa, Jaffa, and Tel Aviv. In 1920, municipal expenditure in Gaza equalled £ 0.26 per capita compared to £ 0.64 in Jerusalem and £ 0.88 in Jaffa. Between 1924 and 1928, Gaza received only £ 2,305 in government grant-in-aids or £ 0.13 per capita compared to a high of £ 63,637 or £ 1.0 per capita for Jerusalem, revealing but one aspect of the economic disparities between the Jewish and Arab sectors. However, among purely Arab towns in those same years, Gaza fared slightly better, as the tiny government grants of £ 0.03 per capita to Khan Younis and £ 0.002 per capita to Majdal would indicate.[84]

By 1944, municipal revenue in Gaza averaged £ 0.70 per capita (and £ 0.40 in Khan Younis), a slight sum when compared with £ 1.7 per capita for Jerusalem, £ 1.65 for Haifa, and £ 5.2 for Tel Aviv.[85] Expenditure on public works, itself an indicator of Gaza's underdevelopment, reveals similar disparities. Between 1936 and 1944, for example, public works expenditure in Gaza town was approximately £ 0.95 per capita. In Jerusalem, by contrast, public expenditure reached £ 1.75 per capita, £ 3.0 in Haifa, and £ 5.8 in Tel Aviv. Thus, whereas public works expenditure in Gaza accounted for only 1.5 percent of total expenditure for Palestine's twelve most prominent localities, public expenditure in Haifa and Tel Aviv equalled 18 percent and 44 percent of total expenditure, respectively.[86] The same pattern is reflected in building activity.[87]

The economic development of the Gaza region, like that of Palestine, was shaped by Britain's need to secure military control of the country and insure the political status quo. In Gaza, these objectives produced an economic policy that promoted commerce and trade without structurally modifying or investing in the economy. Thus, although the Gaza Strip region enjoyed growth associated with population increase, enhanced agricultural production, improved export marketing, and diversified employment opportunities, the precapitalist organization of economic activity and the methods of production underlying it remained largely unchanged, underdeveloped, and highly inefficient. Some local Gazan producers benefitted from the growing commodity market, but this did not represent the penetration of the capitalist mode of production into local agriculture. Rather, this and other changes in the organization of production are better regarded as temporary adaptations within an existing mode of production to "new conditions created by the world market and the embryonic capitalist enclave."[88] Thus, although some prosperity did accrue to the Gaza area during the Mandate, economic development did not.

Conclusion

The Palestinian economy underwent considerable growth between 1917 and 1945 that was largely attributable to the rapid development of the Jewish economy. By 1944, the Jewish community produced £ 73.4 million, or 60 percent of Palestine's national income, whereas the Arab sector of the economy, having experienced considerable expansion as well, accounted for the remaining 40 percent. Yet the Jewish and Arab sectors were becoming more and more segregated, not only by the level of internal growth taking place, but, more importantly, by the nature of that growth. Whereas the Jewish economy was increasingly characterized by structural transformation and the development of a modern sector along capitalist lines, the Arab economy was, at best, experiencing some sectoral expansion with limited structural change within parameters (i.e., system of land tenure, methods of agricultural and industrial production) that had not fundamentally changed since before the Mandate period. The Gaza region was illustrative of this. The evolution of two distinct socioeconomic orbits was neither entirely accidental nor entirely planned, but the result of policies that combined to limit the interaction between Jews and Arabs, and, in effect, promoted the development of one group at considerable cost to the other.

The period between 1917 and 1948 was important for the socioeconomic transformation of Palestine in general and Gaza in particular. The Palestinian economy grew increasingly differentiated as it moved from a predominantly agrarian base to one that possessed a modern industrial sector. The population of the country doubled as a result of high levels of Jewish immigration and natural increase among Arabs. New patterns of economic development emerged due to the introduction of capitalism in Palestine. Both British colonial policy and Zionist colonization played an important role in the economic and capitalist development of the country, and the Arab economy enjoyed marked growth as a result.

Although it never achieved the same degree of structural transformation as did the Jewish economy, the Arab economic sector was not an abandoned entity as it has been described, particularly when compared to other Arab state economies. Better living conditions contributed to the highest rate of natural increase in the Middle East. The influx of over 300,000 Jewish immigrants stimulated the development of an internal market. Capital transfers to the Arab sector (in the form of payments for land, wages, agricultural trade, and rent) amounted to £ 30 million between 1922 and 1941. These transfers catalyzed the horizontal growth of Arab industry as reflected by the greater number of commercial and industrial enterprises, the expansion of Arab citriculture, the increased urbanization of the Arab population, and enhanced opportunities for education and healthcare.[89] Concomitantly, Arab society experienced profound social differentiation with the emergence of new classes: wage laborers and a new Arab bourgeoisie consisting of middle-class capitalist entrepreneurs in industry and agriculture.[90] The Gaza region reflected some of these trends, including an improved standard of living—population growth and a declining infant mortality rate—some occupational diversification and social differentiation, and enhanced agricultural production and marketing. These indicators suggest that a process of development was taking place. Why, then, did the Arab sector fail to achieve any real economic development?

The answer lies in the economic separation of the Arab and Jewish sectors. More importantly, it lies in the dynamics underlying this separation created by the introduction of capitalist relations, which not only produced structural asymmetries between the two national economies or within the larger Palestinian economy, but created internal dislocations within the Arab sector that both distorted and precluded indigenous economic development. Although British policy was meant to appease mounting Arab anger, in the end its primary outcome was to encourage the development of a modern, well-organized, and highly institutionalized society at the expense of a traditional agrarian one. In doing so, the British authorities helped increase the disparities between the Arab and Jewish communities and inflamed existing hostilities (to the point where "Zionism for the Arabs ha[d] become a test of Western intentions"[91]) and created economic dynamics that would persist for decades. By 1939, therefore, the central problem confronting the aggregate Arab economy was not backwardness or the absence of structural change, but underdevelopment, or the deformation of structural change.

The Arab population in Palestine suffered as a result of the socioeconomic changes taking place during the Mandate. The economic dualism of Mandate Palestine not only prevented the emergence of an integrated Palestinian economy and more equitable sharing of resources (as figures comparing municipal revenue and expenditure in Gaza to other cities and towns in Palestine illustrate), but also removed any possibility for intercommunal interaction along social, cultural, political, or national lines. Those benefits that did accrue to the Arab sector were indirect and were obtained at a very high price—dislocation, dispossession, insecurity—and were beneficial only when compared with the position of non-Palestinian Arabs. In Palestine, the growing disparities and deepening separation between the largely traditional Arab economy and its increasingly modern Jewish counterpart were mediated by the fiscal, employment, and development policies of the Mandate administration, and the political-economic imperatives of the Zionist national movement. The former, in effect, succeeded in transferring surplus from the (predominantly Arab) peasant to the (predominantly Jewish) capitalist and was assisted in this endeavor by the collaboration of the nonproductive Arab classes who both benefited from the dualism of the Palestinian economy and willingly reinforced its structure. Indeed, the new demands of the state and of landowners forced the peasant beyond production for the family, or subsistence, into production of a surplus and into debt when a surplus could not be produced.[92] The Jewish community, armed with comparatively great financial resources, aimed at establishing an autarkic national economy, as part of the larger political project that was the Jewish National Home.

Flapan, an Israeli historian, argues that the autarkic aspirations of the Jewish community during the Mandate were not intended to hurt the Arab population but were aimed at the creation of a new society that would reverse the egregious patterns of economic and social organization that had evolved in the diaspora. Intentions aside, the effects were something quite different. The exclusion and expulsion of Arab labor from Jewish enterprises, for example, and the eviction of Arab peasants from land purchased by Jews are but two illustrations of the practical outcomes of Zionist economic policy. Although these events are less important for their actual impact on the Arab economy (which was limited), they are extremely important for what they reveal about the Zionists inability or unwillingness to understand the implications of their policies for the development of the Arab economic sector, and for Arab public opinion.

Consequently, whether by design or defect, the Zionist movement consistently pointed to the obvious and measurable benefits accruing to the Arab economy as a result of Jewish colonization, benefits which, in the Zionist mind, clearly outweighed the gross differences between their two communities. Jewish writers, for example, pointed to the minimal impact of Jewish land purchase on the displacement of the Arab village population and the greater benefits obtained in wage labor over subsistence agriculture. They mistakenly dismissed the widening disparities between the two economies as irrelevant or as the inevitable outcome of Arab backwardness. Laski typified this attitude when he wrote: "If it is true that the Arab transport industry has suffered, this is quite obviously the outcome of the fact that the donkey and the camel do not successfully compete with the motorcar and the railway."[93]

Not only were Zionists oblivious to the problems attending the economic dominance of one community over another, they also saw no need to assist the Arab economy (such as through the provision of credit to the indebted small farmer) in any *direct* or substantive way. The singular focus on the development of an independent and self-contained Jewish economy evinced an unwillingness to initiate any policy of economic cooperation with the Arab community, which did a great deal to nurture the enduring enmity of that community. Not only was the *yishuv* blind to the dislocating impact of capitalist modernization on rural society, it also did not see (or did not care to see) that the problem of acute unemployment and landlessness among the Arab peasantry, to take two examples, could contribute to the political movement against Zionism.[94]

Economic change brought with it acute social change. Traditional Arab society, where cohesion derived from personal rather than economic ties, eventually found itself threatened by dissolution and weakened by the impact of new political and economic forces such as the changing class position of the Arab peasant from cultivator to wage laborer. It has already been noted, for example, that the wartime boom reversed the economic depression suffered by the Arab sector, when increasing numbers of agricultural workers were drawn into casual wage labor in the cities or near their own villages. Having enjoyed the benefits of occupational mobility and higher wages at the expense of traditional social cohesion, many of these workers were reluctant to return to their home villages when the war ended, adding the problems of urban unemployment and rural reintegration to the internal dislocations of the Arab sector.[95]

In an effort to avert looming economic disaster in the wake of postwar demobilization, the Mandate administration implemented a military construction program that continued to provide employment on a number of military works projects, many of them located near Gaza. (One of Britain's three largest military bases was located in Rafah, with other important military facilities at el-Bureij and Nuseirat.) However, the perpetuation of military works was an inadequate measure, at best an economic palliative that temporarily averted the problem of large-scale unemployment among the Arab labor force, but provided nothing else. Rather, by attracting huge numbers of workers from all over Palestine, the Mandate program fueled the process of labor migration and the social dislocations that attended it, and did so under conditions that were no less insecure and that "played a major though forgotten role in the paralysis and panic that overtook the Arab masses in 1948."[96]

Hence, given the critical changes that redefined the Arab sector during the Mandate period, one can also argue that the Jewish and Arab economies did not develop separately, but that the processes that promoted the development of the former created the conditions for the underdevelopment of the latter.

Three important lessons emerge from a study of the Mandate. *First*, a distinction arises between *undevelopment* and *underdevelopment*. In this study, development is seen primarily as a process of economic and social structural change and transformation, which moves from the embryonic and irreducible to the differentiated and complex. By contrast, *un*development, or backwardness, is a static state where no such movement occurs, where conditions are neither appreciably enhanced nor worsened,[97] and where change is primarily functional rather than structural. An undeveloped society is isolated from the world capitalist order, and its productive forces are primitive or precapitalist. Undeveloped societies, therefore, have no market relations with industrialized nations. Certain features of undevelopment characterized the Palestinian economy during the Ottoman period prior to the nineteenth century.

Underdevelopment, however, is characterized by a very different set of socioeconomic conditions. It lies not at the opposite end of the development pole, but somewhere in between and to the side, outside any linear continuum of development. Unlike backwardness, underdevelopment does not describe a static state but a dynamic, ongoing process, which has been shaped by the expansion and consolidation of the capitalist system and has deviated from the path toward development in very specific ways. This deviation is characterized by the introduction and institutionalization of structural changes (by dominant, more powerful economies) whose outward appearances can be positive—economic growth—as well as negative—economic stagnation, social debilitation, poverty, unemployment, and underemployment. Both sets of changes not only hinder the movement toward greater structural differentiation and integration, but distort it as well. In this way, underdevelopment is not to be confused with a precapitalist state of backwardness. Disfigured, the development process assumes a new organic gestalt and internal dynamism that is known as underdevelopment.

Second, the conditions of underdevelopment that have prevailed within the Arab sector, especially since the Mandate, and that have been consistently attributed by Israel and the West to the "natural poverty" of the Palestinians, to reactionary forces within Palestinian society, and to the regressive policies of occupying Arab regimes, are in fact rooted in the policies of the British colonial government and the Zionist national movement. *Third*, the character of Arab underdevelopment introduced during this period differed significantly from that which emerged in the nineteenth century when interaction with Europe began. It was a process that was shaped not by backwardness but by the introduction of capitalism as a mode of production and the dislocating changes to which it gave rise: the transformation of class relations within Arab society and the increasing separation of the Jewish and Arab sectors, which assumed altogether new dimensions in 1948.

Notes to Chapter 2:

1.   See for example, Doreen Warriner, "Land Tenure Problems in the Fertile Crescent," in Charles Issawi (ed.), *The Economic History of the Middle East 1800–1914: A Book of Readings* (Chicago: University of Chicago, 1966), pp. 71–78; and Alexander Schölch, "European Penetration and the Economic Development of Palestine 1856–1882," in Roger Owen (ed.), *Studies in the Economic and Social History of Palestine in the Nineteenth and Twentieth Centuries* (Carbondale, IL: Southern Illinois University, 1982), pp. 10–54.

2.   For a text establishing the Mandate, see Miscellaneous No. 3 (1921), *Draft Mandates For Mesopotamia and Palestine as Submitted for the Approval of the League of Nations* (London: His Majesty's Stationery Office, 1921). The Sykes–Picot Agreement, entered into by the Allied powers in 1916, placed Palestine (including Transjordan) and Iraq under the British sphere of influence.

3.   Anglo–American Committee of Inquiry, *A Survey of Palestine*, 2 vols., and United Nations Special Committee on Palestine, *Supplement to a Survey of Palestine* (Jerusalem: Government Printer, 1946, 1947), p. 372 [Reprinted in 1991 by the Institute for Palestine Studies, Washington, D.C.].

4.   See the Jewish Agency for Palestine, *The Jewish Plan for Palestine—Memoranda and Statements presented by The Jewish Agency For Palestine to the United Nations Special Committee on Palestine* (Jerusalem: The Jewish Agency, 1947), p. 76.

5.   See Kenneth Stein, *The Land Question in Palestine, 1917–1939* (Chapel Hill: University of North Carolina, 1984); Ylana N. Miller, *Government and Society in Rural Palestine 1920–1948* (Austin: University of Texas Press, 1985); Rashid Khalidi, "Palestinian Peasant Resistance to Zionism Before World War I," in Edward W. Said and Christopher Hitchens (eds.), *Blaming the Victims: Spurious Scholarship and the Palestinian Question* (New York: Verso, 1988), pp. 207–33; Abraham Granovsky, *Land Policy in Palestine* (New York: Block Publishing Co., 1940), pp. 3–16; and Yehoshua Porath, *The Palestinian Arab National Movement: From Riots to Rebellion, Volume 2 1929–1939* (London: Frank Cass, 1977), pp. 80–108.

6.   See Philip Mattar, "The Mufti of Jerusalem and the Politics of Palestine," *Middle East Journal* 42, no.2 (Spring 1988): pp. 227–40.

7.   Palestine Royal Commission, *Peel Report* (London: His Majesty's Stationary Office, July 1937), p. 377.

8.   Yehoyada Haim, *Abandonment of Illusions: Zionist Political Attitudes Toward Palestinian Arab Nationalism, 1936–1939* (Boulder, CO: Westview Press, 1983) for a discussion of Zionist responses to the Arab Revolt and the Peel Commission inquiry. Ben-Gurion's views on the problem are discussed in Shabtai Teveth, *Ben-Gurion and the Palestinian Arabs: From Peace to War* (New York: Oxford University Press, 1985), pp. 164–96.

9.   Palestine Royal Commission, *Peel Report*, p. 368.

10.   Sami Hadawi, *Palestinian Rights and Losses in 1948: A Comprehensive Study* (London: Saqi, 1988), pp. 79–80.

11.   Talal Asad, "Class Transformation under the Mandate," *MERIP Reports* 53, (December 1976): pp. 4–5.

12.   Asad, "Class Transformation," p. 4.

13.   Sarah Graham-Brown, "The Political Economy of Jabal Nablus, 1920–48," in Owen (ed.), pp. 88–176, argues that the economic transformation of Palestine during the Mandate was also mediated by the discrepancies between economic life in the coastal plain and big cities, and that of the inland hill area.

14.   *The Jewish Plan for Palestine*, p. 107. See also Walid Khalidi (ed.), *From Haven to Conquest: Readings in Zionism and the Palestine Problem Until 1948* (Washington, D.C.: Institute for Palestine Studies, 1987), pp. 201–11.

15.   *The Jewish Plan for Palestine*, p. 106.

16.   Other crops included dura, fruits, vegetables, and tobacco.

17.   Roger Owen, "Economic Development in Mandatory Palestine," in George T. Abed (ed.), *The Palestinian Economy: Studies in Development under Prolonged Occupation* (London: Routledge, 1988), p. 21. Also see Montague Brown, "Agriculture," in Sa'id B. Himadeh (ed.), *Economic Organization of Palestine* (Beirut: The American Press, 1938), pp. 128–29.

18.   Anglo-American Committee of Inquiry, *A Survey of Palestine, Vol. 1* (Jerusalem: Government Printer, 1946), pp. 461–74.

19.   Anglo-American Committee of Inquiry, *A Survey of Palestine, Vol. 1*, 323–27; Brown, "Agriculture," in Himadeh (ed.), pp. 126–55; and Sir E. John Russell, "Agriculture in Palestine," in J.B. Hobman (ed.), *Palestine's Economic Future* (London: Percy Lund, Humphries & Co., Ltd., 1946), pp. 116–29.

20.   Despite its relative position to Jewish agriculture, however, the Arab sector experienced significant increases in per capita agricultural production.

21.   Nadav Halevi and Ruth Klinov-Malul, *The Economic Development of Israel* (New York: Praeger, 1968), p. 26. However, agriculture's contribution to national income had declined in both the Arab and Jewish sectors.

22.   Halevi and Klinov-Malul, pp. 25–26 and table 6.

23.   Rachelle Taqqu, "Peasants into Workmen: Internal Labor Migration and the Arab

Village Community under the Mandate," in Joel S. Migdal (ed.), *Palestinian Society and Politics* (Princeton, NJ: Princeton University Press, 1980), pp. 260–69; and Graham-Brown, "Political Economy," in Owen (ed.), p. 99.

24.   Graham-Brown, "Political Economy," in Owen (ed.), p. 100.

25.   Taqqu, p. 269.

26.   Shulamit Carmi and Henry Rosenfeld, "The Origins of the Process of Proletarian-ization and Urbanization of Arab Peasants in Palestine," *Annals of the NY Academy of Sciences* 220, Article 6 (March 1974): 470–85.

27.   See Salim Tamari, "The Dislocation and Reconstitution of a Peasantry: The Social Economy of Agrarian Palestine in the Central Highlands and the Jordan Valley 1960–1980," (Ph.D. diss., University of Manchester, Manchester, England, 1983).

28.   Neu, p. 166; P.J. Loftus, *National Income of Palestine 1944* (Palestine: The Government Printer, 1945), p. 27; and Taqqu, p. 267. Although the majority of nonagricultural labor worked in the government and military, between 13,000 and 19,000 were employed in manufacturing, which proved a boost to Arab industry.

29.   Taqqu, pp. 276–77. Another important reason behind the migration of labor was the underdeveloped nature of Arab agriculture, which seldom provided the *fellah* with full time work and created a constant labor surplus. See Henry Rosenfeld, "From Peasantry to Wage Labor and Residual Peasantry: The Transformation of an Arab Village," in Robert A. Manners (ed.), *Process and Pattern in Culture: Essays in Honor of Julian H. Steward* (Chicago: Aldine Publishing Co., 1964), pp. 211–34.

30.   The difference between the size of the Arab and Jewish economies can be seen in industry. By 1945, 31,800 Jews were engaged in manufacturing, an increase of about 30 percent from 1936. Industry's share of national income in the Jewish sector rose dramatically from 26 percent in 1936 to 41 percent in 1945, and the amount of Jewish capital invested in industry rose from £P 2,095,000 in 1930 to £P 20,523,000 in 1944. Corresponding figures from the Arab sector, however, show that the share of manufacturing in national income fell from 13.6 percent to 10.8 percent, indicating not only the lack of structural change and limited industrial capacity, but the concentration of Jewish capital largely if not entirely within the Jewish sector. Jewish industry was producing over 80 percent of Palestine's total industrial output. See Halevi and Klinov-Malul, 26; and Anglo-American Committee of Inquiry, *A Survey of Palestine, Vol. 2* (Jerusalem: Government Printer, 1946–47), pp. 1011–12; and Owen, "Economic Development in Mandatory Palestine," in Abed (ed.), p. 30.

31.   See Graham-Brown, "Political Economy," in Owen (ed.), pp. 144–54.

32.   M.F. Abcarius, "Fiscal System," in Himadeh (ed.), pp. 546–47.

33.   Abcarius, "Fiscal System," in Himadeh (ed.), pp. 551–54.

34. Asad, p. 5.

35. Abcarius, "Fiscal System," in Himadeh (ed.), pp. 515, 530.

36. Abcarius, "Fiscal System," in Himadeh (ed.), p. 531; and David Horowitz and Rita Hinden, *Economic Survey of Palestine* (Tel Aviv: The Jewish Agency for Palestine, 1938), 155. Graham-Brown, "Political Economy," in Owen (ed.), p. 137, citing a communication from the High Commissioner to the Secretary of State for the Colonies on 15 November 1932, offers another interpretation. The communication states that because a large percentage of goods consumed by the rural Arab population were imported duty free from Syria, the burden of indirect taxation fell more heavily on the urban population. Jacob Metzer, "Fiscal Incidence and Resource Transfer between Jews and Arabs in Mandatory Palestine," *Research in Economic History* 7, (1982): 87–132, describes the more progressive aspects of the tax structure.

37. See Albert M. Hyamson, *Palestine under the Mandate: 1920–1948* (London: Methuen, 1950).

38. Asad, p. 5.

39. Graham-Brown, "Political Economy," in Owen (ed.), p. 95.

40. Abcarius, "Fiscal System," in Himadeh (ed.), pp. 520, 555.

41. George Hakim and M.Y. El-Hussayni, "Monetary and Banking System," in Himadeh (ed.), pp. 496–99.

42. Himadeh, pp. 234–45. It should also be noted that the expansion of Arab industrial activity was in part financed by the considerable growth of Palestine's urban population, largely the result of Jewish immigration. The presence of a growing Jewish population created markets for certain Arab-produced commodities.

43. Government of Palestine, *Statistical Abstract of Palestine 1944–45*, pp. 51–62. However, between 1936 and 1945, output per Arab worker increased four times. Simha Flapan, *Zionism and the Palestinians* (New York: Barnes and Noble Books, 1979), p. 197.

44. See Tamari, "The Dislocation and Reconstitution of a Peasantry."

45. Included were the World Zionist Organization and later the Jewish Agency for Palestine, the Palestine Foundation Fund, the Jewish National Fund, and Hadassah. For a discussion of these institutions and their finances, see *The Palestine Economist Annual —1948: A Review of Palestine's Economy* (Jerusalem: Azriel Printing Works, 1948), pp. 10–40.

46. Halevi and Klinov-Malul, p. 29.

47. Government of Palestine, *Statistical Abstract of Palestine 1944–45*, p. 101.

48.   Flapan, p. 199; Halevi and Klinov-Malul, p. 31; and Granovsky, p. 13.

49.   Haim, p. 3.

50.   Teveth, p. 155.

51.   Haim, p. 3. The economic effect of Zionist colonization on the Arab community has been argued from opposing perspectives, a debate that is beyond the scope of this chapter to address.

52.   *The Jewish Plan for Palestine*, p. 340.

53.   Flapan, pp. 197–98, states that whereas Palestinian Arabs obtained an annual per capital income of £ 27 (sterling), Egyptians earned £ 12 per capita whereas Syrians and Lebanese earned £ 16. Similarly, the wages of Arabs in Palestine were four to five times greater than wages obtained in Egypt, and annual government expenditures per capita were £ 4.4 for Arabs in Palestine compared to £ 2.3 and £ 1.8 per person in Egypt and Lebanon respectively.

54.   Flapan, p. 199.

55.   Ibid., pp. 198–99.

56.   Metzer, p. 87.

57.   One of the few areas in which Arabs and Jews cooperated was citrus production. Both communities owned almost equal shares of cultivated land. Both groups worked together in the Palestine Potash Works and more informally in local markets.

58.   Flapan, pp. 200–201. Lowdermilk attempts to rationalize and justify Zionist labor policy, claiming that in the long-term, it would benefit both peoples. (Emphasis added.)

59.   Nathan Weinstock, "The Impact of Zionist Colonization on Palestinian Arab Society before 1948," *Journal of Palestine Studies* 2, no.2 (Winter 1973): 62.

60.   Teveth, p. 166; and Haim, pp. 69–86.

61.   Taqqu, p. 263.

62.   Horowitz and Hinden, p. 206.

63.   See W.J. Johnson and R.E.H. Crosbie, *Report of a Committee on the Economic Condition of Agriculturalists in Palestine and the Fiscal Measures of the Government Thereto* (Jerusalem: Government Printing and Stationery Office, 1930); and Sir John-Hope Simpson, *Report on Immigration, Land Settlement and Development* (London: His Majesty's Stationery Office, 1930). Also see Flapan, pp. 210–11; and Owen, "Economic Development in Mandatory Palestine," in Abed (ed.), p. 21.

64. Graham-Brown, "Political Economy," in Owen (ed.), p. 125.

65. Between 1940 and 1944, Arab land purchases from other Arabs nearly doubled from 33,000 dunums to 34,000 dunums and the value of such purchases increased five-fold. See Government of Palestine, *Statistical Abstract of Palestine 1944–45*, p. 212.

66. Horowitz and Hinden, pp. 204–205.

67. Carol Farhi, *The Gaza Strip* (Jerusalem: Legal Service, Ministry of Justice, 1971), 88; and Robert R. Nathan, Oscar Glass and Daniel Creamer, *Palestine: Problem and Promise—An Economic Study* (Washington, DC: Public Affairs Institute, 1946), p. 187.

68. Porath, p. 85.

69. Anglo-American Committee of Inquiry, *A Survey of Palestine, Vol. 1*, p. 245.

70. Government of Palestine, *Statistical Abstract of Palestine 1944–45*, p. 2; and Anglo-American Committee of Inquiry, *A Survey of Palestine, Vol. 1*, pp. 104–105. The other five districts were Lydda (1,206 sq. kms.); Jerusalem (4,334 sq. kms.); Samaria (3,266 sq. kms.); Haifa (1,021 sq. kms.); and Galilee (2,804 sq. kms.). Palestine had sixteen subdistricts, of which Gaza was the fifth largest.

71. David Gurevich, *Statistical Abstract of Palestine 1929* (Jerusalem: Keren Hayesod, 1930), p. 78.

72. Irrigated cultivation first came to the Gaza Strip region at the turn of the century with the arrival of industrialization and the introduction of machinery to pump water from deep wells.

73. In 1927 and 1928, the Gaza subdistrict was second only to Jaffa in the annual production of wheat, and produced 12.3 percent and 14.3 percent respectively of Palestine's total wheat crop. Barley stood at 15.1 percent of total yield in 1926 and 20 percent in 1928. Gurevich, pp. 82–83.

74. James Baster, "Economic Review: Economic Problems in the Gaza Strip," *Middle East Journal* 19, no.3 (Summer 1955): 323. See also Van Arkadie, pp. 28–29.

75. Calculated from Himadeh, pp. 126–55. Productivity ratios for the Beersheba sub-district were much lower than those of the Gaza subdistrict, which were closer to the average for other subdistricts.

76. Calculated from Himadeh, pp. 126–27, 130, 131, 134, 136, 377. In 1936, the Gaza subdistrict alone accounted for 20 percent of the land planted with dura and 31 percent of grape cultivation, but only 6 percent and 11 percent of total output, respectively. District figures were only slightly higher.

77. Productivity was greater by a factor of five in the Jewish sector for all crops as a whole.

78.   These figures exclude citrus.

79.   Mohammed Ali Khulusi, *Economic Development in the Gaza Strip—Palestine 1948–1962* (in Arabic) (Cairo: United Commercial Printhouse, 1967), pp. 40–43. Khulusi puts that population of the Gaza Strip area at 88,000 in 1947, which is higher than what one might expect based on official population estimates in 1945. See Table 2.2.

80.   Himadeh, pp. 63, 66.

81.   Nimrod Raphaeli, "Gaza under Four Administrations," *Public Administration in Israel and Abroad 1968* 9, (1969): 44.

82.   The Gaza subdistrict consisted of sixty-six villages and localities, fourteen of which were incorporated into the Gaza Strip. Four localities consisted of three bedouin communities (Abu Middain, Nuseirat, and Sumeiri) that were treated as localities with no permanent population, and one locality, Khuza'a, which had no permanent population until 1945. Technically there were sixteen localities but two, Dimra and Beersheba, retained no Arab population after 1948. However, portions of their land were incorporated into the Gaza Strip. See Neu, p. 53.

83.   Government of Palestine, *Statistical Abstract of Palestine 1944–45*, p. 28.

84.   Gurevich, p. 251. Population figures for 1922 were used to calculate per capita averages since population figures for the years mentioned were not available. See Anglo-American Committee of Inquiry, *A Survey of Palestine, Vol. 1*, p. 148.

85.   Government of Palestine, *Statistical Abstract of Palestine 1944–45*, p. 84. Population figures for 1944 were used to calculate per capita sums. See Anglo-American Committee of Inquiry, *A Survey of Palestine, Vol. 1*, p. 150.

86.   Calculated from Government of Palestine, *Statistical Abstract of Palestine 1944–45*, p. 288 and Anglo-American Committee of Inquiry, *A Survey of Palestine, Vol. 1*, 150. Population figures for 1944 were used to calculate per capita averages.

87.   Between 1936 and 1944, 1,414 building permits were issued in Gaza and 434 in Khan Younis, valued at £ 3.4 and £ 1.1 per capita, respectively. By contrast, 5,209 building permits with a per capita value of £ 24.6 were issued in Jerusalem, 5,061 permits worth £ 29 per capita were issued in Tel Aviv, and 6,239 permits totalling £ 121 per capita were issued in Haifa, indicating far greater growth and prosperity in the urban and Jewish sectors. Calculated from Government of Palestine, *Statistical Abstract of Palestine 1944–45*, p. 267, and Anglo-American Committee of Inquiry, *A Survey of Palestine, Vol. 1*, p. 150. Population figures for 1944 were used to calculate per capita averages.

88.   Graham-Brown, "Political Economy," in Owen (ed.), p. 137.

89.   Flapan, pp. 223–24.

90.   By 1947, the Arab community consisted of five distinct social groups: bedouins,

fellahin (peasantry and agricultural labor), urban upper class (effendis), urban middle class (wholesale merchants, shopkeepers, teachers, minor government officials), and urban masses (artisans, unskilled labor, and the unemployed). Rony E. Gabbay, *A Political Study of the Arab-Jewish Conflict: The Arab Refugee Problem (A Case Study)* (Geneva: Libairie E. Droz, 1959), pp. 8–14.

91. Anglo-American Committee of Inquiry, *Report to the United States Government and His Majesty's Government in the United Kingdom* (Washington, DC: United States Government Printing Office, 1946), p. 34.

92. Graham-Brown, "Political Economy," in Owen (ed.), p. 135.

93. Harold J. Laski, "Palestine: The Economic Aspect," in Hobman (ed.), p. 35.

94. Flapan, pp. 223–232, provides more detailed insights on this and other points. Writing in 1946, the Anglo-American Committee of Inquiry *Report to the United States Government*, p. 40, concluded: Too often the Jew is content to refer to the indirect benefits accruing to the Arabs from his coming, and to leave the matter there. Passionately loving every foot of Eretz Israel, he finds it almost impossible to look at the issue from the Arab point of view, and to realize the depth of feeling aroused by his "invasion" of Palestine. He compares his own achievements with the slow improvements made by the Arab village, always to the disadvantage of the latter; and forgets the enormous financial, educational and technical advantages bestowed upon him by world Zionism. When challenged on his relations with the Arabs, he is too often content to point out the superficial friendliness of everyday life in town and village—a friendliness which indubitably exists. In so doing, he sometimes ignores the deep political antagonism which inspires the whole Arab community; or thinks that he has explained it away by stating that it is the "result of self-seeking propaganda by the rich effendi class." It is not unfair to say that the Jewish community in Palestine has never, as a community, faced the problem of cooperation with the Arabs. It is, for instance, significant that, in the Jewish Agency's proposal for a Jewish State, the problem of handling a million and a quarter Arabs is dealt with in the vaguest of generalities.

95. Taqqu, pp. 281–282.

96. Ibid., p. 284.

97. See Walter Rodney, *How Europe Underdeveloped Africa* (London: Bogle-L'Ouverture Publishers, 1972).

3

Gaza under Egyptian Military Administration (1948–1967) — Defining the Structure of the Gaza Strip Economy

Political Developments

1948-1957

As a result of the 1948 war, two-thirds of the district that had been Gaza under the Mandate were incorporated into Israel. The entity known as the Gaza Strip was formally created with the signing of the Egyptian-Israeli General Armistice Agreement on 24 February 1949.[1] This entity, which was just over 1 percent of Mandatory Palestine and less than one-third of the area designated under the UN Partition Plan, included Gaza City and thirteen other Palestinian localities.

Within days of signing the agreement, Israel violated that agreement by taking measures designed to empty the southern area of Israel of its remaining Arab inhabitants.[2] Expulsions took place in al-Faluja and Majdal (now part of the Israeli cities of Qiryat Gat and Ashkelon); the regional director of the American Friends Service Committee, Delbert Replogle, witnessed events in al-Faluja and wrote on 20 March 1949:

> ...when the Jews entered Faluja...[they] systematically, by indiscriminate shooting, not at people but in the air, night and day for some three days, when they first came into the village, by some looting, by assimilated attempts at rape, terrorized the residents so that they would want to leave their homes.[3]

Those evicted or scared out of their homes entered the already swollen Gaza Strip where they were effectively trapped, owing to an Israeli emergency regulation that prohibited anyone from crossing the armistice demarcation line into Israel without a special permit.[4]

Separated from the agricultural area it once served as well as from the rest of Palestine, the Gaza Strip became an occupied territory under Egyptian military rule. During the early years of its military administration, Egypt's policies were designed to centralize authority and power in the military. Little was done to improve the social and economic conditions of the refugee community or of the indigenous (pre-1948) population. The Egyptian army imposed harsh and total control over Gaza's civil and security affairs. All public offices, social services, and legal, judicial, and commercial activities were under the aegis of the Egyptian military governor. Egyptians held all high-level administrative positions and assumed control over appointments in areas such as health, education, and commerce. Refugees were excluded from mainstream social and economic affairs, and indigenous Gazans were carefully monitored. Officially classified as "stateless," Palestinians in the Gaza Strip were ineligible for any passport. Beginning in 1952, special military exit permits were required for travel abroad or to Egypt. A nightly curfew was imposed, and the penalties for breaking it were severe.[5]

The immediate post-war situation in Gaza was extremely difficult. Much of the Strip's agricultural and grazing land had been lost to Israel, and its port had been closed. As a result, the indigenous economy all but collapsed. By 1949, Gaza's small-scale, predominantly rural socioeconomic structure was overwhelmed by masses of new refugees, who presented an urgent problem. Politically, the issues of repatriation and compensation were foremost in the minds of the refugees. The refugees fell under the domain of the United Nations Palestine Conciliation Commission (PCC) and the United States. In his early mediation efforts, Count Bernadotte, the UN Mediator in Palestine, enunciated the absolute right of the refugees to return to their homes as soon as possible, a position that was formalized in UN General Assembly resolution 194 of 11 December 1948.[6] Initially, Count Bernadotte suggested that the emergency situation in which the refugees found themselves was temporary and would be resolved through a peaceful settlement of the Arab-Israeli conflict. However, it soon became clear that Israel would never allow a complete repatriation, and that practically, such repatriation would be impossible. In a letter to Claude de Boisanger, the French chairman of the PCC, the director of Israel's Foreign Ministry wrote:

> The war that was fought in Palestine was bitter and destructive, and it would be doing the refugees a disservice to let them persist in the belief that if they returned, they would find their homes or shops or fields intact. In certain cases, it would be difficult for them even to identify the sites upon which their villages once stood....[The absorption of Jewish immigrants] might have been impossible altogether if the houses abandoned by the Ar-

abs had not stood empty ....Generally, it can be said that any Arab house that survived the impact of the war...now shelters a Jewish family.[7]

The Arab states also refused to absorb the displaced Palestinians, insisting on their return to their homes. This left the refugees in limbo in their ad hoc camps in the West Bank, Gaza, Jordan, Lebanon, and Syria. Predictably, the refugee problem became the focus of the Arab negotiating position, whereas the problem of territory was the focus of Israel's.

Gaza figured prominently in negotiations over the area's fate. Both the sovereignty of the Strip and the fate of its refugees were hotly contested. The Egyptians, Jordanians, Palestinians, and Israelis all vied for control of Gaza. The Egyptians favored an independent, separate Arab state in Palestine, including Gaza, vehemently rejecting any territorial division of Mandate Palestine. The fledgling Israeli government sought additional territories beyond those designated to it by the UN partition plan. Prime Minister Ben-Gurion wanted the remaining portion of the Negev not originally alloted to the Jewish state, as well as the city of Gaza, two areas the Egyptians were using as bases to attack Israel.[8] King Abdullah of Jordan secretly sought to annex the West Bank and Gaza.[9] Abdullah engaged in secret negotiations with Israeli prime minister Ben-Gurion from 1949 to 1950, in which he pushed hard for the Gaza Strip, which would give Jordan access to the sea. In part to thwart King Abdullah's federative ambitions in Palestine, the Arab League established the All-Palestine Government in Gaza in September 1948. This provisional government was committed to Palestine's territorial unity. It represented Palestine's first real experiment with self-government.

Headed by the unpopular Mufti of Jerusalem, the All-Palestine Government was the doomed byproduct of the political struggles between Cairo and Amman.[10] Iraq, Syria, and Lebanon recognized the Gaza government and declared it to be the legitimate representative of the Palestinian people. King Abdullah, who wanted to be declared arbiter of the Palestinian cause, refused to recognize the provisional government and organized the rival First Palestinian Congress, composed of West Bank notables whose political allegiance to the King was unquestioned. The All-Palestine Government ultimately failed, due to inter-Arab struggles and to its own weakness. Its fate was sealed when Abdullah formally annexed the West Bank in December 1948; the Egyptian government signed an armistice with Israel two months later and took over administration of the Gaza Strip.[11]

The Arabs continued to insist that Israel acknowledge the refugees' right of return, whereas the Israelis first demanded a territorial settlement that would provide the context for a resolution to the refugee problem. After months of fruitless negotiations at Lausanne (April to August 1949), the Israeli government, under increasing pressure from the United States and the UN, proposed the Gaza Plan.[12]

The Gaza Plan represented the only official Israeli attempt to address the Palestinian refugee problem since 1948. Under the plan, the entire Gaza Strip and its inhabitants would become a part of Israel upon the signing of a peace treaty. Israel would acquire the strategic Gaza corridor, deprive Egypt of its last military foothold in Palestine (the "sole tangible trophy of [the] Palestine campaign"[13]), and reduce pressure for a full repatriation of the refugees. Egypt would be relieved of its refugee burden but would lose its only wartime acquisition. Several key parties to the conflict had reason to take the Gaza Plan seriously. Cairo feared the territorial ambitions of King Abdullah. U.S. officials latched onto it as the key to resolving the conflict in the region. Consequently, the U.S. State Department became more involved in the negotiations. It insisted that in return for giving up the Gaza Strip, the Egyptians receive a part of the Negev. The Egyptians, outraged at the thought of a refugee-for-territory deal, responded with "great... and...contemptuous surprise that the government of a great nation such as [the] U.S. should lend itself to such [a] disreputable scheme."[14] In the end, the plan died.[15]

In the U.S. view, Israel's refusal to return the refugees had torpedoed the Gaza Plan, and tensions between the two governments escalated. Soon after the Gaza Plan interlude the Lausanne meetings reconvened. Under U.S. pressure, the Israeli government came up with an offer it knew would not be accepted: Israel would reabsorb 100,000 refugees if there was a settlement, and if the Arab states agreed to absorb the remaining majority of refugees within their own boundaries. The latter immediately rejected the offer.[16] The United States protested that under the Gaza Plan, the Israelis had implied their readiness to accept three times as many refugees. By the end of 1949, it was clear that nothing could overcome the impasse between Israel and the Arab states. As the prospects for full repatriation dimmed, the need for resettlement intensified. The United States then turned to the economic domain and together with the United Nations organized the Clapp Commission to investigate the possibilities of generating useful employment for refugees in the Arab host countries. The operating assumption of the commission was that the economic rehabilitation and resettlement of the refugee community would facilitate a political settlement of the Arab-Israeli dispute, an assumption that would prove entirely false.

On 1 May 1950, in response to the commission's findings, UNRWA began relief operations for the Gazan refugees, who were living in open encampments along the seashore and in citrus groves. By 1952, UNRWA had established eight camps in the Gaza Strip and assumed total responsibility for the refugee community, two-thirds of whom were dependent on UNRWA for food, housing, health care, and education. UNRWA initially had a one-year mandate but this has been renewed regularly since 1950. Palestinians have never wanted UNRWA to be more than a provisional body; to accept otherwise would be tantamount to renouncing their right of return.

The refugees were bitter and frustrated by their living conditions, the lack of progress over determining their fate, and their inability to return to their homes across the armistice line. Many began to cross into Israel to search for missing relatives, reestablish contact with family members who remained under Israeli rule, recover valuables left behind in flight, or find food. Some even returned to plough their own fields, which Israel considered "infiltrations for economic reasons." The majority of the Palestinians who infiltrated were unarmed, poor, and hungry. Through the early 1950s, an estimated 5,000–10,000 infiltrations occurred; each year approximately 500 Palestinians were shot on sight and killed.[17] By 1953, incursions assumed violent dimensions, with both sides engaging in a game of retaliation and counterretaliation.

In addition to growing refugee frustration, incursions into Israel became increasingly violent for two reasons: political activity by the Communist party and the Muslim Brotherhood in Gaza, and Israeli provocations. Egypt banned almost all forms of political expression and organization in the Gaza Strip. Consequently, the Communist party and the Muslim Brotherhood, both underground political movements at the time, provided the wells of political activism in the Strip and were strongly supported by the refugee community. Their activity, particularly between 1953 and 1959, included attacks against Israel, which brought Israeli retaliation in the Strip.

Despite the actions of the communists and Muslim Brothers, however, no organized Palestinian resistance movement existed that could seriously threaten Israel. Nonetheless, the Israeli government exploited the situation through a policy of direct provocation that had the intended effect of intensifying Arab anger and exacerbating Jewish fears.[18] A serious incident occurred in August 1953, when an Israeli army unit headed by Ariel Sharon launched a nighttime raid in el-Bureij refugee camp, killing at least fifty Palestinians and wounding many more. The reaction in Gaza was immediate and violent. The Egyptian government, fearing continued Israeli attacks, imposed harsher security measures on Gaza residents, including widespread arrests.

As the violent incidents across the armistice line became more frequent and more serious, the tenuous relationship that had existed between Egypt and Israel since the end of the war began to break down. On 28 February 1955, Israel attacked an Egyptian military installation in Gaza. The attack was unprecedented in scale: thirty-nine people were killed. Less than a month after the attack, Ben-Gurion proposed the permanent occupation of the Gaza Strip, using Israel's provocative act to create a pretext for occupation. Moshe Sharett, Israel's foreign minister, makes it clear that the attack occurred at a time of relative tranquility after Egypt had enforced harsh security measures on Gaza. He also makes it clear that President Nasir sought a peaceful resolution to the conflict but that Ben-Gurion and Dayan sought precisely the opposite, in order to facilitate the expansion of Israel's borders and insure popular commitment to that expansion. Sharett writes:

> The conclusions from Dayan's words are clear: This State has no international worries, no economic problems. The question of peace is nonexistent....It must calculate its steps narrowmindedly and live by the sword. It must see the sword as the main, if not the only, instrument with which to keep its morale high and to retain its moral tension. Towards this end it

> may, no—it must—invent dangers, and to do this it must adopt the method
> of provocation and revenge....And above all—let us hope for a new war
> with the Arab countries, so that we may finally get rid of our troubles and
> acquire our space. (Such a slip of the tongue: Ben-Gurion himself said that
> it would be worth while to pay an Arab a million pounds to start a war).[19]

The proposal was ultimately rejected by the Israeli cabinet.[20]

The Gaza raid proved to be a major turning point in Egyptian-Israeli relations and in Middle East history. It helped convince President Nasir to reorient his foreign policy priorities from a preoccupation with internal and inter-Arab matters to the wider conflict between Israel and the Arab states.[21] The policy of preventing border forays thus gave way to one that actively and openly sponsored guerrilla raids into Israel, and turned the resistance fighters into an official instrument of Egypt's new offensive approach to Israel.[22] Israeli policy completed a similar shift that had begun before the Gaza raid, from one that emphasized defense and restraint (Sharett) to one that favored preventive war (Ben-Gurion), finally culminating in the 1956 Suez war.

The Suez war was precipitated by President Nasir's decision to close the Straits of Tiran and nationalize the Suez Canal, an event that allied Great Britain to Israel and France. Ben-Gurion seized the opportunity and on 29 October 1956, attacked the Gaza Strip with the objectives of eradicating all guerrillas and Egyptian bases, keeping the Straits of Tiran open, and forcing Egypt into a range of territorial concessions. The armistice with Egypt was declared to be "beyond repair" and, in effect, was abrogated.

For the Israelis, the Suez campaign was very successful: Israel soon found itself in possession of Gaza, which it controlled from November 1956 to March 1957, as well as most of the Sinai peninsula.[23] Israel's control over the Gaza Strip, which Ben-Gurion had long anticipated, had been intended as permanent for geographic and defense reasons. The prime minister immediately announced that Israel had no intention of withdrawing from the Gaza Strip, which was declared to be "an integral part not only of the historic Jewish past, but also of the Palestine of the Balfour Declaration, and never a part of Egypt,"[24] and that Egypt would not be allowed to return.

Israel's first occupation of Gaza was two-sided. On one hand, it was extremely harsh. Considerable damage was done to local infrastructure, and clashes with the local population were constant. On the other hand, it brought a degree of normalcy as the government sought to control the situation. On 25 November 1956, Israel's cabinet approved an eight-point plan for the Gaza Strip designed to restore normal life to the territory and institutionalize Israeli control. The eight steps were: (1) the restoration of municipal government in Gaza and other towns in the area; (2) the full cooperation with UNRWA on the provision of food and other social services to the refugees; (3) the full restoration of fishing along the coast; (4) the freeing of communication facilities between the agricultural hinterland of the Strip and the towns and villages; (5) the provision of basic food stocks at subsidized prices from government of Israel stocks to the local nonrefugee population; (6) the marketing of agricultural produce—particularly citrus and dates—from the Strip, and the export of citrus and date surpluses in Israel; (7) the opening of bank and credit facilities; and (8) the improvement of water, electricity, and other services.[25]

Within weeks of occupying Gaza, the government had announced plans for the future development of the Gaza Strip, whose "geographic and economics links...are with Israel and not with Egypt, from which it is separated by scores of miles of desert."[26] For example, the Israel Marketing Board had exported 100,000 cases of Gaza citrus, purchased other agricultural products, and made plans to integrate Gaza's irrigation network into the Israeli national water system.[27] Israel renewed the licenses of 600 fishermen and proposed the marketing of Gaza sardines to Israel at several tons a month. The military government also announced plans to plant 5,100 dunums (one dunum is one-quarter acre) of Gaza's land with fruit trees.[28] The commerce ministry planned to develop certain Gazan industries, and the labor ministry had commissioned population and employment surveys. The transportation ministry was replacing local auto licence plates with new Hebrew ones. Although Israel's occupation of the Gaza Strip at this time was very short-lived, its policy approach foreshadowed official policies after 1967 that resulted in de-development. As it would be later during the second occupation, Israel's aim was to control the land, and the mechanism used to do so was economic integration. The measures implemented suggested that integration was defined to produce better living conditions not structural change.

Israel's withdrawal from Gaza in March 1957 did not occur voluntarily, but under considerable international pressure, most notably from the United States (which threatened to impose economic sanctions) and from the Soviet Union. Not surprisingly, Israel vehemently rejected the reinstatement of Egyptian administration in Gaza. In compromise, the United Nations Emergency Force (UNEF) was assigned responsibility for civil affairs in the territory, but popular support in Gaza for the return of Egyptian rule quickly precluded any but a military role for the UNEF, a reality to which Israel as well as Great Britain vociferously objected.[29] The Egyptians assumed control over the civil administration while the UNEF, stationed on Egypt's side of the armistice line, patrolled the tenuous border with Israel as well as Sharm el-Sheikh at the tip of the Sinai.

1957–1967

The ten years between 1957 and 1967 brought greater Egyptian attention to the needs of Gaza's residents.

The tenor of political discourse in Gaza changed after Israel withdrew. During the Suez crisis and the first Israeli occupation, Gazans, for the first time since 1948, confronted and resisted Israel. Although Palestinian thinking did not undergo major conceptual changes, Suez had a significant impact: it demonstrated that Palestinians could pressure Israel. Within a year of Israel's evacuation of the Gaza Strip, Fateh was born.[30] After 1957, Gamal Abd al-Nasir emerged as a major proponent of the Palestinian cause, as well as the personal embodiment of the Pan-Arab movement.[31] However, competition from political rivals in Amman, Baghdad, and Jerusalem threatened Nasir's strong position among Arabs and among Palestinians in particular, with whom he had few common bonds.[32]

To secure his base of support in Gaza, Nasir expanded the boundaries for political expression. In so doing, he assigned Gaza a position of singular importance in the struggle for Palestine:

> The development of events in the Arab world, including revolutionary movements, has increased the importance of the part played by the Gaza sector as vanguard for the liberation of Palestine. This unyielding sector is the only part of Palestine which still preserves its Palestinian character. It is, therefore, natural that the first shot for the liberation of Palestine should be fired from the Gaza sector....The United Arab Republic...has always been intent on the preservation of the Palestinian structure, and has turned Gaza into the nucleus of the awaited Arab Palestinian state.[33]

Four notable alterations did occur inside Gaza after 1957 that provided the basis for enhanced political activity. The first change originated in Cairo with President Nasir's establishment of the Arab Socialist Union (ASU), the only political party in Egypt at the time.[34] In December 1959, the Palestine National Union (*al-Ittihad al-Qawmi al-Falastini*) was established in the Gaza Strip. In January 1961, the first and last elections to the union in Gaza took place. The second change occurred in 1962 and concerned the leadership of Gaza's legislative council, a political organ established five years earlier. Formerly in the hands of an Egyptian official, the chairmanship of the council was given to a local Palestinian, Dr. Haidar Abd al-Shafi. Half of its representatives were elected by members of the Palestine National Union branches in Gaza; the other half were appointed by the Egyptian governor-general. In March 1962, the government formalized these changes when it issued Law No. 255, which provided Gaza with a constitution and a system of law.[35]

Third, certain kinds of organizations were established. In 1963, the Palestine Student Organization, associated with underground political activism, was permitted to hold a conference in Gaza. The Egyptians also approved the formation of the General Federation of Trade Unions in Gaza in 1964 and the Palestinian Women's Union. However, harsh measures restricting the freedom of the press and of assembly continued as they did inside Egypt itself.[36]

Perhaps the most significant change in the political character of the Gaza Strip during this period was the establishment of the PLO. Sponsored by the Arab League at the first Arab Summit in January 1964, the PLO held its first conference later that year in Jerusalem with several Gaza residents participating. This conference drafted a Palestinian declaration of independence, known as the National Covenant, and the General Principles of a Fundamental Law, which provided the PLO with a constitution. As a result of the Fundamental

Law, the Palestine National Council (PNC) was formed to serve as the PLO parliament; its fifteen-member executive committee included three Gaza residents.

At its inception, the PLO was not meant as a political vehicle for Palestinian liberation, but as an instrument of Arab state control over the disaffected Palestinian masses. In its first three years, the PLO could not engage in real political activity, but it provided an important framework for the development of Palestinian institutions.[37] During this time, however, the military arm of the PLO, the Palestinian Liberation Army (PLA), was established as a conventional force of Palestinian recruits. Given the increasing tension in the Strip, Gazans received Egyptian sanction to open PLA military training camps for refugee youth, where support for the organization was strongest. Despite continued prohibitions on political movements, the Egyptians supplied the PLA with light arms and allowed it to set up a base in Gaza. In 1965, Fateh was formally organized as a liberation movement. After the Arab defeat in 1967, Fateh assumed control of the PLO.

Between the birth of the PLO in Gaza in 1964 and Israel's occupation on 6 June 1967, little violence broke out across Gaza-Israel lines. The UNEF patrolled the armistice line until Nasir replaced it with his own military on 21 May 1967, thereby removing the last restraint on direct confrontation between the Egyptian and Israeli armies. Twenty-four hours later, in a context of acute tension emanating from the growing possibility of an Israeli-Syrian war, Egypt announced a blockade of the Gulf of Aqaba, to which Israel responded on 6 June 1967 by declaring war.

Economic Developments

The creation of the State of Israel in 1948 and the exodus of 55 percent of the Arab population of Palestine, the majority of whom were *fellahin*, completed the socioeconomic transformation of Palestine along the sectoral lines established during the Mandate. The Jewish capitalist sector, now politically as well as economically dominant, assumed control of more than 78 percent of Mandate Palestine, and the process of land rather than labor acquisition that began during the Mandate was dramatically extended. Within months, the Arab sector became dispossessed of its most important natural resource, land, which included the country's best agricultural areas: 95 percent of the "good" soil (of Mandatory Palestine), 64 percent of the "medium" soil, and 39 percent of the "poor" soil. Indeed, those Palestinians who became refugees as a result of the 1948 war possessed 80 percent of the territory and 72 percent of all cultivable land that fell to Israel.[38] Not only was Arab agricultural production largely destroyed, but the "depeasantinization" and the "incomplete proletarianization" of the remaining *fellahin* increased.

Of the 900,000 Arab refugees created by the 1948 war, 170,000 remained within the Jewish state, 350,000 fled to the West Bank, which fell under Jordanian administration, and between 200,000 to 250,000 poured into the newly created Gaza Strip, now under Egyptian control. The remainder were dispersed throughout Lebanon, Syria, Iraq, and the Gulf states. By 1949, only 22 percent of Mandate Palestine remained in Arab hands—the West Bank (20.74 percent) and the Gaza Strip (1.32 percent). The displacement due to Jewish colonization begun during the Mandate thus continued after 1948 with the confiscation of Arab land and the denial of the right of return to the refugees who had lost their land.

The aggregate losses to Arab society and economy were astounding. Palestinian losses occurred in human as well as material wealth. The former—pain, suffering, and psychological damage—are not quantifiable but would certainly swell the value of those losses that are. By 1944, the Palestinian economy was a viable economy in which the Arab community owned a significant share. In 1944, the Arab share of national wealth stood at £P 1,575 million, equally split between property and labor income. The refugees' property wealth alone stood at £P 433 million in 1944 prices.[39] Unestimable loss of human capital included loss of farming potential and proficiency, loss of labor skills through unemployment, and opportunity losses. If values were assigned to opportunity losses and the deterioration of human capital through non-use, economist Atef Kubursi estimates that it would bring total refugee losses to £P 733 million in 1944 prices.[40]

The social dislocations of the Mandate period, particularly as they affected the structure of village life, were carried to their "logical" extreme after 1948. Not only were pre-capitalist social relations of production largely destroyed (or, in the case of those Arabs who remained inside Israel, transformed into capitalist relations of production),[41] and the Arab economic system significantly altered, but the large-scale exodus of the Arab middle class left Palestinian society dominated by one class in the immediate postwar period. In the Gaza Strip, the presence of the refugee population in the urban areas produced a dramatic shift in class structure. The organic integration that the Palestinian economy had known during the Ottoman, and to a lesser degree, British periods, gave way to forced separation into Arab and Jewish sectors after 1948. In this way, the context for economic development was changed once again, and past continuities were accompanied by new discontinuities. The combination proved devastating for all sectors of Arab life.

The structural transformation of Palestinian society, particularly under the impact of the 1948 war, was critical for the future economic development of Palestine. Having been separated from their means of production, not by market forces but by physical dispossession, Palestinian refugees found, for the first time, that economic power could no longer be derived primarily from one's direct control over the means of production, which to varying degrees had still prevailed under the Mandate. After 1948, economic power in the Arab sector became linked to exogenous forces over which Palestinians had little if any control. This was clearly the case in the Gaza Strip under Egyptian occupation, and even more so under Israeli rule, when Palestine not only suffered the effects of economic discrimination and subordination, but also confronted unique attempts at economic dispossession.

The birth of the Gaza Strip was wrenching and traumatic. A new economic unit was created by factors that were entirely noneconomic. In a matter of weeks, the economic reality of the Gaza region was irrevocably altered and redefined by two critical events: the complete loss of its productive hinterland, domestic trade links, and employment opportunities; and the massive influx of 200,000 to 250,000 people. The extreme geographic and demographic changes that attended the creation of the Gaza Strip sent shock waves through the newly formed economy. Whereas before 1948, the introduction of capitalist relations spurred a particular form of underdevelopment, the political and economic situation after 1948 not only insured the continued underdevelopment of the area, but further limited the possibilities for structural change.

The administrative divisions of the previous two decades dissolved without resistance. With the imposition of armistice lines in the immediate aftermath of the war, the Gaza District disappeared. The Arab sector lost 99.5 percent of the Beersheba subdistrict and 73 percent of the Gaza subdistrict (see tables 3.1 and 3.2). For Gaza's Palestinians, this meant the forcible separation from traditional trade areas, agricultural lands that had been worked for generations, and critical markets in Jerusalem and Beersheba. The loss to the Gaza and Beersheba subdistricts in rural land alone was conservatively valued at £P 31,176,000 and £P 25,000,000, respectively, in 1946–47 prices.[42] What remained of the former Gaza District was incorporated into an artificial entity that became known as the Gaza Strip, an area that represented just over 1 percent of Mandate Palestine but contained 18 percent of the total Mandate population, and 27 percent of the Mandate Arab population.[43]

Unlike Arab residents elsewhere in Palestine, few Arab inhabitants of the Gaza subdistrict remained in their homes once the territory fell under Israeli control. Most fled to the Gaza Strip. The influx of between 200,000 to 250,000 refugees increased the indigenous population of at least 70,000 in the Gaza Strip area by more than 300 percent. Population density rose dramatically from 500 people per square mile in 1944 to 2,300 in 1948, which contrasted significantly with the 1948 population density in the West Bank of 360 people per square mile. Per square mile of inhabitable land only, population density in the Gaza Strip increased to 6,000 people, a level equivalent to seven times that of Belgium.[44]

Under the weight of these crushing transformations, Arab economic life and organization prior to 1948 dissipated. Structurally amputated and functionally disfigured, the Gaza economy now found itself isolated and contained to the south by the vast expanse of the Sinai Desert; to the north and east, by the new state of Israel; and to the west, by the Mediterranean Sea. The Egyptians treated the Gaza Strip as a separate economic unit. The drastically reoriented economy became acutely dependent on imports and on one primary employer, UNRWA.

Table 3.1.   Area and Population in Various Gaza Strip Localities, 1945

locality	surface area in dunums*	area in dunums incorp. into the Gaza Strip	area in dunums lost in 1948	population	no. of dunums per person	no. of dunums per person in Gaza Strip localities	population density (no. people/dunum)**
Abasan	16,084	15,000	1,084	2,230	7.2	6.7	.15
Abu Middain	8,821	8,821	0	2,000	4.4	4.4	.23
Bani Suheila	11,128	9,500	1,628	3,220	3.5	3.0	.34
Beersheba***	12,577,000	63,000	12,514,000	2,000	6288.5	31.5	.03
Beit Hanoun	20,025	12,000	8,025	1,730	11.6	6.9	.14
Beit Lahiya	38,376	20,000	18,376	1,700	22.6	11.8	.09
Deir el-Balah	14,735	14,735	0	2,560	5.8	5.8	.17
Dimra	8,492	1,500	6,992	—	—	—	—
Gaza City	170,816	90,000	80,816	34,250	5.0	2.6	.38
Jabalya	11,497	11,497	0	3,520	3.3	3.3	.31
Khan Younis	56,122	56,122	0	11,220	5.0	5.0	.20
Khuza'a	8,179	5,500	2,679	990	8.3	5.6	.18
Nazla	4,510	4,510	0	1,330	3.4	3.4	.30
Nuseirat	10,425	10,425	0	1,500	7.0	7.0	.14
Rafah	40,579	40,579	0	2,220	18.3	18.3	.06
Sumeiri	3,833	3,833	0	1,000	3.8	3.8	.26
Total	13,000,622	367,022	12,633,600	71,470	182.0	5.1	.19

Source: Joseph T. Neu, *Employment, Labor Migration and Economic Development in the Gaza Strip: A Case Study of Rafah* (Ph.D. diss., Fletcher School of Law and Diplomacy, Tufts University, Medford, MA, 1987), p.54.

*   Does not include entire Gaza subdistrict.

**   Population density in the area that became the Gaza Strip before the refugee influx.

*** Refers to the subdistrict.

1 dunum = 1/4 acre.

Table 3.2.   **Area of the Gaza Strip, 1948**

locality	dunums incorporated into the Gaza Strip	dunums incorporated into Israel
Beersheba Subdistrict:	60,000	12,451,769
Gaza Subdistrict:		
Whole Villages		
Abu Middain	8,821	
Deir el-Balah	14,735	
Gaza (urban)	10,072	
Jabalya	11,497	
Khan Younis(urban)	2,302	
Khan Younis(rural)	53,820	
Nazla	4,510	
Nuseirat	10,425	
Rafah	40,579	
Sumeiri	3,833	
	160,594	
Border Villages		
Abasan	14,343	1,741
Bani Suheila	7,503	3,625
Beit Hanoun	12,136	7,899
Beit Lahiya	12,953	25,423
Dimra*	1,883	6,609
Gaza (rural)	72,795	87,949
Khirbet Ikhzaa (Khuza'a)	4,409	3,770
	126,022	
Subdistrict total	286,616	776,280
Total Gaza Strip	346,616	

Source: Atef Kubursi, "An Economic Assessment of Total Palestinian Losses in 1948," in Hadawi, p. 229; and Government of Palestine, *Statistical Abstract of Palestine 1944–45*, p. 273. These figures differ slightly from those presented in Tables 2.1 and 3.1.
* The built-up areas were incorporated into Israel.

    The economic and social development (or lack thereof) of the Gaza Strip during Egyptian occupation falls roughly into two distinct time periods. The first, 1948–57, was characterized by the immediate economic imperatives of coping with the refugee presence. It was UNRWA, not Egypt, that played the predominant role during this period, as Egypt's relationship with Gaza was still legally unclear, despite the many restrictive policies it imposed. Until 1957, domestic conditions in Egypt were alternately in a state of tension and turmoil, which contributed to official behavior toward Gaza.[45]

    The second phase of Egyptian occupation, 1957–67, was marked by a clear shift in policy and posture toward the Gaza Strip. During this period, Egypt played a more active role in the daily life of the Strip. Egypt's reorientation was occasioned by greater domestic stability and a change in approach toward Israel and the Arab states already described. Having legalized its relationship with the Gaza Strip in 1955,[46] and having successfully confronted Israel and the West in Suez in 1957, Egypt regained the nationalist honor it had lost in 1948 and was prepared to assume the mantle of Palestinian liberation and benefit from the considerable political capital to be derived from the exploitation of the Palestinian cause in its struggle for leadership of the Arab world. As a result, the government sought a more substantive role in the Gaza Strip economy. Egyptian policies, however, did little to alter the structural parameters of the past.

1948-1957

The first decade of Egyptian rule was distinguished by massive refugee influx. Without warning, the tiny Strip found itself burdened with a population grossly disproportionate to the material resources available to sustain it. Having lost most of its economic assets, Gaza's predominant agrarian sector could not possibly absorb the number of people who sought to enter it. In a 1949 survey of 20,000 refugees in Gaza, 18 percent were found to be skilled and semi-skilled workers, 17 percent professionals, merchants and landowners, and the remaining 65 percent were farmers and unskilled workers.[47] The population now consisted of four groups of people—Egyptian administrators and military, Bedouins, indigenous inhabitants, and refugees. The refugees found themselves isolated in a sliver of territory; severed from their former homes, relatives, and means of livelihood; unemployed, and totally dependent on external assistance.

As the proportion of urban to rural dwellers swelled dramatically, existing municipal services could not possibly keep pace with the excess demand placed on them. Unemployed, destitute refugees were in no position to pay taxes, and indigenous residents could not make up the difference. Gaza City, for example, with a prewar population of 35,000 and an annual income of £P 100,000, now had to provide services to a population of 170,000 on the same budget. Gaza's tax base quickly collapsed.

The only natural resource (in addition to limited water supplies) was land, itself in very short supply and inadequate to the economic needs of the population now living on it. The Gaza Strip did not "even contain enough building stone to house its population."[48] Any capital assets held by the refugees or indigenous Gazans were quickly depleted, as one observer noted:

> Clothing is worn out, livestock has been killed for food, the area is being completely deforested as the refugees collect wood for fuel and building purposes, and the railroad track has been largely put out of action by the removal of several thousand ties which are invaluable for building timber and carpentry work.[49]

The refugee influx proved especially calamitous for the poorer segments of Gaza's indigenous population. Wage rates for both skilled and unskilled workers fell precipitously by 60-70 percent, below the subsistence level. The Egyptian authorities exacerbated the situation by making it nearly impossible for Gazans to leave Gaza. Those who could leave—mostly skilled professionals—did so early on; those who could not—unskilled workers and farmers whose lands were now inside Israel—had never known such hardship. For, unlike the refugee population, Gaza's indigenous community did not qualify for UN rations or for assistance of any kind. These "economic refugees," who numbered 60,000 in Gaza, suffered even greater deprivation than the refugees did.[50] In response to this extreme and unprecedented situation, UNRWA provided healthcare services to all in need, and the Egyptian government provided each local resident with 7 kilograms (kg) of flour per month, in addition to food aid from UNICEF and the United States government.[51] Indigenous residents who maintained some form of livelihood faced severe hardship as well:

> Competition among small shops and businesses...[was] much more severe. Merchants selling 3 eggplants and 5 tomatoes, farmers cultivating small fragments of sandy soil, men and women bartering manual services for a fragment of a ration—these [were] the symbols of a struggle for life in which there can be little thought of the future.[52]

In the immediate postwar period, the United Nations sustained Gaza's economy and prevented widespread hunger, starvation, and death.[53] Between 1948 and 1950, relief assistance was the primary objective of the various UN agencies assigned responsibility for the refugees: the Disaster Relief Project in 1948, the United Nations Relief for Palestine Refugees in 1949, and UNRWA in 1950.[54] The American Friends Service Committee began what would be a long history of assistance to the Gaza Strip at this time as well. The Egyptian military authorities were far from amicable and cooperative in the implementation of international assistance. Initial relief efforts were highly suspect and deliberately obstructed.[55]

At first, the refugee community was very hostile toward all UN agencies and any schemes of job creation that could be linked to permanent resettlement. They considered their status temporary and awaited their return home. However, by 1950 it was clear that it would be logistically impossible to return Arab refugees to homes and lands now occupied by Jewish immigrants. Moreover, the will of the Western powers to pressure Israel into a substantive repatriation was rapidly waning.[56] Thus, political repatriation became secondary to the more immediate imperatives of economic rehabilitation, and the focus of UN activity in Gaza shifted from emergency relief to sustainable economic assistance.

Economic rehabilitation was a daunting challenge. Indeed, when the Clapp Commission toured all the Middle Eastern countries where Palestinian refugees resided, it found economic possibilities everywhere *except* the Gaza Strip.[57] A Quaker representative working in Gaza at this time wrote:

> The prospects for the early removal from the deadening hardships are dim. Members of the Clapp Commission, who visited the Strip, completed their

work in less than two hours. No other act has recorded so powerfully the impossibility of increasing the productivity of the land so that the local population will be able to maintain itself.[58]

The Clapp Commission's recommendations provided for the formal establishment of UNRWA. UNRWA confronted its greatest problems in the Gaza Strip. The Strip was home to the second largest number of refugees after Jordan (500,000), far more than Lebanon (90,000), Syria (87,000), or Iraq (5,000). Yet Gaza contained only eight camps, the fewest of all host countries,[59] and the highest percentage of refugees, nearly two-thirds, living in organized camp systems. By 1953, the prewar population of the Gaza Strip had increased by 288 percent as a result of the refugee influx, compared to increases of 53 percent in Jordan, 12 percent in Lebanon, and 3 percent in Syria.[60] Unlike Syria or Iraq, for example, where the refugee community enjoyed a high degree of economic assistance and integration, UNRWA found Gaza to be

> a most difficult area in which to provide work for refugees. Overpopulated and lacking any considerable endowment in natural resources as the area is, the Agency has found it possible to do little beyond small jobs such as improvement of the water supply.[61]

UNRWA concluded that not only was the Strip too impoverished to provide employment for the refugees, it was also "too small and barren to provide a satisfactory livelihood for the original population."[62] Egyptian opposition to population transfer or free emigration only exacerbated the problems UNRWA found so impossible to solve. Indeed, government policies did much to shape the economic behavior of Gaza's Palestinians. Unlike their counterparts in the West Bank, for whom outmigration was a natural and viable response to a moribund economy, Palestinians in the Gaza Strip had no such option until later in the decade and even then, to a smaller degree. As a result, the Gaza Strip emerged with an occupational structure quite different from that of the West Bank. As in the Mandate period, and later under the Egyptians and Israelis, the limited availability of alternative employment opportunities both inside and outside the territory was the determining structural feature of village and camp life.

By 1954, however, economic rehabilitation did prove somewhat successful. Refugees no longer lived in tents or in orchard groves as they had in the immediate postwar period but in solid structures that had been built in all the camps. Health and educational services were made available to refugees in proportion to their numbers and quickly institutionalized.[63] Yet the creation of economic opportunity in so deprived an area remained elusive. One dramatic indicator of Gaza's fragile and skewed economy was that UNRWA, in an attempt to stop a continuous decline in local wage rates, had not only become the territory's chief source of employment but also its primary source of market activity. Indeed, the agency became Gaza's largest importer, providing the territory with 75 percent of its imports (60 percent food; 30 percent petroleum products; and 10 percent textiles).

Table 3.3 further indicates that in 1954, UNRWA overwhelmingly provided the largest transfer of payments to the Strip's tiny economy, which served to offset the territory's growing trade deficit (see table 3.4). In 1966, UNRWA wages and contributions equalled 38 percent to 39 percent of the value produced by Gaza's main economic sectors—agriculture, industry, and public services—and 19 percent of Gaza's total national income (see table 3.5).[64] The territory's expanding trade deficit was another indicator of local economic morbidity and stagnation, particularly as it exposed Gaza's heavy reliance on food and energy imports. With no raw materials, no mineral deposits, no access to markets except across 200 miles of the Sinai Desert, and limited amounts of land and water, the Gaza Strip offered little economic potential.

Table 3.3. **Balance of Payments in the Gaza Strip, 1954 and 1966**

| | *1954* | | *1966* | |
	£E	*US$**	*£E*	*US$*
Imports	1,345,000	3,860,150	17,000,000**	39,100,000
Exports	424,000	1,216,880	4,400,000	10,120,000
Deficit	921,000	2,643,270	12,600,000	28,980,000
UNRWA transfers	2,300,000	6,601,000	3,700,000	8,510,000
Expenditure of Egypt	200,000	574,000	3,700,000	8,510,000
(Administration and Army)				
Estimated Earnings				
from Smuggling	100,000	287,000	4,000,000	9,200,000
Purchases by Foreigners			1,000,000	2,300,000
Support from other Institutes			200,000	460,000
Remittances			1,000,000	2,300,000
TOTAL			13,600,000	31,280,000
Reserves			1,000,000	2,300,000

Source: James Baster, "Economic Review: Economic Problems in the Gaza Strip," *Middle East Journal* 19, no.3 (Summer 1955): 325; Aryeh Szeskin, "The Areas Administered by Israel: Their Economy and Foreign Trade," *Journal of World Trade Law* 3, no.5: 539 (also cited in Neu, p.187); and Mohammed Ali Khulusi, *Economic Development in the Gaza Strip—Palestine 1948–1962* (Cairo, 1967), p. 211.

* The 1954 exchange rate was £E 1 = $US 2.87 (£E = Egyptian Pound)
The 1966 exchange rate was £E 1 = $US 2.30.

** Ziad Abu-Amr, "The Gaza Economy 1948–1984," in Abed (ed.), p. 115, places the value of imports and exports in 1966 at £E 11,995,000 and £E 4,349,000 respectively. Szeskin's figures are used for consistency.

Data for 1954 are incomplete and are provided for comparative purposes only. However, it is safe to say that (1) the value of purchases by foreigners was negligible before the liberalization of Egyptian trade policy in the 1960s; and (2) the value of remittances was similarly low given restrictions on emigration during that time.

Against the clear limitations of the area, the hostility of the Egyptian government, the consistent opposition of the refugee community to the development of self-sufficiency large-scale projects, which triggered fears of permanent settlement, as well as its own financial and institutional constraints, UNRWA faced a daunting dilemma in Gaza. The short-term UN objective was to make the refugee community economically self-supporting within existing political and economic circumstances in order to integrate that community over time.[65]

In a peripatetic manner, the agency attempted a number of projects in the early 1950s that were designed to replace direct relief with projects that would generate long-term employment and self-sufficiency. The agency's approach was decidedly tactical rather than strategic. Initially, UNRWA embarked on a public works program that soon proved far more costly than the simple provision of direct relief, and no more productive because it became prohibitive for the agency to pay wages and provide markets simply to hire people. UNRWA next suggested a number of small agricultural development schemes: afforesta-

Table 3.4.   Balance of Trade in the Gaza Strip, Selected Years (in Egyptian pounds)

year	imports (£E)	exports (£E)	deficit (£E)
1950	988,000	137,000	851,000**
1951	1,022,000	170,000	852,000
1952	1,195,000	288,000	907,000
1953	1,189,000	272,000	917,000
1954	1,345,000	424,000	921,000
1955	1,662,000	429,000	1,223,000
1956	1,542,000	163,000	1,379,000
1957	1,565,000	367,000	1,198,000
1958	2,750,000	696,000	2,054,000*
1959	3,400,000	886,000	2,514,000*
1960	3,600,000	985,000	2,615,000
1961	3,950,000	1,100,000	2,850,000
1965	10,674,000	4,297,000	6,377,000
1966***	11,995,000	4,349,000	7,646,000*

Source: Mohammed Ali Khulusi, *Economic Development in the Gaza Strip—Palestine 1948–1962* (in Arabic) (Cairo, 1967), p. 211; (1950–1961), Ziad Abu-Amr, "The Gaza Economy 1948–1984," in Abed (ed.), p. 115.
* Arithmetic wrong in the original (2,052,000, 2,504,000, and 5,646,000).
** The Egyptian Administration in Palestine, *Official Statistics 1954* (Cairo: Department of Surveys and Publications, 1955), p.108, places the deficit for 1950–1954 as follows: 1950—860,550; 1951—851,299; 1952—906,636; 1953—917,173; and 1954—921,310.
*** Szeskin, table 5.6, places the value of imports in 1966 at £E 17,000,000 and exports at £E 4,400,000.

tion of sand dunes, dry farming on sand, and the intensified cultivation of existing cultivable area.[66] The only successfully completed self-supporting activity was the afforestation project, which was implemented in conjunction with the Egyptian government. Over a period of four years, 4.5 million trees were grown in nurseries and transplanted to a 15,000-dunum area of government domain in the Gaza Strip.[67] The project, however, was clearly bounded by the amount of available land.[68]

In 1951, a small-scale weaving and carpet-making industry was promoted; many of Gaza's refugees were from Majdal, which had been an important weaving center before the war. At one time, more than 3,000 people were working on 2,000 handmade looms, and a Gaza Weaver's Union of 1,000 members was formed to market products in Jordan.[69] The industry, however, never became competitive and failed as soon as UNRWA support was withdrawn. In 1952, the

Table 3.5.   **Sources of Income in the Gaza Strip, 1966**

source	£E (millions)	US$ (millions)	percent
GDP			
Agriculture	5.5	12.65	26.2
Industry	0.7	1.61	3.3
Trade and Personal Services*	4.3	9.89	20.5
Transport	0.5	1.15	2.4
Administration and Public Services**	4.0	9.2	19.0
Building and Public Construction	1.0	2.3	4.8
Total GDP	16.0	36.8	76.2
Transfers from Abroad			
UNRWA and other Public Transfers	4.0	9.2	19.0
Remittances	1.0	2.3	4.8
Total	5.0	11.5	23.8
Total Income from all Sources (GNP)	21.0	48.3	100.0
GNP per capita		46.0	106.0

Source: Brian Van Arkadie, *Benefits and Burdens: A Report on the West Bank and Gaza Strip Economies Since 1967* (New York: Carnegie Endowment for International Peace, 1977), p. 31.
* Services included banking and insurance but not house rents, which represent the transfer of income only.
** Includes the activites of the Palestine Liberation Army.
  The 1966 exchange rate was £E 1 = $US 2.30.

search continued for a joint UNRWA-Egyptian project to establish a vocational training school designed to provide courses in a range of skilled occupations including foundry work, carpentry, and auto maintenance and repair. However, the provision of training opportunities was of uncertain benefit in a situation of limited employment. By 1953, for example, the average monthly wage in Gaza for a worker in industry, transport, and services was $11.20, compared to $12.60 in Hebron and $17.50 in Amman.[70] There was growing concern among officials that inadequate job opportunities would create considerable frustration and unrest among the newly trained and better educated and would do little to improve economic conditions in the Strip. There was no employment for those leaving elementary school, and those secondary school graduates who did find jobs found them in teaching. As more graduates entered the job pool, however, teaching diminished as an employment option.[71]

UNRWA again shifted focus from long-term activities to works projects aimed at improving morale and the standard of living to prevent social and political unrest. In 1955, Egypt joined UNRWA in launching a special program of works projects (an approach previously rejected by UNRWA) aimed primarily at providing immediate employment in areas where needs were great and easily addressed.[72] In the end, however, agency politics, Egyptian obstinance, and bilateral tensions prevented the completion of all but one of these projects.

The economic situation in Gaza worsened between 1955 and 1957 during the Sinai campaign and Israel's subsequent four-month occupation. Many UNRWA activities and projects stopped. Unemployment rose when the Egyptian administration was suspended. During Israel's first occupation, its army destroyed some of the existing infrastructure in the Strip, including UNRWA facilities.

1957-1967

The return of Egyptian rule to the Gaza Strip after Israel's forced withdrawal in March 1957 ushered in a new context for economic activity that replaced the crisis management approach of the previous decade with one that was aimed at longer term growth and greater economic diversification. On the one hand, UNRWA's unsuccessful attempts at economic resettlement and rehabilitation, along with consistent financial problems, precluded any real economic role beyond the assigned provision of education, health, and welfare services (in addition to small-scale income-generating projects and a small-grant program initiated in 1955), which by then had become UNRWA's established domain. After 1960, UNRWA placed considerable emphasis on education, in response not only to the need for increased productivity within the local economy but also to the need for skilled workers in the expanding economies of the Arab Gulf states.[73]

On the other hand, the changed and highly charged political environment between Egypt, Israel, and the Arab states after 1957 led Egypt to modify its policy in the Gaza Strip. Official approaches previously aimed at political and economic containment gave way to more liberal economic policies. This change in official attitude is partly reflected in the levels of public expenditure. During the first eight years of Egyptian rule, public expenditure rose by 120 percent, but in the ensuing five years, it increased by 170 percent.[74] Moreover, many of the economic and social changes that were considered acute in the immediate postwar period had, by 1957, become institutionalized features of life, and were not treated with the same sense of urgency, although they remained extreme.

In formulating its policy toward the Gaza Strip after 1957, the Egyptian government made it clear that it had no intention of integrating Gaza economically, as it had rejected the political assimilation of the refugee population. Gaza was to remain distinct and separate, Egypt's Palestinian bailiwick. Official policy, therefore, did not seek the structural transformation of Gaza's economy or any change in existing power relations. To the contrary, Egypt only initiated changes that would not threaten Gaza's domestic status quo. Thus, long-term economic planning in the Gaza Strip was not even an option. Instead, the Egyptians sought a range of improvements that would enhance the level of sectoral output, increase productivity, and improve the standard of living. Formidable constraints existed, however, among them a refugee population with no source of livelihood other than UNRWA allocations and a socioeconomic structure with no real productive base. The dilemma confronting the Egyptians was clearer than its solution: how to promote Gaza's economic growth without major capital investment, while precluding structural integration with the Egyptian economy.

Between 1959 and 1960, the Egyptian government (as part of the United Arab Republic) began to intensify its "development" programs in the Gaza Strip. Some projects were new and some others, begun with UNRWA years before, were expanded and in certain cases reclaimed. They included: an afforestation effort; the reclamation of unproductive state lands; the construction of roads, a small port, and schools; the distribution of land in the Rafah area; and the expansion of small industries engaged in food processing and traditional manufactures.[75]

These projects were part of a larger economic policy that included the following measures: (1) the promotion of agriculture, Gaza's most productive economic sector and leading export, over industry; (2) the expansion of trade and commerce through the creation of new markets in Egypt, the Arab world, and Eastern Europe; (3) the expansion of Gaza's service sector, the largest source of employment and income; (4) the indirect promotion of an illegal but lucrative smuggling trade; and (5) state-sponsored local emigration to the rapidly growing Arab Gulf region, which reduced the burden of employment in the Strip and insured a critical and continuous flow of capital into the territory, which was used to finance other economic activities, notably agriculture and trade. Between 1951 and 1964, approximately 33,200 people emigrated from the Gaza Strip, and 63 percent of them left in the years between 1959 and 1962.[76] Official policies regarding emigration, together with a much improved educational system, became the primary, if not the only, sources of occupational mobility in the Gaza Strip at this time.

Between 1948 and 1967, agriculture was the largest single economic activity in the Gaza Strip, accounting for over one-third of GDP, approximately 35–40 percent of employment, and 90 percent of all exports. However, the new agricultural base created to replace the lost productive hinterland was tiny. When compared to the position of the agrarian sector within the West Bank economy, Gazan agriculture appeared painfully weak. By 1966, for example, only 14 percent of all households in the Gaza Strip had land as a source of income—3 percent of households in the refugee camps and 23 percent of those outside the camps—compared with 42 percent of households in the West Bank—10 percent in the camps and 46 percent in towns and villages.[77] At least 89 percent of Gaza's population lived in urban areas—39 percent in the towns of Gaza and Khan Younis, and 50 percent in the refugee camps—whereas more than 50 percent of West Bankers lived on small farms.[78] At least 20 percent of Gaza's land was concentrated in the hands of the territory's wealthy families and devoted to citrus production. Moreover, at least one-third of all cultivated area in the Gaza Strip was concentrated in farms larger than 100 dunums.[79] The excessive fragmentation of the remaining land holdings, which revealed a striking disparity in the distribution of cultivated area, was a clear problem restricting agricultural production and the development potential of agriculture generally. On the eve of Israeli occupation, the entire farming population of the Gaza Strip numbered only 65,000, or 14 percent of the territory's total population.

Because the Gaza Strip was not an area of concentrated agriculture, the Egyptian government encouraged the maximization of output in areas already under cultivation as well as the expansion of cultivable lands for which the government provided credit. The government conducted surveys of cultivable areas and water resources and implemented projects to protect agricultural lands against the effects of wind and other kinds of environmental aggression. Such measures, between 1948 to 1949 and 1959 to 1960, increased the amount of land under cultivation in the Gaza Strip by 50 percent from 97,192 dunums to 145,826 dunums for a crop valued at 1.5 million Egyptian pounds (£E). The number of unirrigated (*mawasi*) areas increased from 77,470 dunums in 1948 to 110,293 dunums more than a decade later. Irrigated lands increased from 19,722 dunums to 35,533 dunums (80 percent).[80] In 1958, 43 percent of Gaza's total land area, or 75 percent of all arable land, was under cultivation. Between 1959 and 1966, the total area under cultivation increased from 145,826 dunums[81] to 187,000 dunums, just over half the area of the Gaza Strip.[82] Of this, 40 percent were irrigated, indicating that agricultural production was very intensive. By 1966, however, cultivated land accounted for 52 percent of all arable land (and 55 percent in 1968), a decline that in part was due to the excessive fragmentation of land holdings.[83]

Almost by default, agriculture in Gaza centered on the production of citrus fruits, Gaza's largest source of foreign exchange during this period. The authorities actively promoted citrus production, often at the expense of areas cultivated with other crops, because of its greater income earning potential.[84] Between 1948 and 1960, the number of acres devoted to citrus fruits grew from 6,000 dunums to 16,000 dunums; by 1966, the total had reached 70,000 dunums, or 37 percent of all cultivable area.[85] At 55 percent, citrus contributed the largest share of production.[86] The level of citrus exports rose in value from £E 298,557 or 70.5 percent of total exports in 1954 to £E 3,887,000 or 89.4 percent of all exports in 1966, a clear indicator of Gaza's economic vulnerability and structural underdevelopment.[87] Citrus production encouraged the excessive use of water and damaged the regional acquifer by allowing seawater to enter lowered water tables. In fact, the level of water consumption in Gaza's agriculture—100 million cubic meters annually—was equal to that of the West Bank, although the area under cultivation in the West Bank was nearly 10 times greater than the Gaza Strip.[88]

Although Gaza had become virtually a one-crop economy and dependent on a single product for export in terms of value, other crops were also grown and marketed. Approximately 100,252 dunums, or 54 percent of the total area under cultivation in 1966, were devoted to non-citrus commodities. Vegetables, whose cultivation was by then well-developed, were the second most important export crops. However, over the duration of Egyptian rule, vegetable cultivation was subsumed to the more lucrative citrus crop; in fact, some of the lands devoted to vegetable production were converted to citrus orchards, resulting in greater vegetable imports from Egypt at very low prices.[89] By 1964, the amount of land devoted to vegetable production had fallen to 42.7 percent from 65.4 percent a decade prior.[90]

Throughout the period, dates, almonds, and castor and watermelon seeds were produced and exported, but in far smaller quantities than citrus.[91] Gaza was also self-sufficient in milk, poultry, and fish—an industry that employed between 1,200 and 1,500 fishermen.[92] Wheat, barley, corn, apples, figs, guava, apricots, and olives were also produced.

Despite the variety of crops, the agricultural sector was unable to meet consumer demand and keep pace with rural population growth, due to low productivity and the low ratio of cultivated area to population size. The low level of productivity is clear from the fact that agriculture's share of total employment (35 percent to 40 percent) was larger than its share of total GNP output (26 percent). As had been true under the Mandate, low productivity was due to backward and inefficient production methods (particularly concerning the use of water), the traditional farmer's reluctance to invest in more technologically advanced agricultural practices, the presence of disguised unemployment, and fragmented land holdings. Agricultural productivity in the Gaza Strip totalled only 70 kg per dunum, compared with 250 kg in Syria and 320 kg in Egypt.[93]

The amount of cultivated area per person in the tiny Strip was extremely low: in 1966, there were 0.41 dunums of cultivated land for every Gazan.[94] In fact, in 1958, Gaza possessed the lowest ratio of 0.06 hectares per capita compared with 0.20 in Egypt, 0.21 in India, 0.28 in Pakistan, and 0.40 in Lebanon.

Such fragmentation helped keep rural incomes depressed.

The primary position of agriculture had much to do with the weakening of Gazan industry and the lack of employment opportunities therein. By 1966, industry's share of GDP was a paltry 4.2 percent[95] whereas sectoral employment (including workshop and seasonal workers) did not exceed 6,000 (see table 3.6). Characterized by small-scale establishments, an unskilled labor pool, low capital investment, and traditional production, Gazan industry was oriented to production for local consumption.

Industries were confined to three categories. The first consisted of food processing industries that depended on locally available materials, such as grain mills, olive presses, ice factories, soft drinks, sweets, cigarettes, tobacco, clay, citrus processing and organic fertilizers. The second consisted of small workshops that used imported materials and concentrated on the production of textile (carpets, shoes, furniture, ceramics, traditional crafts), and soap production. The textile-weaving and spinning industry was the most important manufacturing enterprise in the Gaza Strip at this time. By 1960, two-thirds of Gaza's industries produced woven textiles. The last category of industries serviced agriculture through the repair and maintenance of agricultural machinery and the manufacture of packing crates.[96] In 1959, 139 such workshops employed 538 workers; by 1966, there were 770 workshops with 1,782 workers.[97]

Table 3.6.   GNP of the Gaza Strip, 1966

sector	JD (millions)	US$ (millions)	percent GDP
Agriculture	3.3	9.2	34.4
Industry	0.4	1.1	4.2
Construction	0.6	1.7	6.2
Public Services	2.4	6.7	25.0
Transport	0.3	1.0	3.1
Trade, Commerce and other Services	2.6	7.3	27.1
GDP	9.6	27.0	100.0
Net Factor Income from Abroad	3.0	8.4	(24% GNP)
UNRWA		(6.7)	
Remittances		(1.7)	
GNP/per capita GNP	12.6/27.7	35.4/78.0	

Source: Fawzi Gharabibeh, *The Economics of the West Bank and Gaza Strip* (Boulder, CO: Westview Press, 1985), p. 17.
JD = Jordanian dinar.
JD1 = $US 2.79.

Industries in all three categories were extremely small and primitive. On the eve of Israeli occupation when there were 1,000 industrial enterprises,[98] only 10 firms in the Gaza Strip employed 10 people or more, and only 2, the largest citrus packing house[99] and the Seven-Up bottling plant, employed over 100. The citrus packing and beverage bottling factories, which numbered fewer than 5 prior to 1967, were the only ones organized along modern lines,[100] a stark illustration of sectoral backwardness and structural underdevelopment.

Such small, backward industries naturally had limited output. In 1960, total industrial output was valued at £E 519,000 based on a capital investment of £E 372,500. By 1966, output in industry had not grown, valued at £E 519,565, or roughly £E 675 per firm,[101] based on an investment of £E 413,043, or a paltry £E 536 per firm.[102] These figures indicate not only the very small investment and output per enterprise, but the gross inefficiencies in production as well as the backwardness of production methods. In 1960, furthermore, only 29 percent of industrial capacity was being used.[103] The Egyptian government did little to spur industry, leaving it to private investors. This precluded capital accumulation and severely constrained the growth of the industrial sector. What growth did occur resulted from the expansion of existing industries, not the creation of new ones.

The character of economic activity in Gaza is also explained by an analysis of trade. Agricultural exports far outnumbered those of industry. The Egyptian government arranged new markets for Gaza's citrus in Egypt (which ended in the mid-1950s when Egypt became self-sufficient in citrus production), Libya, Syria, Lebanon, Eastern Europe, and Singapore. These new markets raised citrus production and export levels and enriched Gaza's merchant class, with whom Egyptian officialdom was clearly allied. Traditional markets established in the 1940s in Western Europe and focused primarily on England continued through Port Said as well. However, the limited trade outlets, underdeveloped trade linkages, and inadequate marketing facilities that characterized the Strip's export trade were problems that similarly constrained the process of economic development. Gaza's heavy dependence on limited markets and a single export was an unhealthy situation that reflected the structural distortions of the local economy and its inability to resolve basic problems. Various problems faced external trade, particularly with regard to citrus. Poor transportation, for example, and the lack of refrigeration would cause much of the fruit to rot, a very simple problem whose persistence revealed the absence of basic modern methods within the local economy. Indeed, it would take as long as one week to ten days to transport produce from Gaza to Port Said in Egypt, a journey of 200 miles.

Moreover, visible trade was consistently characterized by a preponderance of imports over exports, and agricultural commodities dominated both. Egypt supplied Gaza with close to 50 percent of the Strip's imports. The agricultural sector supplied much of the produce required for local consumption and many of the inputs for local production. This was not true of industry, whose small scale and limited technical capacity were sorely inadequate to meet local demand for manufactured goods. Consequently, the bulk of Gaza's industrial imports consisted of manufactured products including clothes items, cloth, fuel, textiles, construction material, metals, motor parts, electrical appliances, and medications.[104] The Gaza Strip did export some of its industrial manufactures, notably manually woven carpets and embroidered cloth[105] for which it is still known, in addition to hides, wool, furniture, brass, and silver products.[106] However, limited export markets placed yet another serious constraint on local industrial development.

Substantial inputs were therefore necessary for the economy to function. Consumer merchandise, particularly large-scale finished products and processed food (largely imported by UNRWA) constituted the largest share of imported items, whereas goods for investment purposes constituted the smallest. Items for use as intermediate inputs for local manufacture were somewhere in between. This composition of imports underscores the lack of capital and intermediate goods in local production, itself indicative of Gaza's underdeveloped production structure.[107]

The limited opportunities in the economy's primary sectors gave rise to a lucrative entrepot and smuggling trade (see table 3.3). This trade evolved in response to government policies that reopened the Gaza port and declared it a free trade zone for industrial and consumer goods, many of which were banned inside Egypt. Egyptians would visit Gaza to purchase items they could not find in Cairo. Moreover, certain imported consumer goods, especially luxury items, were much cheaper in the Strip than in Egypt, which spurred the development of an Egyptian tourist trade to Gaza, a boon for local merchants, and a lucrative but illegal trade of smuggling imports into Egypt for re-export. The Bank of Israel estimated that the trade in smuggled goods accounted for 70 percent of Gaza's imports,[108] with another 20 percent for tourist consumption and 10 percent for local use.[109]

Although agriculture, commerce, and to a lesser degree, industry, provided the greatest opportunities for investment, the service sector evolved into Gaza's largest sectoral employer and largest contributor to GDP. Services developed rapidly due to the presence of the Egyptian army, the PLA (itself an employer), UNEF, and UNRWA. The service sector offered part-time or casual employment at wage rates similar to those in agriculture and industry.[110] For Gaza's poor and for refugees, casual employment in the service sector or in seasonal labor, when supplemented with foreign remittances and UNRWA rations, could provide a livelihood. Indeed, the dominant position of services and agriculture over industry in local employment reveals an occupational structure characteristic of an underdeveloped economy.

The limitations on agriculture and industry sharply restricted employment opportunities in Gaza. Indeed, labor force participation in the Gaza Strip was among the lowest in the world, standing at 23 percent in 1966. In part, this low level was due to male emigration, low female participation rates, and the preponderance of children under fifteen years of age in the population. In 1960, 35 percent of Gaza's indigenous workforce of 69,000 and 83 percent of the refugee workforce of approximately 62,060 remained jobless.[111] Of those 71,000 who did have jobs in 1966, only 21,000 worked in agriculture and 6,000 in industry. The remainder were primarily service-based: 4,000 in transport and communications; 6,000 in the civil service; 3,000 in UNRWA; 1,000 in the UNEF and other international organizations; and 15,000 in trade, commerce, personal services, and construction. Some 10,000 more were absorbed into the PLA, whereas 5,000 worked for the Egyptian military[112] (two sources of employment that disappeared in June 1967). Clearly, Gazans were dependent on sources of employment external to indigenous industry or agriculture. Thus, as in Mandate times, the "transformation" of the Palestinian peasant into a nonvillage worker had little to do with indigenous development. This trend would persist and escalate after 1967.

Although Gaza's economy experienced some growth, differentiation, and sectoral expansion, the economy remained weak and dependent on external income sources in this period. Table 3.6 reveals that whereas agriculture provided the single largest contribution to GDP (34.4 percent), the combined categories of services produced the largest share of gross domestic output (55.2 percent), followed by construction (6.2 percent) and industry (4.2 percent). The trade deficit grew most pronounced in the last decade of Egyptian rule, with imports nearly three times as large as exports in 1966, a direct result of increased expenditure by the Egyptian army and the large-scale smuggling of imported goods through Gaza to Egypt.[113]

Gaza's balance of payments for 1966 indicates the ways in which the deficit was covered. Table 3.3 shows that in 1966 alone, UNRWA covered nearly 30 percent of Gaza's trade deficit; earnings from smuggling absolved another 31 percent. Purchases by foreigners and remittances defrayed an additional 16 percent. Thus, without UNRWA and other nonproductive sources of income, the Gaza Strip could not meet its basic import needs. Unlike the West Bank, where 50 percent of the capital inputs used to cover the deficit were provided by the Jordanian government, Gaza received no such comparable assistance from the Egyptians, leaving little if any financing for the development of the local economy.[114]

The profound weakness of Gaza's economic base is also revealed in its GNP. In 1966, the combined GNP of the Gaza Strip and West Bank equalled only 2.6 percent of Israel's GNP. However, Gaza's GNP totalled just 20 percent of the West Bank GNP, and per capita national product stood at less than half of the West Bank's. Table 3.6 indicates that the GNP of the Gaza Strip in 1966 was estimated at 12.6 million Jordanian dinars (JD; $35.4 million); GDP accounted for 76 percent, whereas the remaining 24 percent, a significant share, derived from unilateral transfers. Using Egyptian census figures of 455,000 for 1966, therefore, per capita GNP ranged from a mere $78 (according to data presented in table 3.6) to $106 (according to data in table 3.5.)[115]

Conclusion

The imbalance between Gaza's wealth of human resources and dearth of natural and material resources could not be corrected. As the Egyptian occupation came to a close, the economy of the Gaza Strip was characterized by a preponderance of services, an agricultural sector devoted almost exclusively to citrus (which occupied a relatively large share of total product), an industrial sector of marginal importance, a high level of private consumption, and a low level of investment in resources. Although some economic growth and social development had taken place since Mandate times, the destruction of pre-capitalist social relations of production, together with the dramatic changes in class structure resulting from the influx of refugees and restrictive Egyptian policies proved imposing constraints on development. On the eve of Israeli occupation, therefore, the Gaza economy remained woefully underdeveloped and fragile, having failed to achieve any real measure of self-sufficiency and structural transformation.

Notes to Chapter 3:

1. A variety of sources were consulted including Sara Roy, "The Gaza Strip: Critical Effects of the Occupation," in Aruri (ed.) pp. 249–96; Graham-Brown, "Impact on the Social Structure of Palestinian Society," in Aruri (ed.), pp. 361–97; Ann Lesch, "Gaza: Forgotten Corner of Palestine," *Journal of Palestine Studies* 15, no.1 (Autumn 1985): 43–59; Ann Lesch, *The Gaza Strip: Heading towards a Dead End*, Universities Field Staff International (UFSI) Reports, Parts 1 and 2, nos.10 and 11 (Hanover, N.H.: Universities Field Staff International, 1984); Ann Lesch, *Perceptions of the Palestinians in the West Bank and Gaza Strip*, Special Study No. 3 (Washington, D.C.: Middle East Institute, 1983); Joan Mandell, "Gaza: Israel's Soweto," *MERIP Reports* (October–December 1985): 7–19; UNRWA for Palestine Refugees in the Near East, *UNRWA: A Brief History 1950–1982* (Vienna: Vienna International Centre, 1983); Benny Morris, *The Birth of the Palestinian Refugee Problem 1947–1949* (Cambridge: Cambridge University Press, 1987); Shamgar (ed.), Vol. 1; *Middle East Contemporary Survey*, Vol. 1 (1976–77) through Vol. 11 (1987); Neu, pp. 100–50; *New York Times*, 1967–1992; and *Jerusalem Post*, 1948–1992.

2. Morris, *The Birth of the Palestinian Refugee Problem 1947–1949*, pp. 243–47. For a copy of the agreement, see "World Documents: Israeli-Egyptian Armistice: Text of Agreement," *Current History* 16, no.92 (April 1949): 232–36.

3. Letter from Delbert Replogle to Clarence Pickett, American Friends Service Committee, Cairo, Egypt, 20 March 1949. Addendums to the letter describe the situation in Faluja in greater detail.

4. In the absence of a peace treaty, that regulation was still in effect in 1994.

5. For an Israeli interpretation of Egyptian occupation, see Eliezer Whartman, "Guileless on Gaza," *The Jerusalem Post*, 16 January 1978. Whartman's main point typifies the government's longstanding position: Israel's occupation of the Gaza Strip is far better than Egypt's was.

6. George J. Tomeh, *United Nations Resolutions on Palestine and the Arab–Israeli Conflict 1947–1974* (Beirut: Institute for Palestine Studies, 1975), pp. 15–17. See also George J. Tomeh, "Legal Status of Arab Refugees," *Law and Contemporary Problems* 33 (Winter 1968): 110–24.

7. Morris, *The Birth of the Palestinian Refugee Problem*, p. 255.

8. Chaim Herzog, *The Arab–Israeli Wars: War and Peace in the Middle East* (New York: Random House, 1982), pp. 91–104. See also Thomas R. Bransten, comp., *Memoirs—David Ben-Gurion*, (New York: World Publishing Co., 1970), pp. 136–37.

9. In a statement repeated on Ramallah radio, the King said, "Gaza must not belong either to the Egyptians or the Jews. This town where my forefathers are buried, belongs to Palestine, and will form an inseparable part of Palestine and Transjordan." See "Abdullah lays claim to Gaza," *Palestine Post*, 23 January 1949.

10. Carol Farhi, "On The Legal Status Of The Gaza Strip," in Shamgar (ed.), p. 75.

11. See Avi Shlaim, "The Rise and Fall of the All-Palestine Government in Gaza," *Journal of Palestine Studies* 20, no.1 (Autumn 1990): 37–53. See also *The Jewish Agency's Digest*, no.3 (29 October 1948): 31–33. For another interpretation, see Avi Plascov, *A Palestinian State? Examining the Alternatives*, Adelphi Papers #163 (London: Institute of Strategic Studies, 1981).

12. Benny Morris, "No Easy Answer," *Jerusalem Post*, 4 July 1986, gives a succinct account of the complexities surrounding the adoption of the Gaza Plan.

13. Neil Caplan, "A Tale of Two Cities: The Rhodes and Lausanne Conferences, 1949," *Journal of Palestine Studies* 21, no.3 (Spring 1992): 21. For an Israeli interpretation of the plan and its significance, see an editorial in *Palestine Post* entitled, "Gaza Plan," 29 May 1949.

14. Caplan, p. 22.

15. Morris, *The Birth of the Palestinian Refugee Problem*, pp. 266–75; and Mordechai Gazit, "Ben Gurion's Proposal to Include the Gaza Strip in Israel, 1949," in *Zionism: Studies in the History of the Zionist Movement and of the Jewish Community in Palestine* 12 (Tel Aviv: Tel Aviv University, 1987), pp. 313–32 (in Hebrew).

16. In this regard, an Israeli scholar, Varda Shiffer, states, "that the offer was made without any intention of implementation and that it would not have been made had there been any realistic prospect of its acceptance by the Arabs." See Varda Shiffer, "The 1949 Israeli Offer to Repatriate 100,000 Palestinian Refugees," *Middle East Focus* 9, no.2 (Fall 1986): 18. Livia Rokach, *Israel's Sacred Terrorism: a study based on Moshe Sharett's Personal Diary and Other Documents* (Belmont, MA: AAUG, 1980), p. 47, indicates that in written instructions to Israel's ambassadors regarding a security pact offered to Israel by the United States in 1955, Foreign Minister Moshe Sharett represented the Israeli government position on refugee repatriation. In his diaries, he wrote:
> there may be an attempt to reach peace by pressuring us to make concessions on the question of territory and the refugees. I warned [the ambassadors] against any thought of the possibility of returning a few tens of thousands of refugees, even at the price of peace.

17. This information was described in a public lecture by Benny Morris, who also described how Jewish settlers on kibbutzim would booby-trap water pumps to prevent Palestinians from removing them. The bodies of those individuals killed by the pump traps were also booby-trapped, so no one could bury them. See *CAABU Bulletin*, 15 February 1991.

18. For an account of how Ben-Gurion and his followers deliberately precipitated war, see Avi Shlaim, *Conflicting Approaches to Israel's Relations With the Arabs: Ben-Gurion and Sharett, 1953–1956*, Working Paper #27, (Washington, DC: International Security Studies Program, The Wilson Center, 23 September 1981), pp. 6–14.

19. Rokach, p. 44.

20. Sharett further wrote:
    ...the occupation of the Gaza Strip will not resolve any security problem,
    as the refugees...will continue to constitute the same trouble, and even more
    so, as their hate will be rekindled...by the atrocities that we shall cause
    them to suffer during the occupation....The problem of the refugees is in-
    deed a problem, but nevertheless we shall chase them to Jordan and even if
    they stay, we'll manage somehow.
Rokach, pp. 48–49.

21. Shlaim, *Conflicting Approaches*, p. 13, states that "while Sharett was exploring
every possible avenue for bringing about an accommodation between Israel and Egypt,
his defense minister [Pinhas Lavon] was being equally energetic in pursuit of his own
goal of escalating the conflict and sowing confusion and chaos in the Arab world."

22. Ibid., p. 16.

23. Details of the Sinai and Gaza campaigns can be found in the personal accounts of
those involved. See Herzog, 129–34; Ariel Sharon (with David Chanoff), *Warrior: An
Autobiography* (New York: Simon and Schuster, 1989), pp. 141–53; and Moshe Dayan,
Moshe Dayan: Story of My Life (New York: William Morrow, 1976), pp. 322–44.

24. "Thoughtless in Gaza," *Jerusalem Post*, 26 December 1956. See also "Permanent
Peace is the Cornerstone of Israeli Policy," *Jerusalem Post*, 8 November 1956.

25. "Cabinet Adopts 8–Point Plan For Gaza Strip," *Jerusalem Post*, 26 November 1956.

26. Government of Israel, Ministry for Foreign Affairs, *The Gaza Strip: Aggression or
Peace* (Jerusalem: The Government Printer, 1958), p. 7.

27. "Premier to Announce Policy on Free Passage, Gaza Development," *Jerusalem Post*,
23 January 1957; and Diana Lerner, "Business Picking Up in Gaza Strip," *Jerusalem
Post*, 14 January 1957.

28. "IL 7,000 Earmarked For Repair of Gaza Streets," *Jerusalem Post*, 23 January 1957.

29. Hamilton Fish Armstrong, "The U.N. Experience in Gaza," *Foreign Affairs* 35,
no.4 (July 1957): 614–17; and Geoffrey Godsell, "Calm Reigns in Gaza Strip," *Christian Science Monitor*, 17 March 1958. Government of Israel, Ministry for Foreign Affairs, *The Gaza Strip*, strongly implies that Israel should maintain control of the Strip
but promises that "Israel is not annexing the Gaza Strip," 10. For a discussion of the
British position, see Farhi, pp. 102–103.

30. Yet, it was still too early for the emergence of a separate political identity among
Palestinian Arabs; it would take the 1967 Arab-Israeli war to organize and institutionalize Palestinian nationalism into a distinct political movement. See Issa al-Shuaibi, "The
Development of Palestinian Entity-Consciousness: Part I," *Journal of Palestine Studies*
9, no.1 (Autumn 1979): 78–79.

31. See Peter Mansfield, "The Rise of Nasserism," in *The Ottoman Empire and its Successors* (London: MacMillan Ltd., 1973), pp. 114–34, for a discussion of Nasir's role in the Arab world.

32. J.A. Marlowe, *A History of Modern Egypt and Anglo-Egyptian Relations 1800–1953* (New York: Praeger, 1954), p. 328. For a discussion of inter-Arab rivalries in the post-Suez period, see Gabbay, pp. 476–536; and Robert W. MacDonald, *The League of Arab States: A Study in the Dynamics of Regional Organization* (Princeton, NJ: Princeton University Press, 1965).

33. United Arab Republic, Gaza, *Gaza: Springboard for the Liberation of Palestine* (Cairo: Information Department, 1962), p. 5, cited in Neu, p. 120. In a similar vein, Articles 1 and 2 of subsection I of Gaza's constitution, personally signed by President Nasir, state:

> The Gaza Strip is an indivisible part of the land of Palestine and its people are part of the Arab nation. The Palestinians in the Gaza Strip shall form a National Union composed of all Palestinians wherever they may be—its aim being the joint work to recover the usurped lands of Palestine, and the participation in fulfilling the call of Arab Nationalism....

34. In 1958, there were rumors that in an attempt to strengthen the newly formed Arab union and Nasir's position in the Arab world, the Egyptian president was arranging for the Gaza Strip to announce its independence as a nation. The residents of the Gaza Strip would then vote themselves into the United Arab Republic and thereby attract the loyalty of the Palestinians living in the West Bank. The struggle between Cairo and Amman continued.

35. The constitution for the Gaza sector appears in its entirety in "Republican Decree Announcing Constitutional System of Gaza Sector, March 9, 1962," *Middle East Journal* 17, nos. 1–2 (Winter–Spring 1963): 156–61. Raphaeli, pp. 46–47, describes the structure of government in Gaza under Egyptian administration.

36. Two newspapers were restricted: a weekly entitled *Gaza*, and *Ahkbar Falesteen* (News of Palestine).

37. Joost Hiltermann, *Behind the Intifada* (Princeton, NJ: Princeton University Press, 1991), p. 38.

38. John Ruedy, "The Dynamics of Land Alienation," in Ibrahim Abu-Lughod (ed.), *The Transformation of Palestine* (Evanston, IL: Northwestern University Press, 1971), p. 135.

39. Atef Kubursi, "An Economic Assessment of Total Palestinian Losses," in Hadawi (ed.), p. 147.

40. Ibid., pp. 147–48.

41. After 1967, this transformation occurred to a lesser degree in the Gaza Strip and

West Bank as well.

42. Kubursi, "An Economic Assessment," in Hadawi (ed.), pp. 167, 171, 315.

43. Anglo-American Committee of Inquiry, *A Survey of Palestine, Vol. 1*, p. 143.

44. Baster, "Economic Review," p. 323.

45. For details of this period, see Gabbay, pp. 412–17.

46. It was not until 1955 that the Egyptian government passed a law clarifying the Gaza-Egypt relationship ("A Law Concerning the Issue of a Fundamental Law for the Region Placed under the Supervision of the Egyptian Forces in Palestine"); see Farhi, p. 93.

47. Baster, "Economic Review," p. 324.

48. Ibid.

49. Ibid., p. 325.

50. United Nations, *General Assembly Official Records*, 6th Session, Supplement #16, 4. For more detailed information, see Neu, p. 172.

51. League of Arab States, *The Palestine Refugees—Information and Statistics* (n.p.: Costa Tsoumas & Co. Press, 1957), p. 77. UNRWA also provided relief for 3,500 bedouins living outside the camps in Gaza.

52. Baster, "Economic Review," p. 326.

53. Gabbay, pp. 118–33, gives a detailed account of relief assistance and the evolution of the UN role.

54. UNRWA rations were provided at an annual cost of $27.00 per person and amounted to 1,500 calories per day in the in the summer and 1,600 calories in the winter. The monthly basic ration for a Palestinian in the summer equalled 10 kg of flour, 600 g of pulses, 600 g of sugar, 500 g of rice and 375 g of oils and fats. In the winter this was increased by 300 g of pulses and 400 g of flour. See Arlette Tessier, *Gaza* (Beirut: PLO Research Center, August 1971), p. 14.

55. Gabbay, p. 139.

56. United Nations, *General Assembly Official Records*, 5th Session, Supplement #18, pp. 2–9, 12–21, 24.

57. *Interim Report of the United Nations Economic Survey Mission*, Vol. 1, UN Document of 28 December 1949, p. 20.

58. Ruth Van Auken, "Hopeless in Gaza," *Jerusalem Post*, 4 April 1950.

59. By contrast, Jordan contained 25 camps, Lebanon contained 16, Syria, 10, and Iraq, none. Gabbay, pp. 179–80. See also League of Arab States, p. 23.

60. James Baster, "Economic Aspects of the Settlement of Palestine Refugees," *Middle East Journal* 8, no.1 (Winter 1954): 55.

61. United Nations, *General Assembly Official Records*, 5th Session, Supplement #19, 9; and Neu, p. 173.

62. United Nations, *General Assembly Official Records*, 8th Session, Supplement #12, p. 11.

63. By 1954, 67 percent of all students were enrolled in UNRWA schools. See The Egyptian Administration in Palestine, *Official Statistics 1954* (Cairo: Department of Surveys and Publications, 1954), pp. 20–21, 24, 27, and 31 for interesting educational data, and pp. 2–3, 10–11, and 17–18 for key health data. (English translation of the Arabic original.)

64. Table 3.6 provides different absolute figures although the ratios are the same.

65. In order to reach this objective, three basic conditions were articulated for the region as a whole: an improvement in the standard of living, enhanced opportunities for vocational training, and a better distribution of refugees in the Middle East. *Middle East Record 1961*, p. 240. See also Neu, pp. 173–78.

66. United Nations, *General Assembly Official Records*, 8th Session, Supplement #12, p. 11.

67. In 1943, 80,549 plants were grown in Gaza out of a total of 1,129,564 for all of Palestine, thus revealing the relatively small scope of the Gaza afforestation project.

68. United Nations, *General Assembly Official Records*, 10th Session, Supplement #15, p. 21; and Neu, p. 175.

69. United Nations, *General Assembly Official Records*, 9th Session, Supplement #17, pp. 13–14; Gabbay, p. 463; and Neu, p. 175.

70. Baster, "Economic Aspects," p. 56.

71. United Nations, *General Assembly Official Records*, 11th Session, Supplement #14, p. 7; and Neu, p. 176.

72. Examples included road construction projects in Gaza City, Khan Younis, and several refugee camps; the construction of new drainage systems in the Gaza municipality; the construction of a new port; and a rudimentary farming project for the mass employment of young people. United Nations, *General Assembly Official Records*, 11th Ses-

sion, Supplement #14, p. 9; and Gabbay, p. 533.

73. Neu, pp. 178–79.

74. Khulusi, p. 266.

75. *Middle East Record*, Vol. 1 (London: Weidenfeld and Nicolson Ltd., 1960), p. 136; and *Middle East Record 1961*, p. 241.

76. However, 10,560 people returned to the Strip between 1956 and 1958 and 160 returned between 1963 and 1964. UNCTAD, in-house, commissioned study on population and demography in the West Bank and Gaza Strip, Geneva, Switzerland, 1992.

77. Roy, *The Gaza Strip Survey*, p. 19; Arieh Szeskin, "The Areas Administered by Israel: Their Economy and Foreign Trade," *Journal of World Trade Law* 3, no.5 (1969): 525, 531; and Eliyahu Kanovsky, *The Economic Impact of the Six-Day War: Israel, the Occupied Territories, Egypt and Jordan* (New York: Praeger, 1970), p. 174.

78. The Jordanian government, by contrast, classified the refugee camp population in the West Bank as rural. David Kahan, *Agriculture and Water Resources in the West Bank and Gaza (1967–1987)* (Jerusalem: The West Bank Data Base Project and the Jerusalem Post Press, 1987), p. 11.

79. Kahan, p. 11, 127, table 2.2.

80. Khulusi, p. 75.

81. Ibid., p. 86, puts this figure at 142,000 dunums.

82. Meron Benvenisti, *The West Bank Data Project: A Survey of Israel's Policies* (Washington, DC: The American Enterprise Institute, 1984), p. 13. Sharif Kan'ana and Rashad al-Madani, *Settlement and Land Confiscation in the Gaza Strip 1967–1984* (Birzeit, West Bank: Birzeit University Center for Research and Documentation, 1985) [English translation of Arabic original], 9, place the total number of dunums under cultivation at 170,252 in 1966.

83. Khulusi, pp. 76–77, 86; Ziad Abu-Amr, "The Gaza Economy 1948–1984," in Abed (ed.), 106; and Fawzi Gharaibeh, *The Economies of the West Bank and Gaza Strip* (Boulder, CO: Westview Press, 1985), p. 65.

84. Government measures that emphasized the continued commercialization of land and labor (as opposed to the structural reform of the agricultural sector) resulted in the development of capitalist agriculture within the tiny, artificial economy of the Gaza Strip that proved extremely lucrative to Gaza's landowning class but only because there were no other ways of realizing comparable profits. See Sarah Graham-Brown, "The Economic Consequences of the Occupation," in Aruri (ed.), pp. 311–25.

85. Figures presented in table 8.1 are slightly different.

86. Gharaibeh, p. 71.

87. Khulusi, pp. 77–78; Abu-Amr, "The Gaza Economy," in Abed (ed.), p. 114.

88. Kahan, p. 3.

89. The cultivation of other fruits including apples, grapes and almonds were also sacrificed. Department of Agriculture, *Vegetable Production in the Gaza Strip* (Gaza Strip: Civil Administration, 1986).

90. Abu-Amr, "The Gaza Economy," in Abed (ed.), p. 107.

91. The Egyptian Administration in Palestine, *Official Statistics 1954*, pp. 104–107.

92. Kanovsky, pp. 175–76; Khulusi, p. 201.

93. Khulusi, pp. 83–84.

94. This figure is based upon an Egyptian population census of the Gaza Strip, which placed the total de jure population at 455,000 in 1966.

95. Bakir Abu Kishk, *The Industrial and Economic Trends in the West Bank and Gaza Strip* (Beirut: United Nations Economic Commission for West Asia, Joint ECWA/UNIDO Industrial Division, December 1981), places industry's contribution to GDP in 1966 at 3.3 percent, or one-eighth the contribution of the agricultural sector. By the same author, see "Industrial Development and Policies in the West Bank and Gaza," in Abed (ed.), pp. 167–68.

96. Abu-Amr, "The Gaza Economy," in Abed (ed.), pp. 109–10; Gharaibeh, pp. 88–89; and Roy, *The Gaza Strip Survey*, pp. 55–56.

97. Khulusi, 159–60; and Abu-Amr, "The Gaza Economy," in Abed (ed.), 110. Khulusi includes a table on p. 160 that appears to be mislabelled. The column beneath the heading "# of workers" refers to the number of workshops.

98. Abu Kishk, p. 13; and Abu Kishk, "Industrial Development," in Abed (ed.), p. 168.

99. The Ahmed Shurab Company employed 195 people, but the work was seasonal.

100. Hisham Awartani, *A Survey of Industries in the West Bank and Gaza Strip* (Birzeit, West Bank: Birzeit University, 1979), p. 9. Awartani states that there were 14 large-scale enterprises: 2 citrus-packing houses, 2 beverage-bottling plants, and 10 carpet and textile-weaving plants.

101. The per firm figure is calculated using the 770 industrial workshops known to exist in 1966. In 1966, 1 Egyptian pound = US $2.30.

102. Abu-Amr, "The Gaza Economy," in Abed (ed.), p. 111; and "Gaza Strip, Sinai

were workless under Egypt," *Jerusalem Post*, 25 July 1967. The latter states that industrial output reached $1,195,000 based on a total capital investment of $950,000.

103. Khulusi, p. 201. This figure was derived by dividing 1,782 laborers by 6,060 workers, which Khulusi estimated to be industry's employment capacity. The occupation able to absorb the single largest number of workers (12,000) was weaving. The shortage of skilled technicians was a major problem affecting local industry and one reason it remained decidely traditional.

104. The Egyptian Administration in Palestine, *Official Statistics 1954*, pp. 70–95, lists at least one hundred industrial imports. In addition, processed foods (including coffee, sugar, and tea) were also imported.

105. Szeskin, p. 538.

106. The Egyptian Administration in Palestine, *Official Statistics 1954*, pp. 106–107; and Khulusi, p. 213.

107. Szeskin, pp. 532–533, makes a similar argument for the foreign trade of the West Bank.

108. Arie Bregman, *Economic Growth in the Administered Areas 1968–1973* (Jerusalem: Bank of Israel Research Department, 1975), p. 82.

109. Szeskin, 538; Kanovsky, 170.

110. Neu, p. 183. Also see Lesch, UFSI Reports, nos. 10–11, p. 4.

111. Elie Rekhes, "The Employment of Arab Laborers from the Administered Areas," *Israel Yearbook of Human Rights* 5 (1975): 390; Khulusi, pp. 61–64; and Abu-Amr, "The Gaza Economy," in Abed (ed.), 102-103. The refugee labor force was calculated using Khulusi's figure of 10,550 refugee workers and Rekhess' figure of 83 percent unemployment among the refugee labor force. Abu-Amr places this number at 64,500. The difference is not significant. Almost 50 percent of employed refugees worked for UNRWA and the Egyptian administration.

112. Kanovsky, p. 177.

113. Szeskin, p. 538; Kanovsky, p. 78.

114. Szeskin, p. 537.

115. Bregman, *Economic Growth*, 14, estimates that per capita GNP in Gaza was $120 in 1965.

4

The Gaza Strip under Israeli Military Occupation (1967–1987) — A Political History

I srael's second occupation of the Gaza Strip began on 8 June 1967. It represented a logical culmination of earlier political intentions to control the area. Policy statements by Prime Minister Levi Eshkol and Defense Minister Moshe Dayan soon after the war conveyed the government's desire to keep the occupied territories, and as far as Gaza was concerned, to avoid the mistakes of 1956, official Israeli support for UN resolution 242 notwithstanding.[1] In 1967, as in 1956, specific economic measures were used to create and insure a new political status quo. This chapter will discuss the political context of Israel's occupation, and later chapters will discuss the economic.

Israel's permanent intentions toward Gaza had immediate implications. As in its first occupation of the area, the government established a military administration which sought to normalize conditions as quickly as possible by restoring services in a variety of sectors—health, education, agriculture, commerce, and law—and easing the restrictions on travel between the Strip and Israel. Institutional development was promoted as well.[2] Having learned its lesson in 1956, the government understood that normalization would not insure control of Gaza. Hence, seven weeks after the war ended, the Israeli cabinet secretly deliberated the Allon Plan, which provided for the formal annexation of the Gaza Strip as well as the resettlement 350,000 Gazan refugees in northern Sinai and the West Bank.[3] Again, as in the Gaza Plan of 1949, the government seemed far more concerned over territory than population.

The Allon Plan was never officially adopted by the government. However, between June and December 1967, the government evicted some 40,000 Palestinians from the Gaza Strip to Jordan, some of them leaving in Israeli buses.[4] Israel also offered Israeli citizenship to the indigenous residents of Gaza, who, unlike the refugees, were not eligible for Jordanian or Egyptian citizenship. Gazans immediately rejected this offer, preferring instead to remain Palestinian and, for the time being, stateless.

Resistance in Gaza

From the beginning, Gazans actively resisted the occupation. Indeed, Gaza once again became the symbol of that resistance. Guided by the principle of armed struggle (*al-kifah al-musallah*), which sought to defeat Israel and replace it with a Palestinian state, the rejection of Israeli rule began in the Gaza Strip and included Arab schoolgirls as well as armed guerrilla fighters. In 1967 as in 1987, "women and children poured into the streets calling upon the Israelis to 'go home.' They built barricades... marched on the offices of the Israeli governor,...stoned vehicles of the Israeli occupation authorities and of Israeli tourists."[5] Within less than a year of Israel's occupation of the Gaza Strip, a protracted period of armed struggle between the PLA and the Israeli military began. Armed struggle was most intense between 1969 and 1971. In the wake of the Arab state defeat, the PLO emerged as a greatly strengthened political force with a committed military presence in Gaza. A guerrilla movement soon developed whose targets included the Israeli Defense Forces (IDF), Israeli establishments inside the Strip, Israeli civilians and civilian settlements, and Arab collaborators, a category that also included Palestinians working in Israel or with Israeli concerns in Gaza.[6] Using bombs, grenades, and sabotage, the PLA operated from within the refugee camps and was largely sustained by the refugees.

Gaza provided fertile ground for a resistance movement. The overcrowded camps provided easy refuge for Palestinian fighters who had been armed and trained by the Egyptian army just years before.[7] Moreover, because Egyptian policy had allowed no local leadership to emerge in Gaza, the resistance fighters and the Israeli military struggled to fill the political vacuum.[8] Unlike in the West Bank, where various political forces strove to control the territory, in Gaza, the IDF and the Palestinian fighters were the only contenders. This day-to-day exposure gained the fighters increasing influence.

In addition to the guerrilla fighting, civil disobedience became widespread.[9] The government found it increasingly difficult to control the territory. A former fighter recounted: "We controlled Gaza by night and the Israelis controlled it by day."[10] In a confidential message to his superiors at *The New York Times*, a Jerusalem-based reporter wrote:

> Try as they might, the Israelis seem unable to solve the problem of how to run restless Gaza. To curb terrorism, the Israelis recently sent in their tough border police to help army units. The terrorism decreased but administra-

tive problems continued. On January 2, the Israelis fired the Egyptian-appointed mayor, Ragheb El-Alami. This weekend, the Israelis dissolved the town's municipal council, placing Gaza temporarily under control of an Israeli army major. The drastic action underlines the continuing troubles Israel is having in Gaza, an old bugaboo.[11]

The government responded by systematically arresting PLA fighters,[12] public demonstrators, and prominent political figures and even expelling them to Sinai or deporting them to Jordan. Between 1968 and 1971, Israel deported 615 Gazan residents, 87 percent of the total number of deportees (705) from the Gaza territory from 1967 to 1988.[13] The military government placed refugee camps under 24-hour curfew and imposed severe restrictions on movement.

When Ariel Sharon became chief of the IDF southern command in 1970, he embarked on a campaign to rid the Gaza Strip of all resistance. Sharon's three-pronged plan aimed to widen camp roads, establish Jewish settlements, and eliminate refugee camps. Only the first two goals received official sanction.

Between July 1971 and February 1972, Sharon enjoyed considerable success. During this time, the entire Strip (apart from the Rafah area) was sealed off by a ring of security fences 53 miles in length, with few entrypoints. Today, their effects live on: there are only three points of entry to Gaza—Erez, Nahal Oz, and Rafah.

Perhaps the most dramatic and painful aspect of Sharon's campaign was the widening of roads in the refugee camps to facilitate military access. Israel built nearly 200 miles of security roads and destroyed thousands of refugee dwellings as part of the widening process.[14] In August 1971, for example, the Israeli army destroyed 7,729 rooms (approximately 2,000 houses) in three volatile camps, displacing 15,855 refugees: 7,217 from Jabalya, 4,836 from Shati, and 3,802 from Rafah.[15] Some 400 displaced families were relocated to el-Arish in north Sinai; 300 individuals were sent to Jericho in the West Bank. The others were left to find their own living arrangements in the Strip, mainly in Rafah. Moreover, 12,000 relatives of suspected guerrillas were deported to detention camps in the Sinai desert.

By early 1972, the Israeli army had achieved its objectives: it had killed large numbers of guerrillas and assumed control over the refugee camps. Having reduced the armed Palestinian presence in Gaza (with substantial help from King Hussein, whose offensive against the PLO in Jordan in September 1970 also weakened the resistance movement in Gaza), Sharon's second objective, the establishment of Jewish settlements (or "Jewish fingers" as he called them) could be implemented.

> I wanted [a settlement] between Gaza and Deir el Balah, one between Deir el Balah and Khan Younis, one between Khan Younis and Rafah, and another west of Rafah....If in the future we wanted to control this area...we would need to establish a Jewish presence now. Otherwise, we would have no motivation to be there during difficult times later on.[16]

Eventually, a settlement pattern close to Sharon's vision emerged.

The Labor government had long before reached the same conclusion as Sharon. One month after Israel assumed control over Gaza, Defense Minister Moshe Dayan stated, "The Gaza Strip is Israel and I think it should become an integral part of the country....I don't see any difference between Gaza and Nazareth anymore."[17] Indeed, one way to insure Gaza's inseparability from Israel was through rapid civilian settlement, an urgent feature of Israel's post-war policy of "creating facts."[18] Minister without Portfolio Israel Galili, who also chaired the Committee for the Settlement of the Gaza Strip, similarly stated that "each visit to the Gaza Strip reconfirmed his identification with the government's conclusion that it must not be separated from Israel territory."[19]

However, given the problems of the Gaza area, the government did not establish many settlements in the territory, as it did in the West Bank and East Jerusalem, but chose instead to establish Jewish settlements at Gaza's southern border with Sinai which it had also captured in the 1967 war. The settlement drive began with the forcible evacuation of 6,000 bedouin from the northeastern corner of the Sinai district.[20] Approximately 33,250 acres of cultivated bedouin land were expropriated, while bulldozers destroyed houses, wells, and other immovable property.[21] By 1978, thirteen settlements had been constructed in the Northern Sinai (and six in the Strip). Their purpose was to serve as a buffer zone between the Gaza Strip and the rest of the desert peninsula.

Appointment of a Municipal Council

Israel's policy of creating facts was indirectly facilitated by the activities of the more traditional and reactionary social circles within Gaza who, since the onset of Israeli rule, had remained largely isolated from political life, cut off from other Arab countries, and extremely concerned with their own material survival. They included Gaza's wealthy citrus merchants and land-owning elite, historically the source of Gaza's political leadership. In the aftermath of the guerrilla violence, these individuals sought to restore to the Strip some semblance of social and economic order, which they felt the resistance had weakened. They also sought to become Gaza's representative voice. At the request of the Israeli authorities, a leading citrus merchant, Rashad Shawa,[22] agreed to become mayor in September 1971. He then formed a municipal council whose members all came from Gaza's upper classes.

Mayor Shawa and the municipal council generated intense controversy, because many nationalists viewed their appointments as a political compromise with the occupier that had little popular support. The PLO, in particular, refused to endorse the municipal council and encouraged armed rather than political struggle. However, with the reinstatement of a local municipal structure and the effective defeat of the resistance movement, political struggle began to challenge armed struggle as a tactical approach for confronting the occupation.

In 1972, the mayor focused on the economic revitalization of Gaza's citrus industry, which had suffered greatly during the fighting, as well as from a variety of Israeli-imposed measures, including the closure of the Bank of Palestine in 1967, the introduction of new trade restrictions, and the levying of new taxes. Export markets were secured through newly established trade routes with Jordan.

The positive effects of the mayor's activities were outweighed by growing public dissent over his support for the creation of the "United Arab Kingdom," a federation between Gaza, the West Bank, and Jordan, proposed by King Hussein in March 1972. Nationalists in the Strip, outraged by Black September, rejected any leadership emanating from Jordan, as did President Sadat, who, fearing a separate agreement between Israel and Jordan, severed diplomatic relations with Jordan and did not renew them until September 1973.[23]

Under intense criticism from both Gazans and Israelis, Mayor Shawa resigned in October 1972.[24] His resignation was followed immediately by the reinstatement of direct military rule in the Gaza Strip. The Israeli military governor assumed all the powers of his Egyptian predecessor. Israelis were appointed to head all social service departments.

Direct Israeli rule over Gaza continued until October 1975, when Shawa agreed to be reappointed as mayor of Gaza City, an act that again angered many Palestinian nationalists who insisted that Gazans reject the Israeli system of appointments and call for elections. This sentiment was heightened by the April 1976 municipal elections in the West Bank, where the victory of pro-PLO candidates eventually prompted Israel to suspend municipal elections in the West Bank as the British had done in Gaza thirty years before. The PLO was extremely popular in the Strip. By October 1977, support for the organization crossed the relatively wide spectrum of political opinion; Gaza was split among pro-Egyptian, pro-Jordanian, PLO nationalist, and religious factions.

Camp David Accords

President Sadat's visit to Israel in November 1977, however, touched off what would be the most explosive phase of Gaza's political history yet. The explosion was fueled by the Camp David Accords and their plan for Palestinian autonomy in the occupied territories. Most Gazans interpreted the Accords as a renunciation by Egypt of all claims on the Gaza Strip. The autonomy plan, moreover, contained many clauses that Palestinians found unacceptable.[25] Objections to the plan emphasized two key points: Israel's continued control over land, water, settlements, and security in the Gaza Strip and West Bank; and continued prohibitions on the establishment of a Palestinian policymaking government. Furthermore, at the end of the process, Palestinians were to choose between Jordanian or Israeli citizenship, neither of which appealed to Gazans.

The Sadat initiative was regarded in Gaza as a political betrayal of the Palestinian cause by a government they had come to trust.[26] Most Gazans saw it as an attempt to bypass the PLO and bargain away national statehood for the Sinai oilfields. Sadat's later suggestion for a "Gaza First" approach to the implementation of the autonomy plan, which was motivated by a need to prove that Egypt was not seeking a separate peace with Israel, did little to mollify local dissent. Under this scenario, autonomy would be "tested" in Gaza before the West Bank, because the Strip was far smaller in size, easier to administer, and less encumbered by disputes over borders. The idea required the establishment of a local ruling council similar to that which existed in Gaza before 1967. The success of the council, it was believed, would entice West Bank Arabs into a similar political experiment, even if it meant defying Jordan and those Arab states opposed to autonomy.

Sadat felt certain he could convince Gazans to adopt his "Gaza First" proposal; he assumed that the mainstream leadership in Gaza was far less opposed to autonomy than their counterparts in the West Bank.[27] His assumption proved embarrassingly incorrect when even Israeli-appointed Mayor Shawa openly rejected the plan. The mayor, who was frustrated by the continued absence of viable political options for the Palestinians, found the autonomy proposals and the Sadat initiative particularly objectionable.

One month after the Camp David Accords in September 1978, a rally was held in Gaza to denounce the accords and to propose comprehensive negotiations for Palestinian self-determination, which were to include the PLO. This rally, the only one allowed in Gaza between 1967 and 1993, brought together individuals and groups from a wide range of political viewpoints, including members of both the indigenous upper classes and the refugee community. Indeed, the differences between these two groups had accounted for the lack of an organized, well-led political movement in the Gaza Strip.

After the rally, the Israelis imposed restrictions on political activity in Gaza, particularly on the organization of public assemblies and meetings. Individuals with known political preferences were confined to the Strip for long periods. Over the next year tensions increased, and various municipalities and local councils issued a communiqué openly proclaiming the PLO as the sole legitimate representative of the Palestinian people. During this time, Egypt, in perceived concert with the Israelis, exerted its own punitive pressures on Gazans. Angered over their rejection of the Camp David Accords and his "Gaza First" proposal, Sadat froze salary payments to officials employed in Gaza by the Egyptian government prior to 1967 and blocked the admission of Gaza students to Egyptian universities.[28]

The rejectionist front, which had developed in the wake of Camp David, resisted Egyptian and Israeli pressures. By 1980, it enjoyed considerable popular support. Despite official announcements of a new, more lenient policy toward the occupied territories, Prime Minister Begin and his defense minister, Ariel Sharon, imposed what came to be known as Israel's "iron fist" policy. The cancellation of promised municipal elections and the expulsion of two West Bank mayors, Mohammed Milhem of Halhoul and Fuad Kawasme of Hebron, were but two examples. An editorial appearing in Israel's independent newspaper, *Haaretz*, said of the government's new policy: "If this is liberalization, it is being applied...with pincers."[29] The autumn of 1981 and the spring of 1982 witnessed a strong resurgence of civil disobedience in the Gaza Strip. A series of Israeli measures imposed on Gaza's residents catalyzed the upsurge in violence.[30]

Soon thereafter, the Israeli government instituted a civil administration in the Gaza Strip and West Bank, structurally parallel to that of the military administration and subject to it. In that sense, the civil administration was, in effect, an integral part of the military structure. Implemented in Gaza on 1 December 1981, the CIVAD, as it came to be known, was given responsibility over all nonmilitary sectors such as health, education, and welfare. Interpreted as the first step toward the implementation of Begin's autonomy plan and the annexation of the territories, the imposition of the civil administration generated considerable frustration and fear in Gaza and once again ignited local passions that took months to quell. Israel's annexation of the Golan Heights in December 1981 did little to appease Arab fears.

On 2 December Mayor Shawa announced a general strike protesting the civil administration. Shawa, in conjunction with West Bank mayors, continued to boycott the CIVAD by refusing to cooperate with its officials. In the spring of 1982, the West Bank mayors were removed and replaced by Israeli military officials; Shawa was ordered to end the strike in Gaza. His refusal to do so culminated in his dismissal and the disbanding of Gaza's municipal council once again. By August 1982, the Israeli interior ministry assumed control over Gaza's municipal structure and direct military rule resumed in the Strip. It was not until 1991 that the defense ministry and local Palestinian leaders agreed to establish a new municipal council in Gaza headed by Fayez Abu Rahme, an attorney and known Fateh activist.

Israel's final withdrawal from Sinai in April 1982 and the Lebanon war that followed heightened tensions and the sense of despair in the Strip. During this time, the Israeli authorities intensified their control over Gaza through a variety of measures, among them increased civilian settlements *inside* the territory.[31]

In the spring of 1986, ex-Mayor Shawa approached Egyptian president Hosni Mubarak with a proposal for returning Gaza to Egyptian administrative supervision, with Israeli approval, pending a final solution to the status of the territory. Shawa had cause for some optimism; the failure of the Jordanian-PLO talks and the assassination of Nablus Mayor Zaafer al-Masri had caused Israeli policymakers to consider a "Gaza First" autonomy scheme.[32] Shawa's autonomy proposal called for setting up Egyptian consular services in East Jerusalem, reestablishing the Palestinian legislative council that existed under Egypt, and opening an Egyptian bank in Gaza.[33] Reflecting an attempt to break through the political impasse confronting the occupied territories by calling for Egyptian-backed Palestinian self-rule in the Gaza Strip, the proposal was ultimately doomed by a clear lack of support from President Mubarak, King Hussein, and Prime Minister Peres.

By the outbreak of the Palestinian uprising on 8 December 1987, Gaza had no elected mayor, no election process, and no right of public assembly. Palestinians had no flag and no sovereignty. Channels for political expression and legal protection did not exist and seemed increasingly improbable in light of the 1985 reinstatement of preventive detentions and deportations. Heightened civilian settlement brought with it contestations over vastly limited natural resources, especially land and water. Economic growth had ended years before, and an array of military restrictions, in effect since 1968, had precluded any form of indigenous economic development.

Conclusion

Gaza's political history under Israeli occupation reveals two facts of particular significance for economic development: Israel's desire for absolute control over land and water, Gaza's critical resources; and Israel's total rejection of any independent indigenous political or economic movement. The "land over people" priority first articulated by the Zionists during the Mandate period was reexpressed in government policies toward the Gaza Strip after 1967, which aimed to insure Gaza's inseparability from Israel.

Political inseparability was fostered through economic integration, through policies that raised Israel's territorial considerations above all others, including the economic. In this way, Israeli policy in Gaza was not motivated primarily by economic rationality but by political ideology. This ideology abhorred the notion of Palestinian sovereignty and rejected any process that might encourage it, especially economic development. Consequently, the government of Israel has pursued a policy of *de-development* in the Gaza Strip which is predicated on the structural containment of the Palestinian domestic economy and the deliberate and consistent dismemberment of that economy over time. However, although radical structural change of the economy was prohibited, individual prosperity was not. Indeed, limited prosperity was meant to mollify Palestinians politically, whereas the loss of their indigenous infrastructural base was meant to insure their continued dependence on Israel economically and preclude the emergence of any nationalist movement or cultural identity from within the occupied territories. In this way, de-development may be regarded as the economic expression (and continuation) of Israel's ideological and political priorities. The conclusion to this book argues that this continues to be case under the Gaza–Jericho Agreement.

Part II of this book, which follows, focuses on de-development, its theory, policy roots, and sectoral manifestations.

Notes to Chapter 4:

1.   See Meir Shamgar, "The Law in the Areas Held by the Israel Defense Forces," *Public Administration in Israel and Abroad* 8 (1968): 40–57; and Mordechai Nisan, *Israel and the Territories: A Study in Control 1967–77* (Ramat Gan: Turtledove Publishing, 1978).

2.   See Don Peretz, "Israel's Administration and Arab Refugees," *Foreign Affairs* 46, no.2 (January 1968): 336–46.

3.   Under the Allon Plan, Israel would return the West Bank to Jordan but would retain a narrow strip of settlements along the Jordan River. The West Bank would be joined to Jordan by a corridor leading from Ramallah through Jericho to the Allenby Bridge. The Dead Sea and the Judean Desert would serve as Israel's defence line in the East. Gaza would revert to Israel but most of Sinai could be returned to Egypt. The Gaza Strip could serve Jordan and the West Bank as an outlet to the Mediterranean with Israel granting certain rights of passage. However, a corridor would not be established.

4.   In 1976, Allon changed his mind and proposed returning Gaza to Arab control. His change in strategy was motivated by the government's failure to fully implement its original plans to settle many of Gaza's 350,000 refugees in el-Arish. Allon's ideas are discussed in Yigal Allon, "Israel: The Case For Defensible Borders," *Foreign Affairs* 55, no.1 (October 1976): 38–53.

5.   John K. Cooley, "Gaza points up strain in Middle East," *Christian Science Monitor*, 31 May 1968.

6. Daniel Dishon (ed.), *Middle East Record*, Vol. 5, 1969–1970 (Jerusalem: Israeli Universities Press, 1977), pp. 395–401.

7.   Dishon (ed.), p. 399. For a study of the role of the fighters within Palestinian society, see Yasumasa Kuroda and Alice K. Kuroda, "Socialization of Freedom Fighters: The Palestinian Experience," in Ibrahim Abu-Lughod and Baha Abu-Laban (eds.), *Settler Regimes in Africa and the Arab World: The Illusion of Endurance* (Wilmete, IL: Medina University Press International, 1974), pp. 147–61.

8.   A. Susser, "The Israeli-Administered Territories," in Dishon (ed.), p. 343.

9.   State of Israel, Ministry of Foreign Affairs, *The Administered Areas: Aspects of Israeli Policy*, Information Briefing 10, Jerusalem, September 1973, p. 35.

10.   For a view of the guerrilla movement from the inside, see Carlos Padilla, "Report on Palestine Resistance," *Arab Palestinian Resistance* 2, no.4 (January 1970): 29–40. A guerrilla fighter in Gaza tells his own personal story in "Highlights of Palestinian Struggle: The Fedayeen Rule the Gaza Strip," *Democratic Palestine* (May 1987): 17–21.

11.   Confidential report dated 15 February 1971, *New York Times* archives, New York.

12.   Between April 1970 and April 1971, 71 guerrilla fighters were killed, 25 captured and 1,219 arrested. See "Aviram: Mood of Gaza population changing," *Jerusalem Post*, 2 April 1971.

13.   Al-Quds Press Office, *Gaza: A Table Explaining the Number of Palestinian Deportees from the Gaza Strip June 1967–October 1988*, Gaza, 1989. The table indicates that after 1973 there were comparatively few deportations from the Strip.

14.   An Israeli colonel, Shumuel Liran, justified the widening of roads as an attempt "to bring some light and space into the camps." Walter Schwarz, "Israel Begins Resettling Gaza Arabs into Better Homes,"*Washington Post*, 5 November 1970. Between 1967 and 1988, the army destroyed a total of 22,230 rooms and displaced 61,401 people. In-house statistics, UNRWA, Gaza Strip, 1989.

15.   In-house statistics, UNRWA, Gaza Strip, 1989.

16.   Sharon, p. 258. See also, "Go to Gaza," *Shdamot* (in Hebrew), no.66 (Winter 1968): 7-13, for the opinions of the Governor of Gaza between 1971 and 1974.

17.   Ze'ev Shul, "Dayan: Gaza Strip should be integral part of Israel," *Jerusalem Post*, 6 July 1967.

18.   Geoffrey Aronson, *Creating Facts: Israel, Palestinians and the West Bank* (Washington, DC: Institute for Palestine Studies, 1987).

19.   "Consolidation in Gaza Strip must be speeded—Galili," *Jerusalem Post*, 8 October 1970. Foreign Minister Abba Eban and Minister of Police Shlomo Hillel were expounding similar viewpoints. See "Eban: Gaza won't be separated from Israel," *Jerusalem Post*, 17 November 1972; and H. Ben-Adi, "Hillel: working toward Gaza's full integration," *Jerusalem Post*, 5 January 1971.

20.   "In high court Rafah Beduin lose case against their eviction," *Jerusalem Post*, 24 May 1973.

21.   Neu, p. 136; and Terrence Smith, "Lines of Israeli Settlements in Occupied Areas Are Said to Reflect Plans for Borders," *New York Times*, 6 November 1975.

22.   David Richardson, "Last of the Aristocrats," *Jerusalem Post*, 17 May 1985, presents an interesting profile of Rashad Shawa, who was a central figure in the history of the Palestinian nationalist movement.

23.   Neu, p. 139.

24.   For an interesting discussion of this period, see Anan Safadi, and Philip Gillon, "Gaza After Shawa," *Jerusalem Post*, 27 October 1972.

25.   William E. Farrell, "Begin Insists Israel Must Keep Troops in West Bank Area," *New York Times*, 29 December 1977, for a text of Begin's plan for the West Bank and

Gaza Strip. For a retrospective view, see "Introduction," in William B. Quandt, *The Middle East: Ten Years After Camp David* (Washington, D.C: The Brookings Institution, 1988), pp. 1–16.

26.   Moslem cleric Sheikh Hasham Hussendeir, supported the idea of autonomy as did other religious figures and some local secular leaders, such as the mayor of Deir el-Balah. They were all threatened and Sheikh Hussendeir was later assassinated.

27.   Colin Legum (ed.), *Middle East Contemporary Survey*, Vol. 3 (New York: Holmes and Meier, 1980), p. 327.

28.   Legum (ed.), *Middle East Contemporary Survey*, Vol. 5, p. 343. For Dayan's interpretation of Sadat's measures, see Moshe Dayan, *Breakthrough: A Personal Account of the Egypt-Israel Peace Negotiations* (New York: Alfred A. Knopf, 1981), pp. 291–93.

29.   William Farrell, "Israeli Shift on Arabs: Real or Mirage," *New York Times*, 19 August 1981.

30.   The first of these measures concerned the government imposition of a special excise tax on professionals, which resulted in a strike on 22 November 1981 by doctors, dentists, pharmacists, veterinarians, lawyers, and engineers. In response, the Israeli government welded shut the doors of 170 shops and 18 pharmacies, imposed heavy fines on doctors, and arrested protesters. The strike, which ended two weeks later, delayed but failed to alter government measures.

31.   See, for example, Joshua Brilliant, "Sharon shuns group on areas after leak of plan for Gaza," *Jerusalem Post*, 15 November 1978; and Ann Lesch, *The Gaza Strip: Heading Towards a Dead End, Part II*, no.11, p. 2.

32.   Benny Morris, "Israel may sound out Murphy on Gaza plan," *Jerusalem Post*, 10 March 1986.

33.   See, for example, Glenn Frankel, "Palestinian Leader Wears Risky 'Moderate' Label: Shawa Tests Political Boundaries with Call for Gaza's Union with Jordan," *Washington Post*, 22 August 1986.

PART II:

Israeli Occupation and De-development

5

Theories of Development and Underdevelopment: The Particularity of Palestinian Dependence

P rior to 1967, underdevelopment was a characteristic feature of Gaza's
economy. De-development commenced only under Israeli occupation. The
distinction is a product of Israeli state policies that differed greatly from those
of previous regimes. Egypt, for example, never aimed to extend its sovereignty
to the Gaza Strip and vigorously maintained the territory as a separate national,
political, and economic entity. For better or worse, the character of economic
reform in Gaza was shaped by this political imperative, which was also linked
to Egypt's own underdeveloped economy. The government did not seek to deprive Gaza of its own economic resources or restructure the domestic economy
to serve Egyptian interests. Israel, by contrast, did, and as a highly industrialized and technologically advanced economy, possessed the power to do so.

Israel's national and political imperatives in the remnant of Mandate Palestine departed significantly from those of its predecessors. The state's national
aspirations extended to the occupied Palestinian territories despite the political
ambiguity surrounding their exact form. The imperatives of expanding Israeli
sovereignty produced an economic policy that prioritized integration over separation, and dispossession over exploitation. Moreover, the expansion of Israeli
sovereignty also demanded the rejection of Palestinian nationalism and the
weakening or suppression of those forces, largely institutional, that could promote that nationalism. These unusual features of Israeli policy, which reflected
the ideological imperatives of Zionism, produced not only underdevelopment
but de-development. Chapters 7 to 9 discuss the policy components of de-de-

velopment: expropriation and dispossession, integration and externalization, and deinstitutionalization.

Thus, during Israeli rule economic policy was used primarily as a form of state control, and only subsequently as a formula for determining economic advantage. This approach and its economic consequences are not easily explained by existing development theories that prioritize the economic over the political. Indeed, such theories fail to explain the economic problems of the Gaza Strip. The reason for their failure is the subject of this chapter. The aim is to provide a conceptual framework for understanding Gaza's de-development.

The development process, which has been the subject of considerable theorizing, began after World War II with the beginning of decolonization and "the revolt against the West."[1] In the newly emerging nations of the third world, economic development was initially seen as a means of achieving political stability and building national identity and, given the example set by the West, was expected to occur rapidly and easily. Development and its counterpart, underdevelopment, have been conceived as many things and explained in many ways, but the theoretical discourse that has emerged around both concepts has attempted to identify their causes and articulate an appropriate response. The focus of the discourse, however, has largely been economic, deriving from a belief among the less developed that economic progress is synonymous with indigenous development.

Development theory can generally be categorized by its response to capitalism. Theories that emphasize the positive impact of capitalist development on third world formations constitute what is termed modernization theory. Those that emphasize the negative impact of capitalist development are termed dependency theory.[2] Born in the cold war era of the 1950s, modernization theory was an attempt to challenge Soviet influence in the third world by offering a Western-style formula for economic growth and social advancement. A decade later, dependency theory arose, in part, as a socialist response to the politics of modernization and modernization's inherent bias towards capitalist-inspired development. After more than four decades of theoretical discourse, the reasons for development and underdevelopment remain unresolved. Despite its inability to *explain* these phenomena, however, development theory has proven particularly useful as a tool for *understanding* them.[3]

Both modernization and dependency theory reveal the difficulties and deficiencies in studying economic change.[4] Both can be used to shed some explanatory light on development in the Gaza Strip, although that light arguably obscures more than it reveals.[5] Modernization theory, for example, points to the lack of capital and absence of innovation as impediments to development, factors that have clearly impeded growth in the Gaza Strip and West Bank. Some theorists argue that the fastest and most efficient way to promote economic growth in less developed nations is to improve the productivity of the agricultural (food-crop) sector, where the majority of the population live and work, whereas others emphasize the development of industry first. Clearly biased toward the Western experience with development and its economic aspects in particular, modernization theorists posit that the West can have only a positive and progressive impact on less developed nations. Hence, they also link the lack of economic development in the third world to the inimical and obstructive nature of traditional values and cultural practices. All these arguments could be used to explain underdevelopment in the Gaza Strip.

Dependency theory elucidates the significance of the structural relationship between a dominant and a subordinate economy and exposes the process by which the latter is exploited to serve the needs of the former. It also reveals that underdevelopment is shaped far more by relations of trade than by relations of production. It is the consequences of markets and trade rather than production patterns in peripheral economies that are the catalysts of underdevelopment. These features also characterize economic conditions in the occupied territories, especially the Gaza Strip. Other applications can be drawn as well.

Both Palestinian and Israeli scholars have used various development theories to describe Israel's economic relationship with the West Bank. Theory, however, has not been used to describe Israel's relationship with the Gaza Strip. Palestinians tend to use the language of dependency theory and use neo-Marxist analyses to define the relationship between Israel and the West Bank as economic and structurally asymmetric. It is a center-periphery relationship between two separate economies, with Israel the dominant "center" economy and the West Bank its subordinated, peripheralized counterpart.

The Palestinian approach characterizes Israel's economy as a highly developed capitalist economy that controls and shapes activity in the far less developed capitalist economy of the West Bank and Gaza. The latter is not freely integrated with the world capitalist system but is instead directed to meet Israeli priorities, both domestic and international. This in turn gives Israel, not the West Bank, a comparative advantage in its exchanges with the world market. Because the Israeli economy has colonized economic activity in the West Bank but has not annexed the territory politically, the two economies remain analytically separate, even though they exist within the same geographical entity. As such, Palestinians characterize the relationship between Israel and the occupied territories as a form of settler colonialism that is external rather than internal in structure.[6]

Palestinians further define the relationship as one of exchange rather than production, in which relations of markets and trade, not class, shape interaction across the green line. However, the exchange relations between Israel and the West Bank are not typical center–periphery relations, which commonly allow for some form of capitalist development in the peripheral economy (although that development is dependent on and disarticulated toward the center). Rather, the exchange relations between Israel and the West Bank are atypical in that they are characterized by a *deliberate* attempt on the part of the dominant power to first incorporate and then pauperize the periphery's productive economic structure through a variety of measures, including land expropriation and the expulsion of the indigenous population.[7] Consequently, any possibility of initiating independent economic activity within the periphery, or those processes essential to such activity (e.g., capital accumulation), are precluded. In this regard, the critique maintains that although the peripheralization of the West Bank and Gaza Strip was not begun by Israel but by the Ottomans (and later perpetuated by the Jordanians and Egyptians), it is being carried to its structural extreme by Israeli policies that aim to repress the development of the periphery's productive economic forces.

Israelis tend to borrow heavily from modernization theory and emphasize Israel's modernizing impact on Palestinian society. They measure this impact by the dramatic material improvements in the Arab standard of living achieved under Israeli rule and by the changing patterns of consumption and production that have accompanied these improvements. Comparisons, typically made with previous Arab occupiers, are drawn along economic, social, and attitudinal lines. First, previous Arab regimes did not foster indigenous economic growth in the West Bank and Gaza Strip. Jordan, for example, clearly favored the economic development of the East over the West Bank. Gaza under Egypt fared no better. Although Egypt did not promote its own economic progress over that of Gaza's, Egyptian policy focused almost exclusively on agriculture, which placed clear limitations on the development of the modern sector and the ability of the local economy to expand. Under Arab regimes, therefore, the traditional nature of economic organization was sustained and reinforced, which precluded enhanced levels of economic growth as well as modernizing innovations.

Second, the absence of economic transformation is correlated with the absence of social transformation. Society remained rural and backward. Commonly cited evidence includes the highly restricted role of women, low levels of educational attainment and limited educational access, particularly among girls, and the inferior quality of health care as reflected in the high level of infant mortality. Without institutional development and change, Palestinians in pre-1967 Palestine remained decidedly traditional in outlook, unexposed to change and unwilling to accept it.

Third, this argument maintains that after 1967, interaction with Israeli society exposed Palestinians to a more modern way of life and inculcated attitudes and values supportive of advanced social and economic change. The argument further maintains that access to the Israeli economy, for example, brought new employment patterns that not only propelled men beyond their own narrow and traditional spheres of social and economic activity, but also created the possibility for women to leave the confines of the private domain. Israel also granted women the right to vote; their political enfranchisement was critical to the promotion of greater gender equality and fair social practice. Under Israeli rule, furthermore, the quality of and access to education and healthcare improved considerably. Universities were established and an increasing number of hospitals built. As a result, popular expectations regarding acceptable standards of education and healthcare, as well as the perceived need for such services, increased significantly. Indeed, widened institutional development in a range of sectors was accompanied by the introduction of new technologies and greater efficiency, which Palestinians came to expect.

Through their exposure to and interaction with Israeli society, therefore, Palestinians in the West Bank and Gaza Strip adopted values and modes of living that were more advanced than the arduous and backward way of life characteristic of traditional societies. The political and economic domains become more distinct, and there was greater differentiation within each domain, particularly with respect to the role of women. Perhaps the most significant changes occurred within the economic sphere, which has been characterized by increased social mobilization and technological diffusion. Common indexes of development used by Israel include the rise in per capita GNP, the significant increase in the number of cars and electrical appliances found in Palestinian homes, and the growth in privately owned residences.[8] Thus, goes the argument, the impact of Israeli rule has been to place Palestinian society in the occupied territories further along the unilinear continuum toward Western-style modernity.

The two perspectives described above are very different, yet both contain incomplete truths. They provide an interesting, albeit competing, set of insights into the same issue, although they are derived from a very different set of ideological assumptions about development. Clearly, no one theory can explain or capture the myriad features and complexities of any development problem, nor is there a universal set of criteria for measuring development. Taken collectively, individual theories can, at best, provide a spectrum of analytic lenses through which to view a given problem and, within the conceptual repertoire currently available, insure as broad and differentiated an interpretation as possible.

This book argues that the relationship between Israel and the Gaza Strip is not easily explained by the available theoretical literature. Indeed, in clear and specific ways, that relationship lies outside existing conceptual paradigms and the assumptions on which they are based. Thomas Kuhn, in *The Structure of Scientific Revolutions,* termed this problem "paradigm exhaustion"; he argued that accepted truths are often inadequate as tools for explaining and organizing varying perceptions of different realities, and that new truths need to be created.[9] Insofar as the Gaza Strip is concerned, any attempt to understand the problems of Palestinian development must ask not only how existing theories facilitate analysis, but, more importantly, how they impede analysis. The issues associated with Palestinian development under Israeli occupation need to be understood in light of what development theory is *unable* to explain, and in light of its consistent failure to identify, let alone incorporate, certain conceptual configurations within its paradigmatic boundaries. Perhaps the reason for this failure lies in the fact that the concept of development, and the ways in which it has been conceived over the last four decades, deny certain possibilities, especially negative possibilities.[10] Yet these possibilities—e.g., destruction of the peripheral economy, suppression of national identity, denial of civil rights—have characterized the relationship between Israel and the Gaza Strip for nearly three decades.

In the absence of adequate theoretical explanations for the peculiar problems confronting development in the Gaza Strip, it is argued that an analytic approach is needed that gives primacy to empirical data. The empirical data should provide the basis for the construction of theory.[11] Development is a relative process that must be understood in its own context and not according to some prescribed theoretical model or externally imposed definition.

Development in the Gaza Strip: The Particularity of Palestinian Dependence

In what ways is the study of development in the Gaza Strip different and how does it contribute to the theoretical discourse? One way to answer these questions is to examine how existing theories fail to explain the condition of the Gaza Strip. Despite their obvious differences, the Palestinian and Israeli approaches described above converge along a number of points that are particularly relevant to this study. Both theories present a notion of development that is teleological and economistic. Change tends to be conceptualized in linear terms and is presumed to be similar in all developing countries. Development is used interchangeably with growth and remains a purely economic concept despite its noneconomic components. Primacy is given to economic relations, often without regard to political, social, and cultural relations. Development is confined to changes in national product or national income, "without substantial change occurring in the structure or locus of social and political power, values, organization or technology—in short, without radical change in the non-economic factors or relevance to the operation of the economy."[12] However, it is precisely the transformation of these noneconomic forces together with those of the economy that underlie development. The cumulative effect of development is not simple growth but a more complex transformation in the structure of the economy and in the political, social, and cultural environment of which it is a part. The theoretical failure to distinguish between growth and development devalues the importance of comparative studies between rich and poor nations that would illustrate their dissimilarities (rather than commonly emphasized asymmetries) and dismisses the less developed country as a unit of analysis.

In this regard, less developed societies are not examined internally; they are not viewed as entities with individual historical experiences, but rather as societies that to varying degrees approximate Western economic, political, and sociological categorizations. There is no differentiation between peripheral nations, only between those of the core and the periphery. This assumption rejects the importance of the periphery as a unit of analysis and in so doing, not only denies the role of class relations and class exploitation in the generation of peripheral underdevelopment, a role of clear import in the Gaza Strip, but denies any possibility of intraperipheral distinctions (economic, political, social, and cultural), themselves a fundamental supposition of this study. By failing to recognize the significance of third world formations, modernization and dependency theory not only err in identifying important factors of underdevelopment, but, in effect, represent an assault on the established institutional order in third world societies. In this case, it is not only the differences between Israel and the Gaza Strip that need to be understood as factors in Gaza's development but also the differences between Gaza and the West Bank.

Both modernization and dependency theory view core–periphery relations as unidirectional—from core to periphery. Neither school sees the periphery as being able to influence the core in any way. The relationship between the Gaza Strip and Israel, however, demonstrates just the opposite. It shows the many ways in which the former can affect the latter (e.g., the growing Israeli dependence on Palestinian labor, especially from the Gaza Strip; the impact of intercommunal violence on Israeli society; popular resistance to the Israeli occupation). The Gaza–Israel relationship extends the dependency relationship to one that acknowledges relations of mutual dependence. More importantly, it redefines the nature of that dependence to include causes that are not primarily economic in character.

Indeed, one way in which the Palestinian case study dramatically departs from conventional development theories concerns the relations of power between Israel and the territories it occupies. First, the periphery is part of the same geographical and economic entity as the center to which it is subordinate and on which it is dependent. Furthermore, it could be argued that the occupied territories are also a part of the same political entity as the center (despite separate political arrangements within each), given Israel's consistent unwillingness to renounce its territorial (and for some, sovereign) claims on Gaza and the West Bank. (As will be demonstrated in the book's conclusion, this has not changed under the terms of the Gaza–Jericho Agreement.) Thus, unlike many of the third world formations described by modernization and dependency theorists, the Israeli-occupied territories are not sovereign states or even entities on the way to achieving sovereignty. As such, they cannot even enjoy the limited or questionable benefits (e.g., infrastructural development, access to financial capital, some sectoral growth) of disarticulated growth associated with "traditional" dependency. The Gaza Strip and West Bank have none of the rights of political independence, such as self-determination, control over economic resources and sectoral development, freedom of cultural expression, unencumbered access to international and national capital, security, and the ability to plan. Hence, the distortion of the Palestinian economy is less the result of international economic relations, the dominance of industrial capitalism, or exploitative market relations (although linkages do exist), than of the imposition of

Israeli military power and physical force.[13]

Israel's relationship with the West Bank and Gaza Strip has been termed a form of settler colonialism and indeed, many features of this model do apply. Colonial settler states are basically characterized by four features: (1) ideological justification (e.g., the Calvinist mission of the Dutch in South Africa, the civilizing mission of the French in Algeria, and the Zionist mission of the Jewish people in Palestine); (2) legal legitimacy (e.g., the 1910 South African Constitution in which the British gave the Boer settlers the right to continue their exclusionary and discriminatory practices toward the native population; the Balfour Declaration, in which the British gave the Jewish population of Palestine the right to settle the land and form their own national body); (3) land acquisition by means such as direct purchase, non-use, public domain, state lands, military declarations (e.g., in 1863, the French took 90 percent of the cultivated lands in Algeria; in 1913, the South African Land Act gave 87 percent of the land to the white settler population; in 1948, the Zionists purchased less than 7 percent of the land of Palestine, followed since by the acquisition of land through state land laws, military closures, and confiscations for security reasons and population settlement); and (4) racism, used to justify discriminatory policies toward the indigenous population.

Although it possesses all these features to varying degrees, Israel differs in marked and important ways. The Jewish population in Palestine settled the land and eventually became the dominant group, but their intent, given their singular mission of creating a safe haven for world Jewry, was not to dominate the native population, keeping them in urban ghettos or separate areas such as bantustans as other settler states had, but to dispossess them of their economic and political resources and physically remove them from the land.[14] It was not the "typical" economic exploitation of the natives for profit that motivated the Zionists, although that did occur, but rather the ideological goal of building a strong Jewish state minus the indigenous Palestinian population that motivated Jewish settlement in Gaza and the West Bank and the large-scale land expropriations that supported such settlement.[15]

However, in order to empower the state, Israel had to increase its own economic strength and viability. Since 1967, it has done so by exploiting Palestinian labor and material resources, by settling occupied Arab lands with Jews, and by promulgating policies aimed at encouraging Palestinians to leave. Furthermore, because of massive amounts of economic aid from the United States and diaspora Jewry, Israel has enhanced its own infrastructure and development without the usual cost constraints or need to balance expenditures with profits from productivity. This, in turn, made it possible for the state to absorb and exploit Palestinian human and material resources and continue its costly settlement policies at the same time. Economic exploitation occurs and contributes to Israel's economic strength, but in a manner that differs from that of other settler states because, over time, such exploitation deprives Palestinians of their own resources.

Hence, whereas dependency theories maintain that the ruling class in both core and peripheral nations is an economic class that rules politically, in this case, the ruling class (whose allegiance is to Zionism) is a political class that rules economically. In this situation, development and underdevelopment are no longer motivated primarily by economic imperatives, but rather by political and ideological ones.

During the formative economic period under the British Mandate, Jewish colonialism sought to acquire Arab land, not Arab labor. This guiding principle did not fundamentally change after 1967. As such, Israeli capitalism never sought to create a capitalist class in the Gaza Strip or West Bank with which it could collude. To the contrary, capitalist development was not what Israel sought to implant in the occupied territories. Consequently, economic relations became a means for fulfilling political objectives, a critical component of Israel's system of control.

Development theories also overlook the link between current problems of underdevelopment and their historical antecedents. Neither development nor the interrelationships identified as impeding it are ahistorical phenomena. The problems of development in the Gaza Strip did not emerge after 1967; they are rooted in the evolution of political, economic, and social relations between Jews and Arabs in Palestine three decades before the Gaza Strip was formally established. Indeed, de-development emanates from the "land over people" imperative formalized during the British Mandate.

The political basis of Israeli policy has resulted in another unusual feature of the Gaza development model: the destruction, of the peripheral entity as an economic, political, and cultural unit. Development and underdevelopment in the Gaza Strip is characterized not only by disarticulation and structural disfigurement of the peripheral economy, but also by its total retrogression.

In Gaza's case, the peripheral economy has been dismembered through a series of measures that precluded the formation of productive forces and sought to dispossess the population of their political patrimony and economic potential. Modernization and dependency theory have never explained a problem of this nature. How, for example, would the theories explain the deliberate uprooting and displacement of the indigenous population, the "de-skilling" and underuse of the Palestinian labor force, the segmentation and fragmentation of the economic sector in the periphery, the usurpation of land and water, the proletarianization of the workforce and the increasing insignificance of the "proletariat," the alienation of the Arab labor force, or the intentional denial of access to the means of production as a form of collective punishment? Moreover, how would existing theories explain the political repression of the Palestinians, the total politicization of social and economic life in Gaza, the harassment of educational institutions, the discriminatory application of economic policy, the denial of legal protections, the destruction of personal property, the deportation of the Palestinian leadership, the arbitrary use of power, the endemic conflict between Israelis and Arabs, and racism? Whereas development theories commonly identify dominance, inequality, and exploitation as reasons for underdevelopment, they fail to account for the dispossession and destruction of productive resources, the principal reason for Gaza's socioeconomic debilitation.

The dismantling of Gaza's economy is in part deliberate, as is the suppression of Palestinian nationalism and cultural identity that motivates it. After all, economic, political, and cultural dispossession are inextricable; the denial of the political and cultural has very much shaped the economic. Hence, development in the Gaza Strip cannot be understood simply as surplus extraction or resource exploitation, but rather as political and cultural aggression. The struggle against Israeli colonization, therefore, does not arise out of the relations of production. Power is no longer defined as mere dominance or control over the means of production but as something far more damaging. Consequently, the study of development and underdevelopment in Gaza includes analytic concepts that remain absent, implicit, or inappropriately defined in other theoretical models. Two such concepts are violence and resistance.

It is an accepted maxim of history that social change is often accompanied by violence and, in some cases, predicated on it. The development literature tends to treat this concept narrowly. Violence and its relationship to development is often regarded as extraordinary: a revolution or rebellion against an authoritarian state or toward the attainment of a new political order. Violence is also regarded as an extrainstitutional phenomenon, existing outside the legitimate institutional structure of a society rather than as an integral part of it. It is consequently portrayed as random, unorganized, episodic, and purposeless, the product of a few deviant minds.[16]

The relationship between the state of Israel and the occupied Gaza Strip and West Bank has been and continues to be characterized by violence of a very different sort. In addition to the accepted characterizations of interstate terrorism, intercommunal terrorism, and the Palestinian uprising, the more common and historic expression of violence between Israelis and Palestinians has gone unnoticed. Violence is defined as a form of interaction that is institutionalized in the structure of military government and legitimized by the system of military law. In Gaza and the West Bank, violence has never been defined solely or even primarily by physical harm to people and their possessions, but rather by the systematic application of measures that encouraged stability in the short term but promoted disintegration in the long term. These measures were designed not only to appease and then fragment Palestinian society, but to render it unviable, and to do so quietly and without notice. These measures variously included: the establishment of Palestinian (health and educational) institutions, followed by their planned and consistent disruption; the promotion of certain grassroots activities, followed by the criminalization of community organizing; the introduction of advanced agricultural technologies concomitant with the steady confiscation of land and water; the introduction of refugee rehousing programs together with the establishment of Jewish settlements on Arab land; improved access to employment in the Israeli economy in conjunction with prohibitions on the development of the domestic Palestinian economy (e.g., restricted access to international markets, control over all forms of indigenous production and over the flow of information, and consistently low levels of government investment in key economic sectors); an improved standard of living tempered by prohibitions on virtually all forms of political and cultural expression; and the denial of civil rights.

This Kafkaesque violence is distinguished by its ordinariness, prosaism, and invisibility. The accepted norms of human behavior such as the need to be fair, consistent, accountable, or reasonable, are delegitimized and cease to define the way people treat each other or what they can reasonably expect. This violence is a form of aggression where randomness of action is the only assurance people have, and lack of predictability their only guarantee. It is violence whose physical manifestations can appear benign if not positive, but whose objectives are highly purposeful: to define the boundaries of daily activity and punish those who exceed them.

Within this construct, violence and development are not simply linked by protest or revolution, nor is violence strictly the unanticipated outcome of successful development.[17] Rather, in Gaza in particular, violence has its own unique totality; it defines development and undermines it at the same time. It characterizes the struggle between integration and disintegration. Violence determines where development begins and where it ends; what it can aspire to and what it cannot; who can participate and who cannot; how it proceeds, and at what pace. David Apter writes:

> Violence is about break, disordering, and ordering. It can do these things because it also has about it a certain starkness, a minimalism that, utterly shocking, pulls away the fabric of decency. It defines and disrupts ordinary rationality....violence today...has a dissolving effect—an alien intimacy— personal yet impersonal, like rape. One experiences it alone.[18]

If violence is a component of development in the Gaza Strip, then so is resistance to violence. Violence and resistance thus form a dialectic in the Gaza Strip. The notion of resistance presumes the periphery can defend itself against external aggression in ways that are nonviolent (although violent means have also been used) and play a role in its own development, another deviation from the theoretical paradigms under discussion that view the periphery as powerless. In Gaza, the periphery has resisted. In the Palestinian context, therefore, resistance is not simply a matter of opposing foreign rule, it is profoundly a matter of survival.

In Gaza and the West Bank, resistance has assumed many forms. One, steadfastness, was supported through a range of economic activities. Another mode of defense is institutional. It involves the establishment of mass-based organizations (e.g., trade unions, women's committees, medical and agricultural relief committees), an "infrastructure of resistance"[19] at the grassroots level, which represents a more active way the Palestinian community can defend itself against the dislocating effects of the occupation. Other means include the preservation of the family unit and the maintenance and strengthening of traditional cultural practices, considered anathema by modernization theorists. Indeed, the use of tradition as a form of resistance has been especially powerful in the Gaza Strip; as such, the Gaza paradigm acknowledges the importance of culture to development, as well as the ability of culture to obstruct development.

Western development theories, whether liberal or Marxist, either assail or ignore the role of religion. Religion, particularly Islam, is considered inimical to capitalism (Weber) and other forms of modernization. However, in the Middle East generally and Gaza specifically, Islam is a central feature of life. It is the source of personal and societal identity, integrity, and legitimacy. It will not be abandoned. Thus, development in the Gaza Strip must include Islam.

The study of the Gaza Strip describes a peculiar set of conditions—new forms and mechanisms of underdevelopment—not commonly seen in other third world settings and that cannot be explained by existing development theories. Underlying Gaza's peculiar form of underdevelopment is an Israeli policy that prioritizes the political-national realm over the economic. This has been expressed in Israel's desire to acquire land rather than exploit the economic potential of the people living on it. Israel's ideological goal of creating a strong Jewish state has always superceded any need or desire to generate profit through economic exploitation of the Palestinian population, although that has occurred. Israel has physically removed segments of the Palestinian population from the land and dispossessed others of their resources and power. Indeed, in the history of modern Palestine, Israel is the first occupying regime that has deliberately and forcibly dispossessed Palestinians of their land, water, and labor. Consequently, in its drive to acquire land, the Israeli government has refused Palestinians in the occupied territories many of the rights often available in other third world societies: political independence and self-determination, control over economic and institutional resources, cultural freedom, civil and human rights, and legal protection. As a result, Palestinians have been unable to create a viable economic base, even one that is distorted, which could support an independent state. Hence, existing development paradigms do not apply to the situation in the Gaza Strip because they see economic gain as the fundamental motivation of state behavior. In the case of Israel and Gaza, underdevelopment gives way to de-development, where economic potential is not only distorted but denied.

The Meaning of De-development

De-development not only distorts development but forestalls it entirely, by depriving or ridding the economy of its capacity and potential for rational structural transformation and preventing the emergence of any self-correcting measures. For example, conventional definitions of underdevelopment *allow* for needed structural change within the weaker peripheral entity, although that change is disarticulated, oriented to, and shaped by the expansion of the dominant external economy to which it is subordinate. An excellent example is peripheral capitalism, which contributes directly to underdevelopment.

Peripheral capitalism is characterized by two key features: economic domination by the center and uneven levels of productivity between sectors. The former is seen in the structure of world trade and in the nature of international capital accumulation, in which the center shapes the periphery according to its own needs and controls peripheral economic production. The latter results from the dual existence of small, highly capitalized industrial sectors on the one hand, and large, backward, and productively inefficient agricultural sectors on the other. Agricultural production is oriented primarily toward export, not domestic consumption. Consequently, dependent economies seeking to expand must do so by dominating the economies of weaker neighbors.[20]

Given the structure of peripheral capitalism, one may conclude that underdevelopment is not manifested in particular levels of production per capita, but in certain structural features that distort the development process in the periphery without eliminating it. Thus, it is possible to sustain economic growth and underdevelopment at the same time. In this way, peripheral capitalism produces a condition of "dependent development" that is predicated on two critical factors. The first is the ability, albeit distorted, of the weaker, or peripheral, economy to industrialize and thereby accumulate capital. Capital accumulation can assume several forms, including large-scale investments in land, human resources, and physical equipment. This ability presupposes access to critical political, financial, and technological resources.

The second factor involves the formation of political and economic alliances among elites within and between the dependent and dominant economies and within the international financial community generally.[21] Thus, the disarticulation of economic activity in the weaker economy does not preclude the formation of internal capacity, or of those critical economic, political, social, institutional, and bureaucratic linkages needed to sustain a process of development, however skewed. To the contrary, the creation of economic capacity (i.e., the ability to accumulate capital) and the synthesis of economic relations within the periphery are crucial to the process of underdevelopment.

De-development, by contrast, is characterized by the negation of rational structural transformation, integration, and synthesis, where economic relations and linkage systems become, and then remain, unassembled (as opposed to disassembled as occurs in underdevelopment) and disparate, thereby obviating any organic, congruous, and logical arrangement of the economy or of its constituent parts. Unlike underdevelopment, some of whose features it possesses, de-development precludes, over the long term, the possibility of dependent development and its two primary features—the development of productive capacity, which would allow for capital accumulation (particularly in the modern industrial sector); and the formation of vital and sustainable political and economic alliances between the dependent and dominant economies and the dependent economy and the international financial system generally.

During Israel's occupation, Gaza's economic de-development has been shaped and advanced by a range of policies, themselves a reflection of the ideological imperatives of the Zionist movement, which may be categorized as follows: expropriation and dispossession; integration and externalization; and deinstitutionalization. Although these categories are not mutually exclusive or inherently sequential, they are delineated here for analytical purposes. These policies, for example, have contributed to de-development by dispossessing Palestinians of critical economic resources or factors of production needed to create and sustain productive capacity; by creating extreme dependency on employment in Israel as critical source of GNP growth; and by restricting the kind of indigenous economic and institutional development that could lead to structural reform and capital accumulation in the industrial sector, in particular.

Policies of expropriation and dispossession are marked by the steady usurpation of economic resources, primarily land and water, and of the capacity (legal, economic, social, and administrative) needed to resist such usurpation.[22] Dispossession, however, is not limited to economic factors but includes aspects of Palestine's political, social, and cultural organization as well. The interrelationship between the economic and noneconomic aspects of dispossession is organic and indivisible, although the economic forms are the most clearly tangible. (Expropriation and dispossession in Gaza are discussed in chapter 7.)

The second category, integration and externalization, is distinguished by policies that promoted Gaza's structural dependence on sources of income generated outside its own economy: the reorientation of the labor force to labor-intensive work in Israel and the Arab states (also a form of economic dispossession); the occupational reorientation of the labor force away from indigenous agriculture and industry, sectors critical to the development of local productive capacity; the redirection of trade to Israel and the Arab states, increasing Gaza's dependence on Israel especially, for trade with the outside world; the increasing and heavy reliance of indigenous agriculture and industry on export trade for sectoral income and growth; the growing linkage between commercial production and external demands; and the extremely low levels of government investment in a productive structure that was weak and underdeveloped to begin with.

Through such policies, not only were local resources transferred away from Gaza's economy to Israel's, but local economic activity—employment, trade, personal income—became unlinked from market forces and increasingly dependent on and subordinated to demand conditions in the Israeli and, to a lesser degree, Arab economies. The primary and most damaging outcomes of economic integration and externalization, therefore, have been the attenuation and disablement of Gaza's internal productive base and diminution of productive capacity, characterized in part by the decline of the agricultural sector in terms of output value, employment, and productivity; a stagnant industrial sector; the expansion of services as the largest source of local employment; and a hobbling of the economic and institutional infrastructure. (Evidence of integration and externalization is provided in chapter 8.)

Deinstitutionalization, which in certain respects can be understood as the logical consequence of dispossession and externalization, describes what in effect has amounted to an attack on institutional development in the Gaza Strip. Not only have Palestinian institutions themselves been harmed, but, more critically, so have their inter- and extra-institutional relationships. Moreover, the linkage system between the formal (governmental) and informal (nongovernmental) sectors, normally used to promote collaboration and coordination to implement development policy, has virtually been destroyed and replaced with a system of restrictions opposed to that very same goal. In this way, government policies have contributed to the debilitation of those institutions required for local development (e.g., financial, credit, and banking systems; local government and authority structures; educational [training, vocational and research centers] and health institutions).

Government policy has also attenuated and, in some instances, destroyed key economic and institutional linkages between governmental and nongovernmental sectors. Consequently, in the absence of major development planning by a national authority and the freezing of most development potential, "development," which in Gaza is often limited to services, has largely fallen to the initiatives of the informal sector and international agencies. Institutional successes, more often than not, occur at the level of the individual and isolated institution and are largely restricted to that institution. They rarely occur as a result of inter- (or intra-) institutional interactions. Thus, even the nongovernmental sector has been enfeebled as a provider of economic and social services.

Deinstitutionalization policies have confined indigenous structural reform, institutional development, and infrastructural growth within narrow structural parameters. One example is found in Palestinian industry where, for more than two decades, product lines have remained labor- rather than capital-intensive. Indeed, the impact of deinstitutionalization on indigenous economic capability and its contribution to the de-development process is strikingly illustrated in the maladministration and distortion of Arab and non-Arab development assistance in the Strip. (Deinstitutionalization is discussed in chapter 9.)

Policies that contribute to de-development include: low levels of government investment in social and economic infrastructure; the absence of a financial support structure for Palestinians, commonly available to their Israeli counterparts; prohibitions on a wide range of economic activities, such as union organizing, the creation of industrial zones, the establishment of factories, cooperatives, and other business enterprises; myriad restrictions on research and training; prohibitions on the development of agricultural, industrial, trade and other credit facilities and financial institutions in both the private and public sectors; the expropriation of land and water, coupled with prohibitions on land and water-use planning; restrictions on the development of public and private utilities and infrastructure; restrictions on foreign trade and the lack of protection from Israeli imports; the inability of Palestinians to determine trade regimes (e.g., tariffs, levies, import/export licensing); limitations on the process of industrial and commercial licensing, agricultural production planning (e.g., planting quotas, marketing, water distribution)[23]; and the lack of political, economic, and social linkages between Israeli and Palestinian groups, elite or otherwise, and between Palestinian and other foreign groups.

Within this scenario, basic economic development and even dependent economic development are suppressed. Thus, although it is possible to increase individual production and improve individual living standards, such indicators do not reflect the development of an indigenous economic base capable of sustained, diversified growth and development. Although a process of structural change was clearly evident after 1967, it was aberrant change that precluded the transformation of positive growth into long-term economic development. The very indicators Israelis have used to measure economic success in Gaza—increased per capita income, increased number of cars per home, increased number of workers in Israel—reveal the failure of real economic development. Furthermore, the singularity of Israeli policy in the Gaza Strip and West Bank has introduced an added, almost surreal and irrational dimension to the process of de-development that exceeds the "simple" distortion of structural change.

The absence of rational structural change and the unprecedented features of Israeli rule have had an exceptional impact on the Palestinian economy, especially in the Gaza Strip. This impact has been distinguished by extreme dependency on Israel, sectoral fragmentation, and internal erosion. This has not changed under partial autonomy. Thus, whereas the effect of underdevelopment is to reorder or recombine economic relations into a less meaningful, less integrated, and disfigured whole, the effect of de-development over the long term is to un-order, un-combine or scramble those relations so that no whole can, in effect, emerge. The de-developed economy is rendered weak, dependent, and underdeveloped; moreover, it soon becomes inanimate and phatic, robbed of dynamism and capacity. This comparison in no way is meant to suggest that underdevelopment is preferable to de-development; rather, it merely attempts to point out the narrow but significant difference between them. De-development and underdevelopment are not mutually exclusive processes—the former *presumes* the existence of the latter. However, it is quite possible to have underdevelopment without de-development.

The progressive dismemberment of the economic structure that distinguishes de-development began with the institutionalization of key Israeli policies in the first six years of the occupation. These policies not only defined the parameters of economic activity in the occupied territories but remained unchanged throughout the occupation. They are the subject of the next chapter.

Notes to Chapter 5:

1.   See Geoffrey Barraclough, *An Introduction to Contemporary History* (Harmondsworth: Penguin Books, 1967) p. 154.

2.   This conceptual framework is described in Ronald H. Chilcote, *Theories of Development and Underdevelopment* (Boulder, CO: Westview, 1984); and Anthony Brewer, *Marxist Theories of Imperialism: A Critical Survey*, Second Edition (London: Routledge, 1990).

3.   See Peter Vandergeest and Frederick H. Buttel, "Marx, Weber, and Development Sociology: Beyond the Impasse," *World Development* 16, no.6 (1988): 687.

4.   This discussion is not intended to be a survey of the literature nor an exhaustive review. Rather, it will address certain key points that illustrate some of the problems involved in studying change.

5.   For purposes of this discussion, the Gaza Strip and West Bank are treated as one entity because the problems of Palestinian development generally apply to both. The specific features of the Gaza Strip will be analyzed in subsequent chapters.

6.   For example, see Adel K. Samara, "The Political Economy of the West Bank 1967–1987: From Peripheralization to Development," in Khamsin, *Palestine: Profile of an Occupation* (London: Zed Books, 1989), pp. 7–31; Jamil Hilal, "Class Transformation in the West Bank and Gaza," *MERIP Reports* 53 (December 1976): 9–15; and Elia Zureik, "The Economics of Dispossession: The Palestinians," *Third World Quarterly* 5, no.4 (October 1983): 775–90.

7.   Samara, pp. 7–31; and Yusif A. Sayigh, "Dispossession and Pauperisation: The Palestinian Economy Under Occupation," in Abed (ed.), pp. 259–85.

8.   Typical of this view are Bregman, *The Economy Growth of the Administered Areas 1968–1973*; and Vivian A. Bull, *The West Bank: Is It Viable?* (Lexington, MA: Lexington Books, 1975).

9.   Thomas S. Kuhn, *The Structure of Scientific Revolutions*, Second Edition (Chicago: University of Chicago Press, 1970); and Paul Rabinow, *Reflections on Fieldwork in Morocco* (Berkeley, CA: University of California Press, 1977).

10.   David Apter, *Rethinking Development: Modernization, Dependency, and Postmodern Politics* (Beverly Hills, CA: Sage Publications, 1987).

11.   See Charles Tilly, *Big Structures, Large Processes, Huge Comparisons* (New York: Russell Sage Foundation, 1984).

12.   Yusif A. Sayigh, *Elusive Development: From Dependence to Self-Reliance in the Arab Region* (London: Routledge, 1991), p. 7.

13. These points are made in Sayigh, "Dispossession and Pauperisation," in Abed (ed.), pp. 259–85; and in "The Dependency Paradigm: Promise, Limitations and Qualifications," in Sayigh, pp. 40–89.

14. Sayigh, "Dispossession and Pauperisation," in Abed (ed.), pp. 259–85.

15. The author acknowledges the contribution of Dr. Elaine Hagopian to this section.

16. See Apter.

17. Apter, pp. 32–48.

18. Ibid., p. 46.

19. Hiltermann, *Behind The Intifada*, p. 14.

20. See Samir Amin, *Accumulation on a World Scale* (New York: Monthly Review Press, 1974); idem., *Unequal Development* (New York: Monthly Review Press, 1976); and Chilcote, pp. 63–64.

21. Sara Roy, "The Gaza Strip: A Case of Economic De-Development," *Journal of Palestine Studies* 17, no.1 (Autumn 1987): 57–58.

22. See, for example, Zureik, pp. 775–90.

23. See United Nations Conference On Trade And Development (UNCTAD), *Palestinian External Trade under Israeli Occupation* (New York: United Nations, 1989), p. 1.

6

The Policy Roots of De-development

T he economic de-development of the Gaza Strip was neither planned nor accidental; rather, it was the outcome of official Israeli policies designed to secure military, political, and economic control over Gaza and the West Bank, and to protect Israel's national interests. These policies and their impact on Gaza's economy are the focus of this chapter. A discussion of Palestinian policies toward development, which (ironically) complemented those of Israel, concludes this chapter.

Chapter 5 argued that the policy basis of Arab de-development, the "land over people" imperative of Jewish settlement in Palestine, was not created or formalized when Israel gained control over the occupied territories, but under the British Mandate when relations between the Jewish and Arab communities took shape. This imperative more than anything else affirmed the primacy of the Jews' sovereign interests over all others and established the political-national realm as the one from which all other realms, including the economic, would emanate.

Within this framework, policies and policy themes emerged from the building of the Jewish National Home that would reemerge after 1967 and greatly affect Palestinian economic development. They included: the belief that the Jewish community was the only legitimate collective in the land of Palestine and that Jewish colonization was therefore in the best interests of all; the pursuit of sovereignty for Jews and autonomy for Arabs; the desire of Jewish officialdom to "Judaize" Arab Palestine; the settlement of Arab land by Jews;

135

the use of economic policy to influence or shape political behavior (i.e., economic appeasement); a total disinterest in and rejection of Arab economic development; the separate, as opposed to collaborative and integrative development of the Arab and Jewish sectors; the concomitant imposition of standards that measured progress in the Arab economic sector against the status quo before the arrival of the Jewish community; and the blindness and disinterest of the Jewish leadership to the long-term impact of their policies on economic (and political) conditions in the Arab community.

With the establishment of Israel in 1948 and the imposition of Israeli control over Gaza and the West Bank in 1967, the policy dynamics initiated under the Mandate and the ideological beliefs they reflected were given institutional and bureaucratic form in the occupied territories, backed by military force. The Israelis created mechanisms of control to translate the imperative of national sovereignty into practicable and implementable measures. Within this framework, the Gaza Strip and West Bank economies were subsumed to security imperatives, and the economic system became a critical component in Israel's larger system of control. This is not to say that the economic exploitation of the occupied territories was not an objective of Israeli policy; it was just not the *primary* objective. It was the ideological need, over the long-term, to insure Israeli control over the occupied areas that set the policy framework for the de-development of the Palestinian economy. Nowhere was this more strikingly accomplished than in the Gaza Strip.

The Imperative of National Sovereignty and the Articulation of an Economic Strategy for the Gaza Strip and West Bank

Among the greatest perceived threats to Israeli sovereignty and its expansion has been and continues to be the establishment of a Palestinian state in the Gaza Strip and West Bank. Israelis have passionately debated the political and national security risks attending such a state since 1967. Any national entity other than Israel is perceived to be illegitimate. Therefore, any claims to such an entity are, by definition, subversive. Although this view was controversial among Israelis ideologically, it served as an unwritten guideline for economic decision makers.[1]

Preventing the emergence of a sovereign Palestine alongside the state of Israel has been a critical focal point of official policy and one reason for Israel's obsession with maintaining control of the occupied territories. However, to deny a people their nationhood and a nation its sovereignty requires much more than the imposition of military power and ideological will. For Israel, it also required the dismantling of those indigenous forces and the relations between them whose growth and development could comprise an infrastructural base—economic, political, social, cultural, physical, and administrative—but more importantly, perpetuate the kind of collective national consciousness needed to sustain that base over time. To preclude the establishment of a Palestinian state, the government had to eliminate any foundation on which it could be built.

Economic policy in the occupied territories became a critical component of this policy. It was characterized by the deliberate rejection of development as a legitimate and rational goal.[2] Since 1967, there has never been an explicit commitment on the part of any Israeli government to advancing the economic interests of the Palestinian population through planned development either in the short or long term. Nor has any Israeli government ever formulated a conscious policy defining the exact relationship between Israel and the occupied territories. (Arguably, the Gaza–Jericho Agreement is an excellent illustration of this.)[3] Development was equated with building the economic infrastructure for a state. In this way, Israel has always seen Palestinian economic development as a zero-sum game. However, interviews conducted with Israeli government officials over several years revealed that Israeli rejection of Palestinian economic development was rooted, not in the fear of economic competition or of a strengthened Palestinian economy per se—which, as dependency theory has shown, a dominant power can turn to its advantage—but in the emergence of sociopsy-chological factors, notably personal and community empowerment, social cohesion, and popular control.

Hence, it was not the restructuring of the economy or the emergence of a definable physical infrastructure that Israelis most feared—a common misconception—but the formation, unification, and consolidation of those relationships required for state-building at its most basic level. The government understood that although Palestinians lacked any national, political, or economic authority, they did possess institutions that enabled them to maintain a sense of national identity, social organization, and internal cohesion. It was at this level of inter- and intrasectoral relations and institutional linkages that official policies, notably in the economic and social realm, would do the profound damage that resulted in de-development.

Having excised "development" from its conceptual and strategic core, Israel's economic policy in the occupied territories was fashioned to achieve two seemingly contradictory ends: improving the standard of living by increasing social and economic *services*, which was attained without any major structural economic change[4]; and progressively weakening the indigenous economic base. Whereas a better living standard was meant to diminish nationalist aspirations and contain violence and popular resentment through a policy of economic appeasement (which also obviated the need for a collaborator class in the Gaza Strip and West Bank that might fulfill the same function), the weakening of the economic base was meant to create ties of dependence that would protect Israel's economic interests by eliminating any threat of competition with, or cost to, the Israeli economy and give Israel complete control over the territories' productive resources and their economic growth potential.

These policy objectives, implemented through a complementary (and discriminatory) system of integration and segregation produced a dual economic outcome, which Meron Benvenisti has aptly characterized as individual prosperity and communal stagnation.[5] Thus, although the integration of Arab labor into the Israeli market economy provided Palestinians with higher incomes and living standards borne of a new consumerist culture, the cost of this inclusion to the Palestinian economy was continued underdevelopment, because Arab employment was geared toward Israeli, not Arab production. Moreover, the decision to seek employment in Israel was not a function of a society experiencing typical patterns associated with industrialization and modernization, in which labor gradually shifts from agricultural to nonagricultural activities, resulting in changes in labor's spatial location and occupational status. Rather, the decision to seek employment in Israel was a reflection of the absence of comparable domestic economic options. As a result, Palestinians were able to generate capital but were unable to accumulate or invest it either in their own weakened economy, which was lacking in viable opportunities, or in Israel's, where such investment by Arabs was strictly prohibited.

The combination of personal prosperity and collective underdevelopment is not as dichotomous as it first appears, particularly in light of official attempts to secure the political status quo through economic means. In fact, given the state's political–national imperative, the prosperity–stagnation outcome came to represent what was maximally allowable within existing constraints as well as what was minimally desirable. Moreover, the dichotomy as framed sets the conceptual and practical stage for de-development, although it fails to account for it specifically.

That prosperity is attainable as underdevelopment proceeds is nothing new; the third world is replete with such contradictions. What is less apparent, however, but pivotal to understanding this particular economic biformity, is the actual complementarity and congruity between its two parts. In the Gaza Strip especially, not only have prosperity and de-development existed side by side, but the systematic dismantling of the economic structure that distinguishes the de-development process has in fact been mediated through the attainment of limited individual prosperity and the horizontal growth on which it was based. This reality has done much to enervate indigenous productive capacity, for which Palestinians and their host of funders must also assume their share of responsibility, and has contributed greatly to the perpetuation in the West of the illusion that Israel's occupation has been benign.

Setting the Structural Stage for De-development: The Political Economy of Pacification, Normalization, and Integration, 1967–73

The first six years of occupation were critical in shaping the structural framework for Israeli policy, in defining its point of departure as well as its point of termination. This period is critical because the policies shaped then have not changed, not even with the implementation of limited self-rule. Within eighteen months of the war, the government achieved full control over all aspects of Palestinian life, the institutionalization and bureaucratization of the new military administration, the physical linking of the Gaza Strip to Israel through the rapid extension of Israeli infrastructural services and networks, notably electricity and water, and the reactivation of prewar economic life by providing public services and alleviating unemployment.

Official policy during this period was characterized by a seesaw between conviction and ambivalence that was related to political uncertainty about the fate of the occupied territories. On one hand, the government was committed to keeping the Gaza Strip and West Bank for the long term.[6] On the other hand, official policy equivocated over the political means to achieve that end—through economic integration with Israel or economic separation. This vascillation completely dissipated after the October 1973 war, when policy goals crystallized.

In the immediate postwar period, the government's commitment to the new political status quo produced what Nimrod Rafaeli, an Israeli policy analyst, has termed a three-pronged policy of pacification, normalization, and integration.[7]

Policies of Pacification

The Israeli government first adopted a pacification policy to secure control over the occupied territories, by bringing a "conquered people from a state of active hostility to a situation of passive obedience."[8] This policy had several objectives:

> to obtain control quickly over the conquered area; to rid the areas of pockets of resistance; to prevent revolt, disturbances, terrorism and sabotage; to bring civilians under control; and to establish peaceful conditions needed by other authorities (such as police, health, education etc.).[9]

In the Gaza Strip, pacification was based not only on the elimination of armed resistance, but also on the alteration of the demographic balance, because it was believed that fewer people in Gaza decreased the probability of turmoil. Between June 1967 and December 1968, for example, Israel evicted approximately 75,000 residents of the Strip, whom Golda Meir referred to as a "fifth column,"[10] lowering Gaza's postwar population of 400,000 (of which approximately 260,000 were refugees) to 325,900.[11] The authorities also prevented the return of between 25,000–50,000 Gazan residents who were unlucky enough to be outside the territory when the war broke out. Thus, between June 1967 and December 1968, using conservative estimates, the Gaza Strip lost 25 percent of its resident prewar population. The June 1967 population was only regained in December 1976.[12]

In October 1969, the government further disclosed a policy whereby Gaza Strip refugees were "encouraged to move to refugee camps in the West Bank which were close to available jobs in Israel and the West Bank itself...."[13] Officially, this policy was intended to alleviate the labor shortage in Israel and the West Bank (especially in the agricultural sector) with excess labor from the Gaza Strip, where unemployment was a severe problem. Unofficially, it was designed to decrease Gaza's population.

Policies of Normalization

The second component of Israeli policy, normalization, aimed to reactivate economic life as soon as possible. The third, integration, was the method by which to do so. As such, normalization and integration established the structural framework for Israel's economic policy in the occupied territories, and the two are difficult to separate analytically.

Political in motivation but economic in form, normalization was primarily a policy of control, not development. The first defense ministry coordinator of government operations in the territories, Shlomo Gazit, explained:

> While unemployment and an atmosphere of crisis encourage [the population] to join sabotage activities, full employment and a flourishing economy discourage such a trend....To work is to occupy oneself in such a way that little time is left for "extra activities" ...and then there is the practical consideration of whether it's worth risking the job and the income.[14]

As a policy of control, normalization operated according to two basic assumptions. The first appeared in *BaMahane*, a publication of the Israel Defense Forces: "What is permitted to and prohibited for the Arabs in the administered areas is not determined by the accepted criteria of past military occupations. It is determined by a single criterion, namely, whatever is not harmful to Israel, is permitted."[15] Second, as a form of control, the restoration of economic order or "business as usual"[16] required immediate and tangible solutions to the most pressing economic problems in a very hostile postwar environment. Toward that end, the military authorities articulated three principles that they hoped would guide their overall policy:

> *non-presence* (minimizing visible signs of the Israeli authorities to lessen friction and conflict with the population); *non-interference* (placing responsibility for economic and administrative activities in Arab hands); and *open bridges* (renewing personal and economic contacts between the population and the Arab world).[17]

The nonpresence principle dictated the transfer of many administrative and social welfare responsibilities to local Palestinian institutions so that Israeli rule could be felt but not seen. The noninterference principle required that local authorities be enlisted in the implementation of Israeli policies. The open bridges principle renewed contact between the occupied territories and the Arab world, relieving economic pressure on Israel while providing the Jewish state with an indirect channel to a vast new market.

Perhaps the most pressing postwar problem the Israeli administration faced in the Gaza Strip was the creation of job opportunities, especially for the refugee community, the locus of resistance to the occupation. Under Egyptian rule, most able-bodied Gazans had held some position.[18] Mordechai Gur, the first Israeli military governor of the Gaza Strip, observed:

> The Egyptians disguised the fact that there weren't enough jobs by em-

ploying many men to do one task. I remember that 80 men were doing the work of seven in the customs office....As I saw it, before we [the Israeli government] occupied the Strip there was no real unemployment...we owed it to them to create or find employment.[19]

The June 1967 war completely dislocated Gaza's economy. The war severed all the economic links between the Gaza Strip and Egypt that had evolved over two decades. Commercial revenue from Egyptian tourism and Gaza's lucrative smuggling trade ended overnight. Traditional export markets were cut off and all public services were disrupted. The departures of the Egyptian army, the PLA, and the UN forces (who were not invited back by the Israeli government) eliminated a critical source of employment and income for local refugees. The many administrative jobs and the vast public works program created by the Egyptian authorities evaporated. In the immediate postwar period, the number of unemployed rose by at least 20,000 above its prewar level, and unemployment remained as high as 17 percent in 1968.[20]

Israel had many alternatives for creating jobs, including through indigenous economic reform. However, the difficulties it faced in providing employment were political, not economic. The structural transformation of Gaza's economy was out of the question. According to one government official: "Israel's present policy is *to change matters as little as possible* in the areas until a peace formula is worked out. On the other hand, time is passing, and human needs do not wait for peace settlements."[21]

In the absence of a planned policy and the will to instigate any real change, creation of jobs was limited and haphazard at first. Initial efforts at job creation in Gaza focused inward, because movement into Israel was prohibited during the first few months after the war.[22] Some 5,000 people were soon employed by the military government and by local municipalities in existing civil service positions.[23] By August 1967, the labor ministry had opened an employment office in Gaza and launched a range of public works projects that employed several thousand people in road and building repair, afforestation, and urban sanitation.[24] The government offered small-scale loans for expansion of local businesses and farms, and municipalities received additional financial support.

Given Israel's national (security)–political priorities, government policy on the provision of domestic employment between 1968 and 1973, admittedly its most "liberal" period, not only established the limits on structural reform in the local economy but, in setting those limits, did little if anything to mitigate and remove the key structural constraints on economic reform in Gaza: a weak agricultural sector incapable of absorbing excess labor, a backward and largely moribund industrial sector, a weak physical and economic infrastructure preventing the accommodation of surplus labor, and a majority refugee population that was underutilized and disenfranchised. As such, the government initiated processes in 1967 that remained fundamentally unchanged in 1987, and that Meron Benvenisti has argued "underline[d] more than anything else, the pervasiveness of the momentum pushing inexorably toward full absorption of the territories into the Israeli system."[25]

Employment in the Gaza Strip was to be encouraged by expanding relief works and capital investment in local industry and agriculture. The former was solely an income-generating activity, bounded in scope. The latter introduced limited structural change, but its effect over time was to retard, not promote, the rational transformation of the indigenous economic structure, since the sources of domestic employment were increasingly linked to Israel's production and economic interests, not Gaza's. The resulting structural pattern tied domestic economic growth and individual prosperity to external sources of income—at great cost to Gaza's economic development.

As part of its employment generation policy, Israel's Cabinet Committee on the Territories decided to make an initial investment of 7.5 million Israeli pounds (£I) in Gaza Strip development.[26] Palestinian entrepreneurs were eligible to receive working capital advances and low-interest loans equal to the amount of their own investment at 6 percent interest, whereas Israeli investors were eligible for loans at 9 percent.[27] Foreign entrepreneurs also received special terms.[28]

Israeli and foreign capital were critical for building an industrial infrastructure in the Gaza Strip, but the territory saw but a minor flow of capital services from Israel. The political and security risks of operating a business in the Strip were certainly a disincentive, but so were government policies that offered outside investors far more attractive terms for investing in development areas in Israel than in the territories. Established businesses in the occupied territories, for example, were not eligible for government grants as were enterprises located across the green line, nor was Israel's Law for the Encouragement of Capital Investments extended to areas under Israeli control. A Jordanian law promoting similar services was suspended.

Of the sixty-five Israeli and foreign enterprises that were established in the occupied territories between 1968 and 1973, only twelve were located in the Gaza Strip in an area known as the Erez industrial zone; all were funded entirely by Israeli capital. Though initially opened to local entrepreneurs, the £I 2.5 million zone was an Israeli concern with a preponderance of Israeli labor from its inception. Its primary commercial linkages were with Israel, not Gaza.[29] Some Erez firms employed Gazans, but not nearly to the degree envisioned by the Cabinet Committee, which had intended to provide 6,000 jobs for local residents.[30] The flow of labor services from the Gaza Strip and West Bank to Israel lessened the need for Israel to export capital services to the occupied territories to take advantage of lower wages.

During this same period, however, local investment did grow, partly due to a government decision to repatriate "to the West Bank and the Gaza Strip persons of means who have been out of the territories since before the Six Day War."[31] Approximately 100 new factories were established and several thousand workers employed. In 1968–69, the government approved 179 applications for working capital amounting to £I 1.1 million.[32] The expansion of local industry resulted from two factors: a growing market for Gazan products in Israel's booming economy, and the expansion of subcontracting arrangements between Israeli contractors and Gazan firms, itself a response to weak domestic opportunities. As a result, the industrial sector experienced impressive annual growth rates of almost 30 percent between 1967 and 1973. These factors, however, not only linked the growth of Gaza's industrial sector primarily to demand conditions and to specific sectoral deficiencies in an external economy, but more importantly, did so without promoting any change in the nature of industrial organization, the character of industrial output, or the methods of industrial production, all of which have remained traditional and labor intensive. A 1971 Bank of Israel report noted: "Industry is adjusting to Israeli demand, mainly by taking subcontracting jobs for Israeli plants and by developing labor-intensive branches such as furniture, sewing, and building materials."[33]

Subcontracting, for example, was entirely dependent on cheap labor, mostly female, and low wages. It involved labor-intensive steps in an industrial process that originated and ended in Israel. The six vocational training centers established in Gaza between 1967 and 1969 offered courses to the unskilled in areas required by the Israeli economy: sewing, shoemaking, bookkeeping, carpentry, building and automobile mechanics, welding, scaffolding, and ironwork.[34] By 1973, more than 15,000 graduates of vocational schools in the occupied territories were working in Israel and within their own economy.[35]

In the agricultural sector, the major change the government introduced called for employment through the development of agricultural exports such as industrial crops and vegetables, which do not compete with Israeli agriculture. Israel quickly dominated Gaza's agricultural exports.[36] Toward this end, the Ministry of Agriculture focused on the introduction of new and more efficient techniques such as drip irrigation, new crops and fertilizers, and mechanization. In Gaza, two mechanized packing houses were established between 1967 and 1969 for efficient citrus export. The government also provided loans to citrus growers and exporters.[37] However, subsidies extended to Israeli dairy and poultry producers were not given to their Palestinian counterparts, forcing many Palestinians out of business.[38] Labor-intensive crops for export and for Israeli industry were also introduced and expanded. Contacts between Israeli entrepreneurs and Gazan farmers focused on agricultural processing and included such labor-intensive activities as almond and grapefruit peeling, and the preparation of peanuts for seeding.[39]

The focus on generating employment within Gaza shifted increasingly to Israel, where manpower shortages were emerging. By early 1968, some Gazans were allowed to work in Israel, despite the ban on border crossing.[40] By that summer, the Israeli economy had recovered and certain sectors (such as construction) were experiencing manpower shortages. Increasingly, Israeli employers illegally hired unemployed labor from the Gaza Strip and West Bank, who were more than eager to earn the much higher wages offered in Israel. The illegal use of unorganized Palestinian labor posed clear problems for the government. To establish control over the employment process, Israel reversed its decision banning Palestinian labor from the occupied territories. By the end of 1968, five labor exchanges had been set up in the Gaza Strip and seven in the West Bank. The needs of the Israeli economy at that juncture dictated the abandonment of the Zionist notion of Jewish labor so prevalent during the Mandate period. The labor exchanges imposed strict quotas on the number of Arab workers entering Israel, and the flow of workers was based on skills and market needs. The government restricted the movement of Gazans in particular, which encouraged them to bypass illegally the labor exchanges,[41] a pattern that has persisted. The Israeli government did have two qualifications, however:

> ...area workers could be employed anywhere in Israel provided that they first received a security clearance from the Military Government and a certificate from a Labour Exchange guaranteeing that their employment would not displace Israeli [i.e., Jewish] workers.[42]

The decision to open the Israeli market to Palestinian labor from the occupied territories dramatically affected employment patterns in the Gaza Strip and West Bank.[43] Between September 1968 and July 1969, for example, the number of workers entering Israel increased from 5,800 to 18,000. Among Gazans alone, the number of laborers crossing into Israel rose from 800 (1.7 percent of the total labor force) in 1968[44] to 5,900 (10.1 percent) in 1970.[45]

More important, wage–labor opportunities across the green line generated the material improvements so critical to normalization and to dependence on Israel. By 1970, for example, income from work in Israel accounted for 15 percent of the territories' total national product compared with only 3 percent in 1968.[46] By 1972, some Israelis were referring to the enhancement of living standards as "the miracle of Gaza."[47] In his memoirs, Dayan observed:

> In the refugee camps in the Gaza Strip, there was a veritable economic revolution. Refugees who for nineteen years had spent their time sitting outside their huts playing backgammon and talking politics, and seldom shedding their pajamas, began going to work... now they could...[bring] home hundreds of Israeli pounds a week in wages...[and] thanks to the high wages in Israel, they were able to improve not only their standard of living but also their way of life. For the first time, they could acquire new clothes, furniture, and kitchen appliances....[48]

Given the rapidly emerging trends in the employment of "area" labor, Israel's Cabinet Committee on the Territories convened in July 1969 and adopted a series of resolutions that defined the problem and some possible solutions. The resolutions were guided by three principles:

> a) The Israeli Administration is the only form of government in the territories with all that this implies;
> b) A reasonable standard of living must be reached by the population of the territories, a standard which must definitely not drop below the pre-war

level. A reasonable standard of living and full employment will have a moderating effect on the population and will counter hostile incitement and influence; and

c)   The government therefore considers it has an obligation to provide work for the unemployed in the territories, without differentiating between refugee and non-refugee.[49]

The problem, as the government saw it, was how to bridge the gap between the "basic desire to find a solution to the matter through increasing natural [rather than relief] employment in the economies of the territories themselves, and the provision of an immediate solution for the unemployed."[50] What emerged was a partial and short-term policy that called for continued employment in Israel, on one hand, and enhanced domestic employment opportunities on the other.

General Gazit explained the government's reactive, nonplanned approach: "In some cases, the realities dictated the resolutions [solutions]. The obvious example was that of Arab labour. It started slowly in a non-organized way....Only when the number grew to thousands was the matter discussed and it was decided to institutionalize the work."[51] Employment in Israel proved to be the immediate solution. The trend toward employment in Israel gained momentum in 1972 when, confronted by King Hussein's plan for a federated state between Jordan, the West Bank and the Gaza Strip, the Israeli government lifted all restrictions on freedom of movement from Gaza to Israel, thereby rejecting the Jordanian initiative.[52] By 1973, over 60,000 workers from the Gaza Strip and West Bank commuted to Israel daily. In the quest for control and in the absence of planning, immediate solutions, with their clear political and economic benefits, became long-term policies.

Another key component of Israel's normalization policy was the resumption of trade between the occupied territories and the Arab world. Incorporated under the rubric "open bridges," this policy had several objectives. The authorities believed that if they were allowed contact with Jordan, Palestinians would not feel isolated politically and any "latent tendency among [them] for self-determination"[53] would be effectively discouraged. Moshe Dayan also argued that continued contact between Palestinians and the Arab world would prevent the "Israelization [of the West Bank and Gaza] from the cultural and social points of view,"[54] and keep the Jewish and Arab populations separate.

However, the primary factor in the open bridges policy was economic. By creating immediate trading outlets for the vast surpluses of (agricultural) goods that had accumulated after the war, the authorities not only provided "a valve on a steam boiler," but eliminated the possibility that Palestinian exports would enter the Israeli market in huge quantities, creating a glut in products and a fall in prices. Indeed, Moshe Dayan argued that without the open bridges policy, any loss accruing to the West Bank and Gaza from the severance of trade relations with Jordan (which he estimated between £I 70–£I 90 million annually) would have to be made up by Israel.[55]

In the Gaza Strip, the open bridges policy provided a solution to an urgent economic problem: citrus marketing. Soon after the war, Israel closed all Western European markets to Gazan exporters in order to prevent competition. However, indirect export to Europe through Israel's citrus marketing board was permitted through 1974, when the government abruptly terminated all such arrangements. Arab markets opened up in and through Jordan, markets that proved increasingly valuable to Gaza and were largely unavailable to Israel. Direct marketing to Eastern Europe also continued. Marketing between the Gaza Strip and West Bank was established for the first time as well. Between 1968 and 1970, the value of exports from the Gaza Strip more than doubled as a result of a rapidly growing trade with Israel and Jordan.

The open bridges policy did much more than enable control over Palestinian export markets. More importantly, it helped transform the occupied territories into Israel's second largest export market (after the United States). Although Israel has claimed to be in a common market relationship with the occupied territories, it has long imposed quotas on Palestinian exports to Israel, whereas Palestinians have been required to pay full tariffs on imports from Israel. Perhaps most significant for Palestinian trade is that, despite restrictions on what Palestinians could export to Israel, Israelis have had total freedom in exporting whatever they chose to the Gaza Strip and West Bank. The restructuring of the territories' terms of trade in this way imposed what was in effect a one-way trade structure that turned the completely unprotected Palestinian market, especially in Gaza, into a virtual dumping ground for subsidized Israeli goods. This trade asymmetry was another major factor restricting indigenous economic development over time.

Government budgets for 1968 and 1969 also reveal the lack of official commitment to economic development in Gaza, a budgetary pattern that has persisted throughout the occupation. Economic targets, a category defined in official government budgets for the Gaza Strip, received only 14.7 percent and 19.7 percent of total expenditure in 1968 and 1969, respectively. Included in this category were traffic and communications projects, which left a small percentage for work in agriculture, industry, and related sectors. The overwhelming majority of funds were allocated to social services and administrative costs.[56]

In 1973 the government produced the "Galili Document," in which it promised to invest £I 1,250 million over five years in development projects in the occupied areas "but with the proviso that such a written promise of future policy did not necessarily mean actual performance."[57] Following the political shock of the October 1973 war, the Israeli economy fell into recession, and the Galili Document was set aside indefinitely with little if any money invested in Gaza and the West Bank. Between 1973 and 1987, therefore, official policy on economic development in the Gaza Strip and West Bank remained the same as in 1969: employment in Israel and limited investment in the territories.

Hence, the employment of Arab labor in Israel and the externalization of Gaza's domestic economy provided the immediate tactical solutions to internal tensions the government was seeking—per capita GNP and private consumption rose immediately.[58] Moreover, they made it possible to tie long-term economic activity in Gaza directly to conditions and interests in Israel, rather than to indigenous structural reform and sustainable economic development. Indeed, after 1973, when this approach solidified and the new structural patterns stabilized, the limited prosperity that did accrue to the Gaza Strip became predicated upon the underdevelopment of its own economy. Thus, what began as a policy of unplanned and short-range control quietly evolved into a deliberate strategy for defining economic relations across the green line.[59]

Policies of Integration

The noncommittal and ad hoc nature of early government policies in the Gaza Strip and West Bank were shaped by concerns that were primarily political. These concerns were articulated in a prolonged public debate within the ruling Labor party over the political future of the occupied territories and Israel's imminent relationship with them. The debate centered around whether the economies of the Gaza Strip and West Bank should be economically integrated into that of Israel. Moshe Dayan, then minister of defense, represented a view that favored integration; Pinhas Sapir, secretary-general of the newly amalgamated Labor party, represented a view that did not. Dayan maintained that any boundary dividing the Israeli economy from that of the occupied territories should be functional, not territorial. The movement of labor and capital should be free (i.e., labor and capital markets should be integrated) and unrestricted by political geography. Sapir rejected as ludicrous any notion of functionalism. He argued that the free flow of Palestinian labor into Israel was "a powder keg under our own society" that would ultimately force a choice on the state that was too painful to contemplate. The free flow of capital into the occupied territories would draw needed funds away from Israel's own development priorities. Thus, Sapir sought "to keep Israel Israeli and to keep the administered territories Arab."[60] Any interaction between them should consist of bringing work to Arabs and not the reverse. In certain exceptional situations, however, labor could be allowed to cross into Israel but never as a permanent reorganization of the Israeli economy.[61] Histadrut Secretary-General Yitzchak Ben-Aharon feared integration as a threat to the values of Labor Zionism, which "never assumed the possibility that the Jewish people in their own land would become a nation ruling over other nations,"[62] thereby changing the important historical role of the Jewish proletariat.[63]

Dayan's view became the dominant policy. With it, the structural foundations for "integration cum segregation" were laid. Dayan was always careful to distinguish between integration (*shilluv*) and fusion (*mizzug*). Although his position was criticized as a form of "creeping annexation," he, like Sapir, did not seek any form of national integration whereby Arabs from the occupied territories would become Israeli citizens or live in Israel. Economic integration was not to be accompanied by the extension of political rights but by de facto political annexation. However, unlike Sapir, Dayan sought to maintain the political status quo and preclude any possibility of changing it. He sought a *modus vivendi* for mediating Israeli rule that did not rely on the creation of a comprador class, although certain attempts were made to create a local base of support inside the occupied territories.[64] Dayan aimed to establish "patterns of life" in the occupied territories "as though peace had already been achieved."[65] He argued that the Israeli government should define its role in the West Bank and Gaza as that of an enduring government, "to plan and implement whatever can be done without leaving options open for the day of peace, which may be far away."[66] Economic integration served these objectives.

In 1974, a Rand Corporation study concluded:

> Dayan seems to be aiming at an arrangement in which the issue of territorial sovereignty will be submerged in the welter of economic and personal ties that will have been created in the area....In this fluid creation, in the process of integration, or what the ECONOMIST has called "osmosis," particular boundaries will assume secondary significance.[67]

The aim may not have been to make the annexation of the Gaza Strip and the West Bank easier, but it was meant to make their separation from Israel harder. Speaking to town leaders of the Gaza Strip, Dayan said, "If it be necessary to pave the roads, expand health and educational services, and install electricity and water services, we will do all of this. And we will not be inhibited from investing the funds needed in the long run by any sense of temporariness."[68]

At the policy level, the battle over economic integration appeared quite contentious; at the practical level, however, the war had already been fought and won. The rapidly growing dependence of Palestinian labor on the Israeli market and Israel's domination of the territories' terms of trade were but two examples of how structural integration was proceeding. However, other illustrations of the integrative process depict how, from the outset, the absorption of the territories into Israel was planned and deliberate.

In the Strip, one striking example was the linkage of the main towns (and eventually, the entire territory) to the Israeli national electrical grid less than three years after the war.[69] In December 1969, Gaza City was linked up, followed by Khan Younis and Deir el-Balah in May 1970. In a meeting with General Dayan, local mayors, led by Ragheb el-Alami and other notables, protested the linkage "as the thin end of the wedge of Israeli annexation,"[70] and requested immediate disconnection. Dayan rejected their request, arguing that the linkage was necessary for several reasons: to facilitate security patrols, to provide less expensive electricity, and to supply areas in need. There is no doubt that the more efficient Israeli grid allowed greater economies of scale and enabled many more homes to be supplied—24,000 in Gaza City alone compared with 5,000 before the war.[71] However, by tying the Strip to the Israeli power supply, Israel assumed control over a resource that would have been an important source of revenue for the local government and, more critically, that was vital to the development of an economic and industrial infrastructure in the Gaza Strip.

Integration was primarily spurred by policies that affected the use of Gaza's water and land. Immediately after the war, the Israeli government assumed control and integrated the water supply of the occupied territories into the Israeli national water network. Israel exploits almost all of its own water potential; the occupation of the Gaza Strip and West Bank gave Israel access to a supplemental and critically needed source of water, portions of which have been redirected to Israeli use. Given the organic and singular importance of water for human survival and economic growth, Israel's control and subsequent exploitation of Gaza's limited water supply was essential to integration for two reasons: (1) it restricted the development of an independent economic sector, insuring Israeli dominance and increasing Palestinian economic dependence on Israel; and (2) it facilitated the emergence and growth of an Israeli presence within the occupied territories that would similarly thwart if not preclude any attempt at political separation. This is further explained in the next chapter.

Control of land, which is intimately connected to that of water, has remained an issue of singular and almost primordial discord between Jews and Arabs. From the beginning, the government made its intentions clear. On 20 May 1969, Deputy Prime Minister Yigal Allon stated that "our weapon for the formation of borders is the weapon of pioneering settlement [as it was] during all the years of the British Mandate....Nothing has changed in respect to the national objective and the manner in which to ensure Jewish presence."[72] According to Dayan, secure borders without peace were preferable to insecure borders with peace, and settlements were to be pursued even if this "did not bring peace closer."[73] These sentiments reflected the prevailing view within the government, although differences of opinion did emerge over whether settlements should be temporary or permanent.

The occupation of the Gaza Strip and West Bank presented Israel with another political imperative as well: to fulfill historic and religious claims to portions of the occupied territories especially in the West Bank.[74] The Gaza Strip, however, did not possess any real historic or religious significance for Israel. Nor did it hold the same degree of strategic importance, although such arguments were sometimes invoked for its retention. The presence of so large and hostile a refugee community, furthermore, was an admitted security problem. Yet the Gaza Strip remained the focus of considerable government attention when it came to land and civilian settlement. Officials from the centrist foreign minister, Abba Eban, to the right-wing minister without portfolio, Israel Galili, argued that the Gaza Strip must never be separated from Israel. Toward that end, the government had instructed Israeli envoys to "act with a view to ensuring that Gaza be an indivisible part of the State of Israel,"[75] a policy that enjoyed a consensus of support in the coalition as well as the opposition. Galili went so far as to state that "even if peace is achieved, the Israel government will not allow Gaza's status to be open to question."[76]

As in the West Bank, the reasons for hastening settlement and land expropriation in the Gaza Strip were largely ideological and political; in Gaza, however, the absence of other plausible explanations made such motivations more obvious. Galili, for one, was quite explicit: "one of the main reasons for the Government's decision to foster settlement in the Gaza Strip was to bring home to inhabitants there that Israel would not leave the area as it did in 1957 at the end of the Sinai campaign."[77]

At the same time, the government was also careful not to demand the legal integration of the Gaza and the other occupied territories (except East Jerusalem), because to do so would have meant assuming the burdens as well as the benefits of integration and extending all the privileges and rights of Israeli citizenship to Palestinian inhabitants, something that was not in Israel's interest to do, especially in the political and economic realms. Hence, there is no paradox in that although the fundamental purpose of Jewish civilian settlement is to "achieve the incorporation [of the West Bank and Gaza Strip] into the [Israeli] national system,"[78] Israeli planning in the occupied territories is based on the complete spatial separation of the Arab and Jewish populations.

Palestinian Policy Roots

To varying degrees, Israeli economic policy in the Gaza Strip and West Bank was complemented by Palestinian development policies. These policies assumed that economic development was not attainable (nor desirable) under occupation and therefore should not be pursued. By refusing to challenge Israeli policies, this static approach to economic change fuelled the de-development process.

Through the late 1970s, the PLO articulated a political–economic conceptual framework that defined the character as well as the scope of economic activity in the occupied territories and secured PLO influence there. This paradigm expressed the shift in political orientation of the Palestinian nationalist movement from liberation (i.e., the creation of a democratic secular state in all of Palestine), which had been popular before the mid-1970s, to sovereignty (i.e., statehood in the West Bank and Gaza Strip only). Compelled by the Palestinians' failure to fulfill their political and revolutionary objectives in Jordan in 1970, in Palestine during the 1973 October war, or in Lebanon after 1975, this shift underscored the political and strategic significance of the occupied territories, particularly because nowhere else in the Arab world did the dispersed Palestinian leadership have such a solid base. It now sought to consolidate that base.

Consequently, economic activity in the occupied territories was defined as a form of political resistance whose objective was to strengthen the ties of the Palestinian people to their land. Known as *sumud*, or steadfastness, this survivalist strategy used economic assistance as a form of cultural insurance and was informed by the need to fight the occupation not develop society. Its primary aims were to facilitate daily life and ensure the continued presence of the Palestinian people in their homeland. Funds from the PLO, a variety of Arab regimes, and diaspora Palestinians were channelled through the Jordanian–Palestinian Joint Committee for the Support of the Steadfastness of the Palestinian People in the Occupied Homeland (Joint Committee) established at the 1978 Arab Summit in Baghdad for the purpose of supporting Palestinian steadfastness. Between 1979 and 1986, committee funds were used to build educational, health, and social service institutions, to support existing institutions (including municipalities), and to build housing. These monies were also used to cement critical political alliances in the territories that would insure PLO control and influence. Economic activity, therefore, was directed toward maintaining, not transforming, economic conditions. Palestinians were to be helped, not empowered. This conservative strategy (ironically similar to that of Israel) was dependent on external sources of finance and support, and encouraged a patronage system that tended to support PLO centrists and their traditional allies in the West Bank and Gaza Strip. Not surprisingly, *sumud* engendered a great deal of criticism, particularly from Palestinians living in the territories. They faulted *sumud* for promoting Palestinian passivity and dependence and weakening the capacity to resist political normalization and initiate independent economic change. They also complained that *sumud* generated corruption, as money was often used to purchase political influence outright.

In 1981, a group of Palestinian academics and professionals from the occupied territories held a conference in the West Bank to challenge the *sumud* approach. The meeting was also committed to finding a new development strategy that would secure an acceptable standard of living and make Palestinians active participants (and not merely recipients) in the process of resisting the negative effects of Israeli occupation. The urgent need for change among West Bankers and Gazans was also motivated by the continued political dominance of Israel's right wing and by the PLO's 1982 defeat in Lebanon. These events made it increasingly clear that: (1) Israeli occupation would take considerably longer to end than Palestinians had assumed; (2) struggle had to be political rather than military; and (3) the arena of struggle had shifted from outside Palestine to inside the West Bank and Gaza Strip. Consequently, if Palestinians were to resist occupation over the long term, they had to develop more effective and empowering means of resistance.[79]

The new model that emerged was conceived as *sumud muqawim*, or resistance *sumud*. At its conceptual core lay the use of development as the primary form of resistance. Resistance development, as it became known, combined the basic needs approach of traditional *sumud* with the dynamism of grassroots change. Resistance development began to challenge traditional institutional structures and patronage with new, more radical mass-based organizations that organized and educated Palestinians from a range of socioeconomic classes. As such, the Palestinian leadership considered *sumud muqawim* a challenge to the Joint Committee model of development and viewed it with suspicion. The women's movement, for example, began to challenge the traditional charitable institutions that had historically dictated both the form and the extent of women's activities in the public domain. This challenge, however, was directed at the political rather than the social status quo. Other mass-based activities included literacy training, preventive-health care for the rural poor, and the provision of agricultural extension services to isolated areas.[80]

Emerging economic strategies variously focused on revitalizing the trade union movement, organizing rural cooperatives, securing regional and international expanded markets for Palestinian commodities, and promoting the entrepreneurship so essential to developing those markets. However, change was slow and problematic, especially in an environment that institutionally reinforced old patterns and attitudes. Moreover, the mass movements that emerged during the 1980s were all organized along factional lines. Although this challenged the traditional patronage structure, it also split the national movement and encouraged internecine battles. However, the changes that occurred during the 1980s set the stage for the intifada, when the issue of development under occupation was carried to its contextual extreme and de-development was finally, albeit temporarily, challenged.

Conclusion

Israeli government policies of pacification, normalization, and integration demonstrated the decisive role of ideological and political factors in the critical early stages of occupation. The emphasis on control and security as the primary national objectives precluded a deliberate and carefully planned program of rational economic development, which the new Israeli administration never considered to be a priority or a real option. Indeed, Israeli capitalism was not interested in creating a satellite capitalist class in Gaza or the West Bank, nor did it seek to turn the occupied territories into a serious investment opportunity. Rather, the state sought to acquire the land, not the economic potential contained within it.

The lack of development planning at the policy level, however, did not absent the emergence of an economic policy that could serve Israel's ideological interests. The policy envisioned economic integration, not structural reform. This approach provided the government with a way of mediating its rule politically. It also encouraged changes in the structure of Gaza's economy that made it more dependent on and reoriented it to the needs of Israeli capital, internal constraints notwithstanding.[81]

Thus, to the extent that economic planning did occur at the official level, it reflected the state's political and economic imperatives and centered on four key areas: the integration of labor into the lowest sectors of the Israeli workforce, the elimination of the "refugee problem," the restructuring of trade, and the expropriation of land and water. The structural patterns established by these four areas, the primary foci of Israeli policy, contributed directly to delimiting and shaping the patterns of structural change in other sectors as well.

Palestinian development policies emphasizing *sumud* perpetuated the economic status quo created by Israel. These policies were survivalist in nature and were based on ensuring a Palestinian presence in the occupied territories through infusions of external Arab aid. It was not until the early 1980s that the static approach to economic activity was challenged by policies of grassroots change aimed at transforming economic and political life.

In the first two decades of interaction between Israel and the Gaza Strip, the major structural constraints on indigenous economic development inherited in 1967 (i.e., an agricultural sector too weak to absorb surplus labor, a tiny and underdeveloped industrial sector, a poor physical and economic infrastructure, and the presence of a majority and disenfranchised refugee community) remained unchanged. In addition, Israel introduced new constraints that reshaped the process of underdevelopment into one of de-development.

Notes to Chapter 6:

1. M. Benvenisti, *The West Bank Data Project—A Survey of Israel's Policies*, p. 12.

2. One government official interviewed physically winced when the word "development" was used and bluntly told the author, "We prefer not to use *that* word in this ministry."

3. Ephraim Kleiman, "The Economic Interdependence of the West Bank, the Gaza Strip and Israel," (paper presented at a symposium entitled "Economic Aspects of a Political Settlement in the Middle East," University of Nijmegen, Nijmegen, The Netherlands, 18–20 April 1990), p. 5. Kleiman also states that the lack of policy formulation occurred "...despite the fact that already by the end of July 1967, the government had before it an evaluation of the expected results of alternative economic policies regarding the West Bank, prepared by the Economic Planning Authority at the Prime Minister's Office."

4. In this regard, M. Benvenisti, *The West Bank Data Project—A Survey of Israel's Policies*, pp. 8–18, has argued that Israeli policy was characterized by attention to improvements rather than transformations.

5. M. Benvenisti, *The West Bank Data Project—A Survey of Israel's Policies*, p. 11.

6. Between 1967 and 1979, the territorial demarcation known as the Strip included the Gaza Strip and Northern Sinai which extended as far west as el-Arish. In 1979, the Sinai was returned to Egypt and the population of el-Arish (approximately 30,000 people) was deducted from official statistics. In 1982, portions of the Rafah area were also returned to Egypt and a population of close to 7,000 was also deducted from official accounts. Because the overwhelming majority of the population resided in the Gaza Strip and the majority of economic activity took place there as well, this chapter will deal only with the Gaza Strip unless otherwise noted.

7. Nimrod Raphaeli, "Problems of Military Administration in the Controlled Territories," *Public Administration in Israel and Abroad 1967* 8, (1968): 50. Also see Raphaeli, "Military Government in the Occupied Territories: An Israeli View," *Middle East Journal* 40 (Autumn 1968): 179.

8. Raphaeli, "Military Government in the Occupied Territories," p. 179.

9. Ibid.

10. A. Susser, "The Israeli-Administered Territories," in Dishon (ed.), Vol. 5, 353. Original citation, *Ma'ariv*, 30 November 1969.

11. Janet Abu Lughod, "Demographic Consequences of the Occupation," in Aruri (ed.), pp. 402, 404–405, states that there were 400,000 de facto residents of Gaza and 450,000 de jure (i.e., 50,000 Gazans were living outside the country).

12.   Abu Lughod, "Demographic Consequences," in Aruri (ed.), p. 404. In 1967, the government of Israel did inaugurate a repatriation scheme under which 25,800 residents (8 percent of the 325,000 people) expelled from the Gaza Strip and West Bank were allowed to return.

13.   Susser, "The Israeli-Administered Territories," in Dishon (ed.), Vol. 5, p. 353. See also Francis Ofner, "Israeli juggles refugee hot potato," *Christian Science Monitor*, 6 February 1969.

14.   Rekhess, p. 392. Rekhess maintains that the primary concern of Israel policy was humanitarian.

15.   Raphaeli, "Gaza under Four Administrations," 50; and "Bar-Lev to Help Gaza Strip Growth," *Jerusalem Post*, 29 June 1972.

16.   Raphaeli, "Military Government in the Occupied Territories," p. 179. For a definition of this concept in the Gaza Strip, see Herbert Ben-Adi, "Gaza: Business as Usual," *Jerusalem Post*, 8 June 1973.

17.   Rekhess, p. 392.

18.   Neu, p. 189.

19.   Joan Borsten, "Newsbeat/The Gaza Connection—I: Low-paid labour—a marriage of convenience," *Jerusalem Post*, 2 February 1983; and Neu, p. 189.

20.   Kanovsky, p. 179; and Roy, *The Gaza Strip Survey*, p. 31.

21.   Dishon (ed.), *Middle East Record 1969–1970*, p. 349 (emphasis added).

22.   Rekhess, p. 393.

23.   Kanovsky, p. 179.

24.   Borsten, quoting Gur.

25.   M. Benvenisti, *1986 Report*, p. 77.

26.   Dishon (ed.), *Middle East Record 1969–1970*, p. 350.

27.   While there were no customs barriers barring Israelis from investing in the Strip, such barriers did exist for Palestinians who might have wished to venture financially into Israel.

28.   Dishon (ed.), *Middle East Record 1969–1970*, p. 350; and Rekhess, p. 398. See also Aaron Sittner, "Labelled 'development' areas: Gov't to boost investment in areas," *Jerusalem Post*, 9 October 1972.

29.   See Hillel Frisch, *Stagnation and Frontier: Arab and Jewish Industry in the West Bank* (Jerusalem: The West Bank Data Base Project, 1983).

30.   Rekhess, p. 398; Kanovsky, pp. 184–88.

31.   Anan Safadi, "New projects aim: Self-sufficient economy in W. Bank, Gaza Strip," *Jerusalem Post*, 6 August 1972.

32.   Ministry of Foreign Affairs, *Two Years Of Military Government 1967–1969: Data On The Activities Of The Civil Administration In Judea And Samaria, The Gaza Strip And Northern Sinai* (Tel-Aviv: Ministry of Foreign Affairs, May 1969), p. 47.

33.   Bank of Israel, Research Department, *The Economy of the Administered Areas in 1970* (Jerusalem: Bank of Israel, August 1971), p. 34.

34.   See International Labour Conference (ILO), *Report of the Director General-Appendices*, 71st Session (Geneva: ILO, 1985), pp. 37–39.

35.   "Work in Israel produces 35% of 'area' income," *Jerusalem Post*, 2 August 1973.

36.   Bank of Israel, *The Economy of the Administered Areas in 1970*, p. 34; Ze'ev Schul, "Citrus Season—In Gaza Too," *Jerusalem Post*, 4 October 1967; Herbert Ben-Adi, "Making Life Better In Gaza," *Jerusalem Post*, 14 June 1970; and "Gaza Strip notes gains but stays tense," *Washington Post*, 1972.

37.   Government of Israel, *Two Years Of Military Government*, pp. 35–36; and Herbert Ben-Adi, "Gaza strawberries to Europe; citrus packing plant opened," *Jerusalem Post*, 6 February 1969.

38.   Ephraim Ahiram, "The Principle Determinants of Economic Cooperation between the People of Israel and Palestine," (Paper presented at a symposium entitled "Economic Aspects of a Political Settlement in the Middle East," University of Nijmegen, Nijmegen, The Netherlands, 18–20 April 1990).

39.   Government of Israel, *Two Years of Military Government*, p. 35.

40.   Borsten; Neu, p. 191.

41.   Neu, 194, points out other reasons for the high number of unregistered workers. In April 1969, Yitzchak Pundak, advisor on the territories to the Minister of Labor, revealed that of the 16,000 Arabs from the West Bank and Gaza working in Israel, 10,000 were employed illegally. Dishon (ed.), *Middle East Record 1969–1970*, p. 349.

42.   Rekhess, p. 394.

43.   See State of Israel, *Labour And Employment In Judea, Samaria And The Gaza District* (Jerusalem: Ministry of Labour and Social Affairs, Department of International Relations, February 1989), p. 16.

44.   See Bregman, *Economic Growth*, p. 29.

45.   See for example, "Influx of workers from Gaza, West Bank on increase," *Jerusalem Post*, 30 November 1969. See also a six-part series by Joan Borsten on Gaza Strip labor entitled "The Gaza Connection I–VI" which appeared in the *Jerusalem Post* in February 1983. See also Raphael Meron, *Economic Development in Judea-Samaria and the Gaza District: Economic Growth and Structural Change 1970–1980* (Jerusalem: Bank of Israel Research Department, May 1983), p. 48.

46.   Bank of Israel, *The Economy of the Administered Areas in 1970*, p. 8.

47.   Yuval Elizur, "Israel to Allow Gaza Arabs to Enter Country," *Washington Post*, 28 April 1972. Avraham Lavine (ed.), *Society of Change, Judaea, Samaria, Gaza Sinai 1967–1973* (Jerusalem: Ministry of Social Welfare, November 1974), p. 16, spoke of the new possibilities created for Palestinians "to peep, for the first time, over the fence of subsistence."

48.   Dayan, *Story of My Life*, pp. 401–402. See also Herbert Ben-Adi, "Life returns to normal in the Gaza Strip," *Jerusalem Post*, 5 May 1972.

49.   Dishon (ed.), *Middle East Record 1969–1970*, p. 349.

50.   Ibid.

51.   Rekhess, p. 396.

52.   Neu, p. 213; "Gov't said for Dayan plan on Gaza crossings: Status Equal to West Bank," *Jerusalem Post*, 24 April 1972.

53.   Raphaeli, "Military Government in the Occupied Territories," p. 180.

54.   Dishon (ed.), *Middle East Record 1969–1970*, p. 351.

55.   *New York Times*, 16 September 1969; *Jerusalem Post*, 3 October 1969.

56.   Government of Israel, *Two Years of Military Government*, pp. 5–6.

57.   Rekhess, p. 399. For a detailed description of the Galili Document, see Susan H. Rolef (ed.), *Political Dictionary of the State of Israel* (New York: Macmillan Publishing Co., 1987), pp. 120–21.

58.   One government publication stated,
  Wages rose from I£ 5 per day in Judaea and Samaria to I£ 13.9 by December 1973. In Gaza, pre-war daily wages had been I£ 3.1; they had risen to I£ 12.9 by December 1972. There was a corresponding growth of the GNP, which, in Judaea and Samaria, went up from I£ 325 million in 1968 to I£ 685 million in 1971; in Gaza, the GNP rose, during this same period, from I£ 126 million to I£ 280 million.

See Israel Information Centre, *The Administered Areas: Aspects of Israeli Policy*, Information Briefing #10, Ministry of Foreign Affairs, 1973, p. 15.

59.   In 1974, the Research Department of the Bank of Israel concluded:
The introduction of Israeli production methods and lifestyle into the areas must be regarded as a leap forward, one which may turn out to be an important precondition for continued growth. Nonetheless, it would seem that in the immediate future the further rapid growth of the administered areas depends on the continued maintenance of ties with Israel.
See Bregman, *Economic Growth*, p. 8.

60.   Dishon (ed.), *Middle East Record 1969–1970*, p. 348; Rekhess, p. 396.

61.   Ibid.

62.   *Israeleft News*, 15 February 1973.

63.   Sheila Ryan, "Israeli Economic Policy in the Occupied Areas: Foundations of a New Imperialism," *MERIP Reports*, no.24 (January 1974): 8.

64.   In the West Bank, this local base was the village league system, and in the Gaza Strip, it constituted support for specific families and groups with pro-Jordanian (as opposed to PLO) leanings.

65.   "Plan for 'less than peace'—Dayan," *Jerusalem Post*, 2 December 1968. See also Ari Rath, "What Should Be Done Until Peace Comes?" *Jerusalem Post*, 2 February 1973.

66.   "Dayan: let's act in areas, not wait and see," *Jerusalem Post*, 20 August 1971.

67.   Abraham S. Becker, *Israel and the Palestinian Occupied Territories: Military–Political Issues in the Debate* (Report Prepared for the Office of the Assistant Secretary of Defense for International Security Affairs, Rand Corporation 1971), cited in Ryan, p. 9.

68.   *New York Times*, 29 July 1968; Raphaeli, "Gaza under Four Administrations," p. 51.

69.   The supply of electricity by private companies continued far longer in the West Bank, where they were more highly developed.

70.   Dishon (ed.), *Middle East Record 1969–1970*, p. 398; "Gaza mayors want to see Dayan on grid," *Jerusalem Post*, 1 December 1969.

71.   "Gaza linked to Israel national power grid," *Jerusalem Post*, 27 November 1969.

72.   Dishon (ed.), *Middle East Record 1969–1970*, p. 356.

73.   Ibid.

74.   William Wilson Harris, *Taking Root: Israeli Settlement in the West Bank, the Golan and Gaza-Sinai 1967-1980* (New York: Research Studies Press, 1980), p. 1.

75.   "Galili again tells Knesset: Gaza musn't be separated," *Jerusalem Post*, 4 May 1972.

76.   Hirsh Goodman, "Galili to the Knesset: Gaza Strip will not be separated from Israel," *Jerusalem Post*, 28 March 1972. See also, "Consolidation in Gaza Strip must be speeded—Galili," *Jerusalem Post*, 8 October 1970; "Eban: Gaza won't be separated from Israel," *Jerusalem Post*, 17 November 1972; and H. Ben-Adi, "Hillel: working toward Gaza's full integration," *Jerusalem Post*, 5 January 1971.

77.   Goodman, "Galili to the Knesset: Gaza Strip will not be separated from Israel," *Jerusalem Post*, 28 March 1972. The article details the debate in the Knesset over Galili's statements but indicates that his position reflected the prevailing view within the government. A brief but succinct synopsis of Galili's speech in the Knesset is presented in "Gaza and Israel," *Jerusalem Post*, 4 May 1972.

78.   M. Benvenisti, *The West Bank Data Project—A Survey of Israel's Policies*, p. 27.

79.   In this regard, see William B. Quandt, "Political and Military Dimensions of Contemporary Palestinian Nationalism," in William B. Quandt, Fuad Jabber and Ann Mosley Lesch (eds.), *The Politics of Palestinian Nationalism* (Berkeley: University of California Press, 1973), pp. 43–148; and Ann Mosley Lesch, *Political Perceptions of the Palestinians in the West Bank and Gaza Strip* (Washington, DC: Middle East Institute, 1980).

80.   See Ibrahim Dakkak, "Development from Within: A Strategy for Survival," in Abed (ed.), pp. 287–310.

81.   See Baruch Kimmerling, *Zionism and Economy* (Cambridge, MA: Schenkman Publishing Co., Inc., 1983), pp. 41–67. See also (Israel) Ministry of Defense, *Development and Economic Situation in Judea, Samaira, the Gaza Strip and North Sinai 1967–1969: A Summary* (Tel Aviv: Ministry of Defense, 1970), which states, "The areas are a supplementary market for Israeli goods and services on the one hand, and a source of factors of production, especially unskilled labor, for the Israeli economy on the other." Cited in Ryan, p. 9.

7

Expropriation and Dispossession

G aza's de-development has been shaped by a range of policies and economic factors that fall under three categories: expropriation and dispossession, integration and externalization, and deinstitutionalization. Each category will be reviewed separately in the next three chapters. Expropriation and dispossession deny a people the full use and benefits of its own economic resources. As a result, their capacity for economic change is constrained and weakened. In Gaza, expropriation and dispossession are most visible and devastating in connection with water and land issues. Israel's disposition of water and land in the Gaza Strip is a powerful illustration of the ideological and political basis of state policy. This policy has removed critical factors of production from the Arab sector, without compensation, for exclusive use in the Jewish sector. This chapter demonstrates that Israeli policy aimed not only to transfer Gaza's economic resources to Jewish use but to deny Arabs the use of those resources and thereby decapacitate them. As such, expropriation and dispossession represent the absolute and irreversible loss of economic assets and their development potential. A third area of expropriation and dispossession is housing; a fourth is illustrated in Israeli expenditure and investment patterns in the Gaza Strip.

Throughout the next three chapters, reference will be made to the Gaza Plan, a confidential document commissioned in 1986 by the defense ministry and Gaza Civil Administration to survey and study Gaza's key sectors and make planning projections through the year 2000. The Gaza Plan is among the most important internal government documents dealing with the Gaza Strip and has not been made public. The Gaza Plan may seem obsolete in light of the Gaza–Jericho Agreement but it reveals official Israeli thinking and strategies on a variety of critical issues that fundamentally remain unchanged in the Gaza–Jericho Agreement. It is cited throughout as a definitive source and key resource with particular relevance for the future.[1]

Water

The issue of water in the Gaza Strip is extremely compelling. In certain respects, water is most crucial for the future of the Gaza Strip and West Bank because without it, nothing is possible. The policies that affect water, therefore, have a defining impact on other factors of production, especially on the economic, social, and political value of land. The singular importance of water for human survival and economic growth, coupled with its rapid depletion in the area and in the region, makes it an issue of extreme political importance and sensitivity. When one considers that today there is not enough water to meet the needs of all Israelis and Palestinians in the area, policies determining water use and allocation assume a level of meaning and significance too costly to ignore. What has Israeli policy done for water in the Gaza Strip?

The problems with Gaza's water supply did not begin during Israeli rule but before it, when the unregulated use of water resulted in chronic overpumping and the depletion of local supplies. Under the Egyptians, water was considered a private resource of which individuals could claim ownership. Water use was based, not on a system of permits, but on customary law, which conferred on all who needed it the right to use water for whatever purpose.[2] After the 1967 war, the Israeli government, through its national water carrier Mekorot, assumed control over all surface and underground water in the occupied territories.[3] Since then, Israeli policy has exacerbated already existing problems. The basic assertion is that the state, motivated largely by political motives, has overregulated water supply to the grave detriment of the resource.

The problem of water is one of quantity as well as quality. The Gaza Strip contains shallow acquifers (natural reservoirs for underground water), about 30 to 40 meters deep, and unconfined by rock. There are no rivers; the only sources of surface water are wadis. If rainfall is low, one must dig deep to find water. If replenished water decreases, then the concentration of contaminants increases and seawater enters underground water, increasing salinity. In recent years, this problem has been aggravated because the Wadi Gaza, whose regular flooding used to supplement the groundwater supply, has been dry.

Water is supplied by 1,800 to 2,150 artesian wells and boreholes, the majority of which are located in the inner Gaza area and used for agricultural purposes.[4] In 1985, the annual output of water in the Gaza Strip was approximately 90 million cubic meters (mcm) per year. In 1990, total water consumption reached 100 mcm. By the year 2000, demand is expected to rise to 113 mcm.[5]

The demand for water in the Gaza Strip, however, has long exceeded the area's existing capacity and natural replenishment, resulting in a deficit of fresh water. As early as 1981, a master plan for the Gaza Strip revealed that the sustainable level for pumping water was estimated at only 44 mcm.[6] In 1986, in the unlikely event that the situation did not deteriorate, this would have produced a deficit of 46 mcm of fresh water. In 1987, Benvenisti estimated the deficit at 60 mcm per year; another study commissioned by the military government in 1986 placed it more conservatively at 15 mcm.[7] Table 7.1 indicates that by the turn of the century, existing resources will only provide one-third of the water projected for agricultural use and 43 percent for domestic use.

The deficit in fresh water causes overpumping of the aquifer, or the extraction of more water than is replenished naturally. This in turn allows seawater seepage into the fresh water acquifer, because Gaza's underground water slopes toward the sea. Furthermore, urbanization has interfered with the percolation of rain into the ground, which renders the groundwater even more saline.[8] In 1987, overpumping resulted in a drop of Gaza's water table by 7 to 20 cubic meters for the entire territory and increased salinity levels.[9]

Table 7.1.   Water Balance in the Year 2000. Sources and Uses in the Gaza Strip (mcm*)

use	*drawn from wells*	*purified sewage*	*other uses*	*total*
Drinking	23	0	30	53
Agriculture	20	40	0	60
Total	43	40	30	113

Source: Gaza Plan, table 14.1.
* millions of cubic meters.

Salinity is measured by the number of milligrams of chlorine per liter (mcl) found in fresh water, and levels falling below 600 mcl are considered acceptable. (In Israel, anything between 200 mcl and 300 mcl is considered dangerous to citrus.[10]) Salinity levels vary across the Strip. According to Tahal, Israel's water planning authority, they are lowest (100 mcl to 200 mcl) in the northern region, which includes Gaza City, Beit Hanoun, and Beit Lahiya, and in the southwestern regions along the coast. However, salinity levels are extremely high in Gaza's central and southeastern regions, notably Deir el-Balah and Khan Younis, averaging between 600 mcl and 1,000 mcl.[11] In some areas, levels exceed 1,000 mcl. Data from the agriculture ministry reveal that the proportion of chlorine reaches as high as 3,300 mcl in some parts of the Strip, such as Deir el-Balah.[12]

Although levels vary, the trend for the entire Strip has been for salinity levels to rise from 1 mcl to 20 mcl per year since the early 1980s.[13] This is reducing the amount of pumped water with an acceptable salinity level at a dramatic rate, from 71 percent of the total water pumped in the Gaza Strip in 1983 to an estimated 54 percent by the year 2000. In November 1987, Gaza's civil administration estimated that at current usage levels, the Strip would be out of fresh water within 20 years unless reparative measures were taken.

Water quality is also damaged by the entry of sewage into underground water supplies, due to the Strip's overall poor sewage system. The sewage infrastructure in the Gaza Strip has been and continues to be sorely inadequate. Approximately 10 percent of the population is not served by any system and are simply dumping raw sewage. Close to 80 percent of the towns and villages possess an extremely inadequate sewage system and rely largely if not entirely on the use of septic tanks and soaking pits for sewage disposal. These pits often overflow into surface drainage systems, which in turn overflow onto roadways and into homes. The Gaza City system, for example, was planned in 1973 to serve a population of 189,000. However, by 1986, the facilities that were constructed could only handle the sewage of 50,000 people, although Gaza City's population approached 200,000. The 1981 Master Plan for the Gaza Strip envisioned the construction of central sewage systems (including treatment facilities) in five places. By the beginning of 1987, however, only the Gaza system had been completed, whereas development of two others had been aborted due to political obstacles created by neighboring Israeli settlements.[14]

The sewage situation is gravest in the refugee camps. By 1989, only two camps, Jabalya and Beach, had partial systems.[15] Although pumping stations and a lagoon had been built, there was no main line or house connections. In Jabalya, Israeli officials prohibited the construction of the main line, arguing that the Jabalya system did not fit in with their master plan for the Gaza Strip, which they refused to make public.[16] By 1992, a more complete system had been built although appropriate treatment facilities were still lacking. The Beach camp network, built in the early 1970s, is in poor condition. Wastes carried by sewers are typically dumped directly into the sea or are carried to nonoperational treatment systems that dump waste directly onto sand dunes where large cesspools then form. Alternatively, wastes are transported through open channels through valleys leading to the sea where they often form temporary lakes that empty into the sea only during the rainy season. There is no control over the disposal of solid wastes and this contributes greatly to ground water contamination.[17] (The implementation of partial autonomy has brought only minor improvements.)

Sewage seepage results in the concentration of nitrates in underground water. A 1983 survey found a high level of nitrates (100 to 400 milligrams per liter) in the Strip's most populated areas, including Gaza City, Jabalya, Nazlah, Beit Hanoun, Nuseirat, and el-Bureij. The Khan Younis and Rafah refugee camps have extremely high concentrations of nitrates (and other chemicals). Given the Strip's population growth and urbanization patterns, this source of contamination will undoubtedly continue.[18] In 1987, in a confidential report to the military government, Tahal wrote: "The rapid salination processes showing an increase of salinity in certain areas of 10–20 mgr chlorine and the increase of infection by nitrates warrant immediate actions to be taken . . . not later than the beginning of the 1990s."[19] In 1993, UNRWA reported that nitrate concentrations increased from almost two times the international standard in the 1980s to more than six times the international standard in 1993.[20] This suggests that Tahal's recommendations were not implemented by the government.

The insufficiency and decreased quality of Gaza's water supply, have been exacerbated by Israel's own, often urgent, need to supplement its own water resources.[21] In accordance with the Israel Water Law of 1959, water was declared to be a public commodity soon after the occupation began. This declaration exceeded the rights of an occupying power under international law.[22] One objective of official policy was to impose needed regulations on water use in order to preserve the supply that had been seriously depleted during Egyptian rule. Prevailing Egyptian law was amended with Military Order 158, which required a license for digging new wells. Given Israel's need to control and use water resources, however, Military Order 158 translated into a prohibition on the development of new water sources by the Arab population *only*. These restrictions have never applied to the Jewish settlers in the Gaza Strip.

Government measures regarding water use have assumed several forms in Gaza. First, despite the restrictions imposed on the Arab population, the authorities bored five 20-inch artesian wells in the Strip that draw water from Gaza's own limited sources for Jewish (including settler) use.[23] Second, Gaza's most important source of surface water and one that it shares in common with Israel, the Wadi Gaza (or *Nahal Bessor* in Hebrew), is diverted wholly for use by Israel. The Wadi Gaza has catchment areas in the West Bank, Gaza, and Israel and arguably provides 20 mcm to 30 mcm of water per year. However, Israel impounds this water before it even enters Gaza.[24] Third, part of the water in Gaza's aquifer—50 mcm to 60 mcm per year—flows from Israel. Although Israel denies it, Palestinian hydrologists claim that Israel intercepts this flow, leaving small quantities for Gaza.[25] Fourth, unofficial reports from foreign development agencies working in the Gaza Strip maintain that in 1985, the government dug between three and five boreholes so close to Israel's border with Gaza that water drawn from them was being drawn from Gaza's own reserves instead.[26] Fifth, government sanction of Jewish settlement in Gaza has further limited the amount of water available to the Arab sector. Water use among Jewish settlers in the Gaza Strip prevents Palestinian agriculturalists from making optimal use of available water, a fact that has no doubt played a role in confining farming methods within a decidedly traditional framework.

Overall, Israeli policy has had a particularly devastating effect on agriculture, the primary consumer of water and the traditional focus of economic activity, as well as on domestic consumption. It is important to examine each area closely to understand fully the effects of Israeli policy.

Agriculture accounts for at least 80 percent of Gaza's total water consumption, a percentage that has increased in direct response to population growth and the demands for expanded agricultural output that naturally attend such growth. Water used for agricultural purposes derives from two sources: pumped well water and purified sewage water. The former traditionally supplied approximately 70,000 dunums of citrus groves, which provided a livelihood for 10,000 of Gaza's farmers. In 1985, agriculture consumed 67 mcm of the 90 mcm used or 74 percent; in the year 2000, agricultural demand is expected to be 60 mcm out of a projected output of 113 mcm, or 53 percent.[27]

The extension of water to the agricultural sector is critical for expansion, capitalization, and modernization. However, Israeli policy measures toward agricultural use have militated against the expansion of Gazan agriculture. Itzhak Galnoor, in his excellent study of water planning in Israel, explains, "If not for the extension of the water supply to agriculture, it would have been impossible to create a modern farming economy with an export market or to consolidate new settlements based largely on agriculture."[28] In the Gaza Strip, however, the reverse has long been true. In the mid-1970s, the authorities imposed water quotas on Arab farmers, restricting them to 800 cubic meters per year for hard soil and 1,000 cubic meters per year for sandy soil.[29] The government placed meters on all wells, even those dug before 1967, and refused Arabs permits to dig new agricultural wells. In fact, the Israeli government has admitted its policy against granting permits to Palestinians for digging new agricultural wells. The official justification for this policy is that greater productivity can be achieved through improved on-farm irrigation methods than by expanding the amount of land under irrigation.[30]

The solution to the problem of agricultural water supply lies largely in the treatment of sewage water. Israeli planners estimated that if the five central sewage systems described above were completed by the year 2000, the purified sewage water produced would irrigate 7,000 dunums in the Beit Lahiya region; 19,000 dunums in and around Gaza City; 3,000 dunums in the area of el-Bureij and the central Gaza Strip; 4,000 dunums in the Abasan region; and 2,500 dunums in Rafah and its surrounding environs, for a total of 35,500 dunums of additional irrigated land. Furthermore, the Gaza Plan stipulates that any supply of purified sewage water over 8.4 mcm per year could replace well water altogether. In fact, treated sewage water could be used as a substitute for well water to the extent of 40 mcm per year. Hence, the absence of effective sewage systems and treatment facilities has grievously constrained the expansion of the agricultural sector by reducing the amount of land under cultivation and unnecessarily depleted existing water supplies.

Growing salinity of local water resources has reduced the amount of water drawn for agricultural purposes, which has in turn lowered the area under cultivation. The Gaza Plan estimated the rate of decline of well water used for agriculture at 1 percent per year in the north, 3 percent in the center, and 2 percent in the south.[31] The problem is particularly ominous for local agriculture, which can only tolerate 11.5 percent of the nitrate levels found in certain regions.[32] Gaza's citrus crop, a primary consumer of water, has suffered considerably from the increasing nitrate contamination, which has lowered citrus output and quality.

In addition to the problems of salinity, the high cost of agricultural water raises production costs and has contributed to the decision of certain farmers in the Gaza Strip to lower water consumption at the expense of quality and productivity. This practice alone has hindered production for competitive export markets.

Israeli policies have had a very different impact on Jewish agriculture in Gaza. Settler consumption per person is vastly greater than that of Arabs for agricultural use. This is not surprising in light of the very small population size of the settler community, their ethnic status, and the fact that settlements are based largely on irrigated farming. Again, despite stated restrictions on the digging of wells by Arabs in the Strip, Israeli settlements have installed 35 to 40 new wells since their establishment over a decade ago. Moreover, these wells are dug on average 300–500 meters deep compared to the average Palestinian well, which is usually no deeper than 100 meters. The greater depth of Jewish wells, combined with the settlers' use of more powerful pumps, has adversely affected some existing Palestinian wells by drawing water away from them.[33] Jewish farmers, unlike their Arab counterparts, do not suffer from imposed water quotas, nor are any Jewish wells metered. In addition to the 3.4 mcm of water supplied by Mekorot for agricultural use in 1986,[34] Israeli settlements in the Gaza Strip drew 2.2 mcm of water from Gaza's own reserves. This supply, in part, would otherwise have been available for Arab use were the settlers not present.[35] Some settlements, furthermore, are critically situated near the *al-mawasi*, a low-lying sandy strip running parallel with and close to the coast, where fresh water oozes just 1 to 2 meters below ground, an area so fertile that one Gaza farmer called it "the earth's womb."

Viewed individually, the difference in total water consumption between Arabs and Jews in the Gaza Strip is striking. In 1986, for example, annual per capita water consumption among the Arab population averaged 142 cubic meters; it was 2,240 cubic meters among Jews, or close to 16 times greater per person. Agricultural consumption rates among Arabs and Jews differed somewhat, standing at 75 percent and 90 percent of total water consumption, respectively. Annual agricultural consumption per capita was 107 cubic meters for Arabs; for Jews it was 2,016 cubic meters, or more than 18 times greater. This per person difference has not narrowed significantly since 1986.[36] The higher consumption rate among Jewish settlers is heavily subsidized by the government. Settlers also receive water development assistance from a variety of Jewish organizations; Palestinians receive no such assistance, due to government restrictions on water development and external assistance.

Domestic (including business) use accounts for the remaining 20 percent of Gaza's water supply. Because population size and living standards are expected to increase, so too is the demand for domestic water; whether such demand will be met is uncertain. In 1985, 23 mcm of water (26 percent of total output) was consumed for domestic use. By the year 2000, residential use will account for 53 mcm, or 47 percent of total output.[37]

Gaza City has fifteen usable municipal wells but needs approximately thirty to meet local demand. Khan Younis has only six wells supplying the majority of its water, five of which were built during Egyptian rule. According to tables 7.2 and 7.3, total demand for water for residential use will more than double between 1986 and 2000, although there will be a 20 percent decline in usable drinking water during that time (see table 7.4 and figure 7.1). Moreover, in the year 2000, the demand for residential water will, if allocations of sub-

Table 7.2.   Forcast of Demand for Water for Residential Use in the Gaza Strip

region	1986 population ('000)	demand/person/year (m³)	total demand (mcm*)
North	329.2	35	11.5
Central	93.7	35	3.3
South	210.7	35	7.4
Total	633.3	35	22.2

region	1990 population ('000)	demand/person/year (m³)	total demand (mcm*)
North	373.1	41	15.3
Central	106.1	41	4.3
South	238.9	41	9.8
Total	718.1	41	29.4

region	1995 population ('000)	demand/person/year (m³)	total demand (mcm*)
North	432.5	48	20.7
Central	123.0	48	5.9
South	276.9	48	13.3
Total	832.4	48	39.9

region	2000 population ('000)	demand/person/year (m³)	total demand (mcm*)
North	497.5	55	27.4
Central	141.5	55	7.8
South	318.5	55	17.5
Total	957.5	55	52.7

Source: Gaza Plan, table 14.2

* mcm = million m³

standard well water are included, be more than twice the supply. Equally striking is the continued absence of usable drinking water in the central region,
despite a projected increase in total demand of 136 percent. Hence, although
the deficit in usable drinking water for the whole Gaza Strip was 2.4 mcm in
1986, the total deficit was expected to increase to a precipitous 36.8 mcm by
2000, a fourteenfold increase in fourteen years. It is also clear that in 1986, the
deficit was covered by pumping and using drinking water that was brackish and
substandard.[38] It is unclear how the deficit will be covered in the future.

Domestic water consumption is an important indicator of local living standards. Israeli policies, particularly with regard to the cost differentials between
Arabs and Jews and the inequitable allocation of permits for well digging, have
affected the absolute amount of water available to Palestinians for domestic
use. The world standard for domestic water consumption is 250 liters/person/

**Table 7.3.   Balance of Drinking Water through the Year 2000: Sources and
Demand in the Gaza Strip (mcm/year*)**

		1986	
region	*sources*	*demand*	*surplus/deficit*
North	15.3	11.5	3.8
Central	0.0	3.3	-3.3
South	4.5	7.4	-2.9
Total	19.8	22.2	-2.4

		1990	
region	*sources*	*demand*	*surplus/deficit*
North	13.8	15.3	-1.5
Central	0.0	4.3	-4.3
South	3.5	9.8	-6.3
Total	17.3	29.4	-12.1

		1995	
region	*sources*	*demand*	*surplus/deficit*
North	13.6	20.7	-7.1
Central	0.0	5.9	-5.9
South	3.1	13.3	-10.2
Total	16.7	39.9	-23.2

		2000	
region	*sources*	*demand*	*surplus/deficit*
North	13.4	27.4	-14.0
Central	0.0	7.8	-7.8
South	2.5	17.5	-15.0
Total	15.9	52.7	-36.8

Source: Gaza Plan, table 14.4.
*mcm = million m³

day (lpd). In the United States and Western Europe, the average is 400 lpd; in Israel, 500 lpd; in North Africa's Sahara, among the lowest in the world, it is 10 lpd. In 1986, according to the Gaza Plan, the average consumption of domestic water in the Gaza Strip was 100 lpd (or 35 cubic meters per person per year); this was expected to rise to 150 lpd by the year 2000.[39] Thus, according to Israeli planners, domestic consumption in the Strip was 10 times higher than the lowest international level, 60 percent below the acceptable world standard, and 20 percent of the consumption rate in Israel.

Table 7.5 details the domestic consumption and source of water for towns and camps, according to local Palestinian officials. The lowest consumption levels are found in Khan Younis City, Khan Younis camp, and the middle camps. Although partially due to salinity, low levels are also due to a common Israeli practice of shutting off water as a form of collective punishment. Areas such as the middle camps that receive a large percentage of their water from Mekorot are most vulnerable to such measures. This measure was used throughout the intifada, especially in the el-Bureij refugee camp.

Domestic water resources suffer from problems of quality as well as quantity. In 1986, Israeli planners stated that rising salinity levels in Gaza's water supply pose a growing public health problem "that is likely to increase kidney disease and dysentery, with children being the primary victims."[40] These same problems, however, do not affect the domestic consumption of water among the

Table 7.4. Forecast of the Depletion of Drinking Water Sources[a] in the Gaza Strip (mcm/year[b])

region	1986	1990	1995[c]	2000
North	15.3	13.8	13.6	13.4
Central	0.0	0.0	0.0	0.0
South	4.5	3.5	3.1	2.5
Total	19.8	17.3	16.7	15.9
Substandard well water used for drinking	3.2	5.7	6.3	7.1
Total well water used for drinking[d]	23.0	23.0	23.0	23.0

Source: Gaza Plan, table 14.3.

[a] Adapted from Tahal, Closed Water System in the Gaza Strip.

[b] mcm = million m3

[c] Yearly average for 1990-2000

[d] In tables 7.2 and 7.3 the demnad for drinking water in 1986 appears as 22.2 mcm/year. The difference is due to the use of different sources for each of the tables in the original text but is small enough to be ignored.

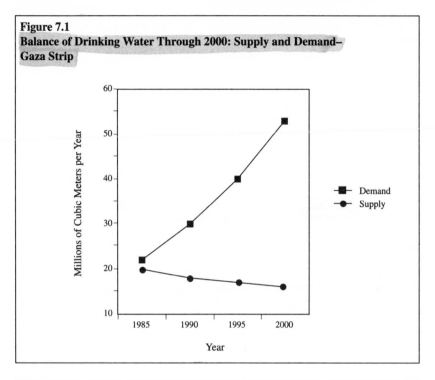

Figure 7.1
Balance of Drinking Water Through 2000: Supply and Demand–Gaza Strip

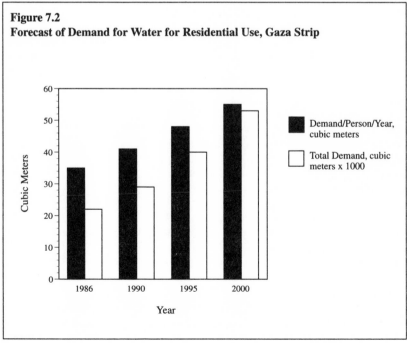

Figure 7.2
Forecast of Demand for Water for Residential Use, Gaza Strip

Jewish population. In 1986, for example, on average, every Gazan Palestinian consumed 35 cubic meters of water for domestic use (100 lpd) or 24 gallons a day, whereas every Jewish settler in the Gaza Strip consumed 224 cubic meters (600 lpd), or 148 gallons a day.[41] Palestinian water is available only during certain hours (especially in the camps); Jewish water is available 24 hours a day. On average, Palestinians pay four times more per unit of domestic water than Jews, who enjoy government subsidies.[42] Moreover, water provided to the Jewish population is of substantially higher quality.

The steady deterioration of the quantity and quality of Gaza's underground

Table 7.5. Domestic Sources of Water and Domestic Consumption by Selected Localities in the Gaza Strip, 1989

locality	source of water	liters/person/day (lpd)
Gaza City	local wells[a]	220
Beach Camp	local wells	160-180
Jabalya Town	local wells	150
Jabalya Camp	local (20%), UNRWA (40%), and private (40%) wells	150
Beit Lahia	local wells	180-190
Beit Hanoun	local wells	180-190
Deir el-Balah[b]	local wells	120
el-Nuseirat	Mekorot (2-3 hrs/day)	100
el-Bureij	Mekorot (2-3 hrs/day)	100
el-Maghazi	Mekorot (2-3 hrs/day)	100
Zawaida	Mekorot (2-3 hrs/day)	100
Rafah City	local wells	200
Rafah Camp[c]	local wells	160
Khan Younis City	local wells (80%), Mekorot (20%)	<100
Khan Younis Camp	local wells (80%), Mekorot (20%)	<100
Bani Suheila	local wells (50%), Mekorot (50%)	150
Abasan el-Kabira	local wells (50%), Mekorot (50%)	150
Abasan el-Saghira	local wells (50%), Mekorot (50%)	150
Kuza'ah	local wells (50%), Mekorot (50%)	150
Other villages	local wells	120

Source: Association of Engineers, Gaza Strip, 1989.

[a] Local wells refer to municipal wells. Gaza City had 17 wells but two were unusable in 1994 due to excessive levels of salinity.

[b] UNRWA has one well each in el-Nuserat and el-Bureij which are unsafe but used in emergency situations. The UNRWA well in el-Maghazi was turned over to the civil administration.

[c] The Water Department at UNRWA, Gaza, stated that UNRWA wells supply 36% and local wells supply 64%.

water supply, combined with the growing demand for water for home and agricultural use, mandate the development of alternative water sources.[43] One suggestion, to import 30 mcm of water from Israel, would meet only 26 percent of Gaza's estimated water demand in the year 2000. Another proposal, to desalinate seawater, is technology intensive and extremely costly. A third proposal, to divert water from the Nile River into Gaza, would require Egyptian cooperation but might be technically feasible, given that water is already piped from the Nile into el-Arish in the Sinai.

Tahal proposed two alternative scenarios that entail additional restrictions on pumping, desalination, importing water from Israel, and treating sewage water. Tahal's recommendations may also seem outdated in light of the Gaza–Jericho Agreement, but they reveal Israeli approaches to the problems of water particularly as it regards Jewish settlements, and are therefore pertinent.

The focus of Tahal's water plan for Gaza was primarily if not exclusively on the provision of supplementary drinking water, given the projected rise in domestic consumption and the immediate human imperative at stake. Tahal did not deal at all with agricultural needs, which appear to be far less important or perhaps unsustainable within existing constraints.[44]

Tahal proposed a two-stage process—intermediate (1990) and permanent (2000 and beyond)—and two different scenarios, one linked to Israel's water supply and the other focused on indigenous sources. For stated reasons of cost, facility, and efficiency, the scenario linking Gaza to Israel's water supply was recommended. Under this scenario, a pipeline would be built to connect the Israeli water network to the north of the Gaza Strip; this pipeline would transfer an additional 7 mcm of drinking water per year to the northern Strip, the Gaza area, and the middle camps. Another pipeline was envisioned to the "Jewish consumers of Gush Katif" in the south, who alone would be supplied with 3 mcm per year. "This [in turn] will enable the transfer of wells, supplying today a quantity of about 2 million cubic meters to the Jewish settlements, to the use of only Arab consumers."[45]

Thus, under this plan, the Arab population would receive an additional 9 mcm of water per year—7 mcm from Mekorot and 2 mcm from its own local sources presently used by Jewish settlements—a supply that would cover only 74 percent of Gaza's projected 1990 deficit in drinking water. The Jewish settlers would receive 3 mcm to cover the loss of the 2 mcm they had previously drawn from local wells, in addition to the 3.4 mcm they already receive from Mekorot. Although the plan does not state this last point explicitly, it is nevertheless a safe assumption.

Consequently, the settler population would, in the end, receive an extra 1 mcm per year. On a per capita basis, therefore, every Arab in the Gaza Strip would receive a supplemental 13 cubic meters per year, whereas every Jewish settler would receive an additional 333 cubic meters per year. Even by restricting the arithmetic to the targeted population in the north and center (approximately 70 percent of the total population), the quantity of additional drinking water per capita amounts to only 19 cubic meters per year for every Arab, for a total per capita allocation in 1990 that would still be 17.5 times smaller than that of the average Jewish settler.[46] Moreover, table 7.4 indicates that even with the additional supply of drinking water from Israeli sources, not all the water consumed for Arab domestic use will be fit for human consumption.

That regulation of Gaza's water supply was necessary is indisputable. However, if regulation and preservation of water resources were the primary goals of Israeli policy, more even-handed policies would have been used and much more stringent efforts would have been applied toward seeking solutions. Instead, Israel depleted a large percentage of Gaza's water for its own use in Israel and for Jewish settlers in Gaza. Palestinians were left with less water and inferior water; agricultural development was handicapped and personal well-being decreased.

Israel's water policy is driven by political, not economic, motives. In Israel, the Zionists declared water a state-owned commodity. Water is part of the ideology of nation-building so central to Zionist thought and to its practical application, land settlement. Therefore, there is no difference between water as a final product (e.g., drinking) and water as a means of production.[47] Water holds great ideological weight among the social priorities of the state and early on assumed archetypal importance as "the blood flowing through the arteries of the nation."[48] In Israel, water is far more than just an economic commodity; it is a precondition for achieving political goals and fulfilling social values. Itzhak Galnoor explains the relationship between national goals and water development in the Israeli experience:

> The vision of opening up the Negev, [for example], never took note of the economic constraints of water but, on the contrary, subordinated consider-ations of development . . . to the vision of making the desert bloom.[49]

This explains why the government has consistently promoted the establishment of Jewish settlements and supported the gross inequities that they have introduced. Indeed, "the question of water was a marginal factor in consider-ations regarding settlement in the territories occupied in the 1967 war and not a constraint affecting policy or planning."[50] Israel's settlement of the Gaza Strip, like that of the Negev, was dictated by ideology, not economy. Only afterwards were the practical problems of water considered, first as they affected Jews, and only then as they affected Arabs.[51]

Israeli policy toward water consumption is a form of control that needs to be understood for both what it has and has not done for Gaza. The policy has consistently reduced the amount of water available to the rapidly growing Gazan Arab population by at least the amount it apportions to Jewish civilian settle-ments, which enjoy disproportionately higher allocations per capita. This amount, in effect, represents the minimum denied; the maximum would include those Arab water sources diverted to Jewish use in Israel. What the policy has not done is augment, supplement, or compensate the absolute loss to the Arab sector nor enhance the quality of the water that is available, a growing percentage of which is unfit for human consumption.

Thus, the problems of water in the Gaza Strip and the government's response (or lack thereof) assume their own internal logic and consistency. The reason for Israel's total control of water has little to do with regulation and a great deal to do with Israel's territorial expansion, itself predicated on the denial of sovereignty to Palestinians. The outcome has been the dispossession and decapacitation of Palestinians in Gaza, and their de-development.

Land and Settlements

Israel's land policies are similar to its water policies. The total area of the Gaza Strip is approximately 140 square miles (365,000 dunums).[52] In 1945, before the state of Israel was established, the entire area was available for Arab use. This meant that there were about 5.1 dunums for every resident of the area that was to become the Gaza Strip. In 1948, with the refugee influx, this figure dropped to around 1.1 dunums. Between 1945 and 1986, the amount of land available to Arabs in the Gaza Strip fell by 39 percent, whereas the population rose by nearly 800 percent. Thus, Gaza's rapidly expanding population has had to make do with an ever-shrinking land base.

The two key determinants of land availability have been government land confiscations and the establishment of Jewish settlements. These have accelerated in recent years. Through 1984, Benvenisti estimated that the government had control over 31 percent of Gaza Strip land; by 1986, the state had assumed possession and/or control over 51.1 percent.[53] Between 1986 and 1990, the amount of area under Israeli control increased to approximately 58 percent, largely due to confiscation.[54]

The acquisition of land in the Gaza Strip (and West Bank) has been facilitated by the existence of certain British and Israeli laws formulated prior to the Israeli occupation. The Emergency Law of 1945 and the Law of Closed Areas (1949) has enabled occupation authorities to close off any area of land for military maneuvres for undefined periods of time. The Law of Security Areas similarly has allowed the confiscation of land for security reasons, forcing residents to leave the land. The Law of Taking Action (1953) states that if lands are not cultivated or used by their owners, the government has the right of repossession for defense and settlement needs. None of these laws and the powers they endow have been subject to any form of judicial review by Israeli courts; all are in violation of international law as set down in the Geneva Convention of 1949. Once the Israeli occupation began, a series of military orders further facilitated the acquisition of land in the Gaza Strip by amending those laws legislated prior to 1967. These orders empowered the government to (1) administer all lands registered as state lands before 1967; (2) seize privately owned land for military purposes; (3) close areas for training purposes; (4) repossess land belonging to Jews before 1948; (5) expropriate land for public purposes; and (6) seize land by declaring it state land. State land declarations view all land as "national patrimony" and consequently require Arab claimants to prove ownership. Furthermore, under this strategy, lands that are uncultivated and unregistered are more vulnerable to seizure.[55]

Portions of the confiscated land were turned over to Jewish settlements. In 1971, only one civilian settlement, Kfar Darom, was established in Gaza; however, following the suppression of all Palestinian resistance in 1971, five additional settlements—Netzarim, Morag, Eretz, Katif, and Netzer Hazani— were set up. They began as paramilitary outposts or *nahals*, which were first inhabited by soldiers who prepared the physical infrastructure for the settlement sites while fulfilling their military duty.

Prior to 1978, settlement activity in the Gaza Strip remained limited as the Labor government pursued a policy of containment, preferring to surround rather than implant the territory with an Israeli civilian presence. By 1978, thirteen such settlements had been built as a buffer zone at Gaza's southern border in northern Sinai. With the installation of the right-wing Likud party, the scale of settlement increased although fundamental policies did not change. Following the Camp David Accords, which raised the specter of Palestinian autonomy, Israel's settlement strategy shifted to a focus on two new objectives: (1) to create a strong Israeli presence in the Gaza Strip that would make it difficult for the Palestinian communities to form an independent state in the event of future negotiations; and (2) to isolate Arab communities from each other physically in order to minimize the possibility of unified political action. In these objectives, the government was largely successful. The border settlements were removed and between 1978 and 1985, eighteen new settlements housing 2,150 people, spaced at more or less regular intervals between the territory's largest population centers, were established in four regional blocs along or near Gaza's coastline.[56] By 1991, the population had increased to 3,500.

By 1993, sixteen such settlements (two had been left due to the intifada) housed 4,000 Jewish settlers, a mere 0.5 percent of Gaza's population. Yet Israel granted this tiny community use of at least 25 percent of Gaza's land; whereas Gaza's 830,000 Arabs had 224,5000 dunums, its 4,000 Jews had 91,000 dunums.[57] Therefore, every Jew in Gaza was allowed 23 dunums, whereas each Arab inhabitant was given 0.27 dunums (see table 7.6).[58] There were 85 times as many people per dunum among Arabs than among Jews in 1993.

The disparities in land allocations between Jews and Arabs are mirrored almost surrealistically in the physical contrast between residential areas. In many Jewish settlements, rows of neatly aligned red-roofed houses enhanced by modern street lights, sidewalks, red brick driveways and carefully manicured lawns appear pristine and serene. Some have swimming pools, palm trees, and riding stables. All are surrounded by electrified security fences or concertina wire, as if to insulate them from the sprawl and squalor of the rest of the Strip.[59] In Palestinian areas, by contrast, overcrowded, decomposing refugee camps dominate. Dilapidated houses appear crammed together absorbing every inch of avail-

Table 7.6. Land Use in the Gaza Strip by Ethnic Group (in dunums)

group/land use	1983	1986
Palestinian		
Built-up areas	50,000	56,500
Agriculture-Cultivated land	200,000	168,000
Total	250,000	224,500
Israeli		
Jewish settlements		
Land allocations	32,300	37,000
Land leased to settlers	58,000	54,000
Other (state-controlled)	23,500	49,500
Total (state/settler)	113,800	140,500
Gaza Strip Total	363,800	365,000
Palestinian land use/ Gaza Strip total	68.7%	61.5%
Israeli land use/ Gaza Strip total	31.3%	38.5%

Source: Calculated from Meron Benvenisti and Shlomo Khayat, *The West Bank and Gaza Atlas* (Jerusalem: Jerusalem Post Press, 1988), pp. 112–13.

able land. Most of Gaza's roads are sand and dirt that easily turn to mud in the rain. Sewage flows on many streets and garbage is a prominent feature of the urban landscape. The sense of physical decay is pervasive.

The increasing absorption of land by the state and the installation of Jewish civilian settlements have had a considerable effect on Gaza's de-development. Land confiscations have removed viable agricultural lands from Palestinians and their economy, displaced people and their resources, weakened linkages, and caused massive overcrowding (and with it, various social and economic ills). Settlements have broken up areas of contiguous Arab settlement and bifurcated private farmers' agricultural lands with roads and other infrastructure.

Population density is perhaps the most visible outcome of Israel's land and settlement policy. On lands available for use by the Arab population, population density was over 14 times greater in 1986 than it was in 1945 (see table 7.7). Between 1966 and 1986, population density for the entire Strip increased by 58 percent. Between 1986 and 1993 alone, it jumped another 31 percent. (See table 7.8).

Table 7.7.   Population Density in the Gaza Strip

	1945 *Gaza Strip localities*	1986 *Gaza Strip*	*% change*
Total Area (in dunums)	367,000	365,000	-0.5
Total Area Available to Palestinian			
Population (in dunums)	367,000	224,500	-39.0
Population	71,500	633,600	786.0
Dunums/Person (total area)	5.1	0.576	-89.0
Persons/Dunum (total area)	0.195	1.74	790.0
Dunums/Person Available			
to Palestinian Population	5.1	0.354	-93.0
Persons/Available Dunum	0.195	2.82	1350.0

Source: Calculated from tables 3.1 and 7.6.

In both 1986 and in 1993, population density for the Gaza Strip more than doubled when calculated on the basis of Arab-owned land alone (see table 7.8). Density levels calculated on the basis of total area are completely misleading, especially when compared to those obtained in Arab built-up areas, notably the refugee camps. In 1993, such comparisons revealled that population density was more than 33 times greater in the camps than in the territory as a whole.

Population density figures for camp and non-camp residents are also quite dramatic. Whereas the camp residents comprised 28.7 percent of the total Arab population in the Gaza Strip in 1986, they lived on only 7.2 percent of the total Arab built-up area. Table 7.8 indicates that population density averaged 115,924 people per square mile in the camps compared with 22,434 people per square mile outside the camps. In 1993, the population density in Gaza's camps rose to 197,070 people per square mile and was 9.6 times that of the non-camp population.

Comparisons with other areas of the world underline the gross overcrowding in the Gaza Strip. Gaza has one of the highest population densities in the world: 5,929 people per square mile (overall). The comparable figure for Israel was 543; for the Middle East as a region, 55; for the United States, 68; for China, 294; and for India, 642. Only the densities of Singapore and Hong Kong (6,734 and 14,763 per square mile, respectively)[60] exceed Gaza's, although not if one considers Arab built-up areas alone.

By contrast, Jewish built-up areas in Gaza had 282 people per square mile in 1993.[61] Thus, each Jewish settler in Gaza had 73 times more land to live on than every Palestinian living in built-up areas outside the camps, and 699 times more land per capita than each camp resident. Moreover, if density levels on lands available to each ethnic group are compared, there are, conservatively speaking, 115 people per square mile of Jewish land in contrast to 9,640 people per square mile of Arab land.

Density in the camps is directly tied to land shortage. Table 7.9 shows that the total area available to camp population declined by 46 percent between 1961 and 1986, with the largest decline (30 percent) occurring between 1961 and 1973. The Gaza Plan does not state the reason for the decline in land. However, it is most likely due to land confiscations by the government. The land available to the camp population—1.57 square miles or 4,084 dunums—represents the area considered "usable" by the Gaza Plan. According to the Gaza Plan, Deir el-Balah camp, which is located on the seashore, is considered unfit for human habitation; the plan recommends its complete evacuation. Consequently, the 156 dunums (39 acres) that today comprise the Deir el-Balah camp were not even factored into the total camp area in the Gaza Plan estimates.

The direct contribution of settlement to Palestinian population density can actually be measured. Assuming the area of inhabitable land was the same

Table 7.8.   Population Densities in the Gaza Strip

year	population	area (square miles)	population density (persons/sq. mile)
1966	400,000	140 (total)	2,857.0
1986	633,600	140 (total)	4,526.0
		68.5 (owned by Arabs)	9,250.0
		86.1 (available to Arabs)	7,359.0
		21.7 (Arab built-up areas)	29,198.0
	451,600	20.13 (built-up areas/non-camp residents)	22,434.0
	182,000	1.57 (built-up areas/camp residents)	115,924.0
	2,500	34.9 (allocated and leased to Jewish settlers)*	71.6
	2,500	14.2 (Jewish built-up area only)	176.0
1989	750,500	140 (total)	5,361.0
		68.5 (owned by Arabs)	10,956.0
		86.1 (available to Arabs)	8,717.0
		27.0 (Arab built-up areas)	27,796.0
	489,700	25.43 (built-up areas/non-camp residents)	19,257.0
	260,800	1.57 (built-up areas/camp residents)	166,115.0
1993	830,000	140 (total)	5,929.0
		68.5 (owned by Arabs)	12,117.0
		86.1 (available to Arabs)	9,640.0
		27.0 (Arab built-up areas)	30,741.0
	520,600	25.43 (built-up areas/non-camp residents)	20,472.0
	309,400	1.57 (built-up areas/camp residents)	197,070.0
	4,000	34.9 (allocated and leased to Jewish settlers)*	115.0
		14.2 (Jewish built-up area only)	282.0

* Does not include other state-controlled lands.

Source: Calculated from tables 7.6 and 7.9.

Table 7.9.   Areas of the Gaza Strip Refugee Camps for Selected Years (in dunums)

camp	1961	1973	1986 (maximum)	1986 (minimum)*
Jabalya	1558	1404	1404	1404
Shati	515	519	519	515
el-Nuseirat	1070	558	559	279
el-Bureij	955	518	528	259
el-Maghazi	844	599	591	300
Deir el-Balah	270	155	156	0
Khan Younis	561	549	549	549
Rafah	1759	978	978	778
Total	7532	5280	5284	4084

Source: The Gaza Plan, table 17.5; UNRWA, *Area and Population of the Camps in the Gaza Strip* (Gaza Strip: UNRWA, 1988); and UNRWA, In-house study, Gaza Strip, 1989.
* The minimum forecast is the area Israeli planners estimated could actually be used.

during Egyptian and Israeli rule (140 square miles), then density levels in 1966, 1986, and 1993 went from 2,857 to 4,526 to 5,929. Measured this way, the difference between them is a function of population increase only. However, if only the land allotted and leased to Jewish settlers is subtracted out (35 square miles), then population density based on total land area increases to 6,034 in 1986 and to 7,905 in 1993. Consequently, Jewish settlement policies *alone* increased the density level among Arabs by 1,976 people per square mile in 1993.

Israel's occupation has been distinguished by the conscious and consistent expropriation of land from Gaza's Palestinian sector and subsequent donation to the miniscule Jewish sector and state control generally. Land confiscation has played a pivotal role in Gaza's de-development. Under the weight of an expanding population competing for a decreasing amount of land, for example, Gaza's physical infrastructure—houses, roads, sewage systems—has suffered marked deterioration, especially in the absence of structural improvements. Deterioration in turn has had a direct impact on Gaza's economic infrastructure, exacerbating Gaza's inability to integrate its own labor force. Moreover, although Jewish settlements remain economically isolated from local economic activity, they impinge on that activity in at least four crucial ways: by expropriating and then incorporating Arab land into their own physical boundaries[62]; by consuming indigenous water resources[63]; by denying work opportunities to all but a handful of the local labor force, a vestige of the old idea of employing exclusively Jewish labor; and by the gross disparities in public and private sector funding for economic development.

In the Gaza Strip, with its acute population density and limited resources, the deliberate confiscation of land, like water, is not as much an expression of economic aim as of political and ideological conviction. Its goal is to support the expansion of a Jewish settler community on Arab land in order to institutionalize Israeli state control and eclipse the possibility of establishing Palestinian sovereignty over those lands. That land confiscation is an act of deliberate dispossession is clear from the gross differences in population densities between the Arab and Jewish sectors and from the apparent refusal of the state to make needed land allocations to the Arab sector for purposes of supporting an expanding population through infrastructural development and for the expansion of Palestinian agriculture and industry.

Indeed, one example of how Israeli land policy dispossesses Arabs is found in the Gaza Plan. In 1986, Israeli planners estimated that a *minimum* of 17,113 dunums would have to be made available to the Palestinian community to meet the basic needs of a growing population through the year 2000.[64] Of this, 13,600 dunums were needed for schools, health facilities, sewage systems, and refugee rehousing. Continuous land confiscations from the Arab sector since 1986, however, suggest that Israel had little intention of following its own planners' recommendations. In fact, the Gaza Plan indicated that the 17,113 dunums required by the Arab sector would have to be met, in large part, through the seizure of privately owned land. The terms of the Gaza–Jericho Agreement, which allow Israel to retain broad authority over all land and full control over the disposition of state lands, zoning, and Jewish settlements, do not suggest any substantive changes in the allocation of the Strip's land.

The Housing Crisis and Refugee Resettlement

The impact of land expropriation and its contribution to de-development is illustrated in Israel's failure to provide adequate housing in the Gaza Strip. Without a physical place to live, people will leave, a quintessential form of dispossession.

The Gaza Strip clearly suffers from a severe housing crisis and has for many years. The Gaza Plan estimates that by the year 2000, the population will reach 957,500. Approximately 555,300 people will be refugees. Of these, only 186,000 or 19.4 percent will be camp residents, although the majority of camp dwellers will be refugees.[65] In the 10 years between 1976 and 1986, for example, an average of 1,940 housing units were begun per year (with the number declining in recent years), whereas the number of new families created each year in the Gaza Strip averaged 5,000. Theoretically, therefore, only 39 percent of Gaza's new families could obtain housing in any given year; the remaining 61 percent had to live in the Strip's already overtaxed housing, which includes many of Gaza's poorest slums (e.g., Zeitoun, Daraj, Sajaia), or in illegally built homes. Housing density is therefore high. Between 1983 and 1986, the percentage of Gaza Strip households with more than three people per room, the international criterion for overcrowdedness, increased from 36.2 percent to 41.5 percent, indicating a deterioration in local living standards. In Israel, by contrast, only 1 percent of Jewish households had more than three people per room.[66] Camp shelters are the most cramped. Although they range in size, 67 percent of all camp shelters contain three rooms or fewer; 64 percent are inhabited by seven to twelve people.[67]

Housing density has been exacerbated by a decrease in the number of houses built. Between 1979 and 1988, there was a significant and absolute decline in completed housing as well as in the number of houses started.[68] Another interesting finding emerges from the number and size of housing units constructed in the Gaza Strip between 1979 and 1987. Although the number of units begun and completed declined, the average number of rooms per unit and the average size of each unit grew.[69] This pattern of fewer but larger housing units is not indicative of decreasing housing density, but rather of growing social disparity between the haves and have-nots in the Gaza Strip.[70]

Another striking indicator of the territory's housing crisis is that between 1968 and 1986, of all buildings completed in the Gaza Strip, 85 percent were residential and 15 percent nonresidential. Of all completed buildings, only 4 percent to 5 percent were government funded.[71] It should also be noted that residential housing provided through the refugee rehabilitation program (see below) comprised 31 percent of all residential building in the Gaza Strip annually through 1987.

If trends remain the same, 84,000 families will have been added to the Gaza Strip population by the year 2000, but only 27,000 additional housing units will have been built. Of these, says the Gaza Plan, the military government was expected to construct 8,600 units for refugee families, or 32 percent of the total units built, which translates into homes for only 10 percent of all the families added by the turn of the century.[72] Given that projected requirements for rehousing in the Gaza Plan were based on camp population estimates that were far lower than those made by UNRWA—a difference of at least 81 percent—one can assume that any upward adjustment in actual population growth rates would strain the system even more, aggravating overcrowding and population densities, infrastructural stress, and health problems, infant mortality, and poverty.

The failure to provide adequate housing in Gaza as of 1994 lies in large part with the government of Israel. It derives not only from the enormity of the task and the natural constraints of the environment but also from policies that assign little value to the economic needs of the non-Jewish population and even less value when those needs conflict with the state's primary interests. The acute housing crisis has arisen due to the government's failure to provide public housing, restrictions on private construction, and control of municipal and extra-municipal zoning, which in part remains with Israel under Palestinian limited self-rule, and urban planning. All of these failures have been fueled and aggravated by repeated land confiscations that have left Gazans little building room. The government has not taken any steps to alleviate this crisis. The only housing program undertaken by the Israeli authorities was the refugee resettlement program. It is the contention here that far from being a benevolent effort in the public interest, official refugee resettlement programs in fact represented just another form of dispossession.

The refugees' need for housing is greater than any other sector in Gaza. In the camps, refugees live in three kinds of shelters: those built by UNRWA, those built by the occupants with UNRWA materials, and those built by the occupants with permission from UNRWA's engineering department. In 1950, camp shelters were built with the agreement of the Egyptian government, which imposed a variety of restrictions on their construction. For political reasons these shelters were meant to be temporary, and so their structure could not demonstrate any intention of permanency.[73] Consequently, shelters could not have solid foundations or attached roofs. Refugees could not build with reinforced concrete, corrugated steel, or asbestos. Typically, shelters were built with cement block walls and cheaply tiled roofs; as a result, dwellings were left partially exposed to the elements. Finally, shelters could have no more than one floor; any expansion had to be horizontal, not vertical.

Today, most of these same physical injunctions remain in place although they have long since lost their political anchor. All sense of the temporary has vanished, leaving people to contend with the objective and prosaic difficulties of the present. As families grew, any space between shelters was used for housing extensions, leaving narrow streets and snakelike alleyways as the only urban boundary between them. The original UNRWA units remain largely unchanged; after more than forty years, most are in extremely poor condition. On average, three to four people live in each room. A typical room in a refugee shelter is between 9 and 12 square meters of inhabitable area. Per occupant, the inhabitable area can be as little as 2 square meters or as much as 20.[74]

Although most shelters have water and electricity connections, environmental sanitation is perilously substandard, which poses a grave public health risk. Pit latrines, for example, commonly serve as toilet facilities, a form of disposal that is hazardous because excreta soak into the soil around the pit. A confidential study commissioned by UNRWA in 1988 described the following:

> Stormwater, and domestic wastewater from cooking and washing, flows in and from the camps along networks of open channels in the roads and pathways. The drainage channels are sometimes also used for disposal of excreta from those shelters where latrine is filled to capacity. This is a very insanitary practice: contact between the refugees and the excreta should be avoided, and the drainage channels should be used only for rainwater and wastewater. Most channels are formed in the concrete surfaces of the access lanes, but in some camps the wastewater finds its own channels along "natural" drainage routes. Water can drain freely away from the camps that are located in hilly sites in the West Bank, but pools of stagnant water can develop in the flatter sites in the Gaza Strip.[75]

The sewage system, also meant to be temporary, has remained largely open and exposed, a common and extremely unsanitary playground for children, especially in the summer.[76] According to one official, UNRWA's decision finally to address the problem of open sewers beginning with Jabalya camp was in part political, based on the acknowledgement "that the [refugee] situation is no longer temporary."[77]

Given these conditions, one could argue that resettlement projects represented a serious effort by the Israeli government to provide housing for the refugees. The government's program to rehouse Gaza's refugees technically began in 1971 but did not get fully underway until 1972. Rehousing was promoted as an opportunity "to improve considerably the living conditions of refugee camp residents and to develop social and community services for them."[78] Through such efforts, the government aimed to have "a positive effect on the remodelling of society in deprived areas of the Gaza Strip."[79] The housing projects were located just outside municipal boundaries near the camps. However, by virtue of their growth and expansion, the projects eventually spilled over into the neighboring municipality where they were legally incorporated. Master plans for some of these areas reflect intentions to design nineteen "housing estates."[80]

The lands allocated to rehousing projects were primarily, if not entirely, unregistered lands that became state property. In the first three to five years of the program, the government built and sold housing units at subsidized prices and leased the land to the owners for ninety-nine years. After 1975, when this arrangement became too expensive for the government to sustain, owners had to pay for materials and construction although they still leased the land at the same ninety-nine-year rate. In some instances, the government gave refugees mortgages to supplement construction costs. Owners were also responsible for linkage to the Israeli electrical grid and connection of water services. In some cases, refugees built their own homes; in others, they hired contractors or the government to do it for them.

Given the financial incentives offered by the government, especially in the early phase of the program, many refugees could have afforded to move. But financial solvency was far outshadowed by three critical political criteria refugees had to meet to qualify for resettlement. Upon acceptance to a project, the refugee had to (a) submit a written statement denouncing his status as a refugee and dropping all claims as such; (b) start construction within six months or lose entitlement to the new plot of land, as well as to his original camp shelter; and (c) demolish his camp shelter. Refugees who failed to demolish camp shelters before moving had to pay an extra $5,000 to the government to do it for them.

Although the Israelis consistently maintained that it was not their intention to change the refugees' status in any way, no refugee wishing to participate in the government housing program could in fact do so without technically renouncing his status. One UN official explained that by providing new housing outside the camps, "the Government could claim the people are resettled in permanent homes,"[81] and that the refugee problem had been resolved. Hence, the real bone of contention between Israeli officials and Palestinian refugees was not the provision of better housing by the former, but an alteration in or the denial of political and legal rights to the latter.

That Israel's motives fall into the second category is clear from the policy toward evacuated shelters. Departing refugees had to destroy their shelters. Once they left, the destroyed shelters became state property and were sometimes used as military outposts. The destruction of shelters reflected an intent to eliminate camps and with them, the possibility that Israel would ever have to contend with refugee claims. If this were not the intent, the government would have responded to rational analyses such as that of a defense ministry report issued in 1975 that stated: "despite 1,500 new housing units which have already been constructed for refugees . . . the camps are still overcrowded, and services far from satisfactory."[82] UNRWA had repeatedly requested use of demolished shelters, because they were sometimes larger, in better condition, and easier to rehabilitate than existing shelters. However, the government consistently refuses such requests and turned a deaf ear on UNRWA proposals to let cramped refugees move to larger demolished shelters and exchange their smaller, evacuated shelters for government use. Similarly, camp shelters that sat on state-owned or privately owned land could not be structurally altered without government approval. Because approval required a lengthy application process, many people began expanding before they obtained official permission. The government considered this illegal; if discovered, the entire house could be confiscated and/or demolished.[83]

The political nature of the refugee resettlement program was made clear by Moshe Dayan in 1971 in his attempt to normalize conditions in the Gaza Strip. Dayan defined the crux of the problem and the basis of a solution: "The critical question . . . is the refugees. We hope that within a couple of years they will be living on an equal footing with the non-refugee population and will no longer think of themselves as refugees."[84] For Dayan, refugeeism was an economic and social stigma that needed to be removed[85]; the refugee and the working man, he said, were mutually exclusive beings. Consequently, Dayan's attempt to change that status could only be interpreted politically. The political denuding of the refugee that Dayan not only sought but deemed possible through economic means appeared twenty years later to be an important objective of the government's resettlement program.

The resettlement program originally began as a rehousing scheme for refugees displaced by Ariel Sharon's "thinning out" operations in the Gaza camps during his campaign against the Palestinian resistance movement in 1971. At that time, 80 percent of the people displaced refused to accept the new housing offered by the authorities and decided to find their own instead.[86] Not long after the program went into effect, the government made clear its long-range goal of turning such rehousing efforts into a full-scale program of "rehabilitation" that would transform the refugee camps into autonomous municipal units so that, in the words of one Israeli official, "in three or four years' time there will be no refugee camps as we know them in Israeli-administered territories."[87] In November 1976, the UN General Assembly voted overwhelmingly to call on Israel to halt refugee resettlement in the Gaza Strip and return all Palestinian refugees to their former camp houses.[88]

The authorities have always claimed that the resettlement program is humanitarian and aims to provide more and better housing, thereby improving local living standards. Political objectives aside, how successful have government efforts been when measured against stated goals? Data from the military itself, extrapolated to the year 2000, explicitly reveal failure when measured in terms of the number of families rehabilitated, population density in the camps, housing density within the government projects, and their infrastructural condition, all of which are tied to the limited amount of land made available for government rehousing.

Gaza has twenty Israeli government housing projects, twelve in which the houses were built by the government and eight comprised of houses built by refugees. The standardized housing units generally have two rooms, sometimes three, and only rarely four, not unlike many camp shelters. These structures are more permanent than camp shelters. They are also more expandable: owners can add two to three floors with municipality approval. Average lot size is 150 square meters (living space and courtyard space).

UNRWA indicates that by February 1989, only 9.2 percent of the total registered refugee population was living in government housing projects, which also represented 7.17 percent of all refugee families. Figures from the Gaza Plan reveal that between 1972 and 1986, close to 8 percent of total refugee families were rehabilitated, with 80 percent leaving after 1975.[89] However, government data also indicate that of the 49,518 people who had departed the refugee camps by 1986 (a number that includes natural growth), 86.5 percent did so through the government rehousing program, whereas the remaining 13.5 percent did so of their own means. Thus, it would appear that the major force propelling people out of the camp system has been the government's housing program.[90]

Although rehousing efforts were comparatively brisk during the second decade of Israeli rule, the pace of rehabilitation could not keep up with the natural growth of the refugee population. The Gaza Plan estimated that even if official efforts excluded new refugee families and focused on the current (1986) 33,000 refugee households only, rehabilitation work would have to continue an additional fifty-four years.[91] Thus, it comes as no surprise that the population of the refugee camps did not decrease as a result of government rehousing efforts; in fact, not only did population size continue to grow and densities remain the same, but future rehabilitation efforts were expected to *exacerbate* conditions in the camps. The Gaza Plan explains:

> Rehabilitation projects were accomplished in the past through the construction of new neighborhoods close to the refugee camps on land that belonged to the state. However the state has almost no available land left

in the Gaza Strip that can be used for the rehabilitation of the refugees. Therefore, any solution for the refugees in the camps will have to be *implemented on the land of the camps themselves*, perhaps with some additional, adjacent land that will be acquired for that purpose.[92]

Judging by the available area within the refugee camps and the population densities therein, it is difficult to imagine how the problem of increasing density among refugees could be solved within the extremely limited area of the camps, especially considering that half the land in the three middle camps is privately owned, and none of the land currently used for housing in the Deir el-Balah camp is suitable for such purposes. Moreover, this suggestion appears to contradict the Gaza Plan itself, which states that rehabilitation efforts will lower the growth rate in the camps. This certainly would not be the case if people were rehabilitated within the camps. The Gaza Plan indicates that in existing master plans, some of the land area in specific refugee camps is designated for open spaces, not housing. The authors assumed that this land could be used for housing purposes, but because open space land is considered more valuable than lands allocated to housing, "other land will be found for this [housing] purpose either through purchase or seizure."[93] The Plan goes on to conclude:

> The rehabilitation activities of the civil administration involve giving a refugee a unit of land on average 150 square meters for purposes of building a house. This means 6.5 housing units per gross dunum or 3.2 units per net dunum, that is, after space for roads, public institutions and unused area has been taken into account. Under this condition of density and given the available land in the camps, it would be theoretically possible to rehabilitate only 13,700 families or 41% of the total families in the camps.[94]

The government has repeatedly asserted that no state lands are available for continued rehousing; large tracts of state land have consistently been allocated to Jewish settlements. The failure of the resettlement program to provide housing to sufficient numbers of refugees is paralleled by the poor quality of the housing provided. There is no doubt that in their infancy, the new government-sponsored "neighborhoods" represented a qualitative improvement over camp life. By the mid-1980s, however, any difference between government housing and the refugee camps had largely disappeared, and with it any meaningful improvement in the refugees' economic conditions. The reasons are several and they are all linked to the denial of land use by the government. First, high population densities and declining land area have made it impossible for the camps to accommodate additional people. Any surplus population is forced to leave and a certain percentage flow into the "new neighborhoods" created nearby. Second, because government housing projects were designed for a specific and finite population size—one lot is suited for one family of 5.5. people—the constant addition of people to a fixed lot size and the natural increase of the resident population have increased population densities within the housing projects to the point where physical conditions, especially the carrying capacity of the infrastructural systems, have been seriously damaged.

One example of this phenomenon can be found in Sheikh Radwan, a government housing project in the Gaza City municipality. Given the extreme overcrowding of the area, the sewage system, built to accommodate a much smaller population, cannot absorb all the wastes put into it. Periodically, sewage backs up into the streets and common areas of the project. It is quite common to see children playing in raw sewage, which they often fall into and sometimes ingest. "Of course," state the authors of the Gaza Plan, "one could have put in larger sewer pipes, but this would have involved much larger investments or, in view of budgetary limitations, it would have meant finding a solution for many fewer families."[95] The idea of placing more land at the disposal of the Arab population in order to avoid such a zero-sum outcome appears not to have been considered.

The high population densities of the housing projects are matched only by the dense coverage of land area. This phenomenon distinguishes these "neighborhoods" from the refugee camps; indeed, in some respects, it makes them less suitable places to live. Again, the Gaza Plan explains why:

> Plots averaging 150 square meters, with a building set back of 1 meter are tolerable when the buildings are one or two stories. However, if buildings of 3 or 4 stories are built on the plots, the density becomes intolerable. There are many examples throughout the world of this phenomenon of blighted neighborhoods with tall buildings. If this intolerable density is added to the phenomenon of infrastructure systems which cannot carry the population, the conditions are in place for the creation of distressed, neglected neighborhoods. Moreover, such neighborhoods are even harder to rehabilitate because of the difficulties in razing multi-story buildings.[96]

In some parts of the Gaza Strip, government housing projects and neighboring refugee camps have become almost indistinguishable. Furthermore, the unavailability of land for physical expansion has actually propelled some refugee camps outward to envelop nearby housing projects, further blurring any social or economic distinctions between them. Jabalya camp and the Beit Lahia housing project, for example, have become virtual extensions of each other.

In summary, the government resettlement program was not a genuine effort to provide housing to a majority of the population who desperately needed it, but rather a political attempt to eradicate the refugee presence and the political responsibilities it carried. As such, the resettlement effort, if anything, represented a deliberate restriction of residential opportunity, not a genuine solution to a crisis.

The failure to provide adequate housing for a people is a quintessential form of dispossession. The failure to provide enough physical living space not only constitutes the denial of tangible economic resources but also of something less measurable but possibly more profound—national identity. Without space to accommodate a growing population, physical structures decay. Without a physical place in which to live, people leave.

Public Finance

Public finance is a key measure of government policy toward development in the Gaza Strip and a revealing measure of resource expropriation and dispossession. Public finance, or the level of government services (expressed monetarily) provided to area inhabitants, is measured in two ways: public expenditure (or consumption) refers to the level of services provided inhabitants; and public investment (or output) refers to the cost of creating physical infrastructure and other fixed assets. The former is expressed in the ordinary (or regular) budget; the latter, in the development budget.

Gaza's ordinary budget is a revealing measure of Israeli priorities. Government consumption expenditure is primarily composed of the budget of the Israeli civil administration (including spending by local authorities), which covers salaries of both local and Israeli employees and the operation and administrative costs of local social services. Table 7.10 indicates that for the years 1984–86, education and health combined accounted for over two-thirds of the regular budget expenditure, followed by welfare. The agricultural and industrial sectors absorbed a negligible percentage of government expenditure in those years, standing at 2.4 to 2.5 percent and 0.3 percent, respectively. In 1986, critically needed water exploration in the Gaza Strip qualified for only 0.1 percent of total expenditure (as did energy), less than the monies spent to run the governor's headquarters in Gaza City.

Table 7.10   Civil Administration—Gaza Strip Regular Budget Breakdown for Selected Years ('000 NIS)

	1984		1985		1986	
	NIS	% of total	NIS	% of total	NIS	% of total
TOTAL	15073	100.0	31145	100.0	68248	100.0
1. Civil Adm. HQ	215	1.4	562	1.8	940	1.4
Governor's HQ					428	
Subdistricts					146	
Dept of Inform					88	
Bureau					278	
2. Office of the						
Prime Minister	76	0.5	137	0.4	308	0.5
Main Services					286	
Bureau					22	
3. Ministry of Finance	513	3.4	1631	5.2	3550	5.2
Head Office					688	
Dept of Income Tax					429	
Dept of Customs					656	
Administration					947	
Personnel					368	
Internal Supervisor					86	
Head Office					110	
Bureau of Income Tax					129	
Customs Bureau					137	
4. Ministry of the Interior	310	2.1	689	2.2	1563	2.3
Head Office					1089	
Fire Extinguishing					168	
Bureau					306	
5. Ministry of Justice	384	2.6	806	2.6	1690	2.5
6. Ministry of Education	5293	35.1	10325	33.2	22411	32.8
7. Ministry of Religion	97	0.6	201	0.6	422	0.6
8. Ministry of Energy	12	0.1	28	0.1	60	0.1
9. Ministry of Labor	304	2.0	623	2.0	1335	2.0
Head Office					435	
Cooperative Services					17	
Vocational Training					753	
Supervision of Labor					23	
Employment Bureau					107	

	1984		1985		1986	
	NIS	% of total	NIS	% of total	NIS	% of total
10. Ministry of Health	5619	37.3	10893	35.0	24003	35.1
11. Ministry of Welfare	948	6.3	2548	8.2	5518	8.1
Head Office					977	
Institutions for Juvenile						
Delinquincy					119	
Relief-Needy					3451	
Community Work & Rehab					635	
Youth Employment Projects					336	
12. Ministry of Agriculture	363	2.4	769	2.5	1620	2.4
General					1103	
Control, Spraying and						
Inspection					185	
Water Exploration					70	
Bureau					262	
13. Ministry of Trade and						
Industry	47	0.3	98	0.3	206	0.3
14. Ministry of Transport	105	0.7	224	0.7	517	0.7
15. Public Works and						
Surveying	107	0.7	266	0.9	570	0.8
16. Ministry of						
Communication	595	3.9	1175	3.8	663	1.0
17. Appointee on Gov't.						
and Abandoned Property	85	0.6	170	0.5	358	0.5
18. Refugee Rehabilitation	0	0.0	0	0.0	250	0.4
19. Reserve for Wages and						
Acquisitions	0	0.0	0	0.0	2264	3.3

Source: State of Israel, *Proposed Budget for the West Bank and Gaza Strip, 1986*; idem., *Proposed Budget for the West Bank and Gaza Strip, 1988*; and West Bank Data Base Project, *Budgetary Data,* Jerusalem, 1989.
Note: The actual budget for FY1986 allocated NIS 20 to the reserve for wages and acquisitions.

The development budget is even more indicative of official priorities. Between 1983 and 1987, the development budget of the Gaza Strip reveals little change in the share of government investment despite small increases in real levels. For example, Table 7.11 shows that the development budget accounted for an average share of 17.6 percent of Gaza's total budget between 1984 and 1988. However, the development budget of the Gaza Strip accounted for only 3.5 percent of total expenditure in the occupied territories in 1986, which was less than the total amount expended on the police force in the occupied territories (see table 7.12).

Table 7.13 shows that despite an increase in Gaza's total development budget through 1987, only 11 categories were slated for investment in the Gaza Strip between 1983 and 1987. Three areas crucial to productive economic development—industry, land, and water—are conspicuous by their absence (although the Gaza Plan indicates an average expenditure on the development of water resources of NIS 1.4 million in the 1980s). Housing is also absent, whereas agriculture accounts for only 0.4 percent. Other low-priority areas during this period were welfare (0.6 percent), roads (2.3 percent), and infrastructure/public works (6.7 percent).

The official position against productive investment stands in sharp contrast to those consumption-based areas that receive the most support: municipalities, education, and health. Although such social services are no doubt indispensable, they do little to alter the structural status quo. Moreover, the lack of infrastructural development, especially within the economic domain, further impedes any possibility of innovation and structural transformation in other sectors. In this regard, despite the relatively large investments made in education (school construction) and health (construction of new facilities), only 0.1 percent of the development budget was apportioned for professional development between 1983–87, the lowest of all investment categories. Once the intifada began, not only were the gains derived from increased budgets quickly reversed, but the development budgets of the Gaza Strip and West Bank were frozen in 1988 and eliminated altogether in 1989.

The sources of income for the regular and development budgets of the Gaza Strip also illuminate the economic relationship between Israel and Gaza and government policy toward Palestinian economic development. Table 7.11 clearly shows that regional income, or internal revenues in the form of collected taxes, financed the overwhelming share—averaging 70 percent—of the budget between 1984 and 1988. The remaining deficit was covered by two sources: transfers from the Israeli state budget and transfers from the deduction fund, also known as the *keren hanikuyum*,[97] deducted at source from Gazan laborers employed in Israel. These sums are national insurance fees that equal 20 percent of the worker's gross wage, the same percentage as that deducted from Israeli workers' wages. However, Palestinian workers are only eligible for only 2 percent of this insurance deduction, whereas Israelis are

Table 7.11.   Total Budget of the Gaza Strip by Destination and Source, 1984-1988 (in 000s)

	1984[a]			1985[b]			1986[c]			1987[d]			1988[e]		
	NIS	$	%	NIS	$	%	NIS	$	%	NIS	$	%	NIS	$	%
Destination															
Total Budget	18,198	36,396	100	36,308	29,519	100	78,730	52,487	100	108,770	65,921	100	146,937	79,425	100
Regular Budget	15,073	30,146	83	31,145	25,321	86	68,248	45,499	87	87,252	52,880	80	111,904	60,488	76.2
Wages	10,996	21,992	60	21,619	17,576	60	50,925	33,950	65	61,121	37,043	56	72,569	39,226	49.4
Operations	4,077	8,154	23	9,526	7,745	26	17,323	11,549	22	26,131	15,837	24	39,335	21,262	26.8
Development Budget	3,125	6,250	17	5,163	4,198	14	10,482	6,988	13	21,518	13,041	20	35,033	18,937	23.8
Source															
Total	18,198	36,396	100	36,308	29,519	100	78,730	52,487	100	108,770	65,921	100	146,937	79,425	100
Regional	12,090	24,180	66	21,015	17,086	58	52,508	35,005	67	87,197	52,847	80	117,085	63,289	79.7
State Budget	6,108	12,216	34	15,293	12,433	42	26,222	17,482	33	21,573	13,074	20	29,852	16,136	20.3

Source: State of Israel, *Proposed Budget for the West Bank and Gaza Strip 1986*; idem., *Proposed Budget for the West Bank and Gaza Strip 1988*; and West Bank Data Base Project, *Budgetary Data*, Jerusalem 1989.

[a] $1 = 0.50 shekels
[b] $1 = 1.23 shekels
[c] $1 = 1.50 shekels
[d] $1 = 1.65 shekels
[e] $1 = 1.85 shekels

Table 7.12.   Distribution of Expenditure and Income for the Budget of the Civil Administration (Gaza Strip and West Bank), 1986-1988 (in 000s)

	1986[a]			1987[b]			1988[c]		
	NIS	$	%	NIS	$	%	NIS	$	%
1. Expenditure — Total	301,440	200,960	100.0	382,821	232,013	100.0	561,048	303,269	100.0
Area of General Activity — Total	32,541	21,694	10.8	37,483	22,717	9.8	108,025	58,392	19.2
General	7,857	5,238	2.6	7,671	4,649	2.0	13,639	7,372	2.4
Refugee Rehabilitation	3,382	2,255	1.1	3,580	2,170	1.0	57,925	31,311	10.3
Police	15,744	10,496	5.3	19,939	12,084	5.2	30,188	16,318	5.4
South Lebanon (Peace for Galilee Aid)	5,558	3,705	1.8	6,293	3,814	1.6	6,273	3,391	1.1
West Bank	190,169	126,779	63.1	236,568	143,375	61.8	306,086	165,452	54.6
Regular Budget	147,784	98,523	49.0	186,654	113,124	48.7	248,904	134,543	44.4
Development Budget	42,385	28,256	14.1	49,914	30,251	13.1	57,182	30,909	10.2
Gaza Strip	78,730	52,487	26.1	108,770	65,921	28.4	146,937	79,425	26.2
Regular Budget	68,248	45,499	22.6	87,252	52,880	22.8	111,904	60,488	20.0
Development Budget	10,482	6,988	3.5	21,518	13,041	5.6	35,033	18,937	6.2
2. Income — Total	301,140	200,759	100.0	385,958	233,914	100.0	561,038	303,264	100.0
From Taxes	213,997	142,664	71.0	316,229	191,654	81.9	423,171	228,741	75.4
West Bank	161,489	107,659	53.6	229,032	138,807	59.3	306,086	165,452	54.6
Gaza Strip	52,508	35,005	17.4	87,197	52,847	22.6	117,085	63,289	20.8
State Participation (allocations from State Budget)	28,155	18,770	9.5	28,155	17,064	7.3	86,112	46,547	15.4
Deduction Fund	58,988	39,325	19.5	41,574	25,196	10.8	51,755	27,976	9.2

Source: West Bank Data Base Project, *Budgetary Data*, Jerusalem, 1989; and State of Israel, *Proposed Budget for Fiscal Year 1988*.

[a] $1 = 1.50 shekels
[b] $1 = 1.65 shekels
[c] $1 = 1.85 shekels

entitled to the full 20 percent. Israel maintains that the remaining 18 percent of Palestinians' deductions is allocated to development work in the occupied territories. Because of this, the deducted funds are transferred from the Employment Service to the Israeli Treasury and not to the National Insurance Institute, where Israeli deductions are sent.[98]

Not all deducted funds make it back to Gaza, however. In 1987, the State of Israel reported a total budget for the Gaza Strip of $65.9 million. Of this amount, $52.9 million constituted the regular budget and $13 million the development budget. Table 7.11 indicates that in that same year, close to $53 million of revenue was collected in the Gaza Strip. (Furthermore, between 1985 and 1987, the contribution of local incomes [collected from taxes] to the total budget increased from 58 percent to 80 percent, respectively, with a concomitant decrease in state participation.) The Israeli government contributed the remaining 20 percent to cover the resulting deficit. In 1987, Gazans employed in Israel paid $3.2 million per month to the Israeli government in direct taxes and social security, producing an annual figure of $38.4 million, well above the $13.1 million government contribution to Gaza's budget. Consequently, it appears that the Gaza Strip did not cost the Israeli taxpayer any money. Moreover, despite the real increase in the income tax component, no appreciable economic change occurred in Gaza. This situation did not change during the intifada when economic conditions deteriorated markedly although taxation increased significantly. Yitzhak Rabin, then defense minister, explained:

> the money of income taxes collected from the inhabitants of the Gaza Strip region working in Israel is not transferred to the civil administration's budget. That is because income tax (as in the whole world) is collected on a territorial basis, and therefore incomes derived from Israel cannot be linked with the Gaza Strip region.[99]

The Gaza Strip also contributed substantial sums to Israeli public consumption through what Benvenisti has termed the "occupation tax." Gaza's balance of payments focuses on what is termed government transfers. These transfers are indicated by credits and debits. Transfers reveal that the deficit of the military government is paid by the Israeli government (credit) minus deductions collected from Gazans working in Israel (debit). Since the late 1970s, deductions collected from Gazans have exceeded Israeli payments, resulting in net transfers of money from Gaza into Israel. Direct tax revenue from income taxes and transfers from Gazans to the Israeli government, for example, increased from $7 million in 1972 to $38.4 million by 1987. However, the revenue accruing to the state in the form of indirect taxation[100] must also be added. Between 1972 and 1987, visible indirect taxes on production in the Gaza Strip increased from $4 million to $15 million, for a total tax revenue of $53 million in 1987.

Thus, government revenues from the Gaza Strip exceeded the levels of government investment in the territory. Moreover, if the Israeli treasury had lost the Gaza market and Gazan laborers in 1987, it would have lost direct and

Table 7.13.   Development Budget for the Gaza Strip, 1983-1987 ($000)

category	actual expenditure '83[a]	% of total	% growth prev. yr. '83-'84	actual expenditure '84[b]	% of total	% growth prev. yr. '84-'85	actual expenditure '85[c]	% of total	% growth prev. yr. '85-'86
Grants to Local Municipalities	3,847	49.3	-23.4	2,946	47.1	-29.7	2,070	49.3	79.5
Welfare				20	0.3	110.0	33	0.8	103.0
Agriculture							42	1.0	30.9
Schools	1,447	18.5	-44.7	800	12.8	26.8	1,015	24.2	33.3
Health	1,365	17.5	-16.2	1,144	18.3	-56.9	493	11.7	180.3
Infrastructure	24	0.3	-66.0	8	0.1	-62.5	3	0.1	13933.0
Telephone				850	13.6	-80.0	170	4.0	-58.2
Reserve							210	5.0	10.5
Roads	658	8.4	-69.0	204	3.3	-100.0			
Professional Development				46	0.7	-100.0			
Misc. (various development works)	471	6.0	-50.7	232	3.7	-30.2	162	3.9	342.0
TOTAL	7,812	100.0	-20.0	6,250	99.9	-32.8	4,198	100.0	66.5

Table 7.13. continued

category	actual expenditure '86[d]	% of total	% growth prev. yr. '86–'87	actual expenditure '87[e]	% of total	total for category	percent of total budgets
Grants to Local Municipalities	3,715	53.2	46.9	5,460	41.9	18,038	47.1
Welfare	67	1.0	65.7	111	0.9	211	0.6
Agriculture	55	0.8	-34.5	36	0.3	153	0.4
Schools	1,353	19.3	34.4	1,818	13.9	6,433	16.8
Health	1,382	19.8	-9.2	1,255	9.6	5,639	14.7
Infrastructure	421	6.0	404.8	2,125	16.3	2,581	6.7
Telephone	71	1.0	947.9	744	5.7	1,835	4.8
Reserve	232	3.3	46.1	339	2.6	781	2.0
Roads						862	2.3
	(1,025)	(14.7)				(1,025)	(2.6)
Professional Development						46	0.1
Misc. (various development works)	717	10.3	60.8	1,153	8.8	2,735	7.1
TOTAL	6,988	100.0	86.6	13,041	100.0	38,289	100.0

Source: West Bank Data Base Project, *Jerusalem 1989*; and State of Israel, *Proposed Budget for Fiscal Year 1986* (translated from the Hebrew original).

[a] $1 = 0.085 shekels
[b] $1 = 0.50 shekels
[c] $1 = 1.23 shekels
[d] $1 = 1.50 shekels
[e] $1 = 1.65 shekels
( ) = Miscellaneous credit

indirect revenues amounting to at least $53 million.[101] Hence, low levels of government investment and high levels of government revenue stand out against the steady deterioration of living conditions and the poverty in the Gaza Strip. Despite the excess of revenues over development expenditures in Gaza, Rabin, responding to written inquiries by Knesset member Mordechai Baron, argued that the government's weak investment performance in the occupied territories was due to budgetary and financial limitations:

> Obviously the State of Israel was keen to invest much more in developing the standard of living for the inhabitants of the territories, but budgetary limits in Israel are known to all. Therefore, we are encouraging every party whomever it may be (local, foreign, a state, an international organization or private initiative) to invest in helping the inhabitants of the territories on condition that this help is not harmful to the interests of the State of Israel and is coordinated with the civil administration.[102]

The Israeli authorities have often pointed to the increases in real terms of both the regular and development budgets of the Gaza Strip, especially in the two years prior to the intifada. Two problems emerge. One concerns the areas (social rather than productive) to which monies are allocated. Another concerns the future social, economic, and infrastructural requirements of the Gaza Strip and whether pre-intifada rates of investment would be sufficient to meet the needs of the Gaza region by the turn of the century. Israeli planners stated that 1986 investment rates would be wholly insufficient; NIS 159 million would be needed for infrastructural improvements alone.[103] A 1993 World Bank mission to the Gaza Strip and West Bank concluded that Palestinian infrastructure stood at one-third its required level. In 1993, the government spent an average of NIS 44 on development for each Palestinian in Gaza compared to an average of NIS 2,100 spent on every Israeli in 1991.[104]

Israeli expenditure and investment in the Gaza Strip illustrate official policy toward local economic development. Investment patterns are the most telling because they show a severe (if not total) lack of government funding for areas essential to the growth of productive capacity. Denying financial support for the development of water, land, housing, industry, and agriculture is a form of dispossession. Doing so with Palestinian tax monies is a form of expropriation.

Conclusion

The cumulative effect of the expropriation of land, water, and housing has been dispossession. The expropriation of key resources critical to socio-economic growth erodes economic capacity or the ability to accumulate capital and invest it in productive activities. Consequently, the economy is unable to compensate for the losses it has incurred, an important factor shaping the de-development process. The denial of land and water, for example, has dramatically and negatively affected the growth and absorptive capability of Gaza's dominant agricultural sector and has forestalled its transformation from a traditional to modernized mode of production. The denial of adequate housing has seriously eroded the living standards of Gaza's Arab population. All three forms of dispossession fuel de-development because they represent an attack on the internal capacity of a community to remain integrated, cohesive, and resilient. So diminished, both society and economy become more and more vulnerable to other, often external forces that can offer any compensation, albeit a palliating one.

The integration of Gaza's economy into that of Israel and its attendant externalization toward economic needs and interests not its own constituted just such compensation. Although expropriation did not necessarily precede integration, the relationship between resource expropriation and economic integration is direct and undeniable. However, the exogenous and "compensatory" shift in economic orientation that occurred after 1967 was not without its costs: structural dependence, sectoral disarticulation, and occupational reorientation. These costs prevented the transformation of Gaza's early economic growth into sustained economic development and contributed greatly to Gaza's de-development, as will be shown in the next chapter.

Notes to Chapter 7:

1.   Civil Administration of Gaza, *A Plan For The Development of the Gaza Strip Through The Year 2000* (Tel Aviv: Ministry of Defense and Gaza Civil Administration, 1986) (hereafter known as the Gaza Plan).

2.   Jeffrey D. Dillman, "Water Rights in the Occupied Territories," *Journal of Palestine Studies* 19, no.1 (Autumn 1989): 52–53.

3.   Mekorot has responsibility for 80 percent of Israel's water supply. See Itzhak Galnoor, "Water Planning: Who Gets the Last Drop?" in Raphaella Bilski et al (eds.), *Can Planning Replace Politics? The Israeli Experience* (The Hague: Martinus Nijhoff, 1980), pp. 148–49, 162–66.

4.   Meron Benvenisti and Shlomo Khayat, *The West Bank and Gaza Atlas* (Jerusalem: The Jerusalem Post Press, 1988), pp. 113–14. They indicate 2,150 boreholes used for agricultural purposes, of which 1,800 were located in the inner Gaza area and 350 by the sea.

5.   Gaza Plan, Section 14.1.1. See also Kahan.

6.   Gaza Plan, Section 14.1.1.

7.   M. Benvenisti, *The West Bank and Gaza Atlas*; Water Planning in Israel Ltd. (WPI), *Closed Water System in the Gaza Strip: Interim Report No. 2* (Tel Aviv: Tahal, May 1987), p. 4. (Confidential Document.)

8.   Director of the Department of Water, United Nations Relief and Works Agency (UNRWA), Gaza, February 1989.

9.   WPI places the drop between 7–10 cubic meters per annum, and Benvenisti and Khayat put it at 15–20.

10.   Zvi Arenstein, "Gaza's water supply is over-exploited," *Jerusalem Post*, 3 June 1977. Saline water impairs the size and quality of citrus fruits.

11.   WPI, *Interim report No. 2*.

12.   Other areas in danger include Mahru' Amer (1,500 mcl to 2,000 mcl), where seawater has penetrated 1.25 kilometers eastward from the coast; Sheikh Ajlein and some areas of eastern Gaza (2,000 mcl); Abu Middain (200 mcl to 2,200 mcl); the western part of Nuseirat (400 mcl to 2,000 mcl); el-Bureij and el-Maghazi (350 mcl to 1,500 mcl); Bani Suheila (500 mcl to 1,500 mcl); the Abasans (700 mcl to 2,000 mcl); and the western part of Rafah (200 mcl to 1,000 mcl). Ministry of Agriculture, *Percentage of Salinity in the Water Wells of the Gaza Strip*, Internal document, Ministry of Agriculture, Civil Administration, Gaza Strip, 1989.

13.   WPI, *Interim Report No. 2*, p. 5.

14.　　These five areas were Beit Lahiya, Gaza, el-Bureij, Abasan, and Rafah. Interviews with engineering consultants to the Save the Children Federation, Gaza City, March 1989, and visits to the sites.

15.　　Confidential study commissioned by UNRWA, 1990. UNRWA requested that the study not be identified (hereafter referred to as UNRWA Internal Report). The report stated that only Beach and Jabalya camps had enough land available to construct appropriate sewage treatment facilities.

16.　　Interview with Richard Larsen, associate director of UNRWA, Gaza Strip, 1989.

17.　　UNRWA Internal report. Another very serious problem caused by unregulated disposal of sewage and solid wastes is insect and rodent infestation. In 1993, further work was planned for the Beach Camp network.

18.　　WPI, *Interim Report No. 2*, p. 6.

19.　　Water Planning in Israel Ltd. (WPI), *Closed Water System in Gaza Strip Intermediate Stage (1990)* (Tel Aviv: Tahal, June 1987), p. 2. (Confidential Document.) According to Israeli planners, in order to deal with all the sewage of the Gaza Strip population through the year 2000, the master plan would require an expenditure of 66.8 million shekels and an allocation of 1,370 dunums of land, some of it to be seized, privately owned land. However, on the basis of government expenditures on sewage systems and treatment facilities through 1986, only 24.0 million shekels would actually be made available through the year 2000.

20.　　UNRWA, Internal Report on environmental problems in the Gaza Strip, April 1993.

21.　　Galnoor, "Water Planning," in Bilski et al. (eds.), pp. 177–89.

22.　　Dillman, 52. Also see Joe Stork, "Water and Israel's Occupation Strategy," *MERIP Reports* 13, no.6 (July-August 1983): 19–24.

23.　　Sharif S. Elmusa, "Dividing The Common Palestinian-Israeli Waters: An International Water Law Approach," *Journal of Palestine Studies* 22, no.3 (Spring 1993): 61.

24.　　Ibid., pp. 61, 63.

25.　　Ibid.

26.　　This claim could not be officially documented but foreign PVOs working in the Strip maintain its validity.

27.　　Gaza Plan, Section 14.1.1.

28.　　Galnoor, "Water Planning," in Bilski et al. (eds.), p. 144.

29.   Roy, *The Gaza Strip Survey*, p. 51.

30.   Dillman, p. 56.

31.   Gaza Plan, Section 14.3.0.

32.   Interview with Dr. Carlo Cammisa, hydrological consultant to UNRWA, Gaza, 1989. Given the deterioration of the water supply since 1989, this is a conservative estimate.

33.   Dillman, p. 56.

34.   State of Israel, *An Eighteen Year Survey (1967–1985)*, p. 78.

35.   WPI, *Intermediate Stage*, p. 3, makes this clear. Kahan, p. 171, provides the figures.

36.   See Elmusa, p. 65.

37.   Gaza Plan, Section 14.1.1.

38.   Gaza Plan, Sections 14.2.2, 14.2.3; M. Benvenisti and Khayat, p. 114.

39.   The figures in table 7.5 are slightly higher.

40.   Gaza Plan, Section 14.2.2.

41.   Domestic consumption rates for Arabs is 25 percent; for Jews, 10 percent.

42.   Dillman, p. 55.

43.   See Elmusa for a discussion of options.

44.   Gaza Plan, Section 14.4.0. Annually, the government spent an average of NIS 1.4 million on the development of water resources in the Gaza Strip through 1986.

45.   WPI, *Intermediate Stage*, p. 3.

46.   These calculations are based on Tahal's projected 1990 Arab population of 686,000. Because no projections for the Jewish community were made, the 1990 figure of 3,000 was used.

47.   Galnoor, "Water Planning," in Bilski et al. (eds.), p. 155.

48.   Ibid., p. 159.

49.   Ibid.

50.   Ibid., 160.

51.   Dillman, p. 49, provides another example of this attitude in his discussion of the Hayes Plan, which called for the diversion of half the water of the Yarmuk River into Lake Tiberias.

52.   The Gaza Strip's total area varies slightly according to source. The Egyptians estimated 360,000 dunums and the Israelis estimate 365,000 dunums. The reason is unclear.

53.   See M. Benvenisti and Khayat.

54.   Interviews with officials in the Ministry of Foreign Affairs, Tel Aviv, 1990, and in the United States Embassy, Tel Aviv, 1990.

55.   Roy, *The Gaza Strip Survey*, pp. 134–35.

56.   See ibid., pp. 137–48, for a detailed description of these settlements; see also Sharif Kana'na and Rashad al-Madani.

57.   The 224,500 dunums made available to the Arab population for domestic and economic purposes represents 61.5 percent of Gaza's total land area. Hence, portions of Israeli-controlled lands are leased to Arabs.

58.   Land allocations to the Jewish and Arab communities are based on 1986 figures because 1993 figures were not available. As such, population densities obtained for 1993 may be considered conservative estimates because of significant increases in the Arab population and because land confiscations from the Arabs and land allocations to the Jewish settlers increased between 1986 and 1993. (The growth in the settler population in these years was not significant.) Furthermore, figures provided for Jewish settlements do not include the availability of other state controlled lands for use by settlers.

59.   For a description of Jewish settlements in Gaza, see Geoffrey Aronson, "Gaza Settlement—Building a Dream World," *Report on Israeli Settlement in the Occupied Territories* 3, no.5 (September 1993): 4–5.

60.   These figures were calculated from The World Bank, *World Development Report 1990* (New York: Oxford University Press, 1990), pp. 178–79. See also Alan Richards and John Waterbury, *A Political Economy of the Middle East: State, Class, and Economic Development* (Boulder, CO: Westview Press, 1990), p. 53.

61.   It is not entirely clear whether the 37,000 dunums allocated for use by Jewish settlers in Benvenisti and Khayat refers to built-up areas only or includes agricultural lands as well. Map 62 (page 116) implies that it is the former, and this is the assumption made in the text.

62.   Between 1978 and 1985, approximately 46,300 dunums of agricultural and nonagricultural land was expropriated from Arab villages and landowners for the pur-

pose of establishing Israeli settlements. Roy, *The Gaza Strip Survey*, pp. 141–45. Between 1985 and 1991, at least 500 hundred additional dunums were expropriated.

63.   International Labour Organization, 71st Session, p. 27.

64.   Various sections of the Gaza Plan.

65.   Some of the assumptions of the Gaza Plan are debatable, especially as they concern the camp growth rate and the impact of rehabilitation efforts on that rate. Other UNRWA projections predict that the camp population will be significantly higher by the year 2000. Given the dearth and accuracy of demographic information, all statistics relating to population size can only be estimates. However, the figures provided by the Gaza Plan are useful because they provide what may be considered a very conservative estimate. Even using these lower estimates, the predicted level of housing is wholly inadequate to need.

66.   Gaza Plan, Sections 3.4.2–3.4.4.

67.   Arab Thought Forum, table 7.

68.   The number of homes completed fell from 247,300 to 230,600 square meters; the number of homes started dropped 30 percent, from 345,600 to 242,500 square meters. Between 1982 and 1985, in particular, there was a 36 percent drop in square meters of finished housing. State of Israel, *Statistical Abstract of Israel* (Jerusalem: Central Bureau of Statistics, 1991).

69.   The number of units begun dropped from 2,401 in 1979 to 1,392 in 1987, and the number of units actually completed declined from 1,757 to 1,247. However, the average number of rooms increased from 3.7 to 4.4. State of Israel, *Statistical Abstract of Israel*.

70.   See Abdelfattah Abu Shokar, "Income Distribution and Its Social Impact in the Occupied Territories," in Kamel Abu Jabber, Mattes Buhbe, and Mohammed Smade (eds.), *Income Distribution in Jordan* (Boulder, CO: Westview Press, 1990), pp. 93–109.

71.   See State of Israel, *National Accounts of Judea, Samaria and Gaza Area 1968–1986*, Special Series No. 818 (Jerusalem: Central Bureau of Statistics [CBS], 1988), p. 162.

72.   Gaza Plan, Sections 17.0.5, 17.6.1–17.6.4. Trends have not changed. According to the World Bank, new household formation in the Gaza Strip and West Bank exceeded 5 percent per annum between 1988 and 1993, a rate that is among the highest in the world.

73.   In the West Bank, camp structures look very different. Many have permanent roofs and are more than one story. (This distinction is due to Jordan's political relationship with the West Bank, which was very different than Egypt's with Gaza.)

74.   UNRWA, in-house statistics, Gaza Strip, 1989. In 1993, UNRWA initiated a small

scale core house replacement program to replace some of the original (and most dilapidated) shelters; a home improvement program to improve the physical condition of some
houses; and, begun in 1992, a roof replacement program to replace damaged roofs.

75.   UNRWA Internal report.

76.   An internal UNRWA report states:

> Recent studies indicated that at Beach camp by the age of four years, from
> 50 to 85% of children are infested with *Ascaris* (roundworms), while even
> among adults over 42% of blue collar workers, and over 27% of white
> collar workers are affected. Other intestinal parasites causing illness such
> as whipworm, amoebae, and *Giardia* are correspondingly excessively
> common.

77.   Interview with official who asked not to be identified, UNRWA, Gaza, 1989.

78.   Abd'al-Latif A'Sha'afi, "From a Refugee Camp to the Dekel Neighbourhood in
Rafah," in Avraham Lavine (ed.), *Community Work in the Gaza Strip* (Jerusalem: Ministry of Labour and Social Affairs, n.d.), p. 13. In the same publication, also see Yaacov
Gal, "Community Work in the New Refugee Neighbourhoods of the Gaza Strip," pp. 9–
12.

79.   Lavine (ed.), *Society of Change, Judaea, Samaria, Gaza Sinai 1967–1973*, p. 11.

80.   "1,500 homes slated for Gaza in 1975," *Jerusalem Post*, 3 March 1975; and "Master
plan approved for Rafah town," *Jerusalem Post*, 24 February 1975.

81.   William E. Farrell, "Israeli Housing for Gaza Refugees Spurs Friction With U.N.,"
New York Times, 24 November 1976. For the opposite interpretation of the rehousing
program, see Alfred Friendly, "Israeli Program for Gaza Misery Encounters Refugees'
Suspicion," *Washington Post*, 27 August 1971.

82.   *Jerusalem Post*, 3 March 1975.

83.   Since 1967, the land in the refugee camps has been either UNRWA-owned or
leased to UNRWA by the Israeli government. Housing changes that occurred on UNRWA
land and were not major (i.e., small vertical additions) qualified for UNRWA assistance
and did not require Israeli approval. Major changes to shelters, no matter whose land
they sat on, required Israeli approval, which was seldom given. Interview with Hashem
Abu Sidu, Public Information Officer, UNRWA, Gaza, 1988. It should also be noted
that, historically, building permits in West Bank refugee camps were granted by UNRWA;
in Gaza's camps, they were issued by the Israeli military government/civil administration. See Cooperative Housing Foundation (CHF), *Housing Needs Assessment for the
West Bank and Gaza* (Washington, D.C.: CHF, 1993), p. 30.

84.   H. Ben-Adi, "Dayan in Gaza: Situation good," *Jerusalem Post*, 24 May 1971.
Emanuel Marx, "Changes in Arab Refugee Camps," *Jerusalem Quarterly* 8 (Summer

1978): 43–52, explains why this did not happen.

85.   Moshe Dayan details his ideas in "A human life for the refugees," *Jerusalem Post*, 27 August 1971. See also Mark Segal, "Dayan wants action to clear refugee morass in Gaza Strip in 2 years," *Jerusalem Post*, 16 September 1969.

86.   "'Do-it-yourself' wrecking operation starts at Rafah," *Jerusalem Post*, 25 December 1972.

87.   Walter Schwarz, "Israel Begins Resettling Gaza Arabs Into Better Homes," *Washington Post*, 5 November 1970; and "Gaza Strip prosperity," *Jerusalem Post*, 12 July 1976.

88.   Peter Grose, "U.N. Calls on Israel to Rescind Resettlement of Arabs in Gaza," *New York Times*, 24 November 1976.

89.   Gaza Plan, Tables 17.3 and 17.4; Section 17.2.4.

90.   Ibid., Table 17.4.

91.   Ibid., Section 17.3.2.

92.   Ibid., Section 17.4.1 (emphasis added).

93.   Ibid., Section 17.4.3.

94.   Ibid., Section 17.4.4.

95.   Ibid., Section 17.5.2.

96.   Ibid., Section 17.5.3.

97.   The defense minister at the time, Yitzhak Rabin, wrote to Knesset Member Mordechai Baron in Jerusalem in August 1986 on the subject of the Gaza Strip and West Bank budgets:

> The collection of deducted money from the wages of inhabitants of the territories working in Israel in an organized manner, and their usage, are stated in the government's resolution of October 8, 1970, which was passed in order to insure conditions for equal competition and determined that: (1) gross wages and net wages be equal to those received by Israeli workers in parallel branches; (2) tax payments, social allocations and deductions enjoyed by those working in Israel will be handled in the same way as in Israel; (3) excess sums and social allocations are transferred to the deduction fund; and (4) the fund will help in developing social services in the territories. In our opinion, there is no need to change the aforementioned government resolution.

98.   The International Center for Peace in the Middle East in Tel Aviv estimated that

as much as 80 percent of the transferred funds never enter the budgets of the civil administration but remain within the treasury for Israeli use. See Hiltermann, p. 22.

99.   Letter, Rabin to Baron, August 1986.

100.   Indirect taxes include: (Israeli) VAT (not Gazan VAT, which remains inside Gaza); other less visible forms such as customs duties and tariffs levied by Israel on imports to the Gaza Strip and West Bank from Jordan and through Israel; and the use of Israeli currency as legal tender, whose inflationary character has widened the deficit with Israel in favor of Israel.

101.   See Roy, "The Gaza Strip: A Case of Economic De-Development," pp. 79–81; M. Benvenisti, *1987 Report.*

102.   Letter, Rabin to Baron, August 1986.

103.   Gaza Plan, various sections.

104.   Samir Abdullah Saleh, "Urgent Priorities for the Development of Physical Infrastructure of the Occupied Palestinian Territory," (Paper presented to the United Nations Seminar On Assistance To The Palestinian People, UNESCO, Paris, 26–29 April 1993), p. 3.

8

Integration and Externalization

The dispossession of essential economic resources has deprived Gaza's economy of vital production factors. This has imposed constraints on internal economic capacity and the economy's ability to sustain its population. Deprived of its own resources, the Gazan economy was forced to rely on external resources for growth. This forced dependence was achieved through integration or incorporation with the Israeli economy and the externalization or reorientation of Gaza's economy toward Israel.

Integration and externalization are distinguished by Israeli policies that encouraged Gaza's dependence on externally generated income sources. These policies include the reorientation of the labor force away from indigenous agriculture and industry to labor-intensive work outside Gaza (also a form of economic dispossession) and the redirection of trade to Israel. Through these and other policies, not only were local resources transferred out of Gaza's economy to Israel's, but local economic activity became increasingly vulnerable to, dependent on, and subordinated to demand conditions in the Israeli economy. As a result, Gaza's internal productive base and capacity were diminished, and de-development was fostered.

This chapter will discuss those sectors where integration and externalization are pronounced and have had marked economic impact: labor and employment, agriculture, industry, and trade.

Labor is a primary axis through which Palestinians are integrated with Israel: Palestinians have comprised approximately 8 percent of the Israeli labor

209

force since the mid-1970s. This is not a reciprocated relationship: Only 0.7 percent of the Jewish labor force has been engaged in production for the occupied territories. However, for certain sectors of the Israeli economy, integration of labor has been very high and Israeli dependence proportionally large. By 1988, for example, Palestinian labor accounted for 42 percent to 45 percent of all workers in Israeli construction, sanitation, and agriculture, and 10 percent to 15 percent of all hired labor in the textile and food industries, garages, and in restaurant and hotel services.[1] Hence, labor is a key structural channel for transferring the problems as well as the benefits of the Israeli economy to the occupied territories.

Labor and Employment

The integration of Gazan labor into the Israeli workforce has been rapid and dramatic. The Bank of Israel reports that between 1970 and 1988, the number of laborers from the Gaza Strip and West Bank working in Israel rose from 22,800 to 109,400, an increase of almost 400 percent. Of the total labor force in the occupied territories, only 13 percent was employed in Israel in 1970; by 1988, this had risen to 38 percent. Relatively speaking, Gazan workers accounted for the largest share of migrant labor in Israel.[2]

The characteristic features of the labor force of the Gaza Strip and its employment patterns are critical pillars of the de-development process. First, Gaza's labor force serves Israel's economic interests, not Gaza's; as a result, Gaza's own productive capacity is eroded. Second, employment patterns in Israel confine workers to manual and menial tasks requiring low skill levels. In such an environment, educational attainment has no bearing on employment opportunity. Without opportunity, the population's skills sink to the lowest common denominator. This, too, contributes to weakening economic capacity. To analyze labor market changes, one must first establish relevant features of the Gaza Strip population.[3]

General Population and Labor Force Characteristics
A. Population Size

Between 1947 and 1987, the population of the Gaza Strip increased from roughly 71,000 to 633,600 people, a rise of nearly 800 percent in just 40 years.[4] This growth rate in this time frame has few, if any, equivalents. After 1967, the growth of the Gaza Strip population was attributable almost entirely to natural increase, which augmented the population and offset the loss of 103,100 emigrants. With the exception of 1973, the migratory balance in the Gaza Strip has always been negative—itself a form of dispossession—and a reflection of growing population densities, the lack of employment opportunities, and constant political pressures.

Gaza's negative migration patterns had a pronounced impact on population size and its ability to grow according to normal demographic patterns.

Levels of out-migration have approached those of natural increase, and it was not until 1979 that the effect of natural increase mitigated the impact of migration loss in the Gaza Strip. Because migratory flows are linked to the very inelastic nature of the labor market and Gaza's productive base, they have considerable implications for indigenous economic development.

In 1993, UNRWA calculated that the Gaza Strip population will double in the next seventeen years and multiply eight times within fifty years.

B. Age Structure

The Gaza Strip population is extremely young. Nearly 50 percent of all residents are fourteen years old or younger; nearly 60 percent are younger than age twenty. Whereas this demographic pattern is found in the Middle East generally, it is even more pronounced among Palestinians. Palestinian fertility rates, among the highest in the developing world, are directly linked to the demographic conflict with Israeli Jews.[5] Little will change in the age structure of the population, as a minimum of 57 percent and a maximum of 60 percent of the population will be nineteen years of age or younger by the year 2000.[6]

C. Gender Composition

Before 1967, women outnumbered men in Gaza, 1,000 to 942. This has since changed, however. By the mid 1980s, the population was equally divided, and by the early 1990s, the number of men exceeded the number of women. A breakdown by age offers some insight into this change. In 1982, the number of men aged 24 years or younger exceeded the number of women in that age group by 12,000 people or 7.6 percent, a pattern that had persisted to varying degrees since 1967. However, for ages 25–49, women consistently outnumbered men by 14,000 and by 10,600 in 1967 and 1982, respectively. The reasons for these demographic trends are largely related to the emigration of males outside the Gaza Strip—more than 94,000 between 1966 and 1987—in search of employment and education.[7] This balance began to change with the intifada, which interrupted the emigration process.[8]

D. Labor Force

The labor force never accounted for more than 19 percent of Gaza's total population, even before 1967. Throughout the occupation, the labor force has remained around 17.5 percent–18.0 percent. The total labor force includes those who are gainfully employed as well as those who are actively seeking employment; it is not to be confused with the employed labor force, or those persons who are actually working. The numerical difference between them has been the subject of much dispute, because Israel has traditionally defined "employed" as persons registered with the Israeli Labor Employment offices and "unemployed" as persons who have unsuccessfully sought work through those offices.

Between 1968 and 1987, Gaza's total labor force increased by 118 percent, from 46,800 to 102,200 people, including children who joined the workforce during the summer and fall harvests. By 1993, there were 120,000 people in Gaza's labor force.

Labor force participation is defined as the number of people participating in the labor force divided by the number of people aged fourteen or fifteen and older. Although participation rates increased over time, throughout the 1980s they remained steady around 33 percent, which is low. Some factors accounting for low participation rates include: the large percentage of people below the age of 15 years; the constant emigration of adults; the high rate of school attendance; and the very limited economic opportunities available to the labor force.

Labor force participation rates among men (aged 14 and older) have exceeded those of women. Between 1968 and 1987, the male participation rate increased from a low of 59 percent to a high of 65.7 percent. Although men comprised around 50 percent of the working age population of the Gaza Strip since 1970, they accounted for well over 90 percent of the total labor force. Participation rates for men in Gaza, the West Bank and Israel (both Arab and Jewish Israeli) are similar: they do not approach the variations in the female population.

Although women accounted for at least 50 percent of the total working age population[9] between 1970 and 1986, they comprised only 8.6 percent and 4.0 percent of the labor force, respectively. Women's labor force participation rate averaged 3.4 percent in 1986, even lower than their absolute presence in the labor force. Unlike the West Bank, where women work primarily in agriculture, in Gaza, over 50 percent of women work in the service sector. In all likelihood, the low and declining female participation rate in the Gaza Strip is occasioned by the limited opportunities for work in agriculture and in the informal economy generally, in addition to shrinking job availability in the formal economy. The extremely low participation rate of women and the loss of productive potential that this represents severely constrains economic development.[10] Moreover, the low female participation rate combined with the small number of working-age males kept the overall labor force participation rate low during the first two decades of occupation, despite the rapid growth of the labor force.

Indeed, the young age structure of the population is the main factor determining the supply of labor. It is also the main reason why labor force growth has been equal to, and sometimes greater than, population growth. Between 1970 and 1987, the labor force grew by almost 70 percent—averaging 3.9 percent annually—whereas the population grew by 63 percent for an average of 3.5 percent annually. The local economy, however, has been unable to keep up with the expansion of the labor force. According to official estimates, although domestic employment has absorbed the larger share of Gaza's labor force since 1967, the level of domestic employment fell dramatically from 97.9 percent of Gaza's total labor force in 1968 to 54 percent in 1987. In 1990–91, 2,750 people were added to Gaza's workforce but only 1,000 were absorbed by domestic industry.[11]

If domestic employment continues to fall behind population and labor force growth, the rate of unemployment will grow.[12] This suggests that unemployment is structural in nature, related to the inability of the local economy to provide new jobs, and not a temporary or transitory phenomenon. In the Gaza Strip, this means that one new job will be available domestically for every eight new entrants to the labor market. (In 1995, according to UNCTAD estimates, close to 22,600 jobs will be needed, rising to 43,000 by the year 2000.)[13]

The inability of Gaza's economy to keep up with labor force growth has been due in part to restrictions on private sector development and a steady decline in public sector activity. As a result, the local economy has not been able to generate sufficient new jobs that would allow it to productively absorb the growing supply of labor increasingly available to it. In fact, domestic output has dropped behind additions to the labor force. The gap between a growing labor force and limited domestic absorption capacity constitutes a major structural constraint on economic development in the Gaza Strip. The deterioration of Gaza's labor absorption capacity creates a very serious imbalance in the structure and future performance of the economy. Without internal structural reform as opposed to a continued reliance on work in Israel, which is becoming increasingly unavailable, Gaza's productive base will deteriorate further and erode.

Employment in Israel[14]

By contrast, the substantive increase in the Gaza Strip labor force is almost entirely due to the growth of employment in Israel, the most significant change affecting the structure of wage labor in the Gaza Strip through 1987. Within the first five years of gaining access to the Israeli market, the number of Gazan laborers commuting to work in Israel increased 27 times and continued to push upward, albeit with minor dips and fluctuations. By 1987, their numbers had swelled to 48,100 wage earners, or 47 percent of the Gaza Strip's total labor force, according to official Israeli estimates. Revised United Nations data, however, indicate that the number of Gazans working in Israel prior to the outbreak of the intifada exceeded 70,000.

Employment in Israel is critical as an outlet for Gaza's domestic labor market. In addition to severely limited domestic opportunities, Gazans have had few possibilities for emigration to the Arab world. The opening of the Israeli economy to Gazan labor affected all sectors of the economy, though some more than others. The most significant transformation occurred in the agricultural sector. As a source of total employment, agriculture suffered the greatest decline between 1967 and 1987, dropping from a high of 33.9 percent in 1971 to a low of 18.3 percent in 1987. This decline was most pronounced in the domestic labor force. Agriculture's share of domestic employment fell from 31.6 percent in 1970 to 16 percent in 1987. By 1984, Israeli agriculture actually employed more Gazan workers than Gazan agriculture. Overall, since 1979, agriculture has employed just slightly more workers than industry, a change without precedent in Gaza's economic history, given agriculture's predominant position during the Mandate period. The reasons for the decline of this sector—both as a whole and domestically—are: the availability of more lucrative income-earning opportunities in Israel; the rise of other sectors, such as construction and services; and the shift to cultivation methods that are less labor intensive.

The sector that was next most affected was construction, whose share of total employment more than doubled from 12.4 percent in 1970 to 29 percent in 1989. None of this growth occurred in Gaza's domestic construction sector, which employed as many people (approximately 4,500) in 1988 as it did in 1967. Israeli construction accounted for all of it, absorbing the losses that accrued to Gaza's own construction sector.

The services sector was likewise dramatically affected by the opening of the Israeli economy to Gazan labor. Overall, the services sector has consistently employed the largest share of Gazans throughout the period of Israeli occupation—from 50 percent to 59 percent of total domestic employment, a pattern which held true before 1967 as well. However, the number of Gazans working in services in Israel rose dramatically from 3.4 percent of all Gazans employed in Israel in 1970 to 18.4 percent in 1987.

Industry remained the smallest single source of total employment, standing at 12.8 percent in 1989. Between 1970 and 1987, industry's share of total employment increased both in Gaza and Israel, although the absolute number of Gazans employed in Israeli industry increased by more than 1,620 percent versus 48 percent in Gazan industry. In Gaza, moreover, industry's historical increase was largely due to the establishment of subcontracting arrangements in the 1970s in which Israeli companies, particularly textile companies, set up "branches" in the territories to take advantage of the cheaper cost of labor. Only the workers' wages from such arrangements accrued to Gaza; all profits returned to Israel. Since they began, subcontracting arrangements have steadily accounted for 15 percent to 20 percent of Gaza's domestic industrial employment.

The presence of growing numbers of Palestinian migrants provided the Israeli economy with a source of cheap and easily exploitable labor that it could use or marginalize without great economic risk. In periods of economic prosperity, for example, the availability of this labor pool had a stabilizing effect on Israeli wages and provided an expanding economy with a competitive advantage in foreign markets without threatening the jobs of any Jewish workers.[15] Given Israel's control over Gaza's economy, wages paid to area workers do not drain the state's economic reserves because the consumption expenditure of Palestinian labor is directly tied to the Israeli economy. The importance of Gazan labor was echoed in a statement by Moshe Baram, Israel's labor minister in 1974, who said, "[T]he Gaza Strip will remain economically integrated with Israel, no matter what the political outcome of the Middle East conflict."[16]

The role of Arab labor in the Israeli economy is further illustrated by the ethnic organization of the Israeli labor market and the concentration of Palestinian workers in confined occupational categories. In 1969, 85 percent of the labor force from the occupied territories were disproportionately represented in 14 out of 83 occupations defined by the Israeli government. Of this group, over 70 percent were concentrated in just five occupational categories: unskilled workers in construction; skilled workers in construction; unskilled laborers in agriculture; laborers in fresh food packaging; and workers in the lumber industry. Although the number of Palestinians working in Israel had increased eightfold over the ensuing decade, Arab workers continued to be confined to certain occupational groups, most of them manual. By 1982, they were concentrated in 20 out of 83 categories; in addition to the five occupational groups listed above, Palestinians were overrepresented in the canned food industry, cleaning services and road construction. Certain categories were completely blocked to Gaza Strip and West Bank labor, notably white-collar or professional occupations (e.g., pharmacists, engineers) and entrepreneurial occupations requiring capital investments and official sanction or security clearance such as the wholesale and retail trade, the insurance industry, and other strategic industries such as aircraft or armaments. Public services were also barred, with the exception of street cleaning and other related services. Only a fraction of other ethnic groups, especially Israeli Jews, are employed in the limited occupations in which Palestinian workers from the occupied territories are concentrated.[17] Indeed,

> [t]he ethnic order of the occupational hierarchy has remained remarkably stable over the years: European-American Jews at the top, noncitizen Arabs [Palestinians from the West Bank and Gaza Strip] at the bottom, and Asian-African Jews and Israeli Arabs between the two extremes. Nevertheless, important changes have taken place in the average occupational status of all ethnic groups. The mean status of the two groups of Jews, as well as that of Israeli Arabs, rose considerably between 1969 and 1982. Each of these three groups improved its status by approximately 10 percent of its mean status at the initial point in time. In contrast, Arabs from the administered territories lost status in both relative and absolute terms.[18]

Indeed, despite prevailing public assumptions in Israel, Arab labor has greatly benefited two economic classes: the Israeli owner/employer, who benefits from the availability of cheap and abundant supplies of labor; and the Israeli working class, primarily the Sephardi Jewish community, whose status and social position as second-class citizens within their own society are enhanced as Arabs assume those forms of employment that no Israeli would ever accept.

Semyonov and Lewin-Epstein further explain that when the Israeli market first opened up to Palestinian labor from the West Bank and Gaza (a stage they call penetration), occupational entry was determined primarily by shortages in given occupational areas. Arab labor was perceived as a temporary solution to an immediate manpower problem. Once it was clear that Palestinians would remain in the Israeli labor market more permanently, "their occupational opportunities were determined mostly by exclusionary processes .... New mechanisms evolved, which placed noncitizen Arabs within the broader stratification system, relegated group members to low-status jobs and barred them from others."[19] The transformation of Arab labor from temporary fill-ins to an integral part of the workforce, combined with their particular ethnic status, delimited their occupational opportunities and institutionalized a caste structure in the Israeli labor system.[20]

Under such conditions of extreme occupational segregation and poor mobility, the educational level of the Palestinian job-seekers is largely irrelevant. Irrespective of their educational degrees, their "job opportunities" are the same: construction worker, dishwasher, garbage collector, and the like. The role assigned to Arab workers in Israel has also alienated them from their Israeli employers and from the dominant culture they enter daily. Sociologist Salim Tamari[21] describes the feelings of rejection, displacement, and dissonance experienced by migrant Arab laborers, who clearly recognize and feel powerless to change the impermeability of a system and society that will give them entry but not acceptance.

In certain key respects, Arab labor patterns after 1967 are no different from what they were under the Mandate. These patterns reveal that labor migration and employment are conditioned by events outside the traditional Arab economy over which the worker has no control.[22] Tamari describes four such patterns that also distinguish Palestinian migratory labor from other third world migratory workers: physical proximity to the Israeli workplace that has enabled workers to maintain their ties to the land and continue their participation in village social life; the ambivalent class identity of workers that derives from their daily interaction with Israeli society; the preponderance of workers in Israeli construction; and the poorly institutionalized labor recruitment process that has resulted in greater exploitation by employers.[23]

In this way, the integrative dynamics introduced during the occupation did not change historical patterns but intensified them. Integration and externalization exacerbated the proletarianization of the Arab workforce; the erosion of traditional social structures; and the transformation of the nonurban Arab economy into something stagnant and nonproductive.[24]

Key Structural Changes

The employment patterns of the Palestinian labor force reflected the institutionalization of two critical structural changes in the Gaza Strip economy. First, Gazan wage earners became increasingly dependent on employment in Israel. The pull of employment in Israel was so strong that by the mid-1970s, open unemployment in the occupied territories had been eliminated, disguised unemployment had virtually disappeared, labor force participation rates had leveled off, and all of the labor reserves in the Gaza Strip had been exhausted.[25] Employment opportunities in Israel rose dramatically, whereas those in Gaza dropped.[26]

Second, attending the rapidly growing dependence of the domestic workforce on employment in Israel has been the increasing importance of incomes earned in Israel to GNP. In fact, income generated by work in Israel was the "single most significant source of external credit to the Palestinian current account since 1980"[27] and a major contributing factor to impressive GDP growth rates. In 1970, for example, external payments accounted for 10 percent of the Strip's GNP[28]; by 1987, 42 percent was generated through factor income and net transfers, the largest component of which was wages earned in the Israeli economy. Moreover, an additional 10 percent to 20 percent of Gaza's GNP derived indirectly from employment in Israel, bringing the real total contribution closer to 60 percent. Gaza's extreme dependency on Israel has been asymmetric: only 1 percent of Israel's GNP has been generated by the Gazan economy.[29]

As early as 1970, furthermore, wages earned in Israel were 110 percent higher than those obtained in the Gaza Strip.[30] The national product, therefore, has consistently been larger than the domestic product, the measure of local production and output. When measured in per capita terms, Gaza's GDP was only 1.7 times as great in 1986 as it was in 1968.[31] Consequently, the Gaza Strip has had an income disproportionate to its productive capabilities; the economy has increasingly been dominated by externally generated resources. As a result, such production-linked indicators as GNP and per capita GNP are inappropriate measures for evaluating the strength and efficiency of the Gaza Strip economy, because they are largely based on transferred resources.[32]

These structural changes have had a profound impact on the growth and transformation of Gaza's domestic economy and the prospects for local development. However, the effect of increasing economic integration between the Gaza Strip and Israel has been viewed as both beneficial and harmful, underscoring the argument made earlier that more than one level of analysis is required. The Israeli government, for one, has consistently underlined what it considers to be the positive outcomes of enhanced integration in the areas of labor and employment. The Ministry of Labour and Social Affairs has defined these outcomes in several ways, most prominent of which is "the significant increase in income, wages, private consumption and standard of living, all of which have more than doubled in real terms."[33] Conditions prevailing before 1967 are held to be the only legitimate basis of comparison, particularly with regard to levels of per capita GNP and unemployment. Officially, unemployment fell from 10 percent to 15 percent before the war to 2 percent to 3 percent after, a situation that the government defines as full employment.[34]

These points are more significant for what they fail to say rather than for what they do say. Economic growth is not the same as economic development. The benefits that have accrued to the Gaza Strip economy as a result of labor integration have been achieved at a high price. For example, the restriction of employment to low-skilled occupations in Israel, eroding domestic opportunities, and the absence of a viable industrial and financial sector have driven out

Palestine's most productive classes—the highly skilled, the professional, and the entrepreneurial. This large-scale emigration has deprived the economy of a critically needed resource for its own social and economic development. This is especially true in the Gaza Strip, where 94 percent of migrant workers abroad are engaged in white-collar work.[35] Strikingly, only 49 percent of the men and 64 percent of the women who were 15 to 24 years old in 1967 remained in the Gaza Strip in 1987.[36]

Moreover, the migration of labor to Israel also meant a loss to those commodity-producing sectors of Gaza's economy in which labor had traditionally been employed, notably agriculture and industry. This loss has had a dislocating impact on the indigenous organization of production, productive capacity, labor productivity, and development potential, despite the significant growth rates achieved during the first decade of Israeli rule. Workers' incomes spent in Israel constituted an additional loss to Gaza's economy as well.

For Gaza, integration has entailed increasing reliance of indigenous economic activity on factors outside Gaza's own productive capabilities, and the transfer of economic resources to Israel or otherwise out of Gaza. The economy becomes vulnerable to events over which it has no control, producing to meet demands that are foreign and of little direct benefit, often at great internal cost. Most detrimentally, the Strip's own development along lines independent of those imposed by the integrative process is effectively precluded. Consequently, Gaza's integration into Israel's economy has a corollary: externalization. Externalization refers to the reorientation of economic activity and domestic production away from Gaza's own economic requirements and desires—production for interests that are not indigenous.

The great demand for unskilled workers in Israel, for example, has "served to distort the Palestinian worker's disposition to acquire advanced education, professional training, or higher skills. There has therefore been a considerable 'de-skilling' of Palestinian manpower under occupation."[37] This de-skilling has severely affected the standards of educational attainment and professional development in the Gaza Strip and the occupied territories generally. The educational and labor (skill) development infrastructure has been reoriented toward Israel's economic interests, which has lowered educational standards, curtailed programs, and discouraged academic and scientific research.[38]

Israeli authorities have consistently cited the "release" of labor from the agricultural sector as a key indicator of economic development in the Gaza Strip and West Bank.[39] However, insofar as development is concerned, the critical question remains: the release of labor toward what end and for whose benefit? In Israel and in many developing economies, the decline in agricultural employment typically resulted in the expansion of the workforce in industry and manufacturing, thus signaling a process of rational transformation within the economy as a whole. In the Gaza Strip, by contrast, the loss of agricultural labor reflected the increasing debilitation of the economy, the inability of domestic employment to keep pace with the expansion of the labor force, and the inability of the economy to mobilize savings from domestic resources and use the benefits of labor migration toward indigenous developmental ends. As such, the decline in domestic employment signified the transformation of the economy from a labor–surplus to a labor–scarce economy unable to compete with the superior income–earning opportunities available in Israel. Indeed, given the vast benefits to Israel of employing Palestinian labor, the argument could also be made that not only did the government have little incentive to promote Gaza's economy, but the continued flow of workers from Gaza was only possible with the continued impoverishment of Gaza's own economy. In this way, integration and externalization can also be understood as a form of expropriation and disinheritance—denying the Gaza Strip the full use of its own human and economic resources.

Furthermore, the migration process has also played an important role in maintaining subsistence, because factor income earned in Israel has enabled Gaza's economy to function in ways that might not otherwise have been possible.[40] For example, as employment in the productive sectors of Gaza's economy declined, little investment or capital formation occurred in those sectors, or in Gaza's own means of production, such as labor, plants and equipment, infrastructure such as transportation and communications, finance and commerce, education, training, and research (especially in the manufacturing process). By 1991, for example, the supply of capital per Gazan worker was $7,000; in Israel, the comparable sum was $40,000. In fact, only 15 percent of Gaza's total resources was directed to investment. This figure is far below investment levels in other third world economies in the Muslim world, Latin America, and non-Muslim Asia. In normal economies, there is a positive connection between the percentage of total resources dedicated to investment and the rate of growth (GNP). The Gaza Strip, however, was able to increase its GNP despite its low investment record because of its heavy reliance on external income from Israel.[41]

Agriculture

The evolution of Gazan agriculture since 1967 provides clear evidence of integration and externalization. In agriculture, the labor force has been redirected into Israel. Production has also been reoriented toward export, tying agricultural production to Israeli technologies. This section will review official Israeli strategies toward agricultural development in Gaza, key sectoral characteristics, and constraints.

Strategy

Since 1967, the agricultural sector has undergone more profound change than any other sector in Gaza. Agriculture has remained the backbone of the Gazan economy. In addition to providing for immediate consumption needs and rural employment, agriculture (especially citrus) has been an important source of foreign exchange and supplier of raw materials for local industry, to which it is strongly linked. During the first decade of Israeli rule, agriculture experienced steady growth; this was followed by equally steady decline over the second decade. In this chapter, only those factors that have contributed to the decline in productive capacity will be discussed.[42] They include market dependencies, tariff barriers (see trade below), competition, the redirection of agricultural labor into Israel, the lack of public and private sources of finance, the absence of a capital market, inadequate infrastructure, and changing output patterns. These factors created overwhelming obstacles for local producers.

Without question, the existing water problem was also a severe constraint on the agriculture sector's development. Other constraints were the presence of a majority refugee population, climate, ecological conditions often inconducive to agricultural mechanization, fragmentation of land holdings, and indigenous production patterns, which sometimes worked against the introduction of modern techniques. Moreover, as with many third world settings, the richer farmers adopted modern technologies before their less privileged counterparts, which fueled income disparities. Although these problems were (to varying degrees) beyond government control, they existed within a government policy framework that made no attempt to empower the economy to address these problems.

The government's strategy for developing Gaza's agriculture reflected its larger economic development strategy. It is discussed in some detail here because it highlights how policy contributed to de-development. The government's immediate objective was to increase agricultural production in order to meet domestic demand.[43] However, in agriculture, as in other sectors, the longer term goal was to prevent the rational transformation of the structural status quo while tying sectoral productivity, income, and growth to an exogenous force, namely Israel. The adoption of this strategy "was justified at the time by uncertainty over the future of the territories and the lack of desire to create an infrastructure that would be politically unacceptable."[44]

The strategy did not attempt to repair Gaza's weak institutional and economic infrastructures, but rather to work within them. That is, the authorities sought to develop Palestinian agriculture within the existing resource base of the local economy rather than through any structural reform of the rural sector. Consequently, the government intentionally did not promote, and in some instances actively prohibited, heavy capital investments in physical infrastructure (i.e., roads, electricity, communications, water supply, sewage systems, deep sea port); institution-building measures (especially in the critically needed financial sector); land and water reform; the development of marketing and credit systems (both public and private); or improvements in trade with countries other than Israel.

Instead, enhanced sectoral productivity was to be achieved through intensive patterns of farming through the transfer of new technologies (e.g., modern, water-efficient irrigation, fertilization, spraying and pest control techniques, upgraded seed varieties, expanded veterinary services) and was to be geared largely toward export. Such new technologies would tie the production process to Israeli suppliers. Prior to 1992, for example, no laboratory facilities for testing soil, water, or the leaves of citrus trees existed in the Strip because of official prohibitions on their establishment. Farmers seeking such testing had to go to Israel, and many did not. Consequently, the application of fertilizer, which the authorities have heralded as an important achievement of agricultural policy, was largely unscientific and unguided.[45]

Technology and markets did not rely on the "dynamics of development," but aimed instead to move traditional subsistence agriculture further toward commercially (and export) oriented farming, and toward the production of cash crops that would further bind the occupied territories directly to Israel and neighboring Arab states through trade.[46] In this regard, official policy also aimed, however unsuccessfully, to orient local production to meet the Israeli market's needs by developing substitutes for foreign products imported to Israel.[47] In this way, the servicing of agriculture for export—or the "externalization" of the agricultural sector—was emphasized over the "internalization" of domestic agriculture through rational structural change.

Given the underdeveloped nature of agriculture at the time, technological inputs, no matter how small, produced clear and positive results, especially in cash crops. New techniques and machinery and other low-cost inputs (which were easily adopted due to increased income earned in Israel) raised productivity and output in relation to labor and land.[48] Between 1972 and 1988, for example, the number of dunums irrigated with new technological methods increased from 3,000 to 57,000.[49] However, increased productivity does not necessarily lead to sustainable growth. The relation of technological change to productivity ultimately depends on the quality of the infrastructural base. In the Gaza Strip, the most significant changes occurred in the improved range of *services* offered farmers, not their infrastructure. The government made virtually no major infrastructural investment (in, for example, transportation, power, irrigation schemes, and research and training facilities) over the course of its rule. For example, agricultural manpower training was almost completely eliminated during Israeli occupation.

Any investment in infrastructure that did occur was mostly private. It revolved around the marketing of citrus, the primary cash crop, and was largely limited to the introduction of drip irrigation systems and the construction of six citrus-packing houses. Government resources, which are essential for increasing agricultural efficiency, were virtually nonexistent. Official prohibitions on the development of a credit support system proved a severe handicap on agricultural development overall. Self-finance, furthermore, was constrained by the weak capacity of the informal financial market to which Palestinians were in large part restricted.

Government efforts directed at the development of an agricultural infrastructure were similarly perfunctory. Before the installation of the Likud government in 1977, for example, the government provided citrus and vegetable growers with limited financial incentives for the export of their crops. Development loans amounting to £I 21.4 million, approximately 10 percent of the total cost of investment, were also provided for the purchase of tractors, agricultural equipment, and machinery; these ceased in 1976. A handful of cooperatives were given permission to operate, some land along Gaza's coastal strip was planted with trees, and a few tracts were prepared for livestock grazing.[50] However, no support was provided for capital investments in areas that would compete with Israeli production such as dairy processing or fish canning. Moreover, in the post-1976 period, most of the infrastructural changes made in the occupied territories benefitted Israeli settlements, not the indigenous population.[51] Thus, agricultural growth in the Gaza Strip was not based on an alteration of structural patterns or the creation of productive capacity that could be sustained over time. Rather, growth evolved haphazardly out of rapid functional change that necessarily accompanied the post-1967 economic transition. In fact, the Bank of Israel reported that despite increases in output and improved growth rates, agricultural production in the Gaza Strip and West Bank was lower than that of many other developing countries at the time. Limited government investment not only bounded sectoral change within traditional parameters, but, in so doing, created disincentives for private entrepreneurs, who had little reason to invest in so fettered an area.

Agricultural growth, therefore, like that of the economy as a whole, could only occur within prescribed constraints, and on the condition that it would neither impose a burden on the Israeli economy nor threaten Israeli agricultural interests. This was true for the Labor and the Likud governments. In 1985, Yitzhak Rabin, then defense minister, put it bluntly: "[T]here will be no development in the Occupied Territories initiated by the Israeli government, and no permits given for expanding agriculture or industry, which may compete with the State of Israel."[52] This attitude reflected an overall government policy of weak public investment in agriculture despite the early provision of limited credit and improved services. Palestinian agriculture was forced to compete on an unequal footing with Israel's highly capitalized, subsidized, and protected agricultural sector, as well as to conform to that sector's needs and demands.

Thus, it is no paradox that between 1967 and 1987, agriculture initially underwent significant growth, then fell into continuous decline. The high agricultural growth rates of the 1970s, for example, began to tumble as the Israeli economy moved into recession and Arab markets contracted. In fact, despite the growth rates achieved during the first decade of occupation, the actual resource base of the Gaza Strip (and West Bank) economy was quietly and steadily eroding, not only because of the expropriation of water and land discussed earlier, which preceded the establishment of Israeli settlements, but because of the transfer of surplus labor to employment in Israel, which began to take its toll on agricultural growth after 1977. Thus, the combined impact of existing factors and government policies on Gaza's agricultural sector was damaging. The absolute loss of land, water, and labor will curtail the future growth potential of Palestinian agriculture as well.

General Characteristics

A. Impact

The study of agriculture in the Gaza Strip can roughly be divided into a period of general growth (1967–77) and relative decline (1977–87). The impact of official policies can be measured according to three macroeconomic indicators: the agricultural share of GNP, the agricultural share of GDP, and the number employed in agriculture. All three demonstrate a virtually continuous decline between 1967 and 1987.

Prior to 1967, agriculture was the largest single economic activity in the Gaza Strip, accounting for over 33 percent of GDP, close to 40 percent of employment, and 90 percent of all exports. Between 1967 and 1987, the position of agriculture in the economy steadily weakened (in both relative and absolute terms) despite increased productivity and high growth rates achieved during the first decade of occupation. The sector's overall decline is evidenced by the drop in agriculture's share of GDP, which fell from a high of 32.5 percent in 1972 to a low of 13.9 percent in 1984, rising only slightly to 17.3 percent in 1987.[53] Similarly, the sectoral share of GNP dropped from a 1968 peak of 28.1 percent to 10.1 percent in 1987 after having dipped to its nadir of 7.8 percent in 1984.

In the first ten years of Israeli rule, agricultural output and productivity rose. Although agricultural employment decreased, production levels continued to rise, a direct result of improved cultivation methods and technology transfer. Toward the end of the 1970s, growth ceased as the sectoral share of GDP and GNP fell to their lowest levels ever, with only minor recoveries thereafter. The cessation of growth is reflected in agricultural employment, which dropped in the early 1980s when the pull of the Israeli market attracted many farmers, slowing the growth of agricultural production. On average, agricultural employment fell by 4 percent and labor productivity by 3 percent during each year from 1982 to 1984.[54]

Agriculture's early growth and subsequent decline were the result of official strategies that tied agricultural production to Israeli technology and the Israeli market. Internal structural reform was never an option. As a result, agricultural development became dependent on and vulnerable to the dynamics of the Israeli economy; Gaza's own economy was incapable of redressing the imbalance. The decline in agricultural employment in Gaza in favor of wage labor in Israel, for example, had a significant impact on slowing agricultural growth and is one expression of how integration and externalization weaken productive capacity and contribute to de-development.

B. Land Use and Agricultural Output Patterns

Slightly more than one-half of Gaza's 360,000 dunums were cultivated in 1966. About half of all cultivated lands were irrigated; of these, citrus occupied the largest share. Some studies of land use in the Gaza Strip (including the author's) maintain a steady increase in the cultivated area over the whole period of Israeli rule, whereas others describe ebbs and flows of varying degrees.[55] Adding fuel to the debate are the data presented in table 8.1, which were obtained by the author in 1989 from a confidential source in the Agriculture Department of the civil administration in the Gaza Strip. These data paint a somewhat different portrait of land use and sectoral growth under Israeli rule.

Perhaps the most striking finding is that in just one year, from 1967 to 1968, the number of dunums under cultivation by Palestinians in the Gaza Strip actually dropped 20 percent, from 187,000 dunums to 150,000 dunums. This was probably due to land confiscation or requisitions through state declarations. The decline in cultivated land continued gradually for several years, nearing its 1958 level of 141,000 dunums in the early 1970s. Only in 1972 did cultivated land regain its immediate postwar level, with 151,000 dunums under cultivation. From 1972 onwards, the area of cultivated land rose incrementally with only minor dips. However, the ratio of cultivated land to total land area did not achieve its prewar level until 1983, and in 1985 exceeded that level for the first time since Israeli rule began.

Politics aside, the decline in cultivable area that appears to have taken place with the onset of Israeli rule represented an absolute and critical loss to the local economy, despite enhanced agricultural output resulting from the increased productivity of labor and land. Not only did it take sixteen years for Gazan agriculture to regain the same amount of cultivated area it had held prior to 1967, but by the time it had done so, the other factors of production—water and labor—had significantly weakened and had lost their cost-efficiency in light of the many other constraints in Gaza's larger economic environment. Hence, the loss of cultivable land could not be compensated, especially in an environment where production, markets, and resource use are linked to external factors beyond indigenous economic control.

The losses in cultivated area are also reflected in changing cropping patterns, which were regulated in large part by the government according to the needs of Israeli agriculture. Although the branches of agriculture have remained largely unchanged, their individual contribution to aggregate output has not. Crops have contributed a majority share to total agricultural output, declining from 77.5 percent in 1967 to 69.5 percent in 1989.[56] Through 1984, citrus, vegetables, and other fruits had, in that order, proved the most productive, although the share of citrus to total output in agriculture had been declining since its peak in the mid-1970s. Perhaps the most significant transformation in agriculture since the 1970s has been the shift away from citrus to vegetables as the primary contributor to output. This shift was largely due to Gaza's water shortage and a variety of Israeli-imposed restrictions (see section on constraints below). In 1985, citrus lost its position as the largest single source of value in agriculture, falling below vegetables probably for the first time since the Mandate period. By 1989, the share of citrus in total crop output value was two-thirds less than that of vegetables.[57] Different branches of agriculture show different patterns (figure 8.1). Some are more dramatic than others; most reflect the pronounced decline of agriculture.

Of all branches of agriculture, citrus has been the most important. Table 8.1 shows that the production of citrus in tons peaked in 1975–76, but by 1988, it had fallen by 46 percent. Thus, between the peak years of 1975 and 1988, 11,000 dunums of citrus went out of cultivation, and production decreased by 108,500 tons (figure 8.2). The high output levels and increased productivity achieved between 1972 and 1976 resulted from the planting of 40,000 dunums prior to 1967, which were just then reaching maturity, and from the use of pesticides, fertilizer, and other inputs, which improved the overall quality of the citrus groves.

However, as the impact of the peak wore off, as financial and technological contributions to agriculture declined, and the problems of water salinity and market share remained unaddressed, agricultural production fell,[58] production costs began to exceed the increase in the citrus sale price, and profits were eroded. Hisham Awartani, a Palestinian economist, explains:

> The drain of labour from agriculture in the occupied territories is almost entirely due to a severe decline in the profitability of all major production sectors. Farmers are being compelled by marginal profits and occasional substantial losses to make the "rational" choice to give up farming and look for an alternative source of income . . . . The crux of the problem, in regard to profitability, stems from the fact that the price system for production inputs and farm produce has been radically restructured to the disadvantage of farmers. The costs of such major inputs as labour, animal-ploughing and irrigation water have risen by 5–18 times, whereas the price of major products . . . has risen by 2–3 times.[59]

Indeed, in 1977, the profitability per dunum for citrus was 160 percent; for vegetables it was 100 percent. By 1987, the profitability per dunum of citrus had declined to 45 percent, whereas that of vegetables remained the same.[60] The loss of profitability resulted in a decline in farmers' income. Between 1979–80 and 1989–90, the farmers' income fell from NIS 162.2 million to NIS 142.7 million, and the average income per self-employed farmer similarly decreased from NIS 22,845 to NIS 17,837.[61] Over time, more and more farmers abandoned their orchards for work in Israel, whereas others replaced their citrus groves with the more cost-effective production of vegetables or other fruits. Hence, between 1967 and 1988, 14,000 citrus dunums went out of cultivation either through uprooting or neglect. By 1987, the citrus branch contributed only 20 percent to agricultural value, half its 1967 share of 40.5 percent.[62]

The vegetable branch of Gazan agriculture, however, has experienced major growth since 1967, a direct result of more efficient cultivation methods and technological innovations (e.g., drip and sprinkler irrigation systems), and of the need to shift production away from citrus to more water-efficient crops. Table 8.1 indicates that the number of dunums planted with vegetables grew steadily from 12,000 to 62,000 between 1967 and 1988. Production likewise increased from 30,000 tons to 150,000 tons (figures 8.1 and 8.3).[63] By 1988, the

Table 8.1.   Agriculture Productivity, 1967-1989

year	citrus dunums	citrus production (tons)	vegetables dunums	vegetables production (tons)	fruits dunums	fruits production (tons)	field crops dunums	field crops production (tons)	fishing production (tons)	total dunum	total production* (tons)
1967–1968	75,000	92,000	12,000	30,000	55,000	20,000	8,000	3,000	2,300	150,000	145,000
1968–1969	71,000	108,000	13,000	33,000	55,000	20,000	8,000	3,000	2,500	147,000	164,000
1969–1970	71,000	140,000	14,500	35,000	54,000	21,500	8,500	3,500	2,450	148,000	200,000
1970–1971	71,000	175,000	16,000	38,000	53,000	22,000	9,000	3,500	2,550	149,000	238,500
1971–1972	71,000	183,000	17,000	40,000	52,000	21,500	9,000	3,500	2,600	149,000	248,000
1972–1973	71,000	178,000	18,000	42,000	52,000	21,000	10,000	4,000	2,600	151,000	245,000
1973–1974	72,000	197,000	19,000	48,000	52,000	22,000	12,000	5,000	2,700	155,000	272,000
1974–1975	72,000	191,000	20,000	50,000	51,800	18,300	13,000	5,000	2,230	156,800	264,300
1975–1976	72,000	237,500	23,000	51,500	49,500	18,500	14,000	4,500	1,770	158,500	312,000
1976–1977	72,000	227,000	25,000	52,500	48,000	18,000	15,000	5,650	2,072	160,000	303,150
1977–1978	70,000	191,000	26,000	54,000	49,000	19,000	17,000	5,000	2,400	162,000	269,000
1978–1979	71,700	176,000	29,000	60,000	49,000	18,500	17,500	5,000	2,320	167,200	259,500
1979–1980	71,700	162,000	30,000	64,000	50,000	19,000	17,500	4,600	2,000	169,200	249,600
1980–1981	71,500	182,000	31,500	70,500	50,000	25,600	21,100	5,100	1,610	174,100	283,200
1981–1982	71,400	201,300	33,200	89,000	47,100	19,500	17,000	2,200	1,240	168,700	312,000
1982–1983	69,000	166,000	35,000	78,000	48,000	23,000	22,000	8,000	1,300	174,000	275,000
1983–1984	67,000	159,500	43,700	104,000	48,350	21,500	26,800	2,500	1,435	185,850	287,500
1984–1985	66,700	175,000	46,200	105,000	48,000	17,000	22,700	1,500	604	183,600	298,500
1985–1986	65,400	147,000	47,100	106,000	45,000	17,100	36,250	2,600	271	193,750	272,700
1986–1987	64,300	191,500	48,700	120,000	44,430	15,900	46,300	14,600	253	203,730	342,000
1987–1988	63,000	190,000	52,200	131,200	45,700	21,300	32,250	6,700	250	193,150	349,200
1988–1989	61,000	129,000	62,000	150,000	46,000	18,000	36,000	13,000	350	205,000	310,000

Source: Agriculture Department, Civil Administration, Gaza Strip, 1989.
* excludes fishing
Note: Melons and pumpkins are not included, but since they provide so small a share of total agriculture output, their exclusion does not significantly change the figures provided.

vegetable branch was tied with citrus in its share of cultivated land, which reflected not only the growth of vegetables but the decline of citrus (table 8.2 and figure 8.4).[64] By 1989, the vegetable branch accounted for 44.7 to 48.0 percent of the total value of agricultural output in the Gaza Strip.[65]

Regarding agriculture production, the value share of fruit (other than citrus), which include almonds (typically 45 percent to 50 percent of total output in the noncitrus fruit branch), olives (20 percent to 25 percent), guava, grape, dates, mangos, and figs, decreased from a high of 13.8 percent in 1967 to 4.6 percent in 1986, as seen in table 8.1.[66] The area planted with other fruits, all of which is cultivated under rainfed conditions, comprised 37 percent of Gaza's total agricultural lands in 1967 but only 22 percent in 1988 (table 8.2). With fluctuations attributable to the vagaries in output of rainfed crops, fruit production increased from 20,000 tons in 1967 to 25,600 in 1980, but fell to 15,900 in 1986, improving only moderately to 18,000 tons in 1988. In light of Israeli competition and a strategy that emphasized intensive crop cultivation, melons and pumpkins were virtually eliminated as an agricultural product, dropping from 4.7 percent of output to 0.2 percent between 1967 and 1987 respectively. Field crops have also added little to agricultural output values overall. Table 8.1 places its value share at 2 percent in 1967 and 4 percent in 1988.[67]

Livestock production contributed 20.6 percent of the value of agricultural output in 1967, 30.5 in 1987, and 30.1 percent in 1989.[68] Meat has

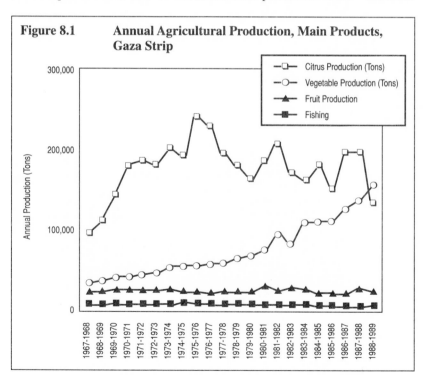

Figure 8.1   Annual Agricultural Production, Main Products, Gaza Strip

remained the largest single contributor to the livestock branch since 1967 and by 1989 was the third largest source of agricultural value after the vegetable and citrus branches.

Of all livestock components, the fishing industry has seen some of the most dramatic declines since 1967. Table 8.1 indicates a drop in annual tonnage, from 2,300 in 1967 to 350 in 1988 (i.e., a decline of 85 percent over 21 years).[69] The decline in fishing was due to a government strategy that dramatically reduced fishing areas and prohibited any form of production that could compete with Israel. Since the intifada, new restrictions involving fishing areas, permits, fines, and taxes have been imposed on the fishing industry, which have further reduced fishing to a marginal activity. Having once contributed as much as 30 percent to total livestock output, fishing contributed no more than 1 percent by 1989.

Overall, agriculture experienced constrained growth under Israeli occupation. Between 1967 and 1988, aggregate production more than doubled but agricultural productivity increased only 56 percent. Gaza's most lucrative agricultural branch, citrus, experienced serious declines in cultivated area and fluctuating declines in output. The amount of land cultivated with fruit crops also decreased, as did production. The vegetable branch increased its value share of agricultural output but did so at the expense of citrus. Although the area cultivated with vegetables was five times greater in 1988 than in 1967, productivity

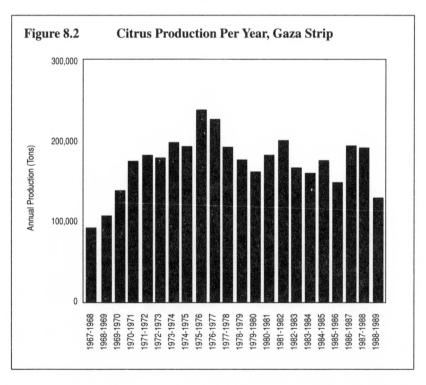

Figure 8.2   Citrus Production Per Year, Gaza Strip

was slightly lower, standing at 2.4 tons per dunum in 1988 (compared to 2.5 tons in 1967). By 1989, agriculture could only add 16.3 percent to the total value of output, a substantial decline from its peak of 57.1 percent in 1976.

Despite some limited growth, agricultural capacity was fundamentally no better in 1988 than in 1967. Agricultural growth occurred within a framework of declining economic resources and increasing constraints; hence, improvements in one agricultural branch could only be achieved at considerable cost to another. Sustainable agricultural development, therefore, was inherently bounded by a variety of constraints, both natural and man-made.

Constraints on Agricultural and Citrus Development

The composition of Gaza's agricultural output changed under the weight of Israeli policy measures and inadequate natural resources, both of which have deprived the Gaza Strip of the potential benefits of economic restructuring. The reduction of cultivated area (through 1985) and citrus output arise from several factors that affect agricultural production generally but citrus most strikingly. Water salinity, insufficient water supply, and high cost of water use have been major constraints on agricultural production and among the most significant factors limiting the impact of increases in productivity. Indeed, as a percentage of total purchased input, water rose from 11.5 percent in 1969–70 to 18.9 percent in 1989.[70] Salinity has had grave implications for Gaza's citrus crop. The

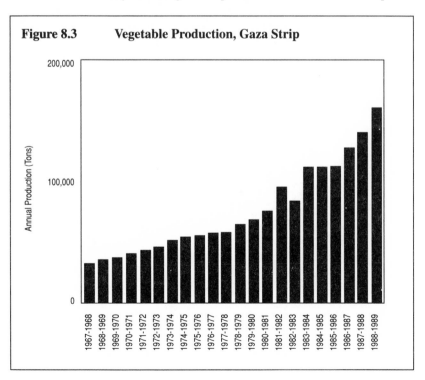

Figure 8.3   Vegetable Production, Gaza Strip

area cultivated with citrus and the size of the annual crop have consistently fallen. By 1988, the Agriculture Department of Gaza's civil administration reported that only 11,000 dunums out of 61,000 dunums planted with citrus (18 percent) were in excellent condition. Vegetables have also been adversely affected, although they do not require as much water as citrus.

Land also poses a severe constraint on agriculture, especially on citrus and vegetable production. Several factors have and will continue to restrict the area under cultivation in the Gaza Strip: (1) the excessive fragmentation of land holdings, with 73 percent of farms smaller than 10 dunums in size; (2) consistent decline in the land available to the Palestinian sector for economic (and residential) use owing to Israeli land confiscation policies; and (3) the acute population growth in the territory, which places increasing pressure on existing land areas and other resources.

Reclamation of land, which could in part have compensated for the absolute loss of land since 1967, was legally prohibited, presenting great difficulties to all farmers. Reclamation involves bulldozing a piece of land in order to remove rocks, boulders, and any other obstructive material to make it cultivable. Gazan farmers were legally forbidden to reclaim their own land unless they obtained permission from the Israeli military authorities.

The decline in citrus output is attributable not only to the lack of fresh water and cultivable land, but to other Israeli policies that have had extremely adverse effects on the development of agriculture, particularly citriculture. Over the past two decades, the Israeli military government imposed restrictions that

Table 8.2.   Breakdown of Total Cultivated Land

	1967	1977	1988
Citrus			
dunums	75,000	70,000	61,000
% of cultivated land	50	43	30
Vegetables			
dunums	12,000	26,000	62,000
% of cultivated land	8	16	30
Fruits			
dunums	55,000	49,000	46,000
% of cultivated land	37	30	22
Field Crops			
dunums	8,000	17,000	36,000
% of cultivated land	5	11	18
TOTAL			
dunums	150,000	162,000	205,000
% of cultivated land	100	100	100

Source: Calculated from Table 8.1.

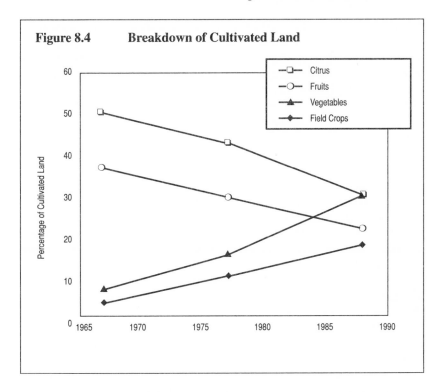

Figure 8.4   Breakdown of Cultivated Land

greatly limited the ability of Gaza citrus producers and merchants to grow as well as market their product. Military orders made it illegal to plant new citrus trees, replace old, nonproductive ones, or plant fruit trees without permission. Permits for these activities had to be secured from the military authorities and could take five years or longer to acquire. As early as 1985, Gaza's agriculture department reported that 10 percent of citrus lands in the northern region and 20 percent in the central region already had old or diseased trees, whereas production levels in the southeast and parts of the center did not even cover costs.[71]

Tax policies further hindered the citrus industry's capacity to grow. Land taxes, perhaps the most severe, were levied according to the number of dunums owned. However, the tax rate used was based on yields per dunum achieved on Israeli citrus farms. Israeli producers and merchants received government subsidies, tax breaks, and other financial supports unavailable to Palestinian merchants and producers. Therefore, Israeli citriculture was far stronger, producing average yields that were substantially higher than those achieved in Gaza. Tax rates on the basis of Israeli production levels did not factor in the different economic conditions confronting Gaza's citrus producers and merchants, nor did they allow for any form of compensation to those individuals in the event of financial loss. A second type of tax, the value added tax, was also applied in a discriminatory manner in Gaza, because Palestinian farmers were not eligible to receive the same VAT rebate on materials as Israeli farmers.[72] Palestinian citrus merchants were subjected to an export tax that they had to pay before being given a permit to export their produce from the Gaza Strip. (The defense ministry denied the existence of the export tax, although local merchants claimed to have paid it.) Finally, the truck tax, which was levied on every truck transporting produce to Jordan, averaged $2,000 per season through 1987, a considerable financial burden in an environment of evaporating profits and spiralling costs.

The complete lack of institutional credit, subsidies, and financial guarantees against loss, as well as the low interest loans that Israeli producers enjoyed further impeded the capacity of Gaza's citrus producers to maintain and expand production of their crop, let alone compete with their Israeli counterparts who enjoyed greater economies of scale as a result. For example, in 1981, the government earmarked $1,448 million in subsidies to Israeli agriculture—almost twice the value of agricultural output in that year. Although subsidies were steadily reduced through the 1980s, they remained high enough to eradicate any competitive threat from Palestinian agriculture.[73] Subsidies and other forms of support[74] allowed Israeli products to flood Palestinian markets uncontested, and Palestinian consumers became increasingly dependent on them. (This has not changed under limited self-rule.)

Furthermore, the economic, political, and legal relationships between Israel and the occupied territories have consistently precluded commercial ventures between Israeli and Palestinian producers, an important factor distinguishing underdevelopment from de-development. Consequently, few if any economic or commercial links ever existed between the two groups. Another less obvious but important problem is the continued absence of agroindustries to absorb surplus products. For example, the government has continuously barred the establishment of juice and other vegetable food-processing factories in the Strip. In 1992, a citrus processing plant was established for the first time since 1967. Juice factories would help absorb crop surpluses and varieties not in demand as a hedge against marketing problems and price declines. Instead, agricultural surplus (mostly citrus) has traditionally been exported to Israeli juice factories at extremely low prices or allowed to rot on the trees.

Among the most severe problems to confront agriculture and citrus products in particular is the lack of markets and marketing facilities for exports. Between 1967 and 1988, markets for Gazan citrus products steadily declined. As noted in chapter three, prior to 1967, Gaza traditionally marketed its produce to parts of Western Europe, Eastern Europe, and Singapore. Trade with Arab countries during this time was minimal.

Immediately after the June 1967 war, Israel banned Gazans from exporting to all Western markets in order to prevent competition with Israeli agricultural producers and then to limit Gaza's access to foreign economic and political circles. However, between 1967 and 1974, Gazans were allowed to market their products in Europe indirectly through Israel's Citrus Marketing Board

(CMB), but at less than competitive prices and under increasingly disadvantageous conditions. The Eastern European market continued and Gaza Strip producers enjoyed the right of direct export to Eastern Europe through the Israeli port of Ashdod. Markets in Arab countries, particularly the Gulf States, opened up through Jordan as well.

Between 1974 and 1979, when Gazan citrus was at its maximum yield, all marketing in Europe through Israel's CMB was stopped. Seeking to reduce the share of Gaza's exports to Europe, the Israeli government encouraged Gazans to seek expanded markets in the Arab world, which Israel itself could not openly enter. A market with Iran opened up that proved extremely lucrative. During this five-year period, the majority of Gaza's citrus was exported to Iran while the Eastern European market, unable to compete with the prices paid by Iran, ended. With the overthrow of the shah in 1979, the Iranian market shut down.

Still denied access to its traditional markets in Western Europe, Gaza again turned to the Eastern European states. However, by 1979, these states had secured other arrangements, mainly with Cuba, with which they dealt in barter trade. Consequently, in order to enter the market, Gazans were forced to trade in barter, not hard currency. Examples of barter include sheep, wood, and crystal products for which Gazans were charged import taxes. With the fall of the communist regimes in 1989, these markets were jeopardized as well, although a new market with the Ukraine opened in 1993.

Through 1987, Gaza's main citrus export markets were Jordan and (through Jordan) other Arab states. However, Arab markets have imposed their own restrictions on Gazan merchants. According to the Arab boycott laws, no Arab country, including Jordan, would import Gazan citrus that may have used raw materials or processing facilities originating in Israel. Consequently, these countries have limited the quantities of citrus that they import from Gaza and, despite promises to import specific quotas, have depended instead on market conditions in Jordan and the Arab world. Between 1975 and 1985, the percentage of Gazan citrus exported to and through East Jordan declined from 68 percent to 55 percent.[75] In addition, markets in the Gulf states were steadily contracting in response to falling oil prices. As a result, many producers turned to the limited local markets in Gaza and the West Bank as a temporary outlet.

Gaza's farmers have always been prohibited from marketing most fruits and vegetables in Israel, a measure designed to shelter Israeli producers from competition with Palestinian products. Products that have not been competitive within the green line such as strawberries, eggplants, and zucchini have been allowed to enter Israel's markets in limited quantities through the Vegetable Marketing Board. Israeli producers, on the other hand, have had unlimited access to Gaza's markets, exporting substantial quantities of fruits and vegetables at prices with which Gazan farmers have been unable to compete.

The instability of Gaza's marketing system has eliminated any linkage between productive yields and external markets. In other words, there is no planned or rational relationship between agricultural production and market forces. This has inhibited long-term expansion of citrus and other crops. Economic activity is determined by state policies, not market dynamics. (This problem has not appreciably changed under the economic terms of the Gaza–Jericho Agreement.) Volatile prices and unreliable markets can result in significant unpredictable losses. In such an environment, where the farmer is buffeted by forces beyond his control, often the only rational decision is to abandon farming.

Market insecurity has made it nearly impossible for the agricultural sector to plan production in line with market considerations. Moreover, other sectors (such as industry) have been equally restricted in terms of their linkages with agriculture and their ability to compensate for agricultural decline by absorbing surplus labor, increasing trade, making new investments, or enhancing output. Thus, the lack of structural development and weak intersectoral linkages, together with official policies adverse to agricultural development, "have rendered agricultural decline the single most identifiable and significant trend in Palestinian economic development."[76] Meron Benvenisti states that the "resources available to the agricultural sector were frozen and all growth potential was transferred to the Israeli economy and the Jewish settlers . . . ."[77] The damage that has already been done will not be easily undone.

Industry

Integration and externalization (and their impact on sectoral transformation) are clearly seen in the lack of structural change and limited growth of Gaza's industrial sector. Government policies hostile to industrial development have been the most serious constraints on sectoral development. The industrial growth that has occurred has been confined within traditional parameters and emerged largely in response to subcontracting arrangements with Israeli enterprises. These arrangements are a form of economic integration and externalization in which control and market demand are totally external. Integration in industry is also apparent in Gaza's industrial trade with Israel in which Israel became Gaza's largest and, at times, only importer and exporter of industrial goods (see the section titled Trade, below). This section will first review the general characteristics of industry and then discuss key constraints.

General Characteristics

The character of industrial activity in the Gaza Strip has remained largely unchanged since 1967, when it was highly underdeveloped. Egypt invested only minimally in Gaza's industry, preferring instead to finance the dominant agriculture. Without any means of capital accumulation, industry stagnated. By 1966, only 1,000 establishments employed an average of two to three persons each. Industry contributed a mere 4.2 percent to GDP. Under Israeli rule, the rate of growth was only slightly better: In 1987, approximately 1,900 establishments employed an average of 4.1–4.7 workers each.[78] Industry continues to provide only a small percentage of Gaza's GDP.

Expansion in the industrial sector has been based on existing production processes (i.e., horizontal expansion) rather than on structural innovation (i.e., vertical expansion). The productive and organizational base of industry remains extremely traditional. It is dominated by small-scale workshops that are owner-operated, labor-intensive, and household in nature, and that primarily service local demand. The share of private investment in machinery and capital stock, for example, has averaged around 8 percent of gross domestic capital formation between 1980 and 1989. Moreover, much of this investment has been used to replace old and obsolete stock. With the exception of 1986, there has been little growth in this component of investment since 1980. In Israel, by contrast, the capital stock of machinery and equipment per worker averaged $30,000, compared with just under $3,000 per worker in the West Bank and Gaza Strip combined.[79]

A 1988 survey of industry conducted in Gaza City (table 8.3), where local industry is concentrated, underscored the traditional nature of sectoral activity. Small workshops and cottage industries engage in a variety of activities. According to unpublished estimates by Israel's Central Bureau of Statistics contained in the Gaza Plan, which were based on two industrial censuses carried out in 1969 and 1984, approximately 1,900 Palestinian industrial establishments employed no more than 9,000 people in 1987.[80]

Though 70 percent of these firms were established after 1967, the industrial sector employed only 9.5 percent of Gaza's total labor force and 17.6 percent of its domestic labor force in 1987. Considering that 46 percent of Gaza's total labor force worked in Israel that year according to official estimates, it is clear that the industrial sector in the Gaza Strip has been unable to absorb surplus labor, notably labor released from the agricultural sector or to compete with employment opportunities in Israel.[81] By 1987, the number of Gazan workers in Israeli industry equalled, and according to some sources, exceeded the number employed in domestic industry.[82]

Not only has the number of industrial workers remained very low over the last two decades, but the size of firms—an important characteristic of economic development—has stayed unusually small. By 1991, only 7.5 percent of total employment in Gazan industry occurred in plants with more than 21 persons per plant. In Israel, by contrast, 36 percent of total employment took place in plants employing at least 300 persons.[83]

The lack of structural reform in Gazan industry is also reflected in the character of industrial output, the source of industrial revenue, the level of industrial productivity and investment, the level of productive capacity, and market size.

Industrial output, for example, has remained largely unchanged since 1967, concentrated in traditional sectors of production—textiles, clothing, and leather. These sectors are highly labor-intensive and continue to employ the majority share of Gaza's industrial labor force. In 1987, the CBS indicated that 43 percent of Gaza's industrial labor force was engaged in the production of clothing, textiles, and leather. Other branches in order of magnitude included basic metals, metal products, and electrical equipment (17.4 percent); other industrial products, of which nonmetallic mineral products constitute the majority share (16.9 percent); wood and its products (15.6 percent); and food beverages and tobacco (7.1 percent).

The Gaza Strip has experienced the growth of two kinds of industries: traditional industries; and industries that complement the Israeli economy, namely textiles, food, and garages.[84] Those complementing the Israeli economy resulted in the growth of small-scale workshops specializing in activities never before known on a wide scale, particularly the low-cost repair of Israeli automobiles, trucks, and agricultural machinery and implements.[85] In short, Gazan industry was externalized to meet Israeli needs. As a result, it developed very slowly, factories remained small, and the distribution of the industrial labor force remained decidedly traditional.

In the virtual absence of structural innovation, the share of traditional branches of industry (food, clothing, textiles) in industrial revenue is quite large— 44 percent of total proceeds, compared with 31 percent in Israel. More technologically advanced industries such as electronics do not exist.[86] In 1987, total industrial revenue amounted to $7,005,000, or $961 per worker, compared with $1,650 per worker in the West Bank. The relative contribution of branches to revenue has remained largely unchanged since 1967, indicating little flexibility, vertical integration, and growth. These factors are also evident in low productivity rates and the character of industrial investment.

Between 1980 and 1987, industrial productivity (GDP divided by industrial employment) in Gaza has been quite low—one-sixth the Israeli rate—in all branches of industry (except for food, beverages, and tobacco). During this period industrial productivity has consistently fallen below $1,000.[87] Low productivity is also a function of low investment rates. Industrial investment depends overwhelmingly on private initiatives, itself a serious constraint on sectoral growth. The remaining sources of industrial capital include partnerships and banks.[88] In 1980, three-quarters of surveyed industrial firms indicated that their initial investment was derived from private sources, resulting in the failure of many of those firms. In 1991, for example, the average investment per employee in clothing workshops was $2,000 in Gaza compared with $40,000 to $50,000 in Israel.[89] The dependence on private sources combined with other limitations such as taxation policies and political instability have produced an environment in which investors are extremely wary.

As a result of these limitations, existing industrial firms have been unable to expand or use their full productive capacity. In 1980, a survey of 94 Gazan firms revealed that only 21 used half or less of their productive capacity; 38 absorbed half of their capacity; 30 achieved a utilization rate of 75 percent; and only 5 were operating at a capacity rate of 90 percent or higher.[90] Utilization capacity has been seriously affected by the dearth of export markets, which have been limited to and controlled by Israel. Thus, capital resources cannot be used efficiently.

Despite its many problems, the industrial sector did experience some growth under Israeli occupation. Its share of GDP rose from 4.5 percent in 1967 to 13.7 percent in 1987. The rise in GDP share was larger than the growth rates experienced by industry in the West Bank. However, this rise was not generated by any genuine internal reform of the sector. Rather, it stemmed from the boom in Israel's economy during the first five years of occupation and the establishment of subcontracting arrangements with Israeli firms.

Subcontracting is a good example of the externalization of Gaza's industrial sector to fulfill Israel's needs. Subcontracting began in 1968 and refers to a widespread practice whereby Israeli contractors provide Gazan industrial firms with semiprocessed raw materials. These firms then complete the processing and deliver the finished product to the Israeli firm at a contracted price. In this way, Gazan industry is integrated with Israeli industry and totally dependent on Israeli demand. Subcontracted products include food, textiles, carpets, clothing, furniture, and shoes. The Gazans who actually do the work may not, in

Table 8.3.   **Industry in Gaza City, 1988**

type of factory	number in Gaza in 1988	average number of employees
Rug	23	—
Polyester/Textiles	15	—
Paper Tissue	7	4.6
Soda	2	20.0
Pottery	4	2.2
Cosmetics	4	3.6
Biscuit	5	12.4
Copybook	2	33.5
Furniture	6	5.1
Solar Heaters	5	3.7
Nylon Mats	1	10.0
Citrus Packing	7	20.7
Battery	3	4.6
Refrigerator	5	12.6
Plastics	2	6.0
Tiles and Cement Blocks	10	6.1
Car Mufflers	1	5.0
Ice Cream	2	47.5
Masonry	1	7.0
Shoe	4	—

Source: American Near East Refugee Aid (ANERA), Internal Report, Gaza Strip, 1988.

fact, be employees of the subcontracting firms, but rather individuals working at home.[91]

Women, who are employed as seamstresses, are paid at relatively lower rates than men; because their task is one they have traditionally performed in the home, their work is considered inferior and unskilled even though it is not.[92] Women working in Gaza are also paid at lower rates than Arab women working in Israel. This wage differential has provided Palestinian subcontractors with a rare comparative advantage that has, in some cases, singularly enabled factories to survive Israeli competition. The use of cheap and unlimited supplies of labor and low overhead costs have made subcontracting a profitable venture for Israeli concerns.

By the end of 1987, for example, between 80 percent and 88 percent of Israeli textile factories were dependent on labor from the Gaza Strip, where most of the factory production was carried out.[93] However, under the best of circumstances, the absence of vertical integration (which refers to a hierarchical structure with integrated and defined lines of command and function) in Gazan industry, paltry financial resources, restricted markets, limited technological advancement, and the comparative advantage of subsidized Israeli firms make subcontracting a tenuous venture for Gazan businessmen despite the considerable revenue it has generated.[94]

Although subcontracting has introduced some degree of specialization in certain industrial branches and limited technology transfer, it has failed to introduce any structural innovation. This is because the subcontracting process requires no investment in new production methods or in the development of new productive capacities that could be used for the benefit of local economic development. Indeed, when one compares industry's share of GDP with the contribution of industrial exports to GDP, the weakness of Gaza's industry becomes painfully clear. The former refers to the low industrial value added in Gaza, which keeps industry's share of GDP low. The latter refers to the higher value of industrial exports, which reflects the total value of locally manufactured goods and goods produced through subcontracting.[95] The difference between the two values is considerable.

Thus, limited improvements in immediate industrial income, employment, and output have produced few spin-off effects for the local economy, especially with regard to human resource development, capital formation, and structural change. In fact, increased specialization, concentration, and economies of scale in the Israeli textile industry have forced some Palestinian contractors out of business, because Israeli enterprises are more efficient and cost-effective. Subcontracting has been Israel's major source of industrial investment in the Gaza Strip economy. It has in effect transformed Gaza's industrial base into a de facto free zone operating for the benefit of Israeli producers, adding to the many anomalies that characterize domestic economic activity and contribute to de-development.

Constraints on the Development of Industry

Palestinian industry has been unable to grow beyond the traditional parameters that were in place in 1967 because of the overwhelming number of constraints it has faced. Chief among these has been the policy of the Israeli government and the innumerable restrictive measures that derive from that policy.

A. Government Policy

Government policy toward the development of Palestinian industry, perhaps more than any other sector, demonstrates official disregard for and outright hostility toward Palestinian economic development in the Gaza Strip. In industry, as in agriculture, economic policy was a product of the state's larger national–political and ideological imperatives. Given the imperatives of insuring Israeli control over the Gaza Strip and protecting Jewish industry from competition of any sort, the government's goals were: (1) to prevent the development of an independent industrial infrastructure in Gaza that could support an independent economic base; and (2) to protect and serve Israeli economic interests by subordinating Palestinian industry and insuring control over areas essential to industrial development: water and land, the registration of companies, trademarks, commerce, tradenames, patents, licenses, taxes, finance, planning, property rights, and trade. This policy has done much to dwarf Gazan industry.

The government never attempted to establish policies, institutions, or regulations that would facilitate development of an industrial base. Early, albeit limited, support for local industry was part of the effort at normalization, which aimed at enabling economic activity to resume, reactivating economic ties, and alleviating unemployment. It was not intended to industrialize the Palestinian economy. The development of a capital-intensive industrial infrastructure, for example, was never a serious option. Government support for local industry dwindled after 1975, particularly as employment in Israel proved to be a more efficient and cost-effective normalization mechanism.[96] Between 1984 and 1986, government expenditure on industry in the Gaza Strip was 3 percent of the total budget, and development expenditure for all three fiscal years did not include any allocation for industry.[97] Since 1980, the trade and industry department of the military government has merely regulated weights and measures, enforced military orders dealing with industry, and actively prohibited many forms of industrial development.[98] In industry as in agriculture, government assistance in the form of tax breaks, export subsidies, subsidized credit,[99] surety bonds, and greater training allowances were not extended to Palestinian industry. No Palestinian firms have ever been registered in the Tel Aviv stock market, nor have Palestinians from Gaza and the West Bank ever been allowed to invest in financial and physical assets in Israel.

The absence of policies, institutions, and regulations not only precluded effective structural change but insured that any local industrial advancements could occur *only* through economic integration with Israel. That is why the comparative advantage offered by lower labor costs in the Gaza Strip never led to any substantive industrial development, as neoclassical economics dictates. Consequently, and in the Gaza Strip especially, Israel promoted the "externalization" of the industrial sector to fulfill its own industrial needs over the "internalization" of industry through indigenous structural reform to meet Gaza's.

As far as industry is concerned, three major factors have militated against the development of the industrial sector in the Gaza Strip: marketing and trade (discussed in detail in the section titled Trade, below), finance (discussed in the preceding chapter), and training (discussed in the next chapter). Government policy has defined activity in all three.

Gaza's terms of trade were shaped by the physical barriers separating the Arab economy from its natural hinterland and controlled by three singular forces: the State of Israel (the most powerful), the government of Jordan, and the domestic market. The Israeli government redefined and reoriented trade to protect Israeli producers from competition and insure their continued domination of domestic and foreign markets. Local businessmen frequently cited the limited size of markets as a major constraint to industrial growth.

Through 1993 Israel imposed a one-way system of tariffs and duties on the importation of goods through its borders; leaving Israel for Gaza, however, no tariffs or other regulations applied. Thus, for Israeli exports to Gaza, the Strip was treated as part of Israel; but for Gazan exports to Israel, the Strip was treated as a foreign entity subject to various "non-tariff barriers."[100] This placed Israel at a distinct advantage for trading and limited Gaza's access to Israeli and foreign markets. Gazans had no recourse against such policies, being totally unable to protect themselves with tariffs or exchange rate controls. Thus, they had to pay more for highly protected Israeli products than they would if they had some control over their own economy. Such policies deprived the occupied territories of significant customs revenue, estimated at $118–$176 million in 1986.[101] (Arguably, the economic terms of the Gaza–Jericho Agreement modify the situation only slightly.[102])

Israel also has imposed quotas on the type and amount of raw materials that could enter the Gaza Strip for use in local manufacturing.[103] Such quotas have particular significance for industry. They have enabled Israel to limit artificially the level of demand for and production of goods manufactured in the territories, thereby imposing clear structural constraints on the industrialization process. (This has not effectively been changed by the 1994 economic protocols.)

Gazan industrialists also have suffered from Arab export restrictions. The Arab boycott has, in effect, left the "open bridges" only partially open, preventing industries established after 1967 and unlicensed by Jordan from exporting to Jordan. Exports could not originate in Israel or contain any Israeli raw materials.[104] This restriction has contributed to the termination of all Gazan industrial exports to Jordan since 1982, effectively closing off the only market where they could possibly compete. Industrial exports to the Jordanian market could therefore contain only raw materials imported through Jordan. The heavy Israeli customs duties and taxes at the bridge[105] and the excessive costs of transportation have undermined trade with Jordan and through Jordan to the Arab world.[106]

Industrial development has also been severely limited by such factors as the absence of financial intermediary institutions, commercial and industrial development banks, and credit of various kinds.[107] Some of these restrictions have been detailed in the section on financial institutions in the next chapter.

Another severe constraint on industry is the lack of a trained industrial labor force. Limited vocational and technical training opportunities and educational attainment of the labor force have contributed directly to the de-development of industry. Inadequate training, in part a function of financial constraints, is also attributable to Israeli government policies that have curtailed or eliminated training opportunities. This is described in greater detail in the next chapter.[108]

The licensing of industry has been another impediment to the sector's development. All powers formally held by local and foreign authorities for regulating industrial activity were transferred to the military government soon after the 1967 war. Authority over licensing decisions has rested with the officer in charge of trade and industry within the military government. Licenses have been required for all forms of industrial activity and have been carefully dispensed and prohibitively expensive. Licenses have been used to regulate industrial activity in Gaza in order to suppress competition with Israel and restructure local industry in line with Israeli needs. Approval by no means ensured the issuance of a license. Many industrialists have waited months and years for a license after receiving official approval for a project.[109] Examples include the denial of licenses for the establishment of fruit-processing factories and a [construction] materials testing laboratory.

The official disregard for Palestinian industry did not extend to Jewish industry. Prior to the election of the Rabin government in 1992, for example, the government provided substantial assistance to local industrial investors in Gaza's Jewish settlements. Investors could choose between a 38 percent bonus or a 66.66 percent loan guarantee with a 10-year tax exemption.[110]

In 1988–1989, furthermore, Israel's employed industrial workforce of 280,452 outnumbered the *total employed labor force* of the Gaza Strip by more than 2 to 1. By 1991, the total revenue from industry in the Gaza Strip was less than 1 percent of what it was in Israel.[111] From 1967 to 1987, government investment accounted for close to 50 percent of gross capital formation in Israeli industry, but close to zero percent of Gaza's industry.[112] Whereas in Israel the government has played the primary role in infrastructural development and in the financing of industry, in Gaza, under the best-case scenario (1969–75), the government restricted its participation to small-scale loans for expanding and retooling local factories and export subsidies for local manufacturers. Measures protecting infant industries, normally found in many less developed economies, were denied in the Gaza Strip, although Israel itself has been granted such privileges by the EEC.[113] Indeed, industrial value-added in the Gaza Strip and West Bank combined has been so low that it fell below the value-added of some individual Israeli firms.[114]

B. Other Constraints

Apart from Israeli-imposed constraints, Palestinian industry—especially the small-scale workshop—has suffered greatly from inadequate quality control. Gazan manufacturers have little experience with standardization, packaging, health, labeling, and content specification requirements expected in most international and regional export markets. Moreover, local industrialists, especially in the isolated Gaza Strip, have little if any experience in satisfying the diversified consumer demand in markets beyond Israel and the Arab states; consequently, they are ill-equipped to produce for and compete in those markets. In part, this shortcoming has derived from Israeli-imposed restrictions on direct trade between the occupied territories and the world market, which have prevented the Palestinian entrepreneur from coming into direct contact with external markets and learning about international trade.

The closure of certain markets and the restricted access to others have forced Gazan manufacturers to focus inward on their own limited domestic markets and fostered intramarket competition. However, without a national trade policy designed to regulate competitive behavior and protect local manufacturing from Israeli competition, the weaker and smaller firms in Gaza have been defeated by their stronger and larger counterparts. Further eroding the possibility for the development of an industrial infrastructure has been the Strip's unchanged adverse balance of payments position and the inability to promote needed industrial development strategies such as import substitution or export promotion.[115] Moreover, there has been very little intraterritorial trade between the Gaza Strip and West Bank in both industrial and agricultural goods, which acts as an additional constraint on the expansion of an industrial base. Indeed, Israeli production and the Israeli market have effectively precluded the development of any significant common market arrangements between Gaza and the West Bank.

Conclusion

The lack of growth and diversification in Gazan industry has resulted from Israeli policies that Meron Benvenisti has termed "integration and exclusion": integration of Gazan industry into Israel's economy when integration benefits that economy, and exclusion when it does not. Without long-term planning or strategy, Gaza's industry has been crippled by many constraints: limited domestic and foreign markets, lack of adequate natural resources, low investment, poor technology, the export of labor, massive industrial imports, low productivity, undercapitalization, and the absence of a developed infrastructure (especially electricity). This combination of constraints has created an industrial base in the Gaza Strip with few means at its disposal to initiate needed structural transformations or "takeoff," particularly with regard to and as measured by the scale or organization of production, the absorption of labor, new investment, productivity, changes in the composition of output, and a widened marketing scope. This in turn has prevented the emergence of those basic or technologically advanced industries commonly seen to "lead" the development process in the third world. Consequently, the Palestinian economy has been incapable of completing a critical stage in structural readjustment, namely, the development of the industrial sector in a manner that would enable the economy to compensate for the decline of agriculture and the problems in other sectors.[116] The Strip has been unable to develop the infrastructure needed to accumulate enough capital to support and promote industrial growth and development. Vulnerable, unprotected, and with limited markets, Gazan industry remains dependent on Israel to generate activity within it.

Israeli forecasts made in 1986 for industry in the year 2000 projected continued stagnation. "New plants will be established to supply the basic needs of the population and traditional exports, but the growth in the number of plants and employment will be less than the growth in population,"[117] a critical indicator of continued de-development. Israeli planners also predicted that if the constraints on industrial development were to be overcome, the initiative would have to be external (i.e., European) and non-Israeli. However, the planners noted that such an initiative would encounter considerable political difficulties given Israel's trade agreements with the common market, and the free trade agreement with the United States in particular.

Although the planners considered the prospect extremely unlikely, they did state that should the Israeli government decide to act, it would have to promote the development of an industrial infrastructure and encourage European investment in joint Israeli–Gaza Strip ventures "whose products could penetrate European and American markets as Israeli goods." Indeed, the planners did add one note of qualification: "The condition for such ideas to succeed, given Israeli economic realities, is that the products would not compete with Israeli goods in the latter's traditional markets."[118]

Trade

General Characteristics

The decline of agriculture, the stagnation of industry, and the disproportionately important role of exports in generating product value point not only to the direct linkage between local production and Israeli demands but to Israel's domination of Gaza's export capabilities. Because the terms of trade of the Gaza Strip were removed from normal market forces and were shaped instead by demand conditions in the Israeli economy, the principles of comparative advantage have been distorted.

Although some of the Strip's prewar trading patterns were maintained during Israeli rule, a few dramatic new changes were introduced. The two most significant were: (1) the redirection of trade to Israel resulting from the closure of traditional trading outlets and Israeli-imposed tariffs that have given Israel a comparative advantage over foreign competitors (as well as changes in the composition of trade); and (2) the institutionalization of a one-way trade structure whereby the Gaza Strip was turned into an open and unprotected market for Israeli exports. In addition, the growth of trade between the Gaza Strip and the Arab world, particularly citrus exports to Arab and Asian countries, has increased significantly since 1967. However, imports from Arab countries have not been allowed in Gaza.[119] In trade, as in labor, structural integration between the economies of the Gaza Strip and Israel has been extensive, as has the externalization of domestic economic activity. Indeed, the disproportionately large percentage of labor obliged to seek work across the green line has helped create a captive market for Israeli goods in the Gaza Strip and West Bank.

Since 1967, exports and imports have filled a significant portion of aggregate demand in the Gaza Strip. However, this trade has been restricted to three key markets. Israel, for one, has become Gaza's largest trading partner, followed by Jordan, the Arab Gulf, and other countries, primarily Eastern Europe. In 1968, for example, exports to Israel accounted for 29 percent of Gaza's total exports, but by 1987, this share had grown to 92 percent. Imports from Israel have been very high from the beginning. The visible trade of the Gaza Strip, furthermore, is characterized by an excess of imports over exports, a pattern established long before Israeli rule but acutely extended during that rule.[120] Imports have escalated as local demand has increased.[121] For much of Gaza's visible trade, both Israel and Jordan act as conduits rather than as final destinations for goods. For invisible trade (i.e., labor services), the direct importance of these two markets has been substantially greater.

However, imports from Israel alone have comprised an overwhelming share of Gaza's trade. In 1986, 86 percent of total imports were industrial, and 93 percent of total industrial imports originated in Israel. Agricultural commodities accounted for only 14 percent of total imports, but again, Israeli agriculture accounted for 84 percent of total agricultural imports. It should be understood, however, that Gaza's import trade has been severely distorted by the growing need to purchase so many consumer goods from Israel. These goods could have been made locally if Israel had not prohibited the development of import substitution industries.

Exports, too, were largely restricted to Israel. In 1986, Israel received 85 percent of Gaza's total exports, which were predominantly industrial products subcontracted by Israeli merchants. Industrial exports constituted 88 percent of Gaza's total exports to Israel. Exports to Jordan and Eastern Europe were strictly agricultural. In 1986, Jordan was Gaza's largest export market for agriculture, absorbing 54 percent of total agricultural exports or roughly 14 percent of total exports. Exports to other countries have steadily contracted since 1973, falling dramatically from 54 percent in 1968[122] to 1.2 percent in 1987.[123]

Similarly, the value of imports has risen steadily and has sometimes grown faster than both consumption and GDP. European imports alone increased in value from approximately $3 million in 1972 to $14 million in 1987.[124] Imports rather than domestic resources have become the critical factor in satisfying consumption demand, yet another indicator of Gaza's limited productive capacity. Conversely, the value of exports, despite a slow recovery, declined by 6 percent between 1972 and 1985 and by as much as 44 percent between 1982 and 1985. The resultant import surplus has accounted for a growing share of Gaza's expenditure on GDP and is another indication of the economy's limited productive capacity and inability to redress the use of its own resources in a more efficient form.

In 1987, Gaza's trade deficit equalled $277.2 million, an increase of 130 percent from 1982. The largest share of the deficit, $259.5 million or 94 percent, was accrued in trade with Israel. Trade with other countries contributed $29.5 million, and trade with Jordan, which gave Gaza a modest surplus, eased the deficit by $11.8 million. Traditionally, the deficit has been financed not by trade but by external remittances and wages earned by Gazans working in Israel, two sources of revenue that have eroded since the Gulf war.

Constraints on Trade

The warped trade performance of Gaza's two most important sectors derives from Israeli and Arab restrictions on the expansion and diversification of exports and limited markets (two problems universally cited by local industrialists in interviews), and heavy dependence on imports for domestic production and consumption needs. Interestingly, there is little relationship between the composition of output and export trade, where normally a relationship should exist. Agriculture's relatively large (though declining) contribution to domestic economic output, for example, is not reflected in its small share of total exports. Similarly, industry's virtual stagnation and minor contribution to local economic growth in the Gaza Strip is inversely related to its predominant share of Gaza's export markets. Consequently, the composition of output has had no discernible influence on the structure of exports, an expression of irrational growth in Gaza's production and export sectors.

This "irrationality" has resulted largely from the distortion and reorientation of Palestinian production and export performance away from the free market, toward Israeli demands and commercial interests. It has also resulted from Israeli and Arab-imposed constraints that have shaped the level and quality of production and export flows.[125] For example, the growing share of industrial goods in Gaza's total exports might appear to be an indication of a stronger industrial sector. In Gaza, however, it reflects a production process that is linked to and driven by Israeli industrial needs, not domestic economic capabilities. Hence, the benefits of trade are not those associated with specialization and higher returns in production. Rather, trade is necessary for basic economic survival. In the final analysis, the issue is not really one of exchange but of how to pay for the goods imported.[126]

Gaza's trade problems are linked to a variety of factors affecting agricultural and industrial production, some of which have already been discussed. Limitations on the development of Palestinian trade are mainly due to the structural underdevelopment of the economy and Israeli measures that have restricted structural reform and external sector performance. Although it is difficult to disentangle organic from imposed constraints, it is easier to understand the impact that such constraints have had. It is beyond the scope of this chapter to detail the many problems affecting trade; however, certain issues of particular relevance to de-development are briefly highlighted here and discussed at length in the next chapter.

Because access to external markets is so restricted, the small size of the domestic market is a critical problem. Gazan manufacturers would have to install expensive new machinery to compete with Israeli product lines in Gaza's markets. However, local markets are so small and export potential so limited that any form of internal expansion would be an exercise in financial folly, especially because production capacity is already underused.

Moreover, the unrestricted flow of Israeli goods into Gazan markets has narrowed the home market further. In fact, prior to the intifada, many Israeli imports competed with goods that were also produced in the Gaza Strip and West Bank, such as soft drinks, cigarettes, clothing, and shoes. Local producers found it difficult to compete because they remained unprotected and Palestinian consumers preferred Israeli over domestic products and had the incomes to purchase them. As such, the Gaza Strip became a captive market for low-priced Israeli agricultural goods and substandard industrial products. Whereas the success of Israeli industrial products could be attributed to the interaction between a highly industrialized economy and one that was comparatively underdeveloped, the decreasing share of local agricultural producers in their own markets leaves perhaps one explanation: Israel has dominated the market and imposed policies that constrain and discriminate against local production.[127]

In the Gaza Strip, only 44.5 percent (on average) of marketed fruits and vegetables were produced locally each year between 1980 and 1986.[128] The domestic consumption of fruits, vegetables, and melons accounted for roughly a quarter of total output in Gaza.[129] Thus, even if local agricultural produce could substitute for Israeli imports, there would still be a large surplus that cannot be absorbed by the limited external markets accessible to Palestinian producers. Consequently, much of this surplus has been marketed locally, and the remainder has simply rotted. Spoilage has been an ongoing and growing problem.[130] With such a limited home market, local development has had to depend largely and disproportionately on Gaza's constrained external trade.

Another serious problem is the virtual absence of an organized and integrated marketing infrastructure.[131] Restricted markets, poor export potential, and the continuing underdevelopment of the economy have done little to reverse the low levels of investment in physical infrastructure needed to promote and expand export marketing and everything to sustain them. The lack of an institutionalized marketing infrastructure has adversely affected the quality of production and export/import patterns in the Gaza Strip, as well as the local economy's ability to compensate and redress these problems. This erosion of capacity is a distinguishing feature of economic de-development.

A Review of Domestic Resources and Uses

The changes wrought by official policies of integration and externalization and their impact on Gaza's productive capacity suggest a critical analytic distinction between aggregate performance and sectoral change. The performance of domestic resources (e.g., GDP, net factor income, national income) and domestic uses (e.g., private and public consumption, national savings, capital formation, exports, and imports) reveals the strength or weakness of an economy.

Domestic Resources (Production)

During the first two decades of occupation, the Gaza Strip economy experienced the unsteady growth of its GDP and GNP along with increases in private consumption and investment. For example, GDP grew from $183.5 million (in constant 1990 dollars) in 1972 to $481.2 million in 1987, an increase of 162 percent. GNP similarly grew by 223 percent between 1972 and 1987, rising from $256.5 million to $828.8 million, respectively.[132] Per capita, GNP rose from $669.9 to $1,492.5.

The period of greatest growth was 1972 to 1975, when Gaza's GDP grew by an annual average rate of 16.9 percent and GNP grew by 18.3 percent. Such impressive growth rates—even higher than Israel's—were in large part spurred by the recovery of the immediate postwar period, interaction with the expanding and prerecessionary Israeli economy, and the indirect effect of the growth of the Arab oil-based economies. Once the adjustment process played itself out, the difference in growth rates between the Gaza Strip and Israel disappeared and eventually reversed itself. Between 1976 and 1980, GDP and GNP dropped to 3.4 percent and 4.4 percent, respectively. Although these rates rose slightly during the 1980s, they never again approached the rates of the early boom period.

Despite this growth, and that of employment, Gaza's economy, with its poor infrastructure and limited capital formation, remained weak and disabled. Looking at the performance of GDP over time, three trends stand out: (1) agriculture's share continued to decline, whereas industry's was always minimal; (2) construction and services generated a disproportionate share; and (3) the growth of GDP was fueled largely by external resources and consumption.

For reasons already discussed, agriculture and industry grew less than other sectors and less than GDP. Thus, productive sectors have played a minor role in economic growth. The progressive weakening of the agricultural sector, for example, left it increasingly unable to satisfy local demand and improve its export performance. Some restructuring of production patterns occurred, particularly in response to the declining availability of water and land, but did not introduce the kind of structural change needed—diversification, expansion, integrated planning, production of inputs, and strengthened marketing infrastructure—to increase employment, enhance income, and improve output performance.

Gazan industry fared no better. Although industry's share of GDP increased during the first two decades of occupation, industrial production and revenue were largely concentrated in traditional areas, linked to Israeli demand, and catalyzed by subcontracting arrangements with Israeli industry. Whereas these factors were largely responsible for generating activity and encouraging some growth, they promoted and reinforced a form of structural dependency that rendered Gaza's industrial sector incapable of achieving adequate economies of scale—the basis of rational economic behavior—and of redressing existing constraints and deficiencies.

By contrast, the construction and services sectors enjoyed a rapid rise in output between 1967 and 1987, and growth rates that often exceeded those of GDP. This strong performance is linked to two factors, neither indicative of rational structural change: the desperate need for housing in the Gaza Strip, and the dearth of investment opportunities outside residential building. Moreover, most of the activity in this sector was financed by private earnings and remittances, not by locally generated revenue or government investment. Indeed, the building and construction sector has received the overwhelming share of private investment since 1981. Investment and capital formation in the private sector have accounted for 85 percent of total capital formation in the Gaza Strip. The services sector, which includes public, community, and private (e.g., transport) services, accounted for the overwhelming share of domestic output—over 50 percent—for the period 1967 to 1987.

The dominance of the services sector is due to the important role of retail and wholesale trade activities in Gaza's economy. These activities were fueled by rapid increases in private consumption and by transport services that benefitted greatly from the daily commute of at least 70,000 Gazans to Israel. Hence, the strength of the services sector, like that of construction, did not derive from or contribute to improved productive capacity or rational structural transformation, but from the declining position of agriculture and industry in domestic production and from the externalization of labor and dependence on Israel.

The performance of individual sectors indicates that despite measurable economic gains, productive capacity did not improve and aggregate performance was bounded by a variety of constraints, including but not restricted to limited markets, poor infrastructure, weak investment, and inadequate financial intermediation. (Financial intermediaries are financial firms such as banks that stand between ultimate lenders—households—and ultimate borrowers—businesses. Lenders place funds with intermediaries, which in turn lend them to borrowers.) Hence, although capital was clearly being generated, there were no mechanisms such as financial and credit institutions through which it could be accumulated and invested in development. Without large capital formation in the different sectors of Gaza's economy, especially the productive areas, economic infrastructure could not be created or strengthened; institutions could not be improved; enterprises could not expand; and new employment opportunities could not easily be created. One important measure of economic weakness—and a distinguishing feature of de-development—is the swift reversal of achieved economic gains. In Gaza, such a reversal occurred during the intifada as is explained in chapter 10. Again this suggests that the "gains" achieved under Israeli occupation did not result from improved productive capacity and structural readjustment or innovation, enabling the mobilization of domestic resources, but from gross structural imbalances such as the economy's heavy reliance on external factors for generating domestic and national growth. As a result, the impact of GDP growth was confined to nothing more than enhanced purchasing power and rapidly rising consumerism.

Domestic Uses (Consumption)

Domestic resources are not the only measures of Gaza's economic distortion. The main components of aggregate demand—consumption (expenditure), savings, investment, and trade—provide equally revealing measures of Gaza's de-development. The most significant component on the demand side of the Palestinian economy has been consumption, the largest portion of which has been private (personal) consumption expenditure. Real levels of private consumption in the Gaza Strip tripled between 1972 and 1987, resulting from a significant rise in earned income, private transfers, and remittances. Notably, the value of consumption (goods consumed) has often been greater than the value of GDP (goods produced), a disparity that underlines the importance of external financial sources in servicing local demand. This fact strongly points to the structural debilitation of the Gazan economy and its de-development.

Given that consumption has often exceeded output, the need for imports has been tremendous. The rapid rise in imports has diverted a considerable share of national resources that under "normal" circumstances would be used to develop a productive base. The rise in aggregate private consumption is not reflected in individual consumption because Gaza's exponential population growth has cut into per capita consumption, particularly after 1980.

The savings component of aggregate demand is another indicator of Gaza's tenuous economic base, especially when measured against the role of external financial resources in generating savings. Given that private consumption consistently outstripped GDP, the ratio of domestic savings (savings drawn from domestic resources) to GDP was consistently negative between 1967 and 1987: –49 percent in the Gaza Strip for a loss to GDP (or domestic dissavings) of $286 million. However, the ratio of national savings (savings drawn from all resources) to GDP was consistently positive given the reliance of national savings on income earned abroad, accounting for 13 percent of the Gaza Strip

GNP in 1987.[133]The difference between domestic savings and national savings points to the importance of external income in generating internal growth and to the increasing morbidity of the economy with respect to mobilizing savings from the resources available to it.

Israel lauds as advances in the local standard of living the growing levels of private expenditure and consumerism; clearly, however, they would not have been sustainable without the contribution of external sources of revenue to savings. Thus, although individual Palestinians were accumulating material possessions and improving their standard of living, their economy was growing weaker. The inability to mobilize financial resources within the local economy (stemming from weak financial institutions capable of saving and investing) progressively encouraged the rechannelling of savings from investment to consumption. In this way, savings were increasingly eroded by expenditure.

The status of investment resembles that of savings. In Gaza, investment is largely a private sector initiative, because government investment dropped from 6.6 percent of GNP in 1972 to 3.4 percent in 1987. Foreign investment has also been negligible. Prior to the intifada, the rate of private investment in the Gaza Strip was high—82 percent and 88 percent of total investment spending in 1972 and 1987, respectively[134]—but the growth or effectiveness of such investment was modest. Investments have been concentrated in two areas: social overhead investment (SOI) and directly productive investment (DPI). The former refers to building and other forms of construction and is not production-oriented; the latter is defined by investment in machinery and new equipment that improves productive capacity. Throughout the occupation, SOI accounted for the largest share of Gaza's fixed private investment. In the early 1970s, SOI absorbed nearly two-thirds of private investment in the occupied territories and DPI accounted for the remaining third. A decade later, the share of DPI had fallen to almost one-fifth. Whereas SOI enjoyed an average annual growth rate of 15 percent between 1972 and 1987, DPI grew at an average annual rate of 9 percent. Between 1980 and 1987, 88 percent of Gaza's fixed capital formation was invested in SOI.

Weak investment patterns in productive activities reflect official priorities and structural constraints that actively opposed the development of a productive economic base in the Gaza Strip. Instead, domestic investment has been channelled largely to the residential sector, not to development-related activities that would transform Gaza's productive capacity and economic structure.[135]

Another distinguishing feature of the Gaza Strip economy is the prominent role played by trade in meeting total local demand. Exports have risen erratically over time, accounting for 56 percent of Gaza's GDP in 1980 and 39 percent in 1987. Imports, however, rose steadily and rapidly, far outstripping exports. Between 1980 and 1985, imports accounted for 133 percent of Gaza's GDP, or more than twice the value of exports, indicating the inefficient and distorted use of domestic resources. Imports absorbed a significant part of consumption demand and grew faster than both consumption and GDP, exacerbating the dramatic trade deficit that has plagued the Gaza economy at least since Egyptian times.

Given the weak performance of exports, increasing reliance on imports, and low domestic output levels, Palestinian national income has had to rely increasingly on external sources of finance—net factor income (the largest component) and net transfers—for generating growth. Net factor income, largely composed of income earned in Israel, equaled 42 percent of Gaza's GNP in 1987. In 1987, income from external factor payments to the occupied territories fell just below total GDP (to which agriculture and industry contribute), another striking indicator of meager productive capacity. Without factor payments, Gaza's GNP would have grown at a rate well below that of domestic output.

Net transfers from abroad have played a supplementary but needed role. They comprised 11 percent of Gaza's GNP in 1980 and 7 percent in 1987. Net transfers are composed of remittances from workers in Jordan and the Arab Gulf; Israeli government transfers to the civil administration budget; Arab government transfers to municipalities; and transfers from international agencies (the largest of which is UNRWA).

With the availability of external sources of finance, Gaza's gross national disposable income (GNDI), like GNP, enjoyed considerable growth. However, the external basis and dependent nature of domestic and national income meant that the gains in income levels had increasingly little to do with Gaza's productive capacity. Since 1967, the ratio between investment in productive activities and national income showed little improvement. This reveals a weak link between growing national income and improved productive capacity.

The growth of Gaza's domestic and national products did not reflect strengthened capacity or the kind of structural transformation that normally accompanies economic growth. If anything, Gaza's growth occurred despite the weaknesses of the domestic economic sector, not because of it. By 1987, the Gaza Strip economy was only capable of generating 50 percent to 60 percent of its national income and employment from domestic sources. Were it not for external financial resources, no savings would have been possible at all (given the weak performance of domestic output). Furthermore, those savings that did accrue were, in the absence of productive investment opportunities, diverted mainly into residential housing. Consequently, local demand was increasingly met through rising imports; the resulting trade deficit has become a permanent feature of the local economy.

Taken together, these pieces of economic performance form a clearly warped whole, a whole that has been de-developed. That Gaza has undergone de-development is clear from its distinguishing economic characteristics: the stagnation and distortion of key productive sectors; the disarticulation between productive sectors (i.e., the uncoupling or disuniting of sectors that leaves them functioning in relative isolation, responding to external forces, not each other); import dependency in lieu of enhanced productive capacity to satisfy local consumption demand; the inability of exports to generate sufficient foreign exchange; the inability of the economy to mobilize domestic savings or finance consumption and investment; rising unemployment and the continued erosion of the economy's ability to absorb labor; and increasing dependence on external sources of finance to generate GDP, GNP, and GNDI growth. These conditions reveal profound structural weaknesses that render the economy unable to readjust or self-correct. They also bring home just how transient Gaza's economic gains have been and how little they have contributed to the rational restructuring of the economy.

Conclusion

Integration and externalization have had a marked impact on Gaza's key economic sectors. Weakened by the expropriation of its own economic resources, Gaza's economy became increasingly and structurally dependent on external (largely Israeli) resources for domestic growth. This dependency was imposed and achieved through economic integration with Israel and Gaza's externalization toward Israel's economic needs.

Integration and externalization resulted in (1) the reorientation of the labor force away from domestic agriculture and industry toward Israel; (2) the reshaping of agriculture toward export production and reliance on Israeli inputs; (3) the realignment of industry with Israel's industrial needs through subcontracting and trade; and (4) the redirection of Gaza's trade to Israel. In this way, local resources were transferred outside Gaza's economy to Israel's and Gaza's own productive capacity was diminished.

Another crucial factor contributing to the dimunition of Gaza's productive capacity has been the lack of an institutional infrastructure capable of supporting structural reform. This was largely due to Israeli policies deliberately restricting the development of a viable institutional base in Gaza, thus compounding the effects of dispossession and integration.

Notes to Chapter 8:

1. Bank of Israel, *Annual Report 1988* (Jerusalem: Bank of Israel, May 1989), p. 84. See also Dan Zakai, *Economic Development in Judea-Samaria and the Gaza District 1985–86* (Jerusalem: Research Department, Bank of Israel, December 1988), pp. 17–21.

2. Calculated from State of Israel, *National Accounts of Judea, Samaria and Gaza Areas 1968–1986*, p. 119; State of Israel, *Judaea, Samaria And Gaza Area Statistics* 18, no.1 (Jerusalem: CBS, March 1988), p. 28; and Bank of Israel, *Annual Report 1988*, p. 85.

3. The problems of obtaining accurate data on population are many, and more than one database can be found including the Central Bureau of Statistics, the Registration of Residents, and various Palestinian studies. See Gaza Plan, Sections 2.1.1.–2.1.4; 2.2.3; 2.3.1–2.3.2; 2.4.5; 2.4.7; 9.4.2; Tables 2.1–2.3; 2.5–2.6; 2.8–2.9; State of Israel, *Projections of Population in Judea, Samaria and Gaza Area up to 2002*, Special Series no.802 (Jerusalem: CBS, 1987); and State of Israel, *Population Forecasts for Judea and Samaria and the Gaza Strip 1983–2002* (in Hebrew).

4. The 633,600 figure is derived from Israel's Central Bureau of Statistics and is lower than Palestinian estimates.

5. Informal interviews with approximately 200 women throughout the Gaza Strip revealed that particularly since the intifada, the rejection of family planning is in part linked to the perceived need to increase the number of Palestinians inside the occupied territories and to compensate for lost lives.

6. CBS, Special Series no.802, pp. 40–41.

7. Neu, pp. 207–208, makes this point as does Van Arkadie, pp. 54–57.

8. CBS, Special Series no.802, pp. 39–41, forecasts a slight to significant preponderance of males over females in all five projections for the year 2002.

9. The total population size does not reflect those living abroad. Ministry of Labour and Social Affairs, *Labour Force Statistics*, Jerusalem, 1988.

10. Comparable participation rates for women in the West Bank and Arab citizens of Israel in 1986 averaged out much higher, at 11.3 percent and 13.5 percent respectively. The labor force participation rate among Jewish women in Israel, by contrast, was 14 times greater than that of women in Gaza. Zakai, *Economic Development 1985–1986*, p. 43. Women in Gaza do not participate in the labor force for a number of reasons that are largely cultural. See, for example, Susan Rockwell, "Palestinian Women Workers in the Israeli-Occupied Gaza Strip," *Journal of Palestine Studies* 16, no.2 (Winter 1985): 119–30.

11. Ezra Sadan, *A Policy for Immediate Economic-Industrial Development in the Gaza Strip: A Summary Report* (n.p.: Ben-Ezra Consultants, Ltd., August 1991), p. 69.

12.   Official Israeli sources put unemployment at 1–2 percent annually between 1967–1987, while Arab and other sources put it much higher, particularly if underemployment and seasonal work are taken into account. See International Labour Organization Vol. 2; and Neu, pp. 200–20.

13.   United Nations Conference on Trade and Development (UNCTAD), In-house, commissioned study on population and demographics in the occupied territories, Geneva, Switzerland, 1992.

14.   Figures in this section are derived from various issues of State of Israel, *Statistical Abstract of Israel* (Jerusalem: Central Bureau of Statistics).

15.   Roy, *The Gaza Strip Survey*, pp. 36–37. See also Salim Tamari, "The Dislocation and Reconstitution of a Peasantry," p. 90.

16.   "Baram: No accord will cut Israel–Gaza labour links," *Jerusalem Post*, 26 July 1974.

17.   Moshe Semyonov and Noah Lewin-Epstein, *Hewers of Wood And Drawers of Water: Noncitizen Arabs in the Israeli Labor Market* (New York: New York School of Industrial and Labor Relations, Cornell University, 1987), pp. 27–29; and Kimmerling, pp. 60–61.

18.   Semyonov and Lewin-Epstein, p. 24.

19.   Ibid., pp. 39, 41.

20.   See Neu, pp. 220–22.

21.   Salim Tamari, "Building Other People's Homes: The Palestinian Peasant's Household and Work in Israel," *Journal of Palestine Studies* 11, no.1 (Autumn 1981): 31–66.

22.   A key distinction is that before 1967 workers emigrated to work; after 1967, they commuted.

23.   Tamari, pp. 33–34.

24.   Ibid., pp. 31–66.

25.   Meron, pp. 48–49.

26.   Bregman, pp. 33–35; and Bank of Israel, *The Economy of the Administered Areas in 1972* (Jerusalem: Bank of Israel Research Department, June 1974), p. 30.

27.   United Nations Conference on Trade and Development (UNCTAD), *Recent Economic Developments in the Occupied Palestinian Territories* (Geneva: UNCTAD, June 1986), p. 13; and UNCTAD, *Palestinian External Trade Under Israeli Occupation*, p. 51.

28.   Bank of Israel, *The Economy of the Administered Areas in 1970* (Jerusalem: Bank of Israel Research Department, August 1971), p. 25.

29.   Sadan, *A Policy for Immediate Economic-Industrial Development*, p. 11.

30.   Bank of Israel, *The Economy of the Administered Areas in 1970*, p. 42.

31.   Kleiman, p. 12.

32.   See United Nations, Economic and Social Council, Economic and Social Commission For Western Asia (ESCWA), *The Occupied Palestinian Territories: Industrial Development Policies, Constraints and Prospects* (Paper presented at a seminar entitled "Prospects for the Palestinian Industrial Sector," UNIDO, Vienna, 11–13 October 1989), pp. 1–3.

33.   State of Israel, *Labour and Employment in Judea, Samaria and the Gaza District*, p. 30. See also Rekhess, p. 412.

34.   State of Israel, *Labour and Employment in Judea, Samaria and the Gaza District*, p. 30.

35.   UNCTAD, In-house population study, Geneva, Switzerland, 1992.

36.   Calculated from State of Israel, *Statistical Abstract of Israel*, various issues.

37.   George T. Abed, *The Economic Viability of a Palestinian State* (Washington, D.C.: Institute for Palestine Studies, 1990), pp. 13–14.

38.   Ibid., pp. 14–15.

39.   See, for example, State of Israel, *Labour and Employment*, pp. 10–11.

40.   UNCTAD, *Recent Economic Developments*, p. 11.

41.   Sadan, *A Policy for Immediate Economic-Industrial Development*, pp. 6–7.

42.   For a comprehensive review of the agricultural sector between 1967 and 1987, see, for example, Kahan, *Agriculture and Water (1967–1987)*; M. Benvenisti, *The West Bank Data Project: A Survey of Israel's Policies*, pp. 12–15; Awartani, "Agricultural Development and Policies in the West Bank and Gaza Strip," in Abed (ed.), pp. 139–64; and Gharaibeh, pp. 59–82.

43.   For an Israeli account of Gaza's agriculture, see Gideon Weigert, "Gaza Farmers Look Forward," *Bulletin of the Jerusalem Chamber of Commerce*, April 1977, pp. 33–36; and Gideon Weigert, *Life Under Occupation* (Jerusalem: Jerusalem Post Press, 1971) for a series of short essays on economic conditions in the Gaza Strip and West Bank.

44.   Kahan, *Agriculture and Water (1967–1987)*, p. 17.

45.   Peter Gubser, *Middle East Trip Report, 4 April 1992–16 April 1992*, (Washington, D.C.: American Near East Refugee Aid [ANERA], April 1992), p. 5.

46.   Kahan, *Agriculture and Water (1967–1987)*, pp. 16–17; and M. Benvenisti, *The West Bank Handbook: A Political Lexicon* (Jerusalem: The Jerusalem Post Press, 1986), p. 2.

47.   See David Kahan, *Agriculture and Water in the West Bank and Gaza, Part One, The Arab Sector* (Jerusalem: West Bank Data Base Project, 1983), pp. 39–40.

48.   UNCTAD, *The Palestinian Financial Sector Under Israeli Occupation*, (New York: United Nations, 1989), p. 17.

49.   Department of Agriculture, *Agricultural Statistics* (Gaza Strip: Civil Administration, 1989).

50.   Kahan, *Agriculture and Water, Part One*, pp. 42–44.

51.   Ibid., pp. 41–42.

52.   *Jerusalem Post*, 15 February 1985.

53.   State of Israel, *Statistical Abstract of Israel*, various issues; and State of Israel, *National Accounts for Judaea, Samaria, the Gaza Strip, and North Sinai For the Decade 1968–77*, Special Series no. 615 (Jerusalem: CBS, 1979).

54.   Kahan, *Agriculture and Water (1967–1987)*, p. 47.

55.   For example, Roy, *The Gaza Strip Survey*, based on Gharaibeh; Kana'na and al-Madani; State of Israel, Ministry of Defense, *Report of the Military Government 1985–86* (Gaza: Ministry of Defense, 1986); and Kahan, *Agriculture and Water (1967–1987)*.

56.   State of Israel, *Agricultural Statistics Quarterly* 21, no.1 (Jerusalem: Central Bureau of Statistics, January–March 1990): 61. See also Sara Roy, "The Gaza Strip: A Case of Economic De-Development," p. 63.

57.   State of Israel, *Agricultural Statistics Quarterly*, p. 61.

58.   At a production level of 1 to 3 tons/dunum, farmers are losing money; at 4 to 5 tons/dunum, there is some margin of profitability; at 5 to 6 tons/dunum (typical Israeli yield) there is a reasonable profit. Farmers need at least 4 tons/dunum to break even, Economic Development Group (EDG), Jerusalem, 1989.

59.   Awartani, "Agriculture Development and Policies," in Abed (ed.), p. 145. See also UNCTAD, *Palestinian External Trade*, Table 5, p. 13.

60.   Statistical Data obtained from the Economic Development Group (EDG), Jerusalem, 1989.

61. State of Israel, *Agricultural Statistics Quarterly*, p. 64.

62. State of Israel, *Statistical Abstract of Israel*, various issues.

63. CBS figures are slightly higher.

64. Department of Agriculture, Civil Administration, Gaza Strip, 1988. See also Department of Agriculture, *Vegetable Production in the Gaza Strip*, Internal Document (Gaza Strip: Civil Administration, 1986).

65. See Department of Agriculture, *Agricultural Production in the Gaza Strip 1987–1988*, Internal Document (Gaza Strip: Civil Administration, 1988); State of Israel, *Statistical Abstract of Israel*, various issues, which provide slightly lower figures.

66. CBS figures are slightly higher.

67. CBS figures are slightly lower. Kahan, *Agriculture and Water (1967–1987)*, p. 43, also presents different figures from those in table 8.1.

68. The 1989 figure is drawn from the State of Israel, *Agricultural Statistics Quarterly*.

69. State of Israel, *Agriculture Statistics Quarterly*, pp. 61–62, states that between 1988 and 1989 alone, the quantity of output in fish declined by 12.9 percent.

70. State of Israel, *Agricultural Statistics Quarterly*, p. 63.

71. Department of Agriculture, *Prospects for the Citrus and Fruits Sector in the Gaza Strip*, Internal Document (Gaza Strip: Civil Administration, 1985).

72. The government of Israel reimbursed VAT to Gazans only if they made above a certain amount and if they banked their money so that it could be converted to shekels. Gazans were reluctant to bank their money for two reasons: currency inflation and possible seizure by the Israeli authorities. If income from VAT rebates was not banked at official exchange rates, exporters were not allowed to export their goods. VAT was charged on crates, wrapping paper, and goods sold.

73. The 1987 Israeli budget proposed a 5 percent subsidy for milk, a 30 percent subsidy for eggs, a 25 percent subsidy for poultry, and a 50 percent subsidy for irrigation water.

74. Other supports available to Israeli agriculture and not available in Gaza include: a price stabilization scheme, an insurance fund against natural disasters, minimum price guarantees, reduced electricity and energy costs, and access to advanced research and extension facilities, which is particularly important for improving productivity and quality. UNCTAD, *Palestinian External Trade*, p. 86.

75. UNCTAD, *Palestinian External Trade*, Table 10, 45. However, when measured in

absolute tonnage the level of exports to Jordan fell by 48 percent between 1976 and 1985.

76.   Ibid., p. 14.

77.   M. Benvenisti, *The West Bank Handbook*, p. 2.

78.   Sources vary. See *Statistical Abstract of Israel 1988*; and Gaza Plan, Sections 7.1.1–7.1.4.

79.   Eli Sagi and Yacov Sheinin, *Israel, the West Bank and Gaza: the Case of Economic Cooperation* (Ramat Gan, Israel: Economic Models Ltd., 1989), p. 17.

80.   The Gaza Plan, Sections 7.1.1–7.1.4. *Published* CBS data, however, indicated only 1,628 plants employing 6,226 people by the beginning of 1987. Consequently, Israeli planners feel it is safe to assume that published data on industrial employment represent only 80 percent of what is actually true.

81.   This may confirm an assertion in the Gaza Plan that a 1981 forecast of rapid growth in Gaza Strip industry had been completely falsified. Gaza Plan, Section 7.7.2.

82.   State of Israel, *Statistical Abstract of Israel 1988*; Palestine Liberation Organization, *Industrial Statistical Bulletin for the West Bank and Gaza Strip 1988* (Damascus: Central Bureau of Statistics, Economic Unit, 1988), pp. 24–30.

83.   Ezra Sadan, *Durable Employment For The Refugee-Populated Region Of Gaza* (n.p., 1993), p. 4.

84.   Gaza Plan, Section 7.4.5.

85.   UNCTAD, *Recent economic developments in the occupied Palestinian territories with special reference to the external trade sector* (Geneva: UNCTAD, 19 September 1988), p. 11.

86.   This branch accounts for 15 percent of industrial revenue in Israel. Sadan, *A Policy for Immediate Economic-Industrial Development*, pp. 27–28.

87.   UNCTAD, *Palestinian External Trade*, p. 17.

88.   Simcha Bahiri, *Industrialization in the West Bank and Gaza* (Boulder, CO: Westview Press, 1987), p. 37.

89.   Sadan, *Durable Employment*.

90.   Abu Kishk, 1981, p. 36.

91.   Indeed, small sewing shops established by Palestinian subcontractors in the refugee camps are the only form of small industry to penetrate the camps.

92. Interviews with owners of subcontracting ventures in the Gaza Strip, 1985. Hiltermann, *Behind the Intifada*, pp. 28–29, makes a similar point.

93. Al-Haq, Law in the Service of Man, Ramallah, West Bank, In-house files, March 1989. Original source: *Yediot Aharanot*, 28 December 1987.

94. Hillel Frisch, *Stagnation and Frontier: Arab and Jewish Industry in the West Bank* (Jerusalem: West Bank Data Base Project, July 1983), p. 56.

95. UNCTAD, *Recent Economic Developments*, p. 9.

96. Frisch, pp. 63–64.

97. State of Israel, *Budget for 1986/87* (Jerusalem: Government Printer, 1986).

98. Bakir Abu Kishk, "Industrial Development Policies in the West Bank and Gaza Strip," in Abed (ed.), p. 168.

99. Israeli manufactured goods enjoyed subsidies and protections estimated at 60 percent of the value of products in the international market. UNCTAD, *Recent Economic Developments*, p. 9.

100. Bahiri, *Industrialization in the West Bank and Gaza*, p. 40.

101. UNCTAD, *Palestinian External Trade*, p. 85.

102. See Sara Roy, "Development or Dependency? The Gaza Strip Economy under Limited Self-Rule," *The Beirut Review* (Fall 1994).

103. Abu Kishk, "Industrial Development Policies," in Abed (ed.), p. 177.

104. Ibid., p. 179, states that in 1979, the Jordanian government allowed a limited number of post-1967 factories to export to Jordan.

105. UNCTAD, *Palestinian External Trade*, p. 77, lists the following Israeli-imposed fees on traffic across the bridges (for early 1988): (1) monthly lorry permit (for an average of five trips per month) = $154; (2) Inspection fee on return (per trip) = $20; (3) Customs service fee (per trip) = $14; Personal exit permit (per trip, for owner of goods) = $176. Therefore, one truckload to Amman incurs a total fee of $65 without the participation of the owner, and $241 if the owner accompanies his merchandise.

106. See Dieter Weiss, *Industrial Development for Palestine—A Conceptual Framework with Special Reference to the Size Constraints*, (Paper presented at a seminar entitled, "Prospects for the Palestinian Industrial Sector," UNIDO, Vienna, Austria, 11–13 October 1989).

107. See, for example, L. Harris, H. Jabr, and R. Shihadeh, *Study for the Establishment of an Industrial Development Bank in the Occupied Territories of Palestine* (Vienna:

UNIDO, 1 August 1988); P.G. Sadler, U. Kazi, and E. Jabr, *Survey of the Manufacturing Industry in the West Bank and Gaza Strip* (Vienna: UNIDO, March 1984); and Monthor Nijim, *Assessment of the Availability and Demand for Credit Financing by the Palestinian Industrial Sector* (Vienna: UNIDO, October 1989).

108.   See UNIDO, *Identification of Priority Projects in the Industrial Sector* (Vienna: UNIDO, 7 September 1989) for a list of projects considered critical for catalyzing the growth of the industrial sector.

109.   See Sadler, Kazi, and Jabr, pp. 55–60. Interviews with a variety of PVO officials in the West Bank and Gaza Strip, 1989; and the president of the Engineers Association in the Gaza Strip, 1989.

110.   "Documents and Source Material," *Journal of Palestine Studies* 21, no.3 (Spring 1992): 154.

111.   Sadan, *A Policy for Immediate Economic-Industrial Development*, p. 24.

112.   See Abba Lerner and Haim Ben Shahar, *The Economics of Efficiency and Growth: Lessons from Israel and the West Bank* (Cambridge, MA: Ballinger Publishing Co., 1975).

113.   Ahiram, p. 10.

114.   See Awartani, *A Survey of Industries in the West Bank and Gaza Strip*, p. 50; Gregory Robison, "Survey of Industries and of Assistance Available to Industries on the West Bank and in the Gaza Strip." First Draft, USAID, Jerusalem, July 1988.

115.   Weiss, p. 27.

116.   UNCTAD *The Palestinian Financial Sector under Israeli Occupation* (1987), 11; and UNCTAD, *The Palestinian Financial Sector*, pp. 20–22.

117.   Gaza Plan, Section 7.7.4.

118.   Ibid., 7.7.8.

119.   The "open bridges" policy enacted within a year of Israeli rule was designed to open trade with Jordan, particularly for Gazan citrus. Imports from Jordan were limited to the West Bank only. This policy has eliminated any competition with Israeli goods in Gazan markets and prevented the development of trade between Jordan and Gaza beyond a specific level.

120.   For actual figures, see State of Israel, *Judaea, Samaria and Gaza Area Statistics* 15, no.2 and 18, no.1; State of Israel, *Statistical Abstract of Israel*, various issues.

121.   Imports range from basic foodstuffs and animal and vegetable products to a variety of manufactured goods such as machinery and mechanical appliances, electrical equipment, and vehicles.

122. The high level of exports in this year was due to the fulfillment of citrus contracts arranged before 1967.

123. See State of Israel, *Judaea, Samaria and Gaza Area Statistics* 18, no.1, p. 7.

124. Civil Administration, Gaza Strip, April 1989. Israeli statistics use current prices, which do not reflect the effect of inflation. Rodney Wilson, *The International Economic Relations of the Palestinian Economy*, (Paper presented at the symposium entitled, "Economic Aspects of a Political Settlement in the Middle East," University of Nijmegen, Nijmegen, The Netherlands, 18–20 April, 1990).

125. For a more detailed discussion of this problem, see UNCTAD, *Palestinian External Trade*, pp. 57–58.

126. R. Wilson, pp. 2–3.

127. UNCTAD, *Palestinian External Trade*, Table 12, p. 61. See R. Wilson.

128. UNCTAD, *Palestinian External Trade*, Table 12, p. 61.

129. Ibid. Calculated using Tables 5 and 12, 13, p. 61.

130. Ibid., p. 61.

131. See ibid., pp. 62–78 for an extensive discussion.

132. Data in this section are derived from UNCTAD, confidential studies prepared by the UNCTAD Secretariat: "Prospects for Sustained Development of the Palestinian Economy of the West Bank and Gaza Strip: A Quantitative Framework, 1991–2010," Geneva, Switzerland, December 1991, pp. 14–32; and "Prospects For Sustained Development of the Palestinian Economy in the West Bank and Gaza Strip, 1990–2010: A Quantitative Framework," Geneva Switzerland, April 1992, pp. 17–32. Quoted and referenced with permission of the director of the Special Economic Unit for the Palestinian People, UNCTAD, Geneva, Switzerland.

133. However, this figure also represents a decline from its 1982 level of 21 percent.

134. This equalled 10.7 percent of GNP in 1972 and 17 percent in 1987.

135. See ESCWA, 1989.

9

Deinstitutionalization

D einstitutionalization is the third critical component of economic development. Deinstitutionalization refers to the direct or indirect restriction and undermining of institutions that could plan for and support productive
investment over time. In Gaza, this restriction has come from the Israeli government. For example, expenditure and investment patterns of Gaza's civil administration have done little to promote institutional growth in economically
critical sectors such as industry and agriculture. In this way, deinstitutionalization
can also be understood as the logical consequence of dispossession and
externalization. This attack on institutional development has been directed not
only at the institutions themselves but at inter- and extra-institutional linkages.
Deinstitutionalization erodes the typical supportive relationship between the
formal (governmental) and informal (nongovernmental) sectors, normally a critical factor in the formation and implementation of development policy. It re-
places that relationship with a system of restrictions opposed to most forms of
economic development. Hiltermann explains:

> Since the authorities have been singularly incapable of forestalling the
> emergence of a Palestinian civil society, they have singled out Palestinian
> institutions and popular organizations for specific repressive measures.[1]

Once key linkages between the formal and informal sectors are eliminated,
any development that occurs is due to the initiatives of the latter. Greatly weakened by the absence of such linkages, the informal sector is poorly equipped to
provide services.

263

Moreover, institutions that successfully provide social or economic benefits often do so in isolation, functioning alone rather than as part of a system. In Gaza, the absence of an appropriate institutional structure together with the erosion of essential resources usually available to politically autonomous authorities and the orientation of the economic structure to meet Israel's, have rendered development planning in the occupied territories virtually nonexistent. Even under the best of circumstances, this situation has produced a fragile collaboration between local and foreign institutions in which individuals and communities work in conjunction with international and voluntary organizations to realize specific objectives. As a result, local initiatives are often dominated by foreign assistance agencies, and considerable infighting takes place among local organizations over increasingly limited resources. (The promise of $2.4 billion in economic assistance as part of the peace initiative could in the continued absence of an institutional infrastructure, worsen this problem rather than resolve it.)

Institutions for industrial and economic development in the occupied territories fall into two main categories: mainstream, formal institutions such as cooperatives, credit organizations, municipalities, and schools; and popular, mass-based organizations. The two categories are distinguished by their primary objectives: economic accommodation to the status quo in the case of the former and political resistance in the case of the latter.

The mainstream organizations were designed to help people withstand military occupation through economic and social means. Although these institutions were not organized along nationalist lines or for explicit political purposes, they have, to varying degrees, been characterized politically by the Israeli authorities. The popular grassroots organizations that burgeoned during the 1980s have a decidedly nationalist orientation and were formed with a clear sociopolitical agenda: to oppose military occupation at the mass level, and to provide what Hiltermann has termed an "infrastructure of resistance."[2]

In this book, only the more "formal" or mainstream institutions will be reviewed. There are two reasons for this: (1) popular organizations in the Gaza Strip, particularly those with relevance for economic activity (e.g., the labor movement), have historically been weak and have had a negligible effect on local economic development; and (2) although both sets of institutions have been subject to similar forms of harassment by the Israeli authorities (e.g., closures, banning, withholding permits, restricting membership, prohibiting meetings, arresting directors, deporting leaders), those in the mainstream have been more typically subject to measures and problems that provide evidence of deinstitutionalization.

In the Gaza Strip, deinstitutionalization is characterized by several features: (1) a disjointed and ad hoc approach to internal planning; (2) a remarkable lack of intra- and interinstitutional coordination and interinstitutional integration; (3) limited horizontal expansion and the near total absence of vertical integration; (4) weak, and in some cases, non-existent linkages with bodies and institutions outside the occupied territories, including in Israel and beyond; (5) uncertain linkages between official Israeli bodies and local institutions that are often based on oppressive control or mutual distrust; (6) the virtual absence of any supportive infrastructure for institutional development; and (7) a dearth of skills required for institutional management and development.

Deinstitutionalization is the product of three factors: restrictive Israeli policies; the motives of Arab and non-Arab foreign donors; and problems endemic to local institutional behavior that are cultural, social, and political in origin. This chapter will focus on the effect of Israeli policies because they have had the most direct impact on deinstitutionalization. An analysis of the roles of foreign assistance and local culture, though important, is beyond the scope of this chapter, but specific points will be noted below.

Israeli restrictions have had the most direct impact on institutional development. These restrictions have made it difficult for institutions to function, let alone maintain any degree of autonomy. Israeli restrictions have been incorporated into military law and mandated that Palestinian institutions must obtain official approval for nearly all of their activities, even the most mundane. Military law controls the external context within which institutions operate and, until the implementation of the Gaza–Jericho Agreement, the internal work of the institutions themselves. Decision-making and control over institutional function, direction, programs, and planning have resided with the Israeli military authorities who aimed to restrict public participation in the running of public affairs. Institutions, for example, had to obtain permission to hold a meeting if it was to consist of three persons or more. Permission was also required for any new program or activity, physical expansion, and personnel change. The authorities determined whether institutions could receive external funding, the amount of that funding, and how it was to be used. They could close institutions at any time for any reason.

Over the long term, institutional growth is dependent on critical factors over which Palestinians have never had any control: land, zoning, and water to establish needed physical infrastructure; development of an economic and legal infrastructure supportive of institutional growth across sectors; and educational, training, and research programs needed to produce a qualified cadre of managers, administrators, and bureaucrats. In short, the institutional development that occurred has done so in spite of Israeli law, not because of it.

Israeli Policy and Deinstitutionalization: Restrictions on Local Institutions

Perhaps the most striking example of deinstitutionalization and its contribution to de-development is found in Palestinian industry. The deficiencies created by deinstitutionalization stand out starkly when one surveys the institutional framework that was supposed to support the growth of the industrial sector, which is vital for economic development.

In Gaza, institutions and services for industry have been steadily eroded. Deinstitutionalization has either weakened or done away with producer/managerial and labor organizations; organizations or associations supporting the development of business and trade; financial institutions able to mobilize savings and channel them into industrial capital, including industrial development banks, credit and investment institutions, finance houses, merchant banks, insurance companies, stockbroking; research and development bodies financed to promote industrial development and innovation; "leading" industries needed to catalyze long-term growth; and government agencies that could provide financial support. The reasons for these deficiencies lie with different actors, the most important being Israel.

Local institutions that do provide assistance to industry and trade in the Gaza Strip are as limited as the assistance they provide. They include: municipalities, chambers of commerce, professional associations, banks, moneychangers, private development and credit organizations, and postsecondary institutes and universities.[3]

Public Institutions

A key indicator of Israeli policy impact on Palestinian deinstitutionalization is found in the serious lack of public institutions in the Gaza Strip. Although this problem was not created by Israel, official policies did little to develop public institutions, which Israel considered an expression of Palestinian nationalism, and a great deal to undermine them. This is illustrated in Israeli measures toward Palestinian municipal government, a potential actor in local industrial growth.

A. Municipal Councils

Municipal councils, a form of local government, are among few remaining indigenous political institutions in Gaza. In the absence of a national authority, municipal councils provided certain necessary public services. The Gaza Strip has four: in Gaza City, Rafah, Deir el-Balah, and Khan Younis. Prior to 1967, they drew their authority from the 1934 Municipal Corporation Ordinance enacted under the British Mandate. The imposition of Israel's Military Orders 194 and 236, however, transferred authority over local government to the Israeli military government (civil administration), invalidating earlier statutes. As a result, the legislative and executive powers of the municipalities have been significantly weakened. Prior to the Gaza–Jericho Agreement, every municipal council activity was subject to military government approval.[4]

Israeli control was visibly manifested in the composition of municipal government. Elections for municipalities were last held in 1946. Between 1982 and 1994, the Gaza municipality was under the direct control of Israel's interior ministry, without mayor or municipal council. Attempts to reestablish the council, begun in 1991, ran into difficulty. In Rafah and Deir el-Balah, the municipal councils were similarly dismissed and replaced with Israeli-appointed mayors.

In the eyes of the populace, Israeli-appointed officials were illegitimate and unrepresentative. Only Khan Younis had an elected mayor and a functioning municipal council.

Given the military government's control over municipal government in the occupied territories, a significant difference existed between the endowed and actual authority of municipal government. According to British law, for example, municipal governments had authority over many areas, including planning, zoning, granting building permits, water usage and allocation, electricity usage and allocation, sewage disposal, public markets, public transportation, public health institutions, budget, expenditure of public funds, and town property and its supervision.[5] Between 1967 and 1994, municipalities were unable to exercise their authority over any of these areas or to initiate new projects without the approval of the military governor. Consequently, they could no longer serve as democratic institutions.

The absence of viable and legitimate municipal government has had a deleterious impact on the ability of municipal institutions to play a positive, catalytic role in industrial and economic development. These problems have resulted in the overall deterioration of town and village infrastructure and services, especially in the Gaza Strip. In Gaza City, for example, raw sewage runs in the streets of several residential areas; many roads remain unpaved and sandy, turning into impassable canals of mud after rain and snow; garbage is strewn along side streets and main thoroughfares as well as sidewalks; and traffic runs amok. The debilitation of municipal function is reflected in four areas: the appointment of Israeli mayors, control over procedures required for industrial development (e.g., zoning, planning, licensing), control over infrastructural resources critical to industrial development (e.g., water, electricity, transportation), and finance.

The appointment by the military government of municipal (and local) councils in the Gaza Strip provided the Israeli authorities with a local power base through which to exercise control. Appointed municipal councils had no authority and little influence of their own. Furthermore, the appointment of Israeli officers as mayors of Arab towns produced direct changes in the physical and economic character of Arab localities. In response to the establishment of the civilian administration in 1981, for example, most municipal institutions in the Gaza Strip suspended operations. In response, Israel deposed Mayor Shawa and replaced him with an Israeli officer. Such appointments "facilitated settlement activity and increased economic integration and land seizures."[6]

Even those municipal councils under elected Arab control exercised limited autonomy over those procedures directly related to the promotion of industrial development. Zoning and planning within the municipal limits of any Arab town, for example, were subject to nullification by military decree at any time. Municipal decisions regarding the use of land were carefully scrutinized by the military government and balanced against the priorities of Israeli settlement activity.[7] (Under the terms of the Oslo agreement, Israel retains ultimate authority over zoning and land use in the Gaza Strip.)

The licensing process was perhaps the major procedural constraint on the development of an industrial infrastructure in the Gaza Strip. Technically, Arab municipalities had the authority to issue license permits for construction within municipal limits, but building licenses, especially for factories, were closely regulated. Fees could be steep and bureaucratic processing lengthy. Israeli environmental regulations, furthermore, forced certain plants into areas unfavorable long-term survival.[8] Israeli officials approved the implementation of certain light industrial projects within municipal boundaries. However, in exchange, some appointed mayors traded their licensing authority for other, often developmentally unsound programs. For example, design of Gazan sewage systems placed the needs of Jewish settlements ahead of those of the indigenous community.

Even if municipal governments had been unencumbered by licensing regulations, their lack of authority over other critical development resources (i.e., land and water, electricity, and transportation) would have impaired their ability to act effectively, particularly with regard to industrial development. For example, all Gaza Strip townships are connected to the Israeli grid. There is not even an unconnected minor station in the entire Strip.[9] Three Israeli power plants supply the entire Gaza Strip through five high tension lines, and this includes nearly all the houses, workshops, and plants in the territory. There are forty-eight utilities which then resell electricity. The majority of Gazans receive electricity in concentrated bursts; Jewish settlements and Israeli institutions receive a direct supply. In 1991, each resident of the Gaza Strip received on average 400 kilowatt hours of electricity; each Israeli received an average of 3,500 kilowatt hours.[10]

Although residents who wished to hook onto the electric grid simply contacted their local municipal authority, individual requests were ultimately subject to the control of the civil administration. (This appears still to be the case under limited self-rule.) Lighting new neighborhoods and industrial areas still requires complex special arrangements. In some instances, industrial and business consumers must finance the electrical connections themselves, creating additional financial burdens in an already cost-ineffective environment. The total reliance on Israel for electricity and other resources has eliminated most vestiges of Gazan institutional control over industrial growth.

The Israeli military government similarly controls the transportation infrastructure in the occupied territories without substantive local input. Road construction, for example, has been designed to service and promote Israeli settlements, facilitate army movements, and integrate the Gaza road system with Israel's. The last point is made extremely clear in Israeli development plans for the Gaza Strip. The Gaza Plan's stated reasons for development of a transportation network in Gaza have little to do with improving Gaza's internal infrastructure. Rather, the reasons revolve around accommodating Israel's need for Gazan labor. The planners predicted that the number of motor vehicles to population would rise rapidly from 39.4 vehicles/1,000 in 1984 to 90.5/1,000 by the year 2000. No clear reason is given for the sharp increase in the rate of motorization, but planners emphasize that the traffic flow from the Gaza Strip to Israel will grow markedly as a result of the projected need to transport Palestinian laborers to and from work inside Israel. They state:

> An outstanding problem is that of Highway 4, from the Erez checkpoint [main border between the Strip and Israel] toward Israel, which has a yearly increase in congestion, particularly during rush hours . . . . According to the employment forecast, about 91,000 workers from Gaza will be employed in Israel in the year 2000, double the number currently employed. About 70 percent of them on average will return home every night, so the number traveling daily between the Gaza Strip and Israel proper will be 64,000. One can assume about 90 percent of these or 57,000 will pass through the Erez checkpoint, in addition to those training who are not employed in Israel. In order to accommodate this flow, two additional lanes leading through the checkpoint and an additional lane at the intersection will be needed.

> The bottleneck at the Erez intersection has two causes: a) the lack of an additional traffic lane, and b) the inspection stations. If there is a desire to maintain a constant flow over additional hours, e.g. requiring the workers to leave for work by 4 in the morning, more efficient inspection stations will have to be developed such as those used at entrances to toll roads.[11]

Road construction is only justified in order to supply Israeli employers with Palestinian labor. Gaza's roads are in terrible condition. Those in refugee camps and in poorer areas of the Strip are unpaved; the rest are potholed and cracked. The best roads are those connecting Israeli settlements. The continued and unattended deterioration of existing roads in the Gaza Strip stands in stark contrast to the 1992 construction of a new forty kilometer road from the Erez checkpoint to Rafah, the entire length of the Strip, for use by Jewish settlers who wish to bypass Palestinian villages. Construction of the seventeen meter-wide road was made possible by the confiscation of private agricultural lands from neighboring Arab villages, especially Beit Lahiya.

Restrictions on municipal budgets also crippled local governments. According to Israeli military law, municipal governments had no legislative authority to generate revenue. They could not introduce new taxes, fees, or rates without approval of the authorities, which was sometimes given. Consequently, municipal governments depended heavily on donations for capital and development expenditure. These funds traditionally came from Israel, Jordan, and other Arab sources. Israel's financial contribution to municipal government was historically weak; gifts and grants to municipalities from other Arab countries were subject to Israeli restrictions on deposit sites, disbursement, and use.[12] Municipalities and other local institutions often were denied access to money already deposited for them by an external party.[13]

Given the many uncertainties surrounding external contributions from

Israel and the Arab world (as measured in the extraordinary budget), the only stable source of revenue accruing to municipalities derived from the ordinary budget. However, ordinary revenues were consistently unable to meet the development requirements of municipalities. As a result, the level of municipal services and development activities declined in real terms.

Weak revenue bases, coupled with a considerable reliance on external funds subject to military control, made it virtually impossible for municipal authorities to promote industrial and economic development in the Gaza Strip. Under present conditions the role of a seriously weakened municipal government in economic development remains problematic.

B. Chambers of Commerce

Chambers of commerce were established in the major cities of the Gaza Strip prior to Israeli occupation. From 1972 to 1992, elections for the chambers of commerce were suspended; terms were simply extended. Some chambers had served since 1965; members who left or died were not replaced.[14]

Chambers of commerce have played an even smaller and more indirect role in industrial and economic development than municipal governments. Although mandated to perform a broad range of functions, local chambers appear to have fulfilled only the following: coordinating agricultural and industrial exports to Jordan; issuing licenses and certificates of origin for exports to Jordan and the Arab world (a function that noticeably declined with Jordan's disengagement from the occupied territories in August 1988); helping local businesses import and market certain products; verifying and authenticating a variety of other documents (travel, biographical); channeling information between the military government and commercial bodies; representing commercial bodies to the military government; and conducting research on topics related to business and trade.[15]

With the intifada, the military government has impeded many of the traditional duties of the chambers of commerce, accelerating their institutional decline. In 1989, one chamber official in Gaza bemoaned, "there is no research, no planning and no support from other institutions here. We do not collect data, which is an important function of a chamber of commerce, and financially, one association cannot help another."[16] During the uprising, Gaza's chamber disseminated information on the effect of government measures on local economic conditions. The chambers of commerce have played a limited role in promoting commerce, and they have had virtually no input into the promotion of economic development generally, and industrial development specifically, either before or since the intifada.

C. Professional Associations

Professional associations, also important catalysts for industrial development, also have had limited economic impact in Gaza. In Gaza, the Association of Engineers (AE), among the largest and most active, is perhaps most important for indigenous economic change. Prior to the intifada, the association succeeded in getting the Gaza municipality to improve local standards of construction by requiring homebuilders to submit their drawings and plans for approval. The AE has encouraged members to design small-scale projects and helped them secure loans from foreign PVOs.

Beyond these limited activities, however, the AE was prohibited from performing functions that would empower it institutionally and enable it to contribute economically. The military government prohibited any action that it perceived might strengthen institutional capacity, wean Gaza's economic dependence on Israel, and compete with Israeli interests. For example, a battle of long duration between the association and the military government concerned the establishment of a materials testing laboratory in Gaza. The AE submitted the original proposal in 1981 through the U.S. Save the Children Federation (SCF) for $70,000 for a laboratory that would test concrete (consistency), steel (tension), and soil (bearing capacity). By 1989, the military government had not responded although it told the SCF to work with another organization on the grounds that the AE worked with the PLO.

Despite its nonresponse, the government conveyed to the AE that the proposal was a bad idea for three reasons. First, the authorities claimed that under Ottoman law associations do not have the authority to run a testing laboratory. Second, factories in Israel produce steel solely for the occupied territories, and the competition is not desired, particularly because this Israeli steel is of substandard quality and unusable in Israel.[17] Third, and perhaps most important from the Israeli point of view, the project would have given the association greater authority over local resources at the cost of Israeli control. In fact, the AE offered to establish a committee of five people, three of whom would be municipal (i.e., Israeli-appointed) officials, to oversee the laboratory. The military government refused. In a meeting between the AE chairman and Gaza's military governor, the former indicated that he was asking for technical, not political, authority for the laboratory and could not understand why the government was so adamant in its refusal. In reply, the governor indicated his concern that the PLO would take credit for the organization's success.[18] It appears that for the government the relationship between institutional success and political empowerment was direct and threatening.

Although successful in initiating a number of individual projects, the association was unable to exceed the parameters imposed on it (for reasons that are both internal and external in origin) and has had minimal influence on shaping local development initiatives, including industry. In this way, government restrictions inhibited the potential of the organization to act as an agent of economic development.

Private Institutions

In Gaza, there are many more private than public institutions. Private institutions were not organized as political or national entities; they were designed to provide needed social and economic services that (from Israel's point of view) provide for order and normalization. However, private institutions also were subject to the regulations described above. Some of these regulations aimed to limit the amount of credit available to local entrepreneurs. In so doing, Israeli policy constricted institutional behavior in order to isolate and fragment economic activity, a characteristic feature of de-development.

A. *Finance and Credit Institutions: Banks, Moneychangers, and Private Development and Credit Organizations*

In 1967, the military government closed all Arab banks operating in the occupied territories and took over the currency and all institutions engaged in financial activities such as post office banking, insurance companies, and cooperative societies.

Israeli banks were allowed to open branches, but only to perform two main functions: (1) to transfer funds and clear checks for Palestinians earning shekels; and (2) to provide services for Arab businesses importing and exporting products. Critically, although Israeli banks dealt in foreign currency, they were not permitted to supply long-term credit for industrial or other forms of productive development, nor did they provide financial intermediation. Indeed, Israeli banks channeled funds deposited by Palestinians to their home offices in Israel rather than lending them to Gazans. Thus, the role of Israeli banks in promoting economic development in Gaza, industrial or otherwise, was negligible.

In 1981, the military government allowed the Bank of Palestine to reopen its Gaza office. This remained the only open branch of a Palestinian bank in Gaza until 1990, when the Khan Younis branch was allowed to reopen. The authorities have prohibited the bank from holding any hard currency; thus, it could not engage in any foreign exchange transactions. Limited to the use of Israeli shekels, the Bank of Palestine has been unable to act as a financial intermediary and has been restricted to short-term, small-scale (primarily agricultural) loans in Israeli shekels. One of the bank's greatest handicaps has been its inability to issue letters of credit. Thus, although it has been the only bank in an area of over 800,000 people, it has not been able to support local enterprises.

Under considerable pressure from the United States, the Israeli authorities opened the Cairo–Amman bank in 1986. It was the only bank in the West Bank serving a population of more than one million people. The bank is allowed to deal in Israeli shekels and Jordanian dinars (JD); however, Gazans wishing to use the bank were restricted to shekels, because the dinar was not a recognized currency in Gaza. Although not as restricted as its counterpart in Gaza, the Cairo–Amman bank did not provide long-term capital, curtailing its significance as a source of finance. Indeed, the bank had approximately 85 million JDs on deposit in 1992, but only 11 million JDs were on short-term loan, such as letters of credit and overdrafts.[19] According to military law, the bank could not accept deposits in excess of a certain amount. On occasion, the government even ordered the bank to lower its interest rate in order to *discourage* deposits. Consequently, the bank has served mainly as a conduit for transfers and remittances, receiving deposits and issuing withdrawals. Because Israeli law has prohibited the bank from issuing loans or providing any credit facilities, most Palestinian financial transactions have taken place abroad, largely in Jordan.

Without Arab banks, moneychangers have become an important, albeit more informal, financial facility. Moneychanging is largely illegal, but many functions are tolerated by the authorities. Though prohibited in the Gaza Strip, moneychanging does occur. Moneychangers exchange currency, transfer money to accounts abroad, receive deposits, and issue loans. Deposits held in dinars and foreign currencies receive interest. Profits accrue in the form of interest on lending and commission on exchange. Most loans are limited to thirty days or (at most) a few months. Moneychangers' loans are rarely directed to high-risk, productive areas. As a result of their questionable legal status, moneychangers are unable to issue letters of credit or credit guarantees. Transactions remain undocumented and are based only on personal trust. In the event of fraud, there is no legal recourse. Thus, whereas some form of financial intermediation does occur (largely between local savings and commercial banks outside the territories), it is highly limited. Moneychangers cannot mobilize domestic savings.[20]

Thus, there has been no source of long-term credit in the Gaza Strip. This gap has been bridged in part by PLO, Arab, and foreign assistance. However, these donors have not always acted in the best interest of Gazan development, as is discussed below.

Israeli constraints on the development of a Palestinian financial infrastructure have eliminated savings institutions and intermediate and long-term lending institutions, a capital market, and working and fixed capital loans. By 1993, all that remained was one commercial bank and short-term internal borrowing. The lack of developed financial institutions also reflects institutional weakness in other, related sectors such as education and information systems. As a result, the services sector has remained woefully underdeveloped, unable to absorb the highly skilled and to make use of local comparative advantage. The limited amount of credit available for industrial and other forms of economic development has forced local entrepreneurs to rely on external economic assistance and expensive private credit.

Private development and credit organizations have tried to fill the credit vacuum. These organizations have played a limited but increasingly important role in the financing of industry and agriculture. Examples of such organizations include the Economic Development Group (EDG) and the Arab Development and Credit Company (ADCC). Although these organizations are based in Jerusalem, their impact extends to Gaza. The EDG has a branch in Gaza as well.

The EDG was established in 1986 in response to the perceived failure of foreign organizations working in the area of economic development. Its aim is to promote small to medium scale development projects in the occupied territories in order to relieve unemployment and encourage local production for local markets. EDG is registered as a nonprofit company based in East Jerusalem, operates according to Israeli law, and, before 1994, was one of very few Palestinian institutions operating in the area of economic development.[23]

The majority of funds disbursed by EDG comes from the European Union (EU) (formerly the European Economic Community [EEC]), the Arab Monetary Fund, and donor countries. By April 1988, EDG had lent more than $500,000 to support over 100 projects in the West Bank and Gaza Strip, including small-scale, labor-intensive light industry and agricultural projects. Between 1989 and 1991, the EEC granted the organization an additional $1 million based on EDG's success. By December 1991, approximately $1.8 million in loans had been disbursed to approved projects with a project average of $60,000.[22] EDG also provides business consulting, and although assistance to industry is limited in scope, EDG projects have generated some local employment opportunities.

In early 1989, the Israeli authorities attempted to interfere with the company's activities and ordered it to suspend its loan program. A conflict ensued over the control of EDG funds. As a licensed authority in East Jerusalem, the EDG is not subject to the same military laws prevailing in the occupied territories, which require organizations to get official permission before accepting outside funds. The EDG was able to distribute its funds in the West Bank and Gaza Strip without government intervention. Because of this, the military authorities wanted the EDG, which one Israeli official termed a "hostile organization," to open a bank account in the West Bank and transfer its funds into it. All transactions from this account would have had to be "coordinated" with the military, who insisted on knowing the amount distributed, the kind of project funded, and the name of the beneficiary. The organization refused, arguing that like its Israeli counterparts doing business in the occupied territories, it was not obliged to submit to such procedures, and that any demand that they do so was political, not legal in basis. In the end, the Israeli government relented, but only because of EEC pressure.

The ADCC has been operating in East Jerusalem since 1987 as a nonprofit credit organization and was similarly established in response to the poor performance of other local and foreign institutions. Before 1994, it operated in the West Bank and Gaza under the supervision of Israeli authorities, a condition of its establishment. It continues to operate under Israeli supervision in the West Bank. In 1987, the ADCC received $400,000 from the EEC and $100,000 from the Welfare Association, and by 1992 it had $2.5 million out in loans with monies received largely from the EU and individual European governments. Loans range in size from $1,000 to $25,000 for use in agriculture in support of such projects as land reclamation, irrigation, grape trellising, agricultural machinery purchases, water networks, greenhouses, and animal husbandry. Interest rates are low (4 percent to 5 percent), and repayment may be spread over five years.[23] The ADCC does not extend credit to industrial activities.

In 1987, the ADCC had a limited capital of 15,000 Israeli shekels (15 shares of 1,000 shekels each). Israeli-imposed restrictions on transferring and increasing these shares limited the company's ability to enlarge its capital. Some of these restrictions have since been lifted; however, the ADCC, together with other "soft" loan institutions, has been restricted by the authorities from having a savings component, a critical constraint on its ability to act as a financial mediator.

In addition to the problems created by Israeli restrictions, local differences between the West Bank and Gaza Strip have worsened existing problems. None of these credit organizations have given Gazan developers a fair share of funds. Of the 330 projects supported by the EDG in 1992, for example, only 25 (or 8 percent) were located in the Gaza Strip. The ADCC funded only one project in Gaza[24] out of 587. Arguably, the economic discrimination against Gaza is local, not foreign in origin. The reasons for this are several. Conceptually, the Gaza Strip has always been treated as an appendage of the West Bank, especially with regard to development planning. West Bankers have always looked down on their Gazan counterparts. Second, the Gaza Strip is a more difficult place in which to work, and one that many West Bank officials do not understand or care to learn about. Consequently, many lending institutions headquartered in the West Bank are unwilling to open branches in the Strip. Third, the occupation authorities have imposed more repressive constraints on development work in Gaza then they have in the West Bank. Fourth, the population is poorer, and much less experienced in entrepreneurship than are West Bankers. This is directly linked to Gaza's gross lack of experience with institutional development, which originated under Egyptian administration when most forms of participatory activity, particularly with regard to political and economic development, were prohibited. This continued under the Israelis and remains unchanged under the new Palestinian Authority. Thus, even despite the success of these organizations, their impact on Gaza has always been marginal, a reflection of cultural differences between the two territories that are not easily bridged.

B. Educational Institutions and Facilities

Education and training are vital for industrial and economic development. Technical and vocational training at all levels of the educational structure is critical for the creation of an industrial labor force. The overall lack of educational institutions devoted to industrial-based and technical/vocational training and restrictions on those few that have existed demonstrate how deinstitutionalization has contributed to the lack of structural reform in industry. This is especially true in the Gaza Strip.

The educational system is plagued by underfunding, overcrowding, inadequate facilities, poor physical infrastructure, and inadequate resources. These and other deficiencies place serious constraints on the physical expansion of classrooms and on the improvement of existing facilities and provide a weak pedagogical and structural framework for other educational initiatives and programs.

The majority of educational institutions in the Gaza Strip have been under the direction of the military government and UNRWA. In addition, a small percentage of private schools operate at the preschool and elementary school levels and in special education.[25] The government has provided education through the secondary school level, in addition to some vocational training, but no university education. Government-run schools have been the responsibility of the staff officer for education in the civil administration.

UNRWA has provided and continues to provide education for the registered refugee community in and outside the camps. UNRWA schools only operate at the elementary (Grades 1–6) and preparatory (Grades 7–9) levels. Refugee youth seeking secondary education transfer to government schools after completion of the preparatory cycle. UNRWA also provides some vocational training.

Under Israeli rule, education in the Gaza Strip suffered from a variety of government-imposed restrictions on the kinds of textbooks and curricula used,[26] the number of schools and classrooms that could be built, the expansion of existing schools, the number of teachers that could be hired, the kinds of courses that could be taught, and the kinds of departments that could be established.

The absence of a public sector and public institutions supporting educational development has been striking in the Gaza Strip, particularly in light of projected increases in enrollments. According to the Gaza Plan, enrollment in Gaza's elementary schools will remain constant at around 95 percent through the year 2000. Given the high rate of population growth, this will mean a 47 percent increase in the last decade of this century alone. Junior high enrollment will also remain steady at 83 percent, which means an increase of 66 percent in the number of students.

Perhaps most ominous for indigenous economic development are the trends among high school students. Between 1978 and 1986, the number in this group attending school steadily dropped from 54.1 to 42.8 percent and is expected to decline even further to 38.5 percent by the year 2000. According to the 1986 Jordanian development plan, 50 percent of Gaza/West Bank students entering first grade dropped out by the time they reached the ninth grade, the majority dropping out between the ages of 13 and 16. By comparison, in the East Bank, only 3.2 percent of students in this age group dropped out of school. Reasons for the decline include the absence of compulsory education beyond the junior high level, the dearth of academic opportunities at the postsecondary level, and the economic need for youth to join the labor force. In fact, student dropouts constituted 40 percent of *all* Arab laborers in Israel in 1986.[27]

High enrollments, especially at the elementary and junior high school levels, combined with government, financial, and spatial restrictions on the construction of new classrooms resulted in undesirably high classroom densities. The Gaza Plan indicates that in 1986, there were 43.6 elementary students per classroom, 44 junior high students per classroom, and 37.1 high-school students per classroom, despite the use of a two-shift teaching day. To lower classroom density to an "optimal" size of 35 students (a level greater than that prevailing in Israel) and eliminate the need for a second shift by the year 2000, the Gaza Plan estimated that 3,360 classrooms in 141 new schools would have to be built at a total cost of NIS 98.2 million.[28]

The deficit of classrooms is directly due to the deficit of land. Arab schools in the Gaza Strip are built on land plots next to other buildings so that there are many classrooms per dunum, although the acceptable standard, according to the Gaza Plan, is one classroom per half dunum. Classroom–land densities are highest in UNRWA schools in the refugee camps. To reach the acceptable standard, the area devoted to existing schools would have to be enlarged by at least 400 dunums. The construction of new classrooms will require an additional land allocation of 1,680 dunums to reach the optimal goal of 3,360 new classrooms.[29] Thus, in order to bring the sector up to minimal classroom–land standards, quite apart from the issue of classroom density, 2,080 additional dunums would have to be allocated to Gaza's educational institutions. Because the institutional structure supporting higher education at the academic and vocational levels has been extremely limited, the impact of this institutional deficiency on economic development has been quite profound.

Beyond the basic level, education for industry has been limited and unpopular. Students could choose postpreparatory vocational training or other vocational programs offered at the preparatory level or below. Both government and private institutions provided basic vocational training programs to students who completed preparatory school but did not enter academic high schools. Through 1993 there were eight vocational secondary schools in the West Bank but none in Gaza (Gazans could enroll in West Bank schools, however).[30] Four were government-run, and four were private. The (three-year) curriculum was both theoretical and practical but lacked scientific content; only men were enrolled. In 1987, only 4 percent of Gazan students at the secondary level were enrolled in vocational training schools; they are far less popular than academic institutions. Low enrollments were not due to lack of demand, however, because applicants outnumbered students three to one. This low percentage of vocational training enrollment contrasted sharply with educational distributions in Israel and other industrialized and industrializing countries.[31] Indeed, in Israel in 1986–87, 48 percent of Jewish secondary students and 16 percent of Arabs were enrolled in vocational institutions.[32] The lack of adequate vocational training institutions was due to government policies restricting their establishment.

Results from a 1988 survey comparing technical and vocational education at the postpreparatory level in the Gaza Strip/West Bank and Israel revealed the following: (1) the number of vocations taught in the occupied territories is less than half that found in Israeli schools; (2) the majority of vocations taught in Gaza and the West Bank are service-oriented (e.g., construction, plumbing, auto mechanics, tailoring, clerical); and (3) vocations *not* taught in the Gaza Strip and West Bank include those related to industrial development (such as fine electronics, mechanics, manufacturing tools, designing machines and industrial chemistry) and skilled vocations requiring high levels of expertise (such as jewelry, diamond cutting, and electronic instrument assembly).[33] Government-imposed restrictions in the occupied territories are largely responsible for these differences.[34]

Various studies conducted on the educational sector in the Gaza Strip and West Bank also reveal the significant shortage of applied education for engineering and industry at the postsecondary level.[35] The lack of such education at the postsecondary level is attributable to two key factors: official restrictions on the development of appropriate programs, particularly on institutions providing middle-level training in the engineering and industrial sciences; and the high premium placed on degree-based education by the local population.

The number of secondary school graduates greatly exceeds the absorptive capacity of existing postsecondary institutes and universities in Gaza. Only a few institutions offer theoretical and applied training in areas relevant to industry and economic development, and the development of new ones was, until 1994, officially restricted.[36] Since 1985, various organizations including American Near East Refugee Aid (ANERA) tried to establish a polytechnic institute in the Gaza Strip. The Israeli authorities refused all such requests. It was not until the spring of 1991, when security considerations prevented the large-scale migration of labor to Israel and worsening economic conditions in Gaza increased tensions, that the authorities gave permission to establish the College of Science and Technology in Khan Younis with European funding. By 1992, the college served 720 students and is projected to serve 2,000. Hence, the number of students entering industry-related areas is very low.

In addition to community colleges, the only existing training programs for specific industry-related fields are in universities. There are two universities in Gaza: Gaza Islamic and al-Azhar (opened only in 1991). Neither have engineering or applied science colleges although in 1993 Gaza Islamic began offering an engineering major. Would-be engineers who are not accepted into these colleges must seek admission to West Bank universities, or leave the country to study. Most Gazans cannot afford to do so.

Thus, available educational data reflect the paucity of institutional development and support for economically and industrially based activities in Gaza. The defining characteristics are: (1) the absence of any formal training in the engineering and industrial sciences; (2) low enrollment in vocational training at the secondary school level; (3) limited opportunities for professional and technical (middle level) training in the engineering and industrial sciences at the postsecondary school level; and (4) low enrollment levels in the engineering and industrial fields compared to other disciplines.

Israeli-imposed restrictions on a range of public and private institutions necessary for industrial development have thwarted the emergence of a viable industrial sector in Gaza. These restrictions, which collectively define deinstitutionalization, have constrained the institutional growth so critical for economic development overall.

Other Factors Contributing to Deinstitutionalization

The problems created for industrial development by Israeli policies leading to deinstitutionalization are exacerbated by two other factors: foreign assistance and local culture. Some key points will be highlighted.

Foreign Assistance

Deinstitutionalization in the Gaza Strip has been fuelled by the policies of foreign donors both Arab (e.g., the Jordanian government, Jordanian NGOs, the Jordanian–Palestinian Joint Committee, other Arab governments and Islamic groups, and the PLO) and non-Arab (e.g., UNRWA, United Nations Development Programme, the EEC, PVOs supported by the United States government and European governments, and a variety of nongovernmental sources). Foreign aid, in large part, has not been informed by development imperatives as articulated by Palestinians but rather by each donor's own political goals and funding priorities. This approach, combined with varying degrees of Israeli control over the receipt of external transfers, the distribution of foreign monies, and the selection of "recipient" institutions, has often served to perpetuate the economic and institutional status quo in the occupied territories instead of transforming it.

Overall, Arab aid, including that of the PLO, has been politically motivated. The criteria for disbursing aid have had little to do with promoting institutional development for economic reform and more to do with creating a political support base in the territories promoting a particular political agenda. Such ineffectivenes has particularly characterized aid to Gaza. The Gaza Strip, an area of decidedly less political importance than the West Bank, has consistently received only 10 percent to 25 percent of Arab aid to the occupied territories.

Jordanian government funding, for example, was motivated by the need to foster a pro-Hashemite constituency in the West Bank and to a lesser degree, Gaza, to protect Jordanian (not Palestinian) interests in the area. This meant protecting the status quo against any radical change and working within the confines of Israeli occupation policy.[37] Given its particular focus, Jordan's support to the industrial sector was extremely weak and indirect. It was largely restricted to guaranteeing long term, low-interest loans to municipalities for local development projects. As has been shown, however, municipal projects involving industry were highly restricted. For similar reasons, the Joint Committee, the primary source of development financing in the occupied territories from its establishment in 1978 through 1988, committed only 4.4 percent of its funds between 1979 and 1985 to industry and to the development of institutions designed to support industrial growth.[38] These monies were used largely to provide inputs into small-scale industry and to help municipalities establish two to three light industrial zones. They were not used to strengthen or promote the industrial sector's institutional base, particularly with regard to technical training. Moreover, whatever support was given to industrial projects went to the West Bank, not Gaza.

More than sixty non-Arab NGOs and international organizations were operating in the West Bank and Gaza Strip in the early 1990s. Non-Arab foreign assistance to the Gaza Strip and West Bank has played a limited role in industrial and economic development and promoting the institutional base needed to support economic reform. The aid has been largely humanitarian and social welfare (as provided by UNRWA, the largest single source of non-Arab foreign aid).[39] In many cases, the Israeli military authorities controlled the disbursement of funding and project implementation. In the absence of a national authority, the military government too often determined where and with whom international agencies could work, often to the exclusion of those institutions and those areas where assistance was most needed, such as industry.

Consequently, non-Arab donors have been criticized for providing services considered the responsibility of the occupying authorities and for providing those services in ways that facilitated occupation and Israeli control.[40] Moreover, in their zeal to "help" the Palestinian community, some international organizations such as UNRWA have unwittingly contributed to deinstitutionalization. For example, by paying their employees higher wages (and often for less work) than they could obtain elsewhere in Gaza, these organizations have made it difficult if not impossible for other local institutions to compete financially.[41]

Furthermore, although many of the assistance agencies resisted (to varying degrees) Israeli intervention in their affairs, their own internal organizational and bureaucratic imperatives, such as the need to expend their budgets by the end of the fiscal year and their unwillingness to confront or challenge the military authorities in any meaningful (i.e., political) way, often produced a situation of political appeasement where program success in the distribution of foreign assistance was measured more by the *number* of projects implemented rather than by the *kinds* of projects implemented.[42] In this way, agencies tried to fill the widening economic, social, and institutional void in Gaza in ways that often satisfied their own agendas rather than met Palestinians' needs. It was the funders and the occupier, therefore, who defined assistance goals, not the beneficiaries. Sometimes the two overlapped; more often, they diverged.[43] (Arguably, these problems have grown worse in the post–Oslo period as the level of donor assistance has increased.)

One example of how donors defined goals is found in donor-supported programs at institutions engaged in professional, technical, and vocational training. Designed to compensate for the deficiencies of existing institutions, these programs tended to be small in scale, to focus on sectors other than industry, and provide basic training and low levels of technical assistance. Comparatively few emphasized industrial development directly.[44] The reasons for the lack of emphasis on industry are two: internal donor priorities that did not include industry and donor programs than accommodated Israeli restrictions on projects that promoted industrial development.[45]

Indeed, studies of pre-1994 foreign-based technical training programs in the Gaza Strip and West Bank reveal clear patterns that not only reflect internal donor agendas but official priorities: a bias toward professional/academic education; an approach that focuses on the improvement rather than the transformation of conditions; the absence of a policy framework for training in all productive sectors; extremely limited resources for investment in technical training; very limited training directed to industrial development specifically and economic development generally; limited absorptive capacity; and weak linkages between existing vocational and technical education programs.[46]

Official hostility toward industrial and economic development created strong disincentives for donors to engage in activities that would be subject to intense scrutiny, harassment, and rejection. Indeed, many foreign assistance officials in Gaza and the West Bank openly admitted that since projects in various areas of training and industry were often rejected by Israel, they did not propose them. Therefore, donor-supported training was, characteristically, provided in isolated, nonintegrated pockets focused on specific institutions and individuals. The outcome was an uneven allocation of resources, as evident from the lack of occupation specializations, trained instructors, and maintenance technicians and low enrollment rates.

In the final analysis, however, the major constraint on institutional development in industry and other sectors was the absence of a central regulating authority operating in the interests of indigenous economic development. Without such an authority, economic requirements could not be linked to educational output. Without an appropriate policy and supporting infrastructure, there could be no accountability, standardized measures, criteria, or goals. In this context, planning for industry or any sector became highly decentralized, uncoordinated, and unchecked, a reflection of the crippled supporting institutional structure and the donors' competing goals. Whether the establishment of the Palestinian National Authority will reverse this situation remains to be seen.

Local Culture

A commonly overlooked problem contributing to deinstitutionalization is cultural. Gaza's historical experience with institutional development is far weaker than that of the West Bank, so there is little precedent for (and some would argue, even a bias against) intergroup cooperation and coordination. Many institutions in Gaza are one-person operations that work in relative isolation. They depend on one individual and, as is often the case, on that individual's political party. While this problem also exists in the West Bank, it is more acute in Gaza.

The Society for the Care of the Handicapped (SCH) in Gaza City is an example of a one-person operation. This organization is virtually alone in providing services to Gaza's approximately 30,000 mentally and physically disadvantaged residents. Through its thirteen programs, the Society now reaches over 4,500 people and employs 360. Despite its problems, the SCH has successfully responded to extant needs in an immediate and innovative way. Evaluations of the organization conducted by American special education professionals rate its performance on par with its American counterparts.

On the other hand, the SCH is dominated by and dependent on its chairman, Dr. Hatem Abu Ghazaleh, who has resisted any attempt to coordinate or integrate its work with other local organizations. The SCH survives entirely because of Dr. Abu Ghazaleh's fundraising acumen and his historical ability to defy Israeli restrictions through sheer strength of character and political savvy. Unlike many other institutional heads in Gaza, he is not affiliated with any political party. Without him, the SCH could not endure financially, an unfortunate but inevitable reality created by external constraints and internal weaknesses. Moreover, the absence of middle management, which characterizes many such organizations, also affects institutional viability. There is no cadre of semi-professional line managers, nor have there been programs to train them. This has been a serious impediment to development, because institutions have had no organizational structure or framework for institutionalizing operating procedures.

Lack of experience with development and national planning in the Palestinian context has perpetuated cultural norms. Although the intifada mitigated this problem, it did not eradicate it. Many local institutions engage in overlapping activities, competing not only for the same limited resources (in order to perform the same function and provide the same service) but for the same client base. Projects are duplicated, forcing some to fold because of limited marketing capacity. Such duplication only feeds de-development. In certain situations, Palestinian institutions have been able to exploit this problem by seeking and receiving services or funds from more than one institutional source with little investment or risk. This has been especially true of many foreign development-oriented initiatives whose resources have been used inefficiently and sometimes wasted.

Institutional development is further constricted by the factional basis on which many local institutions are organized. Political factionalism ties the target population to specific individuals and groups. It also isolates activity and its attendant problems within clearly demarcated and narrowly defined boundaries. The continued segmentation of institutional activities along political lines creates *constituencies* rather than *structures* and reduces the possibility for integrated development planning. All too often, individual institutions and persons benefit at the expense of systemic change. As a result, change or reform at the institutional level has been, at best, functional rather than structural. Although it is possible to capitalize certain kinds of economic activities, it is not yet possible to institutionalize them fully.[47]

Conclusion

Deinstitutionalization policies have been extremely damaging for indigenous structural reform and infrastructural growth. Without institutions and the proper linkages to support them, needed reform and growth, on which rational economic development is based, have been confined within narrow structural boundaries. The local institutional sector in the occupied territories suffers from critical deficiencies, largely Israeli-imposed. These deficiencies have proved particularly damaging for the development of municipal government, and educational and financial institutions. As has been shown, weakened organizational capacity affects both public and private institutions in the Gaza Strip and has resulted directly from Israeli measures designed to weaken the external and internal environment of the institution, leaving little if any control over institutional decision-making in the hands of Palestinians. Such weakness has rendered institutions unable to redress their problems, let alone launch new programs.

To varying degrees and in varying ways, external funders contributed to deinstitutionalization in the Gaza Strip. Despite a clear economic rationale, foreign aid has been largely motivated by political considerations. Programs have been set according to internal bureaucratic priorities rather than prioritized indigenous needs. Together with the constraints imposed by Israeli interventionism and by the local environment, these considerations have (despite notable achievements) created a situation where development assistance has been disbursed in a manner that was unplanned, unorganized, unintegrated, and haphazard. (In the post-Oslo period, little has changed in this regard.)

Furthermore, foreign donors have a poor record of promoting networking and coordination among local organizations in the occupied territories. They have also failed to develop strong relations with indigenous institutions across sectors, or to support productive activities that would encourage vital economic reform. Many of the problems affecting Palestine's institutional structure have been aggravated by these donors, whose selective funding has exacerbated the highly individualistic orientation of local institutions and their unwillingness to work together.

Another serious problem affecting the development of internal capacity has been the remarkable lack of interinstitutional coordination or cooperation that derives from cultural practices that do not favor such cooperation. Funding discrimination against the Gaza Strip, moreover, has fueled deinstitutionalization, making it impossible to speak of integration with West Bank institutions. The almost complete absence of relations with Israeli institutions, a direct outcome of the political situation, has intensified existing constraints on institutional development. The indigenous institutional structure supporting productive change is weakened and productive change is rendered largely impossible, a key characteristic of de-development.

Notes to Chapter 9:

1. Hiltermann, *Behind the Intifada*, p. 54.

2. Ibid., p. 50.

3. See Sara Roy, *The Palestinian Industrial Sector: Structure, Institutional Framework and Future Requirements* (Vienna: UNIDO, 1989).

4. See, for example, Muhammad al-Khass, "Municipal Legal Structure in Gaza, in Emile A. Nakleh (ed.), *A Palestinian Agenda for the West Bank and Gaza* (Washington, D.C.: American Enterprise Institute, 1980), pp. 102–106; Sasson Levi, "Local Government in the Administered Territories," in Daniel J. Elazar (ed.), *Judea, Samaria and Gaza: Views on the Present and Future* (Washington, D.C.: American Enterprise Institute, 1982), 103–122; and Mahmoud Talab Nammoura, "Palestinian Municipal Councils under Israeli Occupation: 1967–1989" (Research paper prepared for the American Near East Refugee Aid [ANERA], Hebron, West Bank, May 1989).

5. Emile A. Nakhleh, *The West Bank and Gaza: Toward the Making of a Palestinian State* (Washington, DC: American Enterprise Institute, 1979), pp. 12–13.

6. M. Benvenisti, *The West Bank Handbook: A Political Lexicon*, p. 157.

7. al-Khass, "Municipal Legal Structure in Gaza," in Nakhleh (ed.), p. 14.

8. P.G. Sadler, U. Kazi, and E. Jabr, p. 58.

9. Gaza Plan, Section 15.1.1.

10. Sadan, *A Policy for Immediate Economic-Industrial Development*, 6.

11. Gaza Plan, Sections 12.2.3–12.2.4.

12. State of Israel, *Statistical Abstract of Israel 1988*.

13. In Gaza, one institution consistently targeted in this way was the Red Crescent Society, the Palestinian version of the Red Cross, under the direction of Dr. Haidar Abd al-Shafi. Not only was Dr. Abd al-Shafi prohibited from having access to money deposited in the Red Crescent account, including USAID funds, but he had to obtain permission from the military authorities for all withdrawal requests.

14. This has also been true of the moribund trade union movement in Gaza, whose seven unions, operating under severe Israeli restrictions, claimed only 500 members, or roughly 1 percent of all workers employed domestically.

15. Interviews with Chamber of Commerce officials in the Gaza Strip, 1989.

16. Ibid.

17. Interview with a former official of the civil administration in Gaza, 1989.

18. Interview with the Chairman of the Engineers Association, Gaza City, April 1989.

19. Gubser, p. 5.

20. Laurence Harris, "Money and Finance with Underdeeloped Banking in the Occupied Territories," in Abed (ed.), pp. 192–99; UNCTAD, *The Palestinian Financial Sector*, pp. 61–65.

21. Economic Development Group (EDG) position paper, Jerusalem, 1987.

22. Ma'an Development Center, *The Role of Credit Institutions in Local Development*, (Jerusalem, 1991), p. 16.

23. Brian Miller, "NGOs working for Palestinian development," *Al-Fajr*, 2 December 1991.

24. Interview with Basil Eleiwa, Program Officer, AMIDEAST, Gaza Strip, 1992. See also Salah Abdul Shafi, "Gaza Strip: The forgotten part of Palestine," *Al-Fajr*, 3 August 1992.

25. See Roy, *The Gaza Strip Survey*, pp. 87–91.

26. In UNRWA school, additional restrictions are imposed by UNESCO, the educational arm of the United Nations system.

27. Hashemite Kingdom of Jordan, *A Programme for Economic and Social Development in the Occupied Territories 1986–1990—Summary* (Amman: Ministry of Planning, November 1986), 7/3–7/4.

28. Gaza Plan, Tables 9.4–9.7.

29. Ibid., Sections 9.0–9.5.

30. See Mahmoud Mi'ari, *Vocational Education in the Occupied Territories* (Bir Zeit, West Bank: Center of Documents and Research, Bir Zeit University, 1988).

31. Mi'ari, p. 7; Atif A. Kubursi, "Jobs, Education and Development: The Case of the West Bank," in Abed (ed.), p. 237.

32. Mi'ari, p. 8. See also Aziz Haidar, *Vocational Education in the Arab Schools in Israel* (Bir Zeit, West Bank: Center of Documents and Research, Bir Zeit University, 1985); and Hasan al-Qeeq, *Vocational Education in the Occupied Territories* (Jerusalem: Arab Thought Forum, 1988).

33. Mi'ari, pp. 7, 12–14.

34. Ibid.

35. In-house studies of the American Middle East Service and Training (AMIDEAST), 1975–1985, Jerusalem and Washington, D.C.

36. Except where noted, the data presented in this section are taken from Munther W. Masri, *The Gaza Technical Center*, Project document prepared for the American Near East Refugee Aid Committee (ANERA), Washington, D.C., and the Benevolent Society, Gaza Strip, June 1988.

37. This point became clear in a series of interviews with officials in the Department of Palestinian Affairs, Ministry of Foreign Affairs, Hashemite Kingdom of Jordan, Amman, December 1988. See also, Hashemite Kingdom of Jordan, *A Note on Jordan's Progress for the Economic and Social Development of the Occupied Territories* (Amman: Ministry of Planning, n.d.).

38. UNCTAD, *The Palestinian Financial Sector under Israeli Occupation* (1987), p. 151. For a discussion of Joint Committee aid, see Ibrahim Dakkak, "Development from Within: A Strategy for Survival," in Abed (ed.), pp. 287–310.

39. See financial statements found in selected years of the *Report of the Commissioner-General of the United Nations Relief and Works Agency for Palestine Refugees in the Near East*, General Assembly, United Nations, New York.

40. This criticism was expressed in a series of interviews with Palestinian, American, and European development consultants between 1985 and 1993.

41. This sentiment was expressed in interviews with officials in several local institutions in the Gaza Strip, 1988–1989.

42. See, for example, Sara Roy, "Development under Occupation?: The Political Economy of U.S. Aid to The West Bank and Gaza Strip," *Arab Studies Quarterly* 13 (Summer/Fall 1991): 65–89.

43. See K. Nakhleh.

44. Based on extensive interviews with PVO officials in the West Bank and Gaza Strip, 1985, 1986, and 1989.

45. See United States Agency for International Development (USAID), *U.S. Economic Assistance to the West Bank and Gaza: A Positive Contribution to the Palestinian People From the American People*, Draft, Washington, D.C., March 1989, p. ii; and M. Benvenisti, *U.S. Government Funded Projects*.

46. USAID, *U.S. Economic Assistance*; Roy, *Development under Occupation*.

47. See Sara Roy, "Gaza: New Dynamics of Civic Disintegration," *Journal of Palestine Studies* 22, no.4 (Summer 1993): 20–31.

PART III:

Continued Economic Dislocations

10

The Intifada—Economic Consequences of a Changing Political Order

A lthough Israel did not start out planning the economic de-development of the Gaza Strip after 1967, precedents for such policy existed, and they were carried to their logical extreme twenty years later when the Palestinian uprising (intifada) against Israeli rule began. In a 1977 *Jerusalem Post* interview, Moshe Dayan commented, "The trouble in Gaza stopped not just because Arik [Sharon] went in there with the army, but because we also let them go to work in Tel Aviv without papers or permits. They're 'hanging loose' now. They don't shoot because they have something better to do."[1] The same faulty assumptions that guided Dayan's thinking in 1977 also shaped the behavior of the prestate *yishuv*. Although structural integration (in the case of the former) and structural separation (in the case of the latter) produced a very different set of economic relations between Arabs and Jews, the political implications of "hanging loose" were much the same in 1977 as they had been four decades earlier. At both times, the Zionist leadership failed to recognize that economic appeasement would not extinguish the need for, or compensate for the loss of, political self-determination. In fact, this same failure crystallized Palestinian nationalism and popular rejectionism prior to 1948 and again in December 1987. In this sense, therefore, the intifada must be understood as a revolt against Zionist colonization, as well as against Israeli military occupation.

Political developments

The intifada, which in Arabic means "the shaking off," broke out in the twentieth year of Israeli occupation in response to the oppressive conditions and erosion of life under occupation. The uprising erupted spontaneously in Gaza's Jabalya refugee camp; within days, it had engulfed the Gaza Strip and the West Bank. Despite its unplanned beginnings, the intifada was rapidly transformed into a highly organized and structured rebellion. It aimed to achieve the very goals the state had consistently sought to eclipse: to decrease Palestine's economic dependence on Israel, make the territories increasingly ungovernable, and end the occupation.

One year after the first demonstration in Jabalya, Yasir Arafat participated in an historic compromise by declaring the PLO's recognition of Israel, acceptance of UN resolution 242 and a two-state solution, and renunciation of terrorism. Neither Arafat nor the PLO would have undertaken a political step of such magnitude without popular pressures from Gaza and the West Bank. The United States responded by opening a dialogue with the PLO in December 1988, and the peace process, which for so long had eluded Palestinians, was finally underway.

Palestinians in Gaza genuinely believed that political progress was possible primarily because of U.S. involvement. Many Gazans were optimistic when the U.S.–PLO dialogue began. During the eighteen months that followed, however, popular faith in America's resolve began to erode. Meanwhile, living conditions in the occupied territories deteriorated rapidly as a direct consequence of Israeli-imposed economic pressures, which the United States refused to condemn officially. Israel's increasingly brutal suppression of the intifada remained similarly unchallenged, as did the government's political intransigence and lack of reciprocity.

Under growing U.S. and international pressure to respond (or at least give the appearance of responding) to Palestinian initiatives, Prime Minister Shamir proposed a plan in February 1989 for elections in the Gaza Strip and West Bank to select Palestinian representatives to negotiations. Shamir ultimately rejected his own plan. However, the election plan was but one part of a four-point agenda originally proposed by Prime Minister Shamir. The full plan, which the United States chose not to publicize at the time, reveals Israeli intentions toward the occupied territories.

In addition to elections, the Shamir plan underscored the return of the Sinai peninsula to Egyptian sovereignty as agreed in the Camp David Accords. The Israeli government argued that by meeting this condition, it had fulfilled UN resolution 242, which calls for the return of territories acquired by Israel in the 1967 war in exchange for peace. Hence, as far as the West Bank and Gaza Strip were concerned, there was nothing to negotiate. Second, the plan called for the normalization of relations between Israel and the Arab states as a precondition for the resolution of the Palestinian-Israeli conflict. The government argued that because the Arab states had no territorial dispute with the state of Israel, the conflict between them would be easier to resolve. Thus, the dispute no longer focused on territory but on political normalization.

The Palestinian agenda, which was centered on territorial return in exchange for peace, was completely submerged. Indeed, in the aftermath of the Gulf war, Palestinians feared the worst from this "two-track" approach. As the United States pursued its own political agenda in the region, which sought greater normalization between Israel and the Arab states, Palestinians feared their priorities might be sacrificed. This fear was reinforced by the third pillar of the Shamir plan, which designated the longstanding refugee situation as a humanitarian rather than as a political problem. Consequently, Palestinian refugees would not be able to make political claims on Israel, nor could they seek redress on political grounds, thereby precluding their stated right of return, as well as the historical reasons invoked in support of this right. (The Gaza–Jericho Agreement, which is discussed in the last chapter, rests on similar assumptions.)

The critical event that finally disabused Gazans of their faith in America and confirmed their sense of betrayal was not the actual suspension of the dialogue between the United States and the PLO in the summer of 1990, but an event that preceded it: the American veto of a UN resolution calling for an observer force in the West Bank and Gaza after an Israeli reservist killed seven Palestinian laborers in Rishon Le Ziyyon in May 1990. For many Gazans, the events in Rishon propelled them to seek different paths to the establishment of their state, and new ways of filling the vacuum created by the "departure" of the United States. In August 1990, Iraq became that way.

Economic Developments

A discussion of the changes imposed on the Gaza economy during the intifada requires two levels of analysis: the external and the internal. At the external level, the government of Israel attempted to quell the intifada through a policy of military action and economic sanction; this policy imposed even greater burdens on an already weakened economy. At the internal Palestinian level, the demand for change on the basis of greater independence from Israeli market forces resulted in a new economic strategy emphasizing production over consumption, and a new turning inward toward local rather than Israeli markets. In the words of one Palestinian economist, We were not weak because we weren't working, we were weak because we never were conserving."[2]

In their efforts to formulate a new strategy, one problem confounding Palestinians in the Gaza Strip was the weak historical precedent for economic reform. There was a lack of entrepreneurship in Gaza; whatever entrepreneurship existed had been depressed by a history of administrative mismanagement and poor planning, lack of capital, and aversion to risk. In Gaza there has been no real accumulation of experience. The historical evolution of the economy has always been almost singularly linked to: (1) the production of citrus, an economic activity traditionally oriented toward export rather than local consumption, and the only activity that involved any degree of long-range planning; and (2) services, the largest sectoral employer.

These problems compounded the already significant constraints on the implementation of new economic initiatives, political success notwithstanding. Consequently, the rare political will and social cohesion generated by the intifada were necessary but insufficient for the economic task at hand. The political will created by the uprising consistently exceeded the economic capabilities needed to translate that will into effective and sustainable change, especially in the Strip. However, important and unprecedented changes did nonetheless take place. How did the uprising affect Gaza's economy, and what were the implications for the de-development process?

Palestinian Measures and Israeli Policy Responses

In the years since the intifada began, the Palestinian economy has experienced basic changes.[3] In the period preceding the Gulf war, these changes were characterized by a lessening of the economic dependence on Israel, achieved to a large extent through the Palestinian boycott of Israeli commodities; a new emphasis on grassroots institution-building; and a willingness to incur and endure economic and social deprivation in order to achieve political independence.

The changed political and economic relationship between Israel and the occupied territories was characterized by other developments as well: the diminished capacity of the domestic economies in the Gaza Strip and West Bank to provide productive alternatives to wage labor in Israel; increasing economic burdens imposed on the Palestinian population; and greater dependence on external aid. In the months following Iraq's invasion of Kuwait, furthermore, economic conditions in the territories rapidly deteriorated. Palestinian popular support for Iraq resulted in a significant loss of economic assistance from the Gulf states, a loss that has imposed considerable damage on the Palestinian economy, especially in Gaza (see chapter 11).

In response to the different conditions that emerged during the intifada, two essential economic changes occurred in the first two years of the uprising. On the one hand, a new development paradigm emerged; on the other, the Palestinian domestic economy was steadily eroded.

The political changes wrought by the Palestinian uprising in its first two years were accompanied by a fundamental attitude change that produced a new development paradigm. This paradigm was characterized by a new emphasis on self-reliance. Two key alterations in economic activity took place: (1) a shift in emphasis from consumption to production; and (2) a reorientation in economic strategy from external competition with and employment in Israel to internal, local production for local markets. Although economic activity in Gaza was geared to addressing the immediate needs and burdens imposed by the intifada, it also aimed to redefine development according to local needs and criteria. These changes represented the first attempt to reverse the de-development process.

The intifada recast the orientation of the economy, but at a considerable price. Before 1967, the Gaza economy was oriented to production for consumption at a subsistence level, but after 1967, consumption levels markedly increased, exceeding those of production.[4] With the intifada, however, and the attempt to disengage structurally from Israel, the economic behavior shifted inward to produce more than was consumed to enable investment and thereby encourage growth. However, this shift was incurred at great economic cost because the local economy not only found itself approaching levels of subsistence and production unknown since before the Israeli occupation, but was unable to pursue any productive investment at the macroeconomic level, the critically needed next step.

The new populist commitment to locally based and indigenously organized change not only represented a departure from earlier Palestinian (and Arab) strategies which emphasized *sumud* or steadfastness, but was also the first attempt on the part of the Palestinians to act collectively as a nation with the objective of wresting some control from the Israeli establishment. In fact, this national coalescing and the changed attitudes that made it possible constituted the greatest threat to Israeli control; they were the driving force behind the official decision to employ economic as well as military means to suppress the intifada.

The Gaza Strip and West Bank economies suffered significant declines during the intifada. The economic sanctions imposed by Israel and the measures demanded by the Unified National Leadership of the Uprising created extreme hardships for Palestinians. In the first three years of the uprising, per capita GNP in the Gaza Strip fell by 41 percent from $1,700 to $1,000, which was below the poverty level for a couple and for a family of four living in Israel in 1989. The fall in GNP resulted from four factors: a 20 percent to 30 percent decline in the value of output in all economic sectors except agriculture which experienced lesser declines (itself originating in the reduced number of hours worked); a significant reduction in the level of trade between Israel and the occupied territories; a dramatic loss in income from work in Israel; and a decline of 70 percent in the level of remittances from the Gulf.[5] Initially, losses were offset by savings, but savings were soon seriously depleted. For an increasing number of Palestinians, net real income dropped by 40 percent to 50 percent compared to pre-intifada levels.[6]

The run on private savings held in Gaza and abroad further curtailed the role of savings and investment in local economic growth. A survey of approximately 300 Palestinians in the Gaza Strip between 1988–89 suggested that personal income for many families had fallen by as much as 75 percent from 1987. Although this finding could not be generalized to the entire population, it indicated emerging trends.[7]

In Gaza, the serious reduction in private income soon changed consumption, savings, and investment patterns. Initially, the drain on household income slowed consumption of luxury goods; by the second year of the intifada, consumption of basic goods was also down sharply as the standard of living plummeted. With continued Israeli restrictions on domestic income generation, employment in Israel, and access to external capital, indigenous financial resources were steadily diminishing and Gazans, in particular, were forced to adopt a range of austerity measures (such as the development of home economies) in order to stave off absolute impoverishment. Ironically, the same conditions that encouraged the creation of a new economic paradigm also imposed severe economic hardship on the population.

Within the first year of the intifada, Israeli policy in the occupied territories grew more restrictive and was shaped by two priorities: to insure and intensify existing economic dependencies in favor of the Israeli economy; and to extinguish the intifada through the use of extreme economic pressure.[8] Toward these ends, Defense Minister Rabin stated in February 1989, "We have to strike a balance between actions that could bring on terrible economic distress and a situation in which [the Palestinians] have nothing to lose, and measures which bind them to the Israeli administration and prevent civil disobedience."[9] Israel's measures together with those imposed by the Palestinian leadership (see below) devastated economic conditions in the Gaza Strip and seriously eroded the ability of the majority of the population to maintain their pre-intifada standard of living. Growing austerity also threatened one of the intifada's greatest achievements—the attitudinal change that catalyzed and supported the very political and economic reforms with which it was associated.[10]

A. *Israeli Restrictions: Curfews and Magnetic Identification Cards—Impact on Laborers*

The most immediate measures used by Israel against Palestinians were curfews and the magnetic identification cards. Curfews were imposed far more often in Gaza than the West Bank and the magnetic ID cards were imposed on Gazans only. These measures were designed to target Gaza's labor force, especially those working in Israel.

In the first year of the uprising, the most populated areas of the Gaza Strip were under curfew an average of 30 percent of the year. In some of Gaza's refugee camps, that average was as high as 42 percent of the year, or 153 days.[11] During curfews residents were forbidden to leave their homes. This meant workers lost a day's wage for each day of curfew. Measures imposed by the Palestinian Unified Leadership hurt Gazan laborers as well. In 1988 and 1989, the Unified Leadership called 152 strike days in Gaza, which meant that travel was prohibited and workers were unable to leave for Israel.

As a result of the various restrictions described, in 1988 and 1989, Palestinians from the Gaza Strip worked in Israel an average of three to four days per week or twelve to sixteen days per month, a decline of 33 percent to 50 percent from 1987. A classified Ministry of Defense report indicated that the average number of work days for the Gaza Strip in the first two quarters of 1989 was 14.2. The report goes on to state that:

[I]f the curfews and strikes in the territory keep the number of days worked in Israel at the current level, the entire sector is likely to disintegrate . . . . the key for improving the economy of the Gaza Strip is the number of work days in Israel and in the area . . . [and the downward trend in the economy] will continue as long as there is no substantial increase in the number of work days.[12]

One measure uniquely affecting Gazan laborers was the magnetic identification card program. Since August 1989, Israeli authorities have required all Gazan laborers to obtain a magnetic ID card in order to enter Israel. In order to qualify for the card, a Palestinian must have no record of "criminal" (i.e., political) activity and must have paid all his taxes. Any history of political activity constitutes grounds for disqualification. As a result, the number of Gazan laborers with permission to work inside Israel averaged 40,000 to 50,000 in 1989, down from 70,000 to 80,000 before the intifada. Furthermore, Palestinians were often assessed exorbitant taxes when applying for the magnetic card. Individuals unable to pay were denied cards; others did not even apply for fear of being targeted by Israeli tax authorities. The card cost $10, a significant sum for many Gazans. According to a Ministry of Defense official, the proceeds were intended to finance the installation of protective windows on vehicles owned by Israeli settlers living in the Strip.[13] The card is still required of Gazans wishing to enter Israel.

Although the magnetic card program was meant to monitor and control the movement of Gazan workers into Israel in order to contain the damage to the Israeli economy, it was, in the words of one Israeli security official, "one of a series of measures aimed at tying the individual to the central authority."[14]

Curfews and general strikes also imposed losses on Gaza's domestic labor force. Additionally, local merchants observed a daily strike that restricted all commerce to the hours of 9:00 A.M. to 1:00 P.M. (This was in force until April 1992, when hours were extended to 3:00 P.M.) Consequently, local businesses remained open four hours per day for an average of four days per week, a decline of 66 percent in the total number of commercial hours per week, which represented a particular blow to the Palestinian middle class. In February 1989, Israel's Ministry of Defense calculated that the number of days worked per month in both Gaza and the West Bank averaged only 10.[15] As a result of the various measures imposed, the Gaza Strip suffered from a severe cash liquidity problem and rising unemployment, which local economists estimated to be as high as 35 percent prior to the Gulf war.[16]

B. The Taxation Campaign

In response to a Palestinian tax boycott that significantly decreased tax revenues during the first year of the intifada especially, the Israeli government began an intensive taxation campaign that proved particularly damaging to the local economy and personal welfare. By 1989, for example, Israeli revenues from income taxes were reduced by $27.9 million, and losses from value added taxes (VAT) amounted to an additional $76.5 million.[17] To compensate for the loss, the government instituted a variety of tax collection methods, both legal and illegal, none of which were coordinated with the state's income tax commissioner.[18]

These methods included tax assessments, the establishment of a border customs office, and changes in tax brackets. Tax assessments were levied against merchants, agricultural producers, factory owners, and businessmen of all incomes. Although the use of assessments was considered legal, taxes were often imposed arbitrarily, levied at excessively high rates with little evidence of proper financial accounting and with little if any possibility of appeal for the taxpayer. This approach to tax collection represented a departure from methods used before the uprising. Assessments ranged from $5,000 to $500,000 and commonly exceeded annual revenues for a given commercial establishment. Often, a merchant would be taxed an amount that was not based on any discernable form of accounting; many reported that their books and accounts showed they owed a much smaller sum than their excessive assessment. Failure to pay an assessment resulted in the revocation of many critical rights and privileges. Informing for the authorities, on the other hand, assured privileges and exemption from untoward taxation.[19]

As a consequence of high assessments, which taxpayers usually could not pay, attachments were placed on private commercial and personal property. Attached assets were sold at public auctions in Israel and were usually valued twice as high as the initial assessments. None of the financial proceeds from the sale of the property were returned to the merchants to whom they belonged. This policy of excessive assessments was not practiced in Israel.

In December 1988, the Israeli authorities also opened a customs office at Erez, the main entrypoint into the Gaza Strip from Israel. The border customs office was used primarily to collect excise-added (VAT) taxes. Customs officials stopped all commercial and private vehicles carrying merchandise across the Gaza–Israel border and required proof of purchase or invoices for all transported items. If appropriate documentation was not provided, goods, including perishable items, would be impounded at the customs checkpoint at a cost of $15 per day until such documentation was obtained. Once goods were seized, an investigation was conducted, which ranged in length from two weeks to two months. All impounded items were held until a settlement was reached. The taxpayer was usually presented with an assessment that could only be challenged within thirty days. Once the taxpayer agreed to a given assessment, it had to be paid together with interest, fines, and inflation differentials. If no formal settlement was reached, the amount of the assessment was treated as the taxpayer's debt that had to be paid.

In January 1988, the Israeli government further introduced a change into its income tax law. This change raised tax brackets for Palestinians and assessed them at a higher tax rate than Israelis. For example, Palestinians earning

$16,000 were taxed at 55 percent; Israelis did not reach the top tax rate until annual income reached $30,000 (even then, the rate was only 48 percent). Based on a direct tax per person, the average family in Gaza (consisting of seven persons) owed a relatively higher tax than the average family in Israel (four persons). At an income level of $100 per person per year, for example, the effective tax in the Gaza Strip was $150, compared to $0 in Israel. At an income level of $200 per person per year, Gazans paid $600 in tax, whereas Israelis paid $200.[20]

Moreover, on tax-related issues, Palestinians (unlike Israelis) did not have recourse to courts of law in their place of residence. Rather, they could only appeal to review boards that were appointed by the military commander of each territory and composed of military officers or officials of the civil administration. Palestinians did not have representatives on these boards, and all decisions were final, with no possibility of appeal.[21]

According to Israel's Ministry of Defence, the government budget for the Gaza Strip and the West Bank in 1987–88 and 1988–89 was approximately $247 million.[22] As a result of the extraordinary tax collection measures in 1988, the Israeli government collected a sum total of tax that exceeded budgetary predictions by $55 million.[23] B'tselem, an Israeli human rights group, reported that $27 million of the surplus was transferred to the budgets of the territories; the other half was deposited into the Israeli treasury, designated for future fiscal use.[24] The government contribution was used largely to maintain a police force in the occupied territories.[25] Approximately $6.5 million was also allocated to IDF salaries, automobile allowances, and reserve duty compensation.[26]

Despite the surplus that accrued to the government treasury, Israeli authorities consistently maintained that a decrease in collected taxes since the beginning of the intifada had forced them to reduce the regular budgets of the Gaza Strip and West Bank by 30 percent, to eliminate the development budget altogether (after 1988), to reduce funds for public services, particularly in the education and healthcare sectors, and to cut welfare payments to thousands of needy families. Given that the budget for 1989 was the same as 1988 (although the population grew by 44,000 people and the currency was devalued), the actual level of services provided to the territories had clearly diminished. Military government officials in Gaza requested that American PVOs working in the area finance projects in education and health, which the government claimed it could no longer finance.[27]

Interestingly, a classified report issued by Israel's defense ministry in 1990 indicated that the original amount allocated for the West Bank and Gaza Strip in 1988 was $346 million, not the $247 million that was actually spent. It appears, therefore, that with the outbreak of the intifada, the budget was cut by $100 million. An additional $62 million budgeted for development was eliminated entirely. The document goes on to speculate what the budget would have looked like had the intifada not occurred. As a result of the intifada, the regular budget of the occupied territories was cut by $347 million and the development budget by $205 million over a three-year period.[28] These cuts may have been punitive or taken in response to declining tax revenues. Clearly, however, some funds were available and were not used.

C. Permits and Licenses

The Israeli government required permits and licenses for many basic activities and economic endeavors. They were important tools used by the Israeli authorities to control and regulate social activity and economic growth in the occupied territories. During the intifada, the Israeli government introduced two regulations that made the acquisition of permits and licenses onerous. Military Order 1262, issued on 17 December 1988, conditioned the acquisition of needed documents on payment of all taxes including income, property, and VAT. This order applied to permits and licenses in twenty-three different categories. Furthermore, before an application for a permit in any one of these areas was considered, approvals had to be obtained from seven authorities: the police; the departments of income tax, property tax, and excise-added tax; the civil administration; the municipality or village head, who was often a collaborator with the military authorities; and the Ministry of Interior. Each charged a fee. The Shin Bet was often included as well.[29] The process was long, cumbersome, expensive, and humiliating. Individuals with prison records or unpaid taxes were denied documents. Given the time and the expense of acquiring permits and licenses, many people went without them. This often happened in the case of home construction and establishment of small-scale businesses or factories. Without the necessary permits, both activities were considered illegal under military law. If discovered, the house or factory would be destroyed and the owner fined.

D. Levies and Fines

The military government charged new levies and fines for a variety of bureaucratic procedures and offenses during the intifada. In Gaza, levies were assessed for the following procedures, all conditioned on the payment of taxes: special car inspections incurring a range of costs (in fact, millions of shekels were invested in building a car checkpoint to which every vehicle with a fault, no matter how minor, was sent for repair)[30]; $10 to $25 for replacing each of the identification cards of the entire adult population[31]; $250 to $440 for replacing license plates on each of Gaza's 25,000 registered vehicles; $20 for what was termed the "Good Gazan" sticker, required of all licensed vehicles traveling to Israel; and between $30 to $315 in registration fees for replacing donkey-cart license plates.

In addition, the government imposed a series of highly punitive fines: $10,000 and five years in jail for shooting firecrackers to celebrate Palestinian holidays; $1,000 to $1,500 assessed to parents of children accused of throwing stones at Israeli vehicles; $400 to $500 for retrieving a child detained by the army or police; and $175 for failing to remove nationalist graffiti from the walls of private homes or public structures. Failure to pay fines could result in imprisonment; parents refusing to post bail for their children could be imprisoned for up to one year.

The Palestinian financial sector, in particular, suffered further erosion resulting from other Israeli measures, including: currency restrictions that limited external capital transfers to the occupied territories to $400 per person per month, down from $5,000 per person per month before the intifada (these restrictions were abolished in 1993); the regular confiscation of money from abroad; and the closure of twenty-two Israeli bank branches in the Gaza Strip and West Bank.

Other Factors Affecting Economic Conditions in the Gaza Strip

The economy of the Gaza Strip was hurt by other factors not directly tied to Israeli government policies. The first event occurred in July 1988, when the Jordanian government severed its legal and administrative links with the occupied territories. Among other things, Jordan's disengagement terminated the government's five-year development plan for the West Bank and Gaza. In an effort to protect Arab producers of similar commodities, Jordan also altered its trade relationship with the occupied territories by importing goods on the basis of market need rather than on the basis of predetermined quotas, as was often the case before the disengagement.

The fall of the Jordanian dinar in 1988–89 also had a direct bearing on the Gaza Strip economy. Used in most personal and commercial dealings in the occupied territories, the dinar had, by January 1989, declined by 40 percent of its 1987 level. Although the exchange rate stabilized soon thereafter, Palestinians experienced noticeable losses in personal income resulting from the decreased value of savings accounts, subsidies, wages, and pensions, as well as remittances received from the Gulf.[32] Conversely, the cost of raw materials and imports increased.

In early 1989, Palestinian financial resources were further depleted by a 15 percent devaluation of the Israeli shekel, which again reduced local purchasing power and increased the costs of basic foodstuffs and Israeli imports.[33] Between 1988 and 1989, considerable damage was also caused by a winter frost and summer heat wave, which resulted in millions of dollars worth of crop damage in both the Palestinian and Israeli economies. Between 1988 and 1990, therefore, Palestinian material and human resource losses were estimated at $260 million.[34]

The Economic Impact of the Intifada Prior to the Gulf War

Gaza's economy weakened as a result of the intifada. Agriculture in the Gaza Strip experienced declines in the value of its output, particularly citrus. Israeli prohibitions on the harvesting and marketing of crops, coupled with the destruction of tens of thousands of trees and crops by the IDF and Israeli settlers between 1988 and 1990 precipitated declines of 40 percent to 50 percent in the value of agricultural (fruit and vegetable) output in Gaza and the West Bank combined.[35] Citrus production in Gaza fell from 190,000 tons in 1987 to 129,000 tons in 1988 and in 1989 before reviving in 1990. Thus, a decline of 32 percent in citrus production between 1987 and 1989 stands in contrast to an increase of 29 percent between 1985 and 1987.[36] Additional restrictions on water consumption, planting, and marketing accounted for the decline.

Industrial output declined significantly, particularly in the first year of the intifada. Classified government figures indicated that in 1988, industrial output in the Gaza Strip fell by 22 percent.[37] By February 1989, industrial production for all industrial branches in the Gaza Strip had fallen by 50 percent, the only exception was food processing, which enjoyed increased levels of output arising from the local boycott of imported Israeli products.[38] Indeed, those branches of Gazan industry that had strong production and marketing links with Israeli manufacturers (e.g., clothing subcontracting, construction materials) suffered declines, whereas those engaged in the provision of basic goods such as soft drinks, detergents, and processed foods—import substitution as it were—experienced increased growth even at the expense of Israeli firms.

Output in Gaza's construction industry also fell by 25 percent to 33 percent in 1988, following annual increases averaging 12 percent in 1986 and 1987. In addition, the commerce and transportation sectors experienced significant declines of 33 percent, whereas activity in the public services sector fell by a dramatic 66 percent.[39]

Trade relations across the green line were virtually transformed as a result of Israeli and Palestinian measures. Israel's export surplus in goods and services to the Gaza Strip and West Bank shrank from $251 million in 1985 to $42 million in 1988.[40] In 1989, Israel's historical trade surplus ended with an unprecedented deficit of $52 million. The decline in Israel's export surplus, however, was incurred largely in merchandise (i.e., Israeli-made goods) rather than service trade, which refers primarily to wages earned by labor from the occupied territories working in Israel.[41]

Despite some short-lived achievements, the structural alteration in trade was incurred at much greater costs to the local Palestinian economy, which was unable to withstand and compensate for the dislocations. The boycott of Israeli goods, for example, sent many merchants, especially those in the highly dependent Gaza Strip marketplace, into bankruptcy. The combination of specifically boycotted Israeli goods,[42] more oppressive taxation, falling prices, and decreased working hours proved devastating for local commerce.

Service trade also experienced some important changes. Although the absolute number of Palestinians working in Israel in 1988 was officially estimated to be equal to its 1987 level, the actual number of hours worked had fallen by 28 percent.[43] Between 1988 and 1990, the average number of days worked in Israel declined by 33 percent to 50 percent. In May 1989, the Bank of Israel reported that during 1988, the Israeli market experienced a 25 percent decline in the *effective* supply of workers from the West Bank and Gaza.[44] This was at a time when the number of job hunters increased due to the closure of secondary schools and the imprisonment of thousands of breadwinners, whose fathers and sons were compelled to enter the workforce.

Thus, significant changes occurred in the size and composition of the Palestinian labor force employed in Israel, and the impact of these changes on private income, factor income, and GNP was negative. Indeed, income earned by Gazans working in Israel equalled $333 million in 1988.[45] However, receipts from Israel were estimated to have declined by 18 percent in real terms in 1988 and by an additional 7 percent in 1989, which resulted in a 20 percent drop in buying power and a 25 percent drop in living standards.[46] Given the weight of this income in total GDP and GNP, the impact of the decline was substantial.

In 1990 and 1991, rising levels of intercommunal violence created public pressure in Israel to separate the Palestinian and Israeli populations. In November 1991, the government announced that in response to a spate of stabbings and attacks against Israelis, 5,000 Gazan workers would be barred from working in Israel.

In January 1991, soon after the outbreak of the Gulf war, a high-level Israeli official predicted that the 120,000 Palestinians then working in Israel would be let go. His predictions were quickly borne out. In February 1991, Israel introduced a new work-permit system, which prevented any Palestinian from working in Israel without a permit obtained from the government labor office. To obtain this permit, the worker's employer had to initiate the application at the labor office at Erez. Only those individuals (and, in some cases, their relatives) who had paid all their taxes (including what the Israelis termed a "life tax" of $1,000 per year)[47] and municipal fees, and who had received a security clearance, were eligible.

Given these requirements, the majority of working-aged people were excluded. Permits had to specify the place of work, to which laborers were confined once in Israel. To work elsewhere was considered illegal unless a new permit was obtained, and to work "illegally" incurred the risk of arrest. In lieu of arrest, however, individuals were usually fined between NIS 500 to NIS 1,000 and stripped of their magnetic cards. Moreover, in another new measure, Israeli employers had to arrange transportation for their workers, because Palestinians were no longer allowed to travel to Israel on their own. If they were caught with illegal workers, employers were fined between NIS 2,000 and NIS 15,000 per worker. If employers failed to provide transportation, workers attempting to reach jobs on their own were vulnerable to harassment and arrest.[48] Furthermore, workers had to pay for their transportation, which often amounted to half their daily wage.

Conclusion

The intifada seriously undermined Gaza's economy. Israeli-imposed measures were designed to further constrain indigenous economic capacity by depleting financial resources, reducing income-earning options, attacking existing institutions, and destroying economic and physical infrastructure. In so doing, the authorities deepened the integrative ties between Israel and Gaza, because employment in Israel increasingly became Gazans' only viable economic alternative for survival. Measures imposed by the Palestinian leadership aimed to wean Gaza of its dependence on Israel; in reality, they only further impoverished the local economy, because no viable income-earning alternatives were made available. As such, the intifada contributed to de-development. The Gulf war dramatically accelerated the process.

Notes to Chapter 10:

1. Lea Ben-Dor, "Dayan and the Territories," *Jerusalem Post*, 12 September 1977.

2. Interview with Hisham Khatib, Economic Development Group (EDG), Jerusalem, April 1989.

3. The discussion of Palestinian measures is drawn from Roy, "Development Under Occupation?" pp. 80–83.

4. Because production was oriented to consumption at the subsistence level, much of the production did not even enter government statistics.

5. In the first two years of the uprising, remittances fell from $250 million to $75 million per year, a trend that continued unabated.

6. Ministry of Defense, Internal document reviewing economic conditions in the occupied territories during 1988 (in Hebrew), Tel Aviv, February 1989. See Sara Roy, "The Political Economy of Despair: Changing Political and Economic Realities in the Gaza Strip," *Journal of Palestine Studies* 20, no.3 (Spring 1991): 61.

7. Data collected by the author in interviews, Gaza Strip, 1988–89.

8. See *International Herald Tribune*, 26 July 1988.

9. *Jerusalem Post*, 17 February 1989.

10. Sara Roy, "From Hardship to Hunger: The Economic Impact of the Intifada on the Gaza Strip," *American-Arab Affairs*, No. 34 (Fall 1990): 117.

11. Information supplied by the Database Project on Palestinian Human Rights, Chicago, IL, August 1990. The discussion of Israeli restrictions is drawn from Roy, "From Hardship to Hunger," pp. 118–23.

12. Ministry of Defense, *Economic Survey for 1988 and 1989: The Economy of Judea, Samaria and the Gaza Strip—After Two Years of Events [i.e. the Intifada]*, Classified document, Ministry of Defense, Tel Aviv, 1990.

13. Joost R. Hiltermann, "Workers' Rights during the Uprising," *Journal of Palestine Studies* 19, no.1 (Autumn 1989): 86. See also *New York Times*, 23 June 1989.

14. Hiltermann, "Workers' Rights," p. 86.

15. Ministry of Defense, Internal document, 1989.

16. Hisham Awartani, "The Palestinian Economy Under Occupation," (paper presented at a symposium entitled "The Economic Aspects of a Political Settlement in the Middle East," University of Nijmegen, Nijmegen, the Netherlands, 18–20 April 1990), p. 10.

17.   Atif K. Alawnah, "The Impact of the Intifada on the Palestinian and Israeli Economies," *New Outlook*, 1990, p. 23.

18.   Data on tax collection measures are drawn primarily from B'tselem–The Israeli Information Center for Human Rights in the Occupied Territories, *The System of Taxation in the West Bank and Gaza Strip as an Instrument for the Enforcement of Authority During the Uprising* (Jerusalem: B'Tselem, 1990), pp. 7–40. See also Marc Stephens, *Taxation in the Occupied West Bank 1967–1989* (Ramallah: Al Haq, March 1990).

19.   Based on 50 interviews with merchants in the Gaza Strip, 1988 and 1989.

20.   Sadan, *A Policy for Immediate Economic-Industrial Development*, p. 63.

21.   See Sidney J. Baxendale, "Israeli taxes discriminate against Arabs," *Christian Science Monitor*, 19 October 1988.

22.   Ministry of Defense, *Economic Survey for 1988 and 1989*. Original figures appear in New Israeli Shekels and have been converted into dollars at an exchange rate of $1 = NIS 1.7. These figures differ slightly from those in table 7.12 and may be due to the fact that the Defense Ministry figures were compiled one year after those presented in table 7.12. Consequently, they may reflect revisions to the budget, or the difference between proposed and actual expenditures.

23.   Ministry of Defense, Internal document, 1989.

24.   B'tselem, 12. B'tselem reported a total budget of $243 million. Ministry of Defense, Internal document, 1989; and *Economic Survey for 1988 and 1989* put the transferred amount at $21 million.

25.   Ministry of Defense, Internal document, and *Economic Survey for 1988 and 1989*. [Note: original figures appear in New Israeli Shekels.]

26.   Ministry of Defense, *Economic Survey for 1988 and 1989*. One component of the regular budget of the occupied territories is allocated to these activities.

27.   Interviews with PVO officials who asked not to be identified. Confirmed in interviews with officials in the Ministry of Defense, 1990.

28.   Ministry of Defense, *Economic Survey for 1988 and 1989*. The conversion rate in 1989 was $1 = NIS 1.85; in 1990 it was $1 = NIS 2.00.

29.   See Joost R. Hiltermann, "Israel's Strategy to Break the Intifada," *Journal of Palestine Studies* 19, no.2 (Winter 1990): 88–89.

30.   Michal Sela, "By bread and olives alone," *Jerusalem Post*, 17 February 1989.

31.   Don Shomron, the army chief of staff, described the reason for the changing of the

ID cards: "All the identity cards in the Gaza Strip are being changed in order to increase the dependence on the civil administration. If the aim of the uprising was to shake off this dependence, our aim is to increase it." *New York Times*, 15 May 1988.

32. See "The Effects of the Dinar's Collapse," *Israel Economist*, March 1989, pp. 17–19.

33. UNCTAD, *Assistance to the Palestinian People: Recent Economic Developments in the Occupied Palestinian Territory* (Geneva: UNCTAD, 1989), p. 23.

34. Ibid., p. 10.

35. Ibid., p. 16.

36. Civil Administration of Gaza, *Gaza Region Agricultural Development*; Citrus Producers Union for the Gaza Strip, *Annual Report 1987* (Gaza Strip, 1987), 8. Certain agricultural branches enjoyed growth. Egg and honey production increased by 50 percent and 45 percent, respectively in 1989.

37. Ministry of Defense, *Economic Survey for 1988 and 1989*.

38. Economic Department, United States Embassy, Tel Aviv, 1989; and Roy, "From Hardship to Hunger," p. 125.

39. Economic Department, United States Embassy, 1989. Classified government figures put this figure minimally at 21 percent.

40. Bank of Israel, *Annual Report 1988*, p. 204.

41. See Joel Greenberg, "Sharon: Palestinian boycott of Israeli goods effective," *Jerusalem Post*, 30 March 1989; and Roy, "From Hardship to Hunger," p. 125.

42. Only specific items that could not be reproduced locally could be imported. Exports to Israel were not opposed.

43. Ministry of Defense, *Economic Survey for 1988 and 1989*.

44. Hiltermann, "Worker's Rights," p. 85.

45. Ministry of Defense, Internal document, 1989.

46. Ministry of Defense, *Economic Survey for 1988 and 1989*. An inflation rate of 11 percent and 16 percent was assumed for Gaza in 1988 and 1989, respectively. See also Roy, "From Hardship to Hunger," p. 126.

47. See interview with Muhammad Quneitah, head of the Federation of Palestinian Labor Unions in the Gaza Strip, *Al-Fajr*, 6 May 1991.

48.   See the newsletter of *Kav La'oved*, entitled *The Workers' Hotline for the Protection of Workers' Rights*, Tel Aviv, November 1991.

11

The War in the Gulf and the March 1993 Closure
— Gaza's Economic Dismemberment

B etween December 1987 and January 1991, the Palestinian economy came under considerable pressure as a result of measures imposed by the Israeli government and the Palestinian Unified Leadership in response to the uprising. During that period, the GNP of the West Bank and Gaza Strip fell by 30 percent to 35 percent. For Gaza, in particular, where workers' movements were more easily restricted, these measures took a steep toll. The number of Gazans working in Israel declined unofficially from 70,000–80,000 to 56,000, or just under half Gaza's total labor force of 120,000. Their pre-intifada income accounted for at least 35 percent of GNP and 70 percent of GDP. The loss of income from work in Israel was therefore dramatic, representing no less than $300 million.[1] Consumption, savings, and investment patterns changed, and the standard of living dropped precipitously.

The Gulf War

The Gulf war had a devastating impact on Gaza's economy. Remittances and direct aid ceased, and employment in Israel slowed to a trickle. Gaza's economy was totally dependent on all three. Palestinians paid dearly for their support of Iraq. Gaza's economy, already weary after three years of intifada, was dealt its most damaging blow. Whatever minimal support had previously gone to development was redirected to relief.

On 16 January 1991, Israel imposed a comprehensive and prolonged curfew on the Gaza Strip (and West Bank), which lasted as long as seven weeks in some areas and virtually shut down the economy. This curfew alone is estimated to have cost Gaza at least $84 million. This loss resulted from a total work stoppage and extreme cutback in the number of workers allowed into Israel that "pushed thousands of families to the brink of economic collapse."[2] By May 1991, at least one out of three Gazans was unemployed. Of the approximately 80,000 people who were employed, 28,000 worked in Israel (down from 56,000 just before the Gulf war); 12,000 were employed by UNRWA, the civil administration, and local municipalities; and 40,000 worked in other sectors of the Gaza Strip. The assumption of total employment in Gaza's other sectors was probably incorrect, increasing the unemployment rate well above 33 percent.[3] Local economists placed the unemployment rate between 35 percent to 40 percent. Personal income fell precipitously, and savings were eroded.[4] During the curfew and just after it, thousands of Gazan workers were summarily fired by their Israeli employers. They had no appeal or recourse. The majority did not receive the severance pay to which they were entitled, nor were people able to travel to Israel to collect wages owed them. The resultant loss in wages was estimated at $11 million per month when compared with wages obtained before the war.[5] National income plummeted during this period, as prices spiralled up.

For those with jobs in Gaza, curfew losses reached $11.5 million. The agricultural sector was hit especially hard because the curfew coincided with the citrus harvest and summer planting season. Irrigation and insecticide spraying activities ceased at least two weeks, destroying many irrigated crops. The curfew came on the heels of a severe drought that already hit farmers hard. Gaza lost its principal export markets in the Gulf, which historically absorbed 30 percent to 60 percent of local citrus exports. After the start of the Gulf crisis, Gaza's principal buyers of citrus—Iraq, Kuwait, Saudi Arabia, and the United Arab Emirates—closed their markets. Trade with Europe was severely interrupted but not terminated. Of the 140,000 tons of citrus produced by February 1991 (down from 175,000 tons a year before), only 15,000 tons were exported. A small portion was sent to Israeli juice factories; the majority spoiled on trees.

The resulting glut, accompanied by rising production costs (for fertilizer, pesticides, and transport) and diminishing returns, posed an immediate threat. Citrus prices plummeted: from 1990 to 1991, lemons fell from $100 to $20 a ton; grapefruits from $100 to $50 a ton, and oranges from $150 to $50 a ton. In 1990, the value of one ton of citrus could buy three tons of fertilizer; in 1991, however, it took six tons of citrus to purchase only one ton of fertilizer.[6] The unprecedented winter of 1991–92 imposed further damage on the Palestinian agricultural sector, which amounted to at least $77 million in direct costs.

A cash liquidity crisis ensued. Consumers stopped buying and drew on what remained of their savings. In late February 1991, sales of red meat had dropped by 80 percent, and vegetables by 70 percent.[7] The citrus industry lost

$8 million and other sectors lost $2 million.[8] By early 1992, with no alternative, some citrus farmers and merchants were selling unpackaged goods to Israeli companies, who would apply a "Product of Israel" stamp and export them as Israeli produce.

The most significant impact of the Gulf war was the loss of remittances from Palestinians living in the Gulf, combined with the termination of direct aid from the Gulf states, notably Kuwait and Saudi Arabia, and the abrupt decline in PLO transfers. Of the 800,000 Palestinians in the Gulf sending money home, 165,000 were from the occupied territories; 30,000 of these had residency in Gaza and the West Bank. In 1987, total remittances from the Gulf countries equalled $250 million, or 10 percent of the territories' GNP. However, given that the GNP of both territories had declined by 30 percent to 35 percent, the proportional value of Gulf remittances to GNP had risen to approximately 15 percent. Kuwait's contribution alone accounted for more than half of this sum.[9] Indeed, between 1988 and 1990, Kuwaiti remittances to the Gaza Strip and West Bank equalled $35 million and $105 million, respectively.[10] Remittances from some countries ended immediately, whereas the value of those that continued, particularly from Kuwait, diminished by more than two-thirds before terminating completely.

Direct aid from the Gulf countries to local institutions in both territories, which amounted to $70 million in 1989 alone, was terminated as well. The loss of this source of financing jeopardized the continued functioning of specific health and educational institutions, in addition to certain development projects. Together with the decline in the level and the value of remittances from Palestinians employed in Israel, the loss of remittances from the Gulf had a devastating effect on the Palestinian economy. By April 1991, the loss of remittances and other direct aid (in addition to the loss of exports) amounted to $350 million.

The PLO lost $480 million in direct aid from Gulf sources; a large percentage of these monies was funnelled into the occupied territories. At one time, in fact, Saudi Arabia's contributions to the PLO were equivalent to 10 percent of the GDP of the West Bank and Gaza Strip combined.[11] Moreover, between 1980 and 1990, the PLO is estimated to have received approximately $10 billion from Kuwait, Saudi Arabia, and the United Arab Emirates, monies that ended with PLO support of Iraq.[12] By 1993, the PLO found itself bankrupt, and the rapid erosion of PLO revenue imperiled local institutions in particular, many of which broke down or closed.

A critical factor affecting local economic conditions during this period, especially in Gaza, was a series of closures and curfews. From May to July 1992, for example, the Gaza Strip was closed for five weeks. UNRWA estimated that between 24 May and 5 July (when workers were allowed to return to Israel), losses from wages alone reached $500,000 per day.[13] During this time, farmers were unable to sell their vegetables in the West Bank, an important market for Gaza, and the resulting surplus caused a precipitous fall in local vegetable prices. Additional restrictions on the export of Gaza produce to Israel were announced by the minister of agriculture (although Israeli farmers still had unlimited access to Gazan markets).[14] Commercial strikes called two to three times per month by Palestinians aggravated an increasingly desperate situation. Indeed, by June 1991, UNRWA was feeding an unprecedented 120,000 families in the Gaza Strip, both refugee and nonrefugee. During 1992, UNRWA distributed an additional 430,000 family food parcels in Gaza.[15]

The economic degeneration worsened in the fall of 1992 under the newly installed government of Yitzhak Rabin. The security situation, after a period of some quiet, began to deteriorate in September. Between December 1992 and March 1993, 57 Palestinians, among them 17 children under the age of 16, were killed in Gaza by the Israeli army; 400 children were shot with live ammunition. Strip-wide closures were imposed for three days in September, nineteen days in December (in addition to a ten-day curfew after the deportation of 415 Palestinians), and six days in early March. For December alone, UNRWA estimated that Gazans working in Israel lost income amounting to at least $13 million, whereas those with jobs in Gaza (including the transportation sector) lost $8 million. Agricultural export losses incurred an additional $3 million, bringing total losses for the month of December alone to $24 million.[16]

In late fall 1992, UNRWA in Gaza advertised eight jobs for garbage collectors and received 11,655 applications, a number one and one-half times Gaza's industrial workforce and close to 10 percent of its total labor force.[17] By January 1993, hunger was clearly a growing problem, especially among children.

The March 1993 Closure

On 30 March 1993, in response to some of the highest levels of Arab–Jewish violence since the beginning of the Palestinian uprising, the Israeli government sealed off the West Bank and Gaza Strip, barring 130,000 Palestinians from their jobs in Israel. The March closure was the longest ever imposed lasting into the post-Oslo interim period; the degree of hardship created the most severe. The economic damage incurred by the Palestinian economy after March 1993 had no precedent under Israeli occupation: for the first time, a large and growing segment of people were *permanently* unemployed, and the basis of the economy underwent a structural shift from cash to credit.

The closure separated the occupied territories into four distinct and relatively isolated areas: the north and south of the West Bank, East Jerusalem, and the Gaza Strip. At least 56 military roadblocks were established along the green line, 27 in Gaza and 29 in the West Bank.[18] All four regions were cut off from each other and from Israel as well. Special civil administration permits were required by people moving between areas. The geographic segmentation of the territories, coupled with severe prohibitions on entry into Israel, proved ruinous for the Palestinian economy, with the labor force enduring the greatest damage. Prior to the closure, 30,000 Gazans (25 percent of the total labor force) were commuting to work in Israel. The income generated by these workers accounted for 50 percent of Gaza's GNP.

Gaza faced an "unnatural slow-onset disaster likely to spiral out of control, possibly resulting in the total disruption of people's lives."[19] By December 1993, only 20,000 Gazans were working in Israel. Unemployment stood at 55 percent. Nonetheless, work in Israel remained Gaza's most important source of income.[20]

The closure resulted in an absolute loss of income at a time when personal savings had been virtually depleted. According to UNRWA, in the first two months of the closure, Gaza was losing $750,000 in wages alone each day. (Monthly losses equalled $19 million, the equivalent of what UNRWA spends in wages in eight months.) The loss of wage income and the accompanying decline in disposable income resulted in a significant loss of purchasing power and local demand for consumer and processed products. The Gaza Strip, which was closed off for more than two of the first five months of 1993, experienced a major, rapid drop in food purchases, a dramatic fall in the volume of consumption, and marked changes in food consumption patterns. Overall food purchases (except for essential commodities) declined by 50 percent to 70 percent and sales of red meat by 70 percent to 90 percent.[21] Sales of certain pharmaceuticals fell by as much as 70 percent, whereas purchases of "luxury" items such as clothing plummeted by almost 90 percent.

One month into the closure, UNRWA was planning four emergency distributions in the Gaza Strip, one every two months, for 90,000 refugee families and 30,000 nonrefugee families for a total of 480,000 family rations. Requests from refugee and nonrefugee alike for food, cash aid, and work exceeded the agency's capacity to provide them. Three months into the closure, the diet of many Palestinian families, especially those in the refugee camps, consisted of bread, lentils, and rice. Shoppers were purchasing only a fraction of the produce they bought before the closure. UNRWA's medical experts stated in June that if the closure were to continue without immediate food relief, "there will be a rise in the incidence of growth-retardation among children under three years of age. This means that there will be more children suffering from malnutrition; as this is closely associated with child and infant mortality rates, there could be an increase in child deaths."[22]

Although some workers were allowed to return to work by the summer and economic activity picked up slightly, monthly losses remained high. Ezra Sadan, former director general of the finance ministry and advisor to the government on economic policy in the occupied territories, stated that "severance of the economies means immediate poverty for [the Palestinians], deep poverty, no hope for development."[23] Sadan predicted that a closure would result in a 50 percent drop in Gaza's per capita GNP, from $1,200 to $600, a level found among the poorest third world nations.

The loss of purchasing power brought about dramatic declines in the production of manufactured goods for local markets. As a result, local wage rates fell—by as much as 30 percent in some sectors[24]—and domestic employment declined. In the first two months of the closure, the primary if not only source of purchasing power in the Gaza Strip was the monthly salaries of UNRWA and civil administration employees. That is, the public sector was the largest sector providing income within the local economy. These salaries amounted to $5 million per month, a small sum when compared to a monthly loss of $19 million in Israeli wages.

Blanket export restrictions imposed at the time of the closure created agricultural surpluses local markets could not possibly absorb. The elimination of export markets combined with declining purchasing power caused food prices to plummet by 50 percent to 90 percent.[25] For example, within two weeks of the closure, the price of Gazan tomatoes for example, had dropped by 65 percent, cucumbers by 81 percent, and squash by 91 percent.[26] Israeli imported foodstuffs, however, doubled in price due to higher transportation costs. That purchasing power remained very weak at a time when food prices had plunged and surplus food stocks increased underlines the extremity of the situation. Moreover, the unprecedented loss of export markets in Israel, the West Bank, and overseas affected the structure of local production, especially in Gaza, because many production processes require a minimum market size if they are to achieve economies of scale required to operate with a modicum of profit.[27] Consequently, a growing number of retail and wholesale establishments went out of business.

Gaza's smaller subcontractors working for the Israeli textile industry reported a complete halt in production, because the closure prevented them from purchasing raw materials in Israel. Gazan merchants reported incidents of price gouging by Israeli buyers seeking to take advantage of the restricted access to Israel and increased economic hardship of the closure to force Gazan subcontractors to sell at below agreed-upon prices. Those larger subcontractors who were not affected by the closure became the targets of regular tax raids conducted by Israeli tax officials at Erez, the Gaza–Israel border, where subcontractors exchange goods with their Israeli buyers.

After wages earned in Israel, citrus production is the most important source of income for the Gaza Strip. By the end of May 1993, the citrus sector was in crisis due to official measures that resulted in shipping delays. Specifically, the civil administration issued export permits to Jordan valid for only one week. Long security checks at the Allenby Bridge, the border crossing between the West Bank and Jordan, exceeded the length of the permit. Trucks carrying Gaza produce, therefore, were caught in the West Bank with expired permits and could not cross into Jordan, and there were not enough trucks available to transport all citrus exports.

Toward the end of May, one hundred trucks—25 percent of the entire fleet—were detained by the Israeli authorities. As a result, between 25,000 and 30,000 tons of Valencia oranges, Gaza's main cash crop, remained unpicked and left to rot. Farmers reported that between the closure and the shipping delays, the price they were paid for Valencia oranges dropped from $140 per ton in May 1992 to $80 per ton in May 1993, a decline of 43 percent. Producers of lower quality oranges used in Israeli juice factories were paid 50 percent less in 1993 ($55 per ton) than in 1992 ($110 per ton).[28] The price of vegetables also dropped, so much that many farmers doubted if they would plant the following season.[29]

The precipitous loss in income, coupled with eroding savings, rising unemployment, and declining wage rates produced an acute cash shortage (that remained after the implementation of self-rule). This in turn resulted in a pattern of asset liquidation and a partial return to a barter economy. Jewelers reported that within the first month of the closure, the resale of gold jewelry, an important source of savings, increased from three or four sales per month to as many as five and six transactions per day. Television sets, radios, VCRs and other appliances, and secondhand cars were also sold on a wide scale.[30]

The conversion of assets to cash, a finite process, was accompanied by the extensive use of credit for basic food purchases. Retailers reported that in Gaza's refugee camps, demand for food on credit grew by 200 percent to 350 percent.[31] Typically, poorer households obtained lines of credit from small retailers who in turn obtained credit lines from their suppliers. Small retail food outlets were ill-equipped to support rising credit demand, especially in a contracting economic environment.

In such an environment, people could not afford to pay for essential services. The Jabalya municipality, for example, estimated that 60 percent of the population were unable to make utility payments. In response, the Israeli authorities introduced coercive measures to insure payment. Households in arrears received surprise military raids at night. Individuals owing more than NIS 400 ($148) had their identity cards confiscated. In this way, failure to pay a bill became a security offense. In panic, many Gazans liquidated what little savings they held in reserve to pay municipal, utility, and tax bills. Payment of bills and taxes has long been a requirement for Gazans wishing to obtain a magnetic identity card, itself a requirement for work in Israel. After the closure, however, the magnetic ID card became a prerequisite for participation in Civil Administration job creation programs *in* Gaza.

The closure created two new problems for the Gaza Strip economy: an unprecedented number of permanently unemployed people, and a growing dependence on credit combined with new levels of indebtedness. The income shortage produced widespread food shortages and brought the economy almost to a point of total collapse. The provision of basic relief, long restricted to a small minority, became the concern of a growing majority. Production gave way to survival; unity to fragmentation. Malnourishment, unemployment, and violence became part of daily life.

Official Israeli Responses to the Closure

The Israeli government responded to the crisis in two ways: by allowing a significantly reduced number of workers back into Israel, and by creating domestic employment. The former was tempered by a commitment not to return to preclosure levels of Arab labor in Israel, thereby increasing pressure on the latter. However, the job creation schemes were decidedly ad hoc in nature, occurring outside any context of integrated planning. They resembled the job creation programs developed by UNRWA in the 1950s, which were designed to provide short-term relief rather than long-term development. Workers, who had to be at least 25 years old, married, and in possession of a magnetic ID card, were directed to sweep sidewalks (often moving sand from one side of the street to another), clean streets and beaches, paint signs, whitewash, and dig ditches. By July 1993, 8,700 workers in Gaza and 7,500 workers in the West Bank were employed largely as street cleaners and painters.[32] Workers were paid a daily wage of NIS 25 ($9), half of what they earned in Israel, and were usually employed for no more than fifteen days at a time.

Gaza's weak and de-developed economy did not possess the capacity or the strength to withstand such extreme economic pressures, particularly in a context of acute political and institutional disintegration. The positive effect of allowing more workers into Israel, for example, the most important factor mitigating the crisis, was countered by forced layoffs by Gazan enterprises. Indeed, income earned in Israel and in local work schemes did not strengthen purchasing power to the point of producing the demand needed to generate jobs locally. These conditions, coupled with Gaza's near-total dependence on Israel for income generation, actually deepened Palestinian dependence on Israel at a time when Israel was preparing to transfer political control over the territory to a new Palestinian authority. This transfer, formalized in the Gaza–Jericho Agreement signed by Israel and the PLO in September 1993, promises Palestinians a form of limited autonomy and a much-needed political separation between Gaza and Israel. In terms of the economy, however, the opposite is true: Integration, not separation, defines the relationship between Israel and Gaza. Indeed, the economic crises precipitated by the Gulf war and accelerated by the March closure allowed Israel to begin restructuring economic relations with a much weakened Gaza Strip along new integrative lines that the Gaza-Jericho agreement both sanctioned and formalized. The policy changes promoting this new integration and their implications for de-development are discussed in the next and final chapter.

Notes to Chapter 11:

1. Sara Roy, "The Political Economy of Despair," p. 61; and idem., "Separation or Integration: Closure and the Economic Future of the Gaza Strip Revisited," *Middle East Journal* 48 (Winter 1994): 11–30. Portions of this chapter are extracted from these two articles with permission of the publishers.

2. UNRWA, *Situation of Palestinian Civilians under Israeli Occupation: Gaza Strip, March–May 1991* (Vienna: UNRWA, May 1991), p. 1.

3. Ibid.

4. Bishara A. Bahbah, "The Economic Consequences on Palestinians," *The Palestinians and the War in the Gulf* (Washington, DC: Center for Policy Analysis on Palestine, 1991), pp. 17–21.

5. UNRWA, *Situation of Palestinian Civilians*, 2. See also, Oded Lifshitz, "You are killing us without guns," *Hotam, Al Hamishmar Friday Supplement*, 26 April 1991.

6. See *Tanmiya*/Development, The Welfare Association, Geneva, Switzerland, 1991, and cited in *Al-Fajr*, 9 December 1991.

7. Frank Collins, "The rescue of the Palestinian economy," *Al-Fajr*, 3 June 1991.

8. Ibid., pp. 2–3.

9. Roy, "The Political Economy of Despair," p. 62.

10. Economic Department, U.S. Embassy, Tel Aviv, September 1990.

11. Sara Roy, "Gaza: New Dynamics of Civic Disintegration," p. 21.

12. See Youssef M. Ibrahim, "Arafat's Support of Iraq Creates Rift in PLO," *New York Times*, 14 August 1990.

13. UNRWA, *The Continuing Emergency In The Occupied Territory And Lebanon And Structural Socio-Economic Problems* (Vienna: UNRWA, March 1993), p. 3. As of 4 July 1992, work permits were only issued to Gazan men aged 20 years or more. Previously, the minimum age was 16 years.

14. "No Gaza produce to be sold in Israel," *Jerusalem Post*, 22 July 1992; and "Israeli competition destroys the potato season in Gaza," *An Nahar* 12 September 1992. According to reports in the Israeli press, "collaborators from Gaza receive special permits to transfer agricultural produce across the Green Line, despite the fact that this was a crime," in Israel. Moreover, the Israeli government, working through collaborators, imported vegetables from Gaza as a way of regulating the price of vegetables in Israel, and as a way of bringing down Israel's consumer price index. See Ronal Fisher, "The government caused the Israeli negative index by flooding the market with vegetables from the

Gaza Strip," *Hadashot*, 19 June 1992; and idem., "A senior government source confirms: Gazans received special permits to transfer vegetables," *Hadashot*, 22 June 1992.

15.   UNRWA, *The Continuing Emergency*, p. 6.

16.   Interview with a staff person of an international NGO who asked not to be identified, Spring 1993.

17.   Interview with UNRWA Director Klaus Worm, Gaza Strip, January 1993.

18.   Palestine Human Rights Information Center, "Israel's Closure of Occupied Territories Creates Military Enclave; Strangles East Jerusalem; Spells Loss of Income to Families, Denies Access to Medical Care, Schools, Jobs, Place of Worship," Press Release, Jerusalem, 15 April 1993.

19.   "A Disaster Preparedness Report: A Preliminary Assessment of the Impact of the Closures on the Population of the Gaza Strip," Draft, 17 June 1993, p. 5. The author of this report, a European NGO, asked to remain unidentified.

20.   The United Nations estimates that in order to reduce unemployment in Gaza by just one-half would require at least $500 million in sustainable investment. UNRWA, *UNRWA Statement to the Nineth North America Seminar on the Question of Palestine*, New York, 28–29 June 1993, p. 8.

21.   UNRWA, "UNRWA Commissioner-General warns Arab League of socio-economic emergency in the occupied territory; appeals for additional funding for Arab sources," Press Release CLO/1/93, Vienna, 18 April 1993, p. 1.

22.   UNRWA, *UNRWA Statement*, p. 5. See also Sara Roy, "Joyless in Gaza: Apartheid, Israeli-Style," *The Nation*, July 26/August 2, 1993, p. 138.

23.   "Investing in Peace," *Jerusalem Post*, 14 May 1993.

24.   UNRWA, The Gaza Strip, 21 July 1993.

25.   Co-ordinating Committee of International NGOs, "The Economic Impact Of The Israeli Military Closure Of The Palestinian West Bank and Gaza Strip," CCINGO Brief, Jerusalem, 26 May 1993, p. 2.

26.   UNRWA, The Gaza Strip, Summer 1993. Toward the end of July, when the glut of vegetables dried up, prices returned to their preclosure levels although demand remained depressed.

27.   "A Disaster Preparedness Report," p. 7.

28.   UNRWA, The Gaza Strip, Spring 1993.

29.   "A Disaster Preparedness Report," p. 26.

30.   UNRWA, The Gaza Strip, Spring 1993.

31.   North American Coordinating Committee for NGOs on the Question of Palestine, "Emergency in the Gaza Strip," *The Fax Tree*, Washington, D.C., 16 July 1993, p. 4.

32.   Institutional sources in Gaza that asked to remain unidentified, May 1993.

PART IV:

The Face of the Future

12

The Gaza–Jericho Agreement:
An End to De-development?

T his study has shown that Israeli occupation has been malefic. Israel's occupation of Palestinian lands after 1967 has expressed far less concern
with the people living on those lands then with the lands themselves. Historically, this was first illustrated in the evolution of Arab–Jewish relations during
the Mandate, then in the Gaza Plan of 1949, and in the Sinai and Gaza campaigns of 1956. Indeed, while the lessons of Gaza's history were certainly not
lost on the Israeli government,[1] it was not Gaza's strategic significance that
impelled the imposition of Israeli control *primarily*, but the state's desire to
expand. For Israel, territoriality is raised above strategic, political, and economic considerations. "Land over people" has remained a national imperative
since the British Mandate era. It is *the* critical and distinguishing feature of de-
development.

When full control over the Gaza Strip was finally achieved after the 1967
war, the government embarked on a policy of institutional integration that was
designed to insure that the territory would not revert back to its pre-1967 status,
although its postwar status remained a source of political dispute. Thus, official
objectives may not have been directed at making political annexation easier,
but they were clearly directed at making territorial separation harder. After 1967,
Israeli policy in the Gaza Strip was driven less by what it aimed to do than by
what it aimed never to do: return the territory to its former sovereign, let alone
to the Palestinians who lived there.

The integration the government sought to promote had to be institution-

323

alized in a manner that not only insured Israeli control over the Gaza Strip but strengthened Israeli domination. Integration, therefore, was predicated on three conditions: the political pacification of the Palestinian population, the increased dependence of that population on Israel, and the suppression of any independently organized or indigenously based political movement in the Gaza Strip. The primary mechanism chosen to achieve these ends was economic.

After 1967, Gaza's underdeveloped economy came in direct contact with Israel's highly industrialized one, against which it could not compete. As such, Israel's overwhelming economic advantage provided the means through which to channel Palestinian disaffection with Israeli rule and thereby mollify it. What emerged, particularly in the first decade of occupation, was a policy of economic appeasement that brought not only prosperity to individual Palestinians but considerable advantages to the Israeli economy. However, although official policy allowed Palestinians economic growth (or the *generation* of surplus), it did not permit economic development (or the *accumulation* of surplus). The former reinforced the political status quo; the latter threatened to change it.

Pointing to selected indicators of economic well-being, Israel has consistently argued that its policies modernized the Palestinian economy and brought it benefits unimaginable under previous regimes. However, when compared to the standard of living of their counterparts in Israel or Jordan, Gazans have never before suffered such extreme economic disparities. The reasons can be summarized in the following fact: the Israeli government, unlike its political predecessors, has attempted to dispossess Palestinians of their political and cultural patrimony through the direct expropriation of their economic resources, notably water, land, housing, and public finance. In so doing, the government has not only restricted any form of Palestinian economic development, which it equates with political independence—something abhorrent to Israel—but has insured that such development in any of its dimensions will not occur within the context of Israeli rule. Indeed, these measures have resulted in precisely the opposite: the undoing of development or de-development.

In August 1993, in a totally unexpected and surprising move, the Israeli government and the PLO announced a resolution to their conflict. An agreement, known as Gaza–Jericho was reached to implement partial autonomy in the Gaza Strip and in the West Bank town of Jericho as a possible first step on the road to peace. The Agreement generated a great deal of excitement, particularly because it had the official support of both sides. Israeli supporters were tantalized by the prospect of a real peace, while their Palestinian counterparts hoped for a sovereign state. Once again, Gaza was first.

The Gaza–Jericho Agreement is not about how Palestinians and Israelis should live separately but about how they should live together, at least during the five years of interim rule called for by the Agreement. Unlike Israel's peace agreement with Egypt, where land was divided and returned, Israel's agreement with the Palestinians calls for a continued "sharing" of the land while Israel maintains ultimate control over it. The question immediately arises: Will

Palestinian–Israeli coexistence in the future be any different from the past? Will occupation end and its structures be dismantled? Will de-development be arrested under the terms of the proposed peace?

The end of de-development is directly tied to the degree to which expropriation, integration, and deinstitutionalization are reversed and to the establishment of Palestinian independence. This reversal, in turn, is based on future economic and political relations between Palestinians and Israelis and, most importantly, on the terms of those relations. For example, how far will Israel go to protect its economic interests in the Gaza Strip? Who will control Palestinian land and water and in whose interests will these resources be used? Who will control Palestinian trade and access to world markets? To what degree and in what manner will Palestine's profound economic dependence on Israel be lessened? Who will determine Palestine's economic future and how will it be determined? Only when the issue of control is resolved will it be clear whether de-development can be reversed.

Under the terms of the Agreement and its Declaration of Principles, the Israeli government transferred limited political and municipal control over Gaza to the PLO. (Critically, Israel retains authority over security and foreign affairs.) Economic control, however, was not as easily transferred. The Declaration calls for joint arrangements between Israel and the Palestinians in almost every economic domain: water, electricity, energy, finance, transport and communications, trade, industry, infrastructure, social rehabilitation, business development, agriculture and tourism. Is meaningful cooperation possible between two unequal actors in a context where power is so asymmetrical? The answer is in large part grounded in Israeli objectives. The government revealed these objectives in measures and policy changes in the occupied territories that first emerged in the aftermath of the Gulf war, took formal shape with the initiation of the Middle East peace process, and culminated in the Gaza–Jericho Agreement. These policy changes clearly promote the greater integration of the Palestinian economy into Israel's and the deepening dependence of the former on the latter. In fact, the Israeli conception of self-rule in Gaza contains very specific economic arrangements that preclude any radical alteration of the economy, the establishment of an independent Palestinian economy, and, by extension, an independent Palestinian state. In this way, the Israeli government has not attempted to institutionalize an economic separation of the Gaza Strip and Israel as is commonly thought, but has pursued a restructured form of integration, particularly since 1991. Indeed, long before the Gaza–Jericho Agreement was reached, Israel was already creating new integrative ties with Gaza.

Israeli Policy Changes: An Economic Framework for the Gaza–Jericho Agreement[2]

The need to address the severe economic dislocations created in the Gaza Strip by the Gulf war was certainly not lost on Israel. The start of the peace process in 1991 provided Israel with a dual and somewhat paradoxical opportunity. On the one hand, it had the chance to capitalize politically on the economic reforms being planned for Gaza. On the other hand, Israel, responding to U.S. pressure for confidence-building measures and to the rapidly deteriorating situation in Gaza especially, articulated a more detailed economic policy for the occupied territories, something it always had been unwilling to do.

At its conceptual level, Israel's economic policy for the territories is clearly based on a specific political arrangement, autonomy or self-rule, and on a specific economic arrangement, unity. In an official briefing on the subject of the economy of the territories, Danny Gillerman, president of the Federation of the Israeli Chambers of Commerce, stated, "Our stand is that the desirable model as far as autonomy is concerned is one entity—the territories and Israel—we see no possibility and no sense in creating any borders or customs post . . . ."[3]

Within this political framework, the main policy goal is economic revitalization through job creation and increased investment. By 1992, the new economic strategy for the occupied territories was slowly being implemented, a strategy devised by Ezra Sadan in his now famous Sadan Report, commissioned by the Ministry of Defense in 1990. This strategy, first developed for the more impoverished Gaza Strip, is based first and foremost on "trade, particularly free trade with and through Israel,"[4] and the expanded production of exportable goods. Given Gaza's devastating experience during the Gulf war when it was separated from its markets, it is clear that "[w]ithout free trade, there is no real economic subsistence in Gaza and—and it is of no consequence whether one likes it or not."[5]

Free trade underlies the development of certain kinds of industries (e.g., electrical appliances) including industrialized agriculture (e.g., horticulture) that seek to exploit Gaza's comparative advantage—labor—and compensate for its lack of natural resources—water and land. Given Gaza's level of economic dependence on Israel, the orders of magnitude difference in the size of their economies,[6] and the underdeveloped and distorted character of Gaza's economic structure, Sadan argues that economic development in Gaza must, logically and of necessity, occur as a branch plant economy to Israel.

For example, when referring to the future development of "industrialized" farms and the production of exportables such as tomatoes and strawberries, Sadan states that "Palestinian marketing reaching to the gates of the lucrative export markets in the West is [now] limited in scope. But, the services of large forwarding facilities, established marketing channels and the option of brand names provided by several firms in Israel guarantee an immediate access to the export markets."[7] He calls on the government to consider subsidies, loan-guarantees, credit, and foreign-trade insurance "as legitimate tools to overcome the limited capacity of the [Palestinian] markets,"[8] in addition to the liberalization and elimination of various military restrictions on economic transactions across the green line. The introduction of carnation production to

Gaza provides a good example of Sadan's policy intentions.

In April 1993, for example, the agriculture department of the civil administration in Gaza approved a near 100 percent increase in the production of carnations (from 57 dunums in 1992 to 107 dunums in 1993), one of several horticultural projects proposed by Sadan. However, the terms under which Palestinians could produce carnations were imposed totally by Israel.

In a measure virtually unprecedented for Palestinian farmers, the Israeli government provided subsidies of between NIS 4,000 ($1,481) and NIS 4,500 ($1,667) per dunum of carnations. In addition, the government expanded the production of strawberries, zucchini, potatoes, and tomatoes. This production was also supported through Israeli government subsidies, the opening of Israeli and foreign markets, and guaranteed crop purchases, also unprecedented for Palestinians. According to Israeli regulations, however, all produce had to be purchased by Israeli agents for sale in Israel or export through Agrexco.[9]

Although the carnation crop has been successful, Palestinians have suffered considerable losses due to the terms of the arrangement imposed on them by Israel. First, Palestinians can only grow those varieties of carnations for which they are given seedlings by government controlled sources. Second, Palestinians can only market their carnations through Agrexco. However, quality control decisions are made by Agrexco, *after* the Gazan merchant has turned over his flowers. Any flowers Agrexco deems unsuitable for marketing must be taken as an absolute loss, since Agrexco does not return them to Gaza for local sale.[10]

Flower growing has no history as a productive enterprise in Gaza. Furthermore, it is a water-intensive activity and therefore highly inappropriate for Gaza given its serious water problem. However, carnation production is very labor-intensive and provides Israel with a cheap labor input into the production of an important export commodity.

In discussing the development of a canned sardine branch in Gaza, long prohibited by the authorities due to fears of competition, Sadan further argues:

> A significant part of the value that would be added with the increasing industrial activity in the Gaza Strip would accrue in Israel, almost certainly in the Tel-Aviv area and the center . . . . [the] finding presented here points up the fact that development of the canned sardine branch in the Gaza Strip would create competition with Israeli producers of canned sardines, *but* it turns out that this would be competition between the Israeli product and a new product that is half Gazan and half Israeli (in terms of value added).[11]

Moreover,

> . . . the Gazan manufacturer is likely . . . to import various inputs—the most important being tin cans—from Israel. If he does not do that, he will have to import those cans from Europe . . . . In the second case, the [Gazan] plant would have to market the entire output of the finished product outside Israel; under those circumstances, it is doubtful if it could stay in business very long.[12]

In 1992, the government abolished certain protectionist practices militating against industrial development in the occupied territories.

Israel's vision of its restructured relationship with Gaza is first and foremost a self-serving one. Gaza will no doubt reap certain new economic benefits under Sadan's scheme but on terms that, once again, are not its own or necessarily in its own best interests. The cost to local economic development will be as high as it has always been. The Gazan economy will remain tightly linked to that of Israel, dependent, auxiliary, vulnerable to closure, and Israeli recession. The degree of benefit Gaza will be allowed to enjoy will be entirely determined by Israel. The development of an independent, self-sustaining, Gazan economic base will remain an impossibility. This will be true under any political arrangement, including the Gaza–Jericho Agreement, that does not give Palestinians full decision-making control over their own resources, especially land and water, and free and independent access to capital and to external markets. Sadan maintains that Gaza has no alternative but to maintain an economic relationship with Israel. He is correct. The issue, however, is not whether or not structural ties between a Palestinian and Israeli economy should exist, but the terms on which those ties are based.[13]

Conclusion

The inability to solve Gaza's economic problems does not derive as much from the backwardness of the local economy as from the particular ideological and national imperatives that inform Israeli policies. These imperatives have led to de-development. The Gaza–Jericho Agreement and its promise of autonomy will not eliminate de-development because, politically and economically, autonomy remains within Israel's ideological mandate.

It was argued earlier that Gaza's peculiar form of underdevelopment was shaped by an Israeli policy that prioritizes the ideological–political realm over the economic. Israel's ideological goal of creating a strong Jewish state always superceded the desire to exploit Palestinians economically although that did occur. Political not economic gain was the fundamental motivation of state behavior. Israel's rejection of Palestinian sovereignty and control over foreign policy, security, and the economy, and its refusal to transfer decision-making authority over areas critical to development planning strongly suggest that little has changed under the Gaza–Jericho Agreement, Israeli concessions notwithstanding. For example, under the plan's terms, the master keys of territorial jurisdiction (and, hence, political sovereignty)—land, water, and zoning—remain under complete Israeli control. The Palestinian National Authority has few powers over land, despite the existence of a land authority. Water issues also are subject to an Israeli veto. Moreover, if the Palestinian economy is to reduce its extreme dependence on Israel and end de-development, it needs to establish relations with economic partners other than Israel, particularly Europe, the Arab states, and the United States. The present terms of the Agreement do not bode well for the establishment of such direct bilateral arrangements.

Although the Israeli government has transfered limited political authority over Gaza to the PLO, it has not renounced its claim to the occupied territories. The military government has been withdrawn, not abolished. The army has been redeployed, not withdrawn. Israel continues to control the land and Jewish settlements remain under the protection of the Israeli army. Israeli military power and physical force continue to determine Gaza's political and economic framework. Political and ideological imperatives continue to motivate state policy, and economic relations remain a critical channel for fulfilling political objectives. The "land over people" principle that distinguishes Israeli colonialism and defines Israeli policy remains intact. In this context, Israeli control of the Palestinian economy continues to have little to do with promoting sustainable economic development and more to do with protecting the state's economic interests in the occupied territories, pacifying a hostile population, and normalizing Israel's relations with the Arab world. Indeed, PLO officials openly admitted that in order to secure U.S. and European funding for Palestinian autonomy, they had to "accommodate Israel's aim of gaining full acceptance in the Arab world."[14]

According to the DoP, Gaza's economic future will be mediated through joint arrangements between Israel and the Palestinians (and subject to Israeli veto) in a broad spectrum of areas. Critically, Israel remains responsible for all international agreements. Palestinian access to external markets, a key factor in establishing an independent economy, will have to be negotiated with Israel. Furthermore, Israel retains decision-making authority over sectors crucial to Palestinian economic development such as finance. For example, approximately $300 million in housing loans were allocated by international donors to the Gaza Strip in 1994, but there is no banking structure through which to disburse them. Under the proposed new arrangements, however, a new banking structure, whose development the Israeli government has actively prohibited for more than two decades, can only be established with Israeli approval. Economic benefits in lieu of sovereignty and in the presence of gross asymmetry will not end de-development, only mitigate its effects.

Consequently, it is not Israeli control over Gaza's key economic resources and foreign policy that is the problem per se but what the retention of such control still makes possible: territorial expansion and the preclusion of Palestinian statehood. This will insure the continuation of those processes—dispossession and expropriation, integration and externalization, and deinstitutionalization—perhaps less extreme in scale or degree, that produce de-development. The growth of capitalism, for example, will not be possible under conditions of autonomy if and when capitalist growth in Gaza conflicts with Israeli interests or is not geared toward Israeli needs. The ultimate solution to the problem of de-development, therefore, is not simply a matter of giving Palestinians greater control within a system of constrained power, but of removing key constraints and the defining ideological strappings to which they are tied. In its current structure, the Gaza–Jericho Agreement does not remove those constraints; it merely reshapes them.

Israeli policy in the Gaza Strip continues to be defined by what it does not allow rather than by what it does. What it does not allow is real Palestinian control over key economic resources (independence). What it does allow is a form of economic growth linked to and mediated by Israel (dependence). Israeli proposals calling for self-rule in the occupied territories therefore envision an economic future for the Gaza Strip that is essentially no different from its economic past.

The combination of "political divorce and economic marriage"[15] articulated by the Gaza–Jericho Agreement will not alter the underlying relationship between occupier and occupied, only its form. The economic fundamentals of occupation remain unchanged. Gaza's de-development will continue as long as Israel has decision-making control over areas critical to Palestinian sovereignty: the economy, foreign policy, and security. Israeli rule may be less direct but it is no less powerful.

Many have stated that economic reform must be implemented quickly or the momentum for peace will be lost. Over the long term, however, what is most important for an end to de-development is not the number of reforms implemented but the *terms* on which they are implemented. That is, will Gaza have free access to markets or will Israel use free markets to control Gaza? The answer will shape Gaza's future economic and national survival.

In the robes of a hungry woman, Gaza came to me
Rested her tired head on my arm
And we cried.
The black trees in our eyes became wet.
And the sea encircled me
So I washed in it my clothes and veins
Who would believe I'm bearing Gaza with me?
All I remember of Gaza is an eagle
Who has devoured its wings
And a woman-child
I carry and walk on the edge of the
    sword
(It was said that the bridge was wide open
This summer,
So where is the child?)
Gaza

       Walid al-Hallees
       1978[16]

Notes to Conclusion:

1. See H. Zeev, M. Gihon, and Z. Levkowich, *The Gaza Strip: Background Paper* (Jerusalem: Carta, 1974), pp. 6–16. The authors state that in the past 3,500 years, the area that is today the State of Israel has been invaded eighty-five times from the area that is now the Gaza Strip, and in all but two campaigns (the Napoleonic invasion of 1799 and Great Britain's in WWI), the invasions were led by Egypt.

2. Parts of this section are drawn from Roy, "Separation or Integration," with the permission of the publisher.

3. State of Israel, *Briefing on the Economy and Autonomy in the Territories*, Government Press Office, Economic Desk, Jerusalem, 8 February 1993.

4. See Sadan, *Durable Employment*, p. 13; idem., *A Policy for Immediate Economic-Industrial Development*, which contains details of the development scheme for Gaza.

5. Press Briefing (1993).

6. In 1992, Israel's GNP was $60 billion while the occupied territories' GNP was $3 billion, of which more than $1 billion was derived from income earned in Israel. Although the Palestinian and Israeli economies are interdependent, Israel contributes close to 50 percent of Gaza's GNP and over 30 percent of the West Bank's, while Palestinians contribute at most 3 percent to Israel's GNP.

7. Sadan, *Durable Employment*, p. 4.

8. Ibid., p. 7.

9. Interview with officials of international organizations working in Gaza who asked not to be identified, April 1993.

10. Ibid.

11. Sadan, *A Policy for Immediate Economic-Industrial Development*, p. 53.

12. Ibid., pp. 53–54.

13. For more details on Sadan's recommendations see Roy, "Separation or Integration," and Sadan, *A Policy for Immediate Economic-Industrial Development.*

14. Lamis Andoni, "Arafat's Deal Could Leave the Palestinians Isolated," *Christian Science Monitor*, 8 September 1993, p. 6.

15. Graham Usher, "Why Gaza Mostly Says Yes," *Middle East International*, 24 September 1993, p. 20.

16. Hannan Mikhail Ashrawi, "The Contemporary Palestinian Poetry of Occupation," *Journal of Palestine Studies* 7, no.3 (Spring 1978): 94.

Selected Bibliography

Newspapers
Al-Fajr
Al Hamishmar
Christian Science Monitor
Ha'aretz
In These Times
Jerusalem Post
Jerusalem Post, International Edition
New York Post
New York Times
Palestine Post
Washington Post
Yediot Ahronot

Government and Official Documents
A. United States
United States Agency for International Development. *Strategy Statement: The Direct West Bank/Gaza Program and the Jordan West Bank/Gaza Development Program.* Washington, DC: n.p., October 1987.

————. *USAID Program Strategy for The West Bank And Gaza Strip 1993–1997.* Near East Bureau. Washington, DC: n.p., 1992.

————. *U.S. Economic Assistance to the West Bank and Gaza: A Positive Contribution to the Palestinian People From the American People.* Washington, DC: n.p., 1989.

B. British
Anglo–American Committee of Inquiry. *Report to the United States Government and His Majesty's Government in the United Kingdom.* Washington, DC: United States Government Printing Office, 1946.

————. *A Survey of Palestine.* Jerusalem: Government Printer, 1946–47.

Commonwealth War Graves Commission Cemetery Register: the War Graves of the British Empire—Gaza War Cemetery, Palestine. London: Imperial War Graves Commission, 1929.

Draft Mandates For Mesopotamia and Palestine As Submitted for the Approval of the League of Nations, Miscellaneous No. 3. London: His Majesty's Stationery Office, 1921.

Franco–British Convention of December 23, 1920 on Certain Points Connected with the Mandates for Syria and the Lebanon, Palestine and Mesopotamia, Miscellaneous No. 4. London: His Majesty's Stationery Office, 1921.

Government of Palestine. *Statistical Abstract of Palestine 1944–45*. Jerusalem: Government Printer, 1946.

Palestine Royal Commission. *Summary of Report (with Extracts)*. London: His Majesty's Stationery Office, 1937.

C. Israeli
Gaza Civil Administration. *Gaza Region Agricultural Development (Internal Document)*. Gaza: Civil Administration, Gaza Strip, 1989.

———. *A Plan for the Development of the Gaza Strip through the Year 2000*. Tel-Aviv: Ministry of Defense and Gaza Civil Administration, 1986.

Gaza Department of Agriculture. *Agricultural Production in the Gaza Strip 1987–1988* (Internal Document). Gaza: Civil Administration, 1988.

———. *Agricultural Statistics*. Gaza: Civil Administration, Gaza Strip, 1989.

———. *Prospects for the Citrus and Fruits Sector in the Gaza Strip* (Internal Document). Gaza: Civil Administration, 1985.

———. *Vegetable Production in the Gaza Strip* (Internal Document). Gaza: Civil Administration, 1986?

Israeli Information Centre. *The Administered Areas: Aspects of Israeli Policy, Information Briefing 10*. Ministry of Foreign Affairs, 1973.

Jewish Agency for Palestine. *The Jewish Case before the Anglo–American Committee of Inquiry on Palestine: Statements and Memoranda*. Jerusalem: The Jewish Agency, 1947.

Jewish Agency for Palestine. *The Jewish Plan for Palestine—Memoranda and Statements presented by the Jewish Agency for Palestine to the United Nations Special Committee on Palestine*. Jerusalem: The Jewish Agency, 1947.

Ministry of Agriculture. *Percentage of Salinity in the Water Wells of the Gaza Strip* (Internal document). Gaza City: Ministry of Agriculture, Civil Administration, 1989.

Ministry of Defense. *Development and Economic Situation in Judea, Samaira, the Gaza Strip and North Sinai 1967–1969: A Summary*. Tel-Aviv: Ministry of Defense, 1970.

———. *Economic Survey for 1988 and 1989: The Economy of Judea, Sama-ria and the Gaza Strip—After Two Years of Events [i.e. the Intifada], (Classified Document)*. Tel-Aviv: Ministry of Defense, 1990.

———. *Report of the Military Government 1985–86*. Tel-Aviv: Ministry of Defense, 1986.

Ministry of Foreign Affairs. *The Administered Areas: Aspects of Israeli Policy*. NTIS,

Information Briefing 10. N.p.: Ministry of Foreign Affairs, 1973.

Ministry of Foreign Affairs. *The Gaza Strip: Aggression or Peace*. Jerusalem: The Government Printer, 1958.

Ministry of Foreign Affairs. *Two Years of Military Government 1967–1969: Data on the Activities of the Civil Administration in Judea and Samaria, the Gaza Strip and Northern Sinai*. Tel-Aviv: Ministry of Foreign Affairs, May 1969.

Ministry of Labour and Social Affairs. *Labour Force Statistics*. Jerusalem: Ministry of Labour and Social Affairs, 1988.

State of Israel. *Agricultural Statistics Quarterly (ASQ)*. January–March 1990. Jerusalem: Central Bureau of Statistics, 1990.

———. *Budget for 1986/87*. Jerusalem: State of Israel, 1986.

———. *An Eighteen Year Survey (1967–1985)*. Tel Aviv: Coordinator of Government Operations in Judea & Samaria and Gaza District, Ministry of Defense, 1986.

———. *Judaea, Samaria and Gaza Area Statistics* 15, no.2. Jerusalem: Central Bureau of Statistics, 1985.

———. *Judaea, Samaria and Gaza Area Statistics* 18, no.1. Jerusalem: Central Bureau of Statistics, 1988.

———. *Judea, Samaria and Gaza Area Statistics*. Second edition. Jerusalem: Central Bureau of Statistics, 1989.

———. *Judea–Samaria and the Gaza District—A Sixteen Year Survey (1967-1983)*. Tel Aviv: Ministry of Defence, 1983.

———. *Labour and Employment in Judea, Samaria and the Gaza District*. Jerusalem: Ministry of Labour and Social Affairs, Department of International Relations, 1989.

———. *National Accounts for Judaea, Samaria, the Gaza Strip, and North Sinai For the Decade 1968–77, Special Series No. 615*. Jerusalem: Central Bureau of Statistics, 1979.

———. *National Accounts of Judea, Samaria and Gaza Area 1968–1986, Special Series No. 818*. Jerusalem: Central Bureau of Statistics, 1988.

———. *Projections of Population in Judea, Samaria and Gaza Area up to 2002, Special Series No. 802*. Jerusalem: Central Bureau of Statistics, 1987.

———. *Statistical Abstract of Israel*. Selected years. Jerusalem: Central Bureau of Statistics, various years.

D. Arab

Central Bureau of Statistics. *Industrial Statistical Bulletin for the West Bank and Gaza Strip 1988*. Damascus: Economic Department, Palestine Liberation Organization, 1988.

Citrus Producers Union for the Gaza Strip. *Annual Report 1989*. N.p.: Citrus Producers Union For the Gaza Strip, 1989.

Egyptian Administration in Palestine. *Official Statistics 1954*. Cairo: Department of Surveys and Publications, 1954.

Hashemite Kingdom of Jordan. *The Economic and Social Development of the Occupied Territories—A Five Year Programme (1986–1990) Summary*. Amman: Ministry of Planning, 1986.

———. *A Note on Jordan's Progress for the Economic and Social Development of the Occupied Territories*. Amman: Ministry of Planning, n.d.

———. *A Programme for Economic and Social Development in the Occupied Territories 1986–1990—Summary*. Amman: Ministry of Planning, 1986.

League of Arab States. *The Palestine Refugees—Information and Statistics*. N.p.: Costa Tsoumas & Co. Press, 1957.

United Arab Republic, Gaza. *Gaza: Springboard for the Liberation of Palestine*. Cairo: Information Department, 1962.

E. United Nations

Conference on Trade and Development. *Assistance To The Palestinian People: Recent economic development in the occupied Palestinian territories, with special reference to the external trade sector (Conference resolutions 146 (VI) of 2 July 1983 and 169 (VII) of 3 August 1987)*. Geneva: UNCTAD, August 1988.

———. *Assistance to the Palestinian People: Recent Economic Developments in the Occupied Palestinian Territory*. Geneva: UNCTAD, 1989.

———. *Developments in the Economy of the Occupied Palestinian Territory*. Geneva: UNCTAD, July 1993.

———. *Palestinian External Trade under Israeli Occupation*. New York: United Nations, 1989.

———. *The Palestinian Financial Sector under Israeli Occupation*. Geneva: UNCTAD, July 1987.

———. *Prospects for Sustained Development of the Palestinian Economy in the West Bank and Gaza Strip*. Geneva: UNCTAD, September 1993.

———. *Recent Economic Developments in the Occupied Palestinian Territories*. Geneva:

Special Economic Unit (Palestinian People), UNCTAD, June 1986.

————. *Recent Economic Developments in the Occupied Palestinian Territories with Special Reference to the External Trade Sector.* Geneva: UNCTAD, September 1988.

Economic and Social Commission For Western Asia. *The Occupied Palestinian Territories: Industrial Development Policies, Constraints and Prospects.* Vienna: United Nations Industrial Development Organization, 1989.

Educational, Scientific and Cultural Organization. *Study on the Needs of the Palestinian People in the Field of Education and Training.* Paris: UNESCO, 1990.

Industrial Development Organization. *Identification of Priority Projects In The Industrial Sector.* Vienna: UNIDO, September 1989.

International Labour Conference. *Report of the Director–General—Appendices.* Geneva: International Labour Office, 1985.

International Labour Organization. *Report of the Director–General—Appendices.* Selected years. Geneva: International Labour Organization, various years.

United Nations. *Addendum to the Report of the Commissioner-General of the United Nations Relief and Works Agency for Palestine Refugees in the Near East, 42nd session.* New York: UN General Assembly, 1988.

————. *General Assembly Official Records.* Selected sessions and supplements. New York: United Nations, various years.

————. *Permanent Sovereignty over National Resources in the Occupied Arab Territories—Report of the Secretary–General.* New York: UN General Assembly, 1981.

————. *UNRWA, Financial Report and Audited Financial Statements of the Year ended 31 December 1987 and Report of the Board of Auditors.* New York: UN General Assembly, 43rd Session, 1988.

United Nations Economic Survey Mission. *Interim Report of the United Nations Economic Survey Mission, Volume 1.* New York: United Nations, 1949.

United Nations Relief and Works Agency. *Information of UNRWA Vocational and Technical Training Programmes in Gaza and the West Bank.* N.p.: UNRWA, 1989.

————. *Registration Statistical Bulletin for the First Quarter 1/91 & 1/93.* Vienna: UNRWA, April 1991.

————. *Situation of Palestinian Civilians under Israeli Occupation: Gaza Strip, March–May 1991 (Internal Document).* N.p.: UNRWA, 1991.

————. *UNRWA: A Brief History 1950–1982.* Vienna: Vienna International Centre, 1983.

UNRWA, Office of the Commissioner-General. *Bulletin (Internal Document)*. Vienna: United Nations Relief and Works Agency, 1991.

———. *Report of the Commissioner-General of the United Nations Relief and Works Agency for Palestine Refugees in the Near East*. Selected volumes. New York: United Nations General Assembly, various years.

Books, Papers, and Articles
A'Sha'afi, Abd'al-Latif. "From a Refugee Camp to the Dekel Neighbourhood in Rafah." In *Community Work in the Gaza Strip*, edited by A. Lavine. Jerusalem: Ministry of Labour and Social Affairs, n.d.

Abcarius, M.F. "Fiscal System." In *Economic Organization of Palestine*, edited by S.B. Himadeh, 545–54. Beirut: The American Press, 1938.

———. *Palestine: Through the Fog of Propaganda*. London: Hutchinson & Co., 1946?

Abed, George T. *The Economic Viability of a Palestinian State*. Washington, DC: Institute for Palestine Studies, 1990.

Abercrombie, Thomas J. "Ibn Battuta: Prince of Travelers." *National Geographic* 180, no. 6 (December 1991).

Abu Kishk, Bakir. "Industrial Development Policies in the West Bank and Gaza Strip." In *The Palestinian Economy: Studies in Development under Prolonged Occupation*, edited by George T. Abed, 165–89. London: Routledge, 1988.

———. *The Industrial and Economic Trends in the West Bank and Gaza Strip*. Beirut: United Nations Economic Commission for West Asia, Joint ECWA/UNIDO Industrial Division, 1981.

Abu Shokar, Abdelfattah, Kamel Abu Jabber, Mattes Buhbe, and Mohammed Smad. "Income Distribution and Its Social Impact in the Occupied Territories." In *Income Distribution in Jordan*, 93–109. Boulder, CO: Westview Press, 1990.

Abu-Amr, Ziad. "The Gaza Economy 1948–1984." In *The Palestinian Economy: Studies in Development under Prolonged Occupation*, edited by George T. Abed. London: Routledge, 1988.

———. "Class Structure and the Political Elite in the Gaza Strip: 1948–1988." In *Occupation: Israel Over Palestine*, second edition, edited by N. Aruri. Belmont, MA: Association of Arab–American University Graduates (AAUG), 1989.

Abu-Lughod, Janet. "Demographic Consequences of the Occupation." In *Occupation: Israel Over Palestine*, second edition, edited by N. Aruri. Belmont, MA: Association of Arab–American University Graduates (AAUG), 1989.

Ahiram, Ephraim. "The Principle Determinants of Economic Cooperation between the People of Israel and Palestine." Paper presented at the University of Nijmegen, Nijmegen, The Netherlands, 18–20 April 1990.

Alawnah, Atif K. "The Impact of the Intifada on the Palestinian and Israeli Economies." *New Outlook*, 1990.

Allon, Yigal. "Israel: The Case for Defensible Borders." *Foreign Affairs* 55, no.1 (October 1976): 38–53.

American Cooperative Development Incorporated. *Extension Proposal for the West Bank and Gaza Strip*. ACDI, 1988.

American Middle East Service and Training. *Progress Report-West Bank/Gaza Human Resource Development Project. October 1, 1987–March 31, 1988*. AMIDEAST.

————. *Progress Report–West Bank/Gaza Human Resource Development Project. April 1, 1988–September 30, 1988*. AMIDEAST.

————. *Progress Report–West Bank/Gaza Human Resource Development Project. October 1, 1988–March 31, 1989*. AMIDEAST.

American Near East Refugee Aid. *Addendum to ANERA Proposal: Cooperative, Municipal and Business Development Projects in the West Bank/Gaza*. Washington, DC: ANERA, May 1988.

————. *The Gaza Technical Center—Project Document*. ANERA, 1988.

————. *Preliminary Business Plan: Cooperative Finance Bank—West Bank/Gaza*. Washington, DC: ANERA, 1992.

Amin, Samir. *Accumulation on a World Scale*. New York: Monthly Review Press, 1974.

————. *Unequal Development*. New York: Monthly Review Press, 1976.

Amiran, D.H.K. "The Patterns of Settlement in Palestine." *Israeli Exploration Journal* 3, nos.2–4 (1953): 65–78, 192–209, 250–60.

Amor, Meir. "The Fact of War." In *Walking The Red Line: Israelis in Search of Justice for Palestine*, edited by D. Hurwitz, 66–76. Philadelphia: New Society Publishers, 1992.

Apter, David. *Rethinking Development: Modernization, Dependency, and Postmodern Politics*. Beverly Hills: Sage Publications, 1987.

Arab Thought Forum. *Statistics*. Gaza City: Arab Thought Forum, 1991.

The Arabs under Israeli Occupation, 1979. Beirut: Institute for Palestine Studies, 1980.

Armstrong, Hamilton Fish. "The U.N. Experience in Gaza." *Foreign Affairs* 35, no.4 (July 1957): 600–19.

Aronson, Geoffrey. *Creating Facts: Israel, Palestinians and the West Bank*. Washington, DC: Institute for Palestine Studies, 1987.

———. *Report on Israeli Settlement in the Occupied Territories, Volume 1, No. 2*. Foundation for Middle East Peace, 1991.

Asad, Talal. "Class Transformation Under the Mandate." *MERIP Reports* 53 (December 1976): 3–9.

Asfour, Edmund. "The Economic Framework of the Palestine Problem." In *Backdrop to Tragedy*, edited by W. R. Polk, David M. Stamler, and Edmund Asfour. Boston: Beacon Press, 1957.

Ashrawi, Hannan Mikhail. "The Contemporary Palestinian Poetry of Occupation." *Journal of Palestine Studies* 7, no.3 (Spring 1978).

Avi-Yonah, Michael. *Encyclopedia of Archaeological Excavations in the Holy Land*. London: Oxford University Press, 1976.

———. *The Holy Land from the Persian to the Arab Conquests (536 BC–AD 640): A Historical Geography*. Grand Rapids, MI: Baker Book House, 1977.

———. *The Jews Under Roman and Byzantine Rule: A Political History of Palestine from the Bar Kokhba War to the Arab Conquest*. New York: Schocken Books, 1984.

Awartani, Hisham. "Agricultural Development and Policies in the West Bank and Gaza Strip." In *The Palestinian Economy: Studies in Development under Prolonged Occupation*, edited by George T. Abed, 139–64. London: Routledge, 1988.

———. "The Palestinian Economy under Occupation." Paper presented at Nijmegen University, Nijmegen, The Netherlands, 18–21 April 1990.

———. *A Survey of Industries in The West Bank and Gaza Strip*. Birzeit, West Bank: Birzeit University, 1979.

Bahbah, Bishara A. "The Economic Consequences on Palestinians." In *The Palestinians and the War in the Gulf*, edited by The Center for Policy Analysis on Palestine. Washington, DC: The Center for Policy Analysis on Palestine, 1991.

Bahiri, Simcha. *Economic Consequences of the Israel–PLO Declaration of Principles: An Israeli Perspective*. Jerusalem: Israel/Palestine Center for Research and Information, 1994.

———. *Industrialization in the West Bank and Gaza*. Boulder, CO: Westview Press, 1987.

————. *Peaceful Separation or Enforced Unity: Economic Consequences for Israel and the West Bank/Gaza Area*. Tel-Aviv: International Centre for Peace in the Middle East, 1984.

Bank of Israel. *Annual Report 1988*. Jerusalem: Bank of Israel, 1989.

————. *Annual Report 1989*. Jerusalem: Bank of Israel, 1990.

————. *The Economy of the Administered Areas in 1970*. Jerusalem: Research Department, Bank of Israel, 1971.

————. *The Economy of the Administered Areas in 1972*. Jerusalem: Research Department, Bank of Israel, 1974.

Bar Zohar, Michael. *Ben–Gurion*. Translated by Peretz Kidron. London: Weidenfeld and Nicolson, 1978.

Barraclough, Geoffrey. *An Introduction to Contemporary History*. Harmondsworth: Penguin Books, 1967.

Baster, James. "Economic Aspects of the Settlement of Palestine Refugees." *Middle East Journal* 8, no.1 (Winter 1954): 54–68.

————. "Economic Review: Economic Problems in the Gaza Strip." *Middle East Journal* 19, no.3 (Summer 1955): 323–27.

Bauer, P.T. *Dissent on Development*. Cambridge, MA: Harvard University Press, 1976.

Benvenisti, Eyal. *Legal Dualism: The Absorption of the Occupied Territories into Israel*. Boulder, CO: Westview Press, 1990.

Benvenisti, Meron. *1986 Report: Demographic, Economic, Legal, Social and Political Development in the West Bank*. Jerusalem: West Bank Data Base Project, 1986.

————. *1987 Report*. Jerusalem: West Bank Data Base Project, 1988.

————. *U.S. Government Funded Projects in the West Bank and Gaza (1977–1983) (Palestinian Sector) Working Paper #13*. Jerusalem: The West Bank Data Base Project, 1984.

————. *The West Bank Data Project: A Survey of Israel's Policies*. Washington, DC: The American Enterprise Institute, 1984.

————. *The West Bank Handbook: A Political Lexicon*. Jerusalem: The Jerusalem Post Press, 1986.

Benvenisti, Meron, and Shlomo Khayat. *The West Bank and Gaza Atlas*. Jerusalem: The Jerusalem Post Press, 1988.

Binder, Leonard. *Islamic Liberalism: A Critique of Development Ideologies*. Chicago: University of Chicago Press, 1988.

Brand, Laurie. "Nasir's Egypt and the Reemergence of the Palestinian National Movement." *Journal of Palestine Studies* 17, no.2 (Winter 1988): 29–45.

Bransten, Thomas R. *Memoirs—David Ben-Gurion*. New York: World Publishing Co., 1970.

Bregman, Arie. *Economic Growth in the Administered Areas 1968–1973*. Jerusalem: Research Department, Bank of Israel, 1975.

———. *The Economy of the Administered Territories 1968–1973*. Jerusalem: Bank of Israel, 1975.

———. *The Economy of the Administered Areas 1974–75*. Jerusalem: Research Department, Bank of Israel, 1976.

Brewer, Anthony. *Marxist Theories of Imperialism: A Critical Survey*. Second ed. London: Routledge, 1990.

Brown, Montague. "Agriculture." In *Economic Organization of Palestine*, edited by S.B. Himadeh. Beirut: The American Press, 1938.

Bruhns, Fred C. "A Study of Arab Refugee Attitudes." *Middle East Journal* 9, no.2 (Spring 1955): 130–38.

Bruins, H.J., A. Tuinhof, and R. Keller. *Water in the Gaza Strip*. The Hague: Ministry of Foreign Affairs, Government of the Netherlands, 1993.

B'tselem–The Israeli Information Center for Human Rights in the Occupied Territories. *The System of Taxation in the West Bank and Gaza Strip as an Instrument for the Enforcement of Authority During the Uprising*. Jerusalem: B'tselem, 1990.

Bull, Vivian A. *The West Bank: Is It Viable?* Lexington, MA: Lexington Books, 1975.

Caplan, Neil. *Palestine Jewry and the Arab Question 1917–29*. London: Frank Cass, 1978.

———. "A Tale of Two Cities: The Rhodes and Lausanne Conferences 1949." *Journal of Palestine Studies* 21, no.3 (Spring 1992): 5–34.

Carmi, Shulamit, and Henry Rosenfeld. "The Origins of the Process of Proletarianization and Urbanization of Arab Peasants in Palestine." *Annals of the NY Academy of Sciences* 220, Article 6 (March 1974): 470–85.

Chilcote, Ronald H. *Theories of Development and Underdevelopment*. Boulder, CO: Westview Press, 1984.

Cohen, Amnon. *Palestine in the 18th Century: Patterns of Government and Administration*. Jerusalem: Magnes Press, Hebrew University, 1973.

Cohen, Amnon, and Gabriel Baer. *Egypt and Palestine: a Millennium of Association (868–1948)*. New York: St. Martin's Press, 1984.

Cohen, Michael. *Palestine: Retreat from the Mandate: The Making of British Policy 1936–45*. London: Paul Elek, 1978.

Dajani, Souad R. "Health Care and Development: A Case Study of the Israeli-Occupied West Bank." Ph.D. diss., University of Toronto, 1984.

Dakkak, Ibrahim. "Development from Within: A Strategy for Survival." In *The Palestinian Economy: Studies in Development under Prolonged Occupation*, edited by George T. Abed, 287–310. London: Routledge, 1988.

Davies, Rhona, and Peter R. Johnson. *The Uzi and The Stone*. Calgary, Alberta: Detselig Enterprises Ltd., 1991.

Dayan, Moshe. *Breakthrough: A Personal Account of the Egypt–Israel Peace Negotiations*. New York: Alfred A. Knopf, 1981.

———. *Moshe Dayan: Story of My Life*. New York: William Morrow, 1976.

Dillman, Jeffrey D. "Water Rights in the Occupied Territories." *Journal of Palestine Studies* 19, no.1 (Autumn 1989): 46–71.

Dishon, Daniel. *Middle East Record (MER) 1969–1970*. Jerusalem: Israeli Universities Press, 1977.

"Documents and Source Material." *Journal of Palestine Studies* 21, no.3 (Spring 1992).

Dothan, Trude. "Excavations at the Cemetery of Deir El-Balah." In *Qedem: Monographs of the Institute of Archaeology*. Jerusalem: Hebrew University, 1979.

———. "Gaza Sands Yield Lost Outpost of the Egyptian Empire." *National Geographic* 162, no.6 (December 1982): 739–69.

Doukhan, Moses J. "Land Tenure." In *Economic Organization of Palestine*, edited by S.B. Himadeh. Beirut: The American Press, 1938.

Downey, Glanville. *Gaza in the Early Sixth Century*. Norman, OK: University of Oklahoma, 1963.

Drori, Moshe. "Local Government in Judea and Samaria." In *Military Government in the Territories Administered by Israel 1967–1980: The Legal Aspects*, edited by M. Shamgar, 237–84. Jerusalem: Faculty of Law, Hebrew University, 1982.

Drury, Richard Toshiyuki and Robert C. Winn. *The Economics of Occupation in the West Bank*. Boston: Beacon Press, 1992.

Efrat, Elisha. "Settlement Pattern and Economic Changes of the Gaza Strip 1947–1977." *Middle East Journal* 31, no.3 (Summer 1977): 349–58.

Elmusa, Sharif S. "Dividing the Common Palestinian-Israeli Waters." *Journal of Palestine Studies* 22, no.3 (Spring 1993): 57–77.

Farhi, Carol. *The Gaza Strip*. Jerusalem: Legal Service, Ministry of Justice, 1971.

———. "On the Legal Status of the Gaza Strip." In *Military Government in the Territories Administered by Israel 1967–1980: The Legal Aspects*, edited by M. Shamgar. Jerusalem: Faculty of Law, Hebrew University Press, 1982.

Fischer, Stanley, Dani Rodrik, and Elias Tuma. *The Economics of Middle East Peace*. Cambridge, MA: MIT Press, 1993.

Fitzgerald, Dean. *A History of Gaza*. Gaza City: Baptist Mission, 1986.

Flapan, Simha. *The Birth of Israel: Myths and Realities*. New York: Pantheon, 1987.

———. *Zionism and the Palestinians*. New York: Barnes and Noble Books, 1979.

Foundation for Middle East Peace. *Report on Israeli Settlement in the Occupied Territories*. Washington, DC: Foundation for Middle East Peace, 1992.

Fox, Frank. *The History of the Royal Gloucestershire Hussars Yeomanry 1898–1922: The Great Calvalry Campaign in Palestine*. London: Philip Allan & Co., 1923.

Frisch, Hillel. *Stagnation and Frontier: Arab and Jewish Industry in the West Bank*. Jerusalem: The West Bank Data Base Project, 1983.

Fruzzetti, Lina, and Akos Ostor. *Culture and Change Along the Blue Nile*. Boulder, CO: Westview Press, 1990.

Gabbay, Rony E. *A Political Study of the Arab–Jewish Conflict: The Arab Refugee Problem (A Case Study)*. Geneva: Librairie E. Droz, 1959.

Gal, Yaacov. "Community Work in the New Refugee Neighbourhoods of the Gaza Strip." In *Community Work in the Gaza Strip*, edited by A. Lavine. Jerusalem: Ministry of Labour and Social Affairs, n.d.

Galnoor, Itzhak. "Water Planning: Who Gets the Last Drop?" In *Can Planning Replace Politics? The Israeli Experience*, edited by R. Bilski et al. The Hague: Martinus Nijhoff, 1980.

Gaza: A Table Explaining the Number of Palestinian Deportees from the Gaza Strip

June 1967–October 1988. N.p.: Al Quds Press Office., 1989.

Gazit, Mordechai. "Ben Gurion's Proposal to Include the Gaza Strip in Israel, 1949." In *Zionism: Studies in the History of the Zionist Movement and of the Jewish Community in Palestine*, 313-32. Tel Aviv: Tel Aviv University, 1987.

George, David Lloyd. *War Memoirs*. London: Oldhams, 1934.

Gharaibeh, Fawzi. *The Economies of the West Bank and Gaza Strip*. Boulder, CO: Westview Press, 1985.

Gibb, H.A.R., and H. Bonen. *Islamic Society and the West*. London: n.p., 1950.

Gichon, Mordechai. "The History of the Gaza Strip: A Geo-Political and Geo-Strategic Perspective." In *The Jerusalem Cathedra*, edited by L.I. Levine, 282–315. Jerusalem: Yad Izhak Ben-Zvi, 1982.

Glucker, Carol A.M. *The City of Gaza in the Roman and Byzantine Periods*. Oxford, England: B.A.R. International, 1987.

"Go to Gaza" (in Hebrew). *Shdamot* 66 (Winter 1968): 7–13.

Goulet, Denis. *The Cruel Choice: A New Concept in the Theory of Development*. New York: Atheneum, 1971.

Graham-Brown, Sarah. "The Economic Consequences of the Occupation." In *Occupation: Israel Over Palestine*, edited by N. Aruri, 311–25. Belmont, MA: Association of Arab-American University Graduates (AAUG), 1989.

———. "Impact on the Social Structure of Palestinian Society." In *Occupation: Israel Over Palestine*, second edition, edited by N. Aruri, 361–97. Belmont, MA: Association of Arab–American University Graduates (AAUG), 1989.

———. "The Political Economy of the Jabal Nablus, 1920–48." In *Studies in the Economic and Social History of Palestine in the Nineteenth and Twentieth Centuries*, edited by Roger Owen. Carbondale, IL: Southern Illinois University, 1982.

Granovsky, Abraham. *Land Policy in Palestine*. New York: Block Publishing Co., 1940.

Gruenbaum, Ludwig. *Outlines of a Development Plan for Jewish Palestine*. Jerusalem: The Jewish Agency, 1946.

Gubser, Peter. *Middle East Trip Report, 4 April 1992–16 April 1992*. American Near East Refugee Aid (ANERA), 1992.

———. *Middle East Trip Report, 7 November 1992–22 November 1992*. American Near East Refugee Aid (ANERA), 1992.

Guillou, A. "Prise de Gaza par les Arabes au vɪɪ Siecle." *Bulletin de Correspondance Hellenique* 81 (1957): 396–404.

Gurevich, David. *Statistical Abstract of Palestine 1929.* Jerusalem: Keren Hayesod, 1930.

Hadawi, Sami. *Bitter Harvest: Palestine Between 1914–1967.* Delmar, N.Y: Caravan Books, 1979.

———. *Palestinian Rights and Losses in 1948: A Comprehensive Study.* London: Saqi, 1988.

Haddad, Hassan. "The Biblical Bases of Zionist Colonialism." In *Settler Regimes in Africa and the Arab World: The Illusion of Endurance,* edited by I. a. A.-L. Abu-Lughod Baha, 3–19. Wilmete, IL: Medina University Press International, 1974.

Hagen, Everett E. *The Economics of Development.* Homewood, IL: Richard D. Irwin, 1980.

Haidar, Aziz. *Vocational Education in the Arab Schools in Israel.* Bir Zeit, West Bank: Center of Documents and Research, Bir Zeit University, 1985.

Haim, Yehoyada. *Abandonment of Illusions: Zionist Political Attitudes toward Palestinian Arab Nationalism, 1936–1939.* Boulder, CO: Westview Press, 1983.

Hakim, George, and M.Y. El-Hussayni, "Monetary and Banking System." In *Economic Organization of Palestine,* edited by S.B. Himadeh. Beirut: The American Press, 1938.

Halevi, Nadav, and Ruth Klinov-Malul. *The Economic Development of Israel.* New York: Praeger, 1968.

Hamilton, R.W. "Two Churches at Gaza as Described by Choricius of Gaza." *Palestine Exploration Fund* (January 1930): 178–91.

Harris, Laurence. "Money and Finance with Underdeveloped Banking in the Occupied Territories." In *The Palestinian Economy: Studies in Development under Prolonged Occupation,* edited by George T. Abed, 191–222. London: Routledge, 1988.

Harris, L., H. Jabr, and R. Shihadeh. *Study for the Establishment of an Industrial Development Bank in the Occupied Territories of Palestine.* Vienna: United Nations Industrial Development Organization, 1988.

Hazboun, Samir, Tariq Mitwasi, and Wajih El-Sheikh. *The Economic Impact of the Israel–PLO Declaration of Principles on the West Bank, Gaza Strip and the Middle East Region.* Jerusalem: Israel/Palestine Center for Research and Information, 1994.

Herzog, Chaim. *The Arab–Israeli Wars: War and Peace in the Middle East.* New York: Random House, 1982.

Hilal, Jamil. "Class Transformation in the West Bank and Gaza." *MERIP Reports* 53 (December 1976): 9–15.

Hiltermann, Joost R. *Behind The Intifada*. Princeton, NJ: Princeton University Press, 1991.

———. "Israel's Strategy to Break the Intifada." *Journal of Palestine Studies* 19, no.2 (Winter 1990): 87–98.

———. "Workers' Rights during the Uprising." *Journal of Palestine Studies* 19, no.1 (Autumn 1989): 83–91.

Himadeh, Sa'id B. "Industry." In *Economic Organization of Palestine*, edited by S.B. Himadeh. Beirut: The American Press, 1938.

Hirschman, Albert O. *The Strategy of Economic Development*. New Haven, CT: Yale University Press, 1961.

Hooper, C.A. *The Civil Law of Palestine and Trans-Jordan*. Jerusalem: The Azriel Printing Works, 1933–36.

Hooper, Rick. *Presentation of UNRWA to the United Nations Seminar on Assistance to the Palestinian People*. Paris: United Nations, 1993.

Hope-Simpson, Sir John. *Report on Immigration, Land Settlement and Development*. London: His Majesty's Stationery Office, 1930.

Horowitz, David. "Arab Economy in Palestine." In *Palestine's Economic Future*, edited by J.B. Hobman, 55–65. London: Percy Lund, Humphries and Co. Ltd., 1946.

Horowitz, David, and Rita Hinden, *Economic Survey of Palestine*. Tel Aviv: The Jewish Agency for Palestine, 1938.

Hurewitz, J.C. *The Struggle for Palestine*. New York: Norton, 1950.

Hyamson, Albert M. *Palestine under the Mandate: 1920–1948*. London: Methuen, 1950.

Ilchman, Warren F., and Norman Thomas Uphoff. *The Political Economy of Change*. Berkeley: University of California Press, 1969.

Issawi, Charles. "Decline and Revival of the Middle Eastern Economy." In *The Economic History of the Middle East 1800–1914: A Book of Readings*, edited by C. Issawi, 3–13. Chicago: University of Chicago, 1966.

———. *An Economic History of the Middle East and North Africa*. New York: Columbia University Press, 1982.

———. *The Fertile Crescent 1800–1914: A Documentary Economic History*. New

York: Oxford University Press, 1988.

The Jewish Agency Digest 3 (29 October 1948): 31–33.

Jewish Currents 46, no. 11 (December 1992).

Johnson, W.J., and R.E.H. Crosbie. *Report of a Committee on the Economic Condition of Agriculturalists in Palestine and the Fiscal Measures of the Government Thereto.* Jerusalem: Government Printing and Stationery Office, 1930.

Kahan, David. *Agriculture and Water in the West Bank and Gaza, Part One, The Arab Sector.* Jerusalem: West Bank Data Base Project, 1983.

———. *Agriculture and Water Resources in the West Bank and Gaza (1967–1987).* Jerusalem: The West Bank Data Base Project and the Jerusalem Post Press, 1987.

Kahn, Alfred E. "Palestine: A Problem in Economic Evaluation." *American Economic Review* 34 (1944): 538–60.

Kahn, Herman. *World Economic Development: 1979 and Beyond.* London: Croom-Helm, 1979.

Kana'na, Sharif, and Rashad al-Madani. *al-Istitan was Musadarat al-Aradi fi Qita Ghazza 1967–1984* (Settlement and Land Confiscation in the Gaza Strip 1967–1984). Birzeit, West Bank: Center for Research and Documents, Birzeit University, 1985.

Kanovsky, Eliyahu. *The Economic Impact of the Six-Day War: Israel, the Occupied Territories, Egypt and Jordan.* New York: Praeger, 1970.

Kasher, Aryeh. "Gaza During the Greco-Roman Era." In *TheJerusalem Cathedra*, edited by L.I. Levine. Jerusalem: Yad Izhak Ben Zvi, 1982.

Kedourie, Elie. *The Anglo–Arab Labyrinth.* Cambridge: Cambridge University Press, 1976.

———. *England and the Middle East: The Destruction of the Ottoman Empire 1914–21.* Sussex: Harvester Press, 1978.

Khalidi, Rashid. "Palestinian Peasant Resistance to Zionism before World War I." In *Blaming the Victims: Spurious Scholarship and the Palestinian Question*, edited by Edward Said and Christopher Hitchens, 207–233. New York: Verso, 1988.

Khalidi, Walid. *From Haven to Conquest: Readings in Zionism and the Palestine Problem until 1948.* Washington, DC: Institute for Palestine Studies, 1987.

———. "The New Middle East Security Environment." In *The Saladin Syndrome: Lessons from the Gulf War*, edited by Z. Schiff and W. Khalidi. Cambridge, Massachusetts: International Security Studies Program, American Academy of Arts and Sciences, 1991.

Khalidi, Walid, and Jill Kedourie. *Palestine and the Arab–Israeli Conflict: An Annotated Bibliography*. Beirut: Institute for Palestine Studies, 1974.

al-Khass, Muhammad. "Municipal Legal Structure in Gaza." In *A Palestinian Agenda for the West Bank and Gaza*, edited by E.A. Nakhleh, 102–106. Washington, DC: American Enterprise Institute, 1980.

Khulusi, Mohammed Ali. *Economic Development in the Gaza Strip "Palestine" 1948–1962*. Cairo: The United Commercial Printhouse, 1967.

Kimmerling, Baruch. *Zionism and Economy*. Cambridge, MA: Schenkman Publishing Co., Inc., 1983.

Kindleberger, Charles P. *Economic Development*. Second edition. New York: McGraw Hill, 1965.

Kleiman, Ephraim. "The Economic Interdependence of the West Bank, the Gaza Strip and Israel." Paper presented at the University of Nijmegen, Nijmegen, The Netherlands, April 1990.

Klijn, Jacqueline. "European Economic Policy toward Israel and the Occupied Territories." Paper presented at the University of Nijmegen, Nijmegen, The Netherlands, 18–21 April 1990.

Kubursi, Atif. "An Economic Assessment of Total Palestinian Losses." In *Palestinian Rights And Losses In 1948: A Comprehensive Study*, edited by S. Hadawi. London: Saqi, 1988.

———. "The Economic Benefits of Palestinian Statehood." *Middle East Focus* 9, no.1 (Summer/Fall 1986): 27–29.

———. "Jobs, Education and Development: The Case of the West Bank." In *The Palestinian Economy: Studies in Development under Prolonged Occupation*, edited by George T. Abed, 223–43. London: Routledge, 1988.

Kuhn, Thomas S. *The Structure of Scientific Revolutions*. Second edition. Chicago: University of Chicago Press, 1970.

Kuroda, Yasumasa, and Alice K. Kuroda. "Socialization of Freedom Fighters: The Palestinian Experience." In *Settler Regimes in Africa and the Arab World: The Illusion of Endurance*, edited by I. a. A.-L. Abu-Lughod Baha, 147–61. Wilmete, IL: Medina University Press International, 1974.

Laski, Harold J. "Palestine: The Economic Aspect." In *Palestine's Economic Future*, edited by J.B. Hobman, 34–42. London: Percy Lund, Humphries and Co. Ltd., 1946.

Laufer, Leopold Yehuda. "U.S. Aid to the West Bank and Gaza: Policy Dilemmas." In *Dynamics of Dependence: U.S.–Israeli Relations*, edited by G. Sheffer, 165–200. Boulder, CO: Westview Press, 1987.

Lavine, Avraham. *Society of Change, Judaea, Samaria, Gaza Sinai 1967–1973*. Jerusalem: Ministry of Social Welfare, 1974.

Legum, Colin. *Middle East Contemporary Survey*. Selected years. New York: Holmes and Meier, 1980, 1982.

Lerner, Abba, and Haim Ben Shahar. *The Economics of Efficiency and Growth: Lessons from Israel and the West Bank*. Cambridge, MA: Ballinger Publishing Co., 1975.

Lesch, Ann Mosley. *Arab Politics in Palestine 1917–1939: The Frustration of a Nationalist Movement*. Ithaca, NY: Cornell University Press, 1979.

———. "Gaza: Forgotten Corner of Palestine." *Journal of Palestine Studies* 15, no.1 (Autumn 1985): 43–59.

———. *The Gaza Strip: Heading Towards a Dead End*. Universities Field Staff International (UFSI) Reports, 1984.

———. *Perceptions of the Palestinians in the West Bank and Gaza Strip*. Washington, DC: Middle East Institute, 1983.

Levi, Sasson. "Local Government in the Administered Territories." In *Judea, Samaria and Gaza: Views on the Present and Future*, edited by D.J. Elazar, 103–122. Washington, DC: American Enterprise Institute, 1982.

Lewis, Bernard. *The Arabs in History*. New York: Harper and Row, 1966.

Lewis, W. Arthur. *The Theory of Economic Growth*. Homewood, IL: Richard D. Irwin, 1965.

Lock, Major H.O. *The Conquerers of Palestine through Forty Centuries*. London: Robert Scott, 1920.

Lockard, Joe. "U.S. Aid: Subsidizing Collective Punishment." *American–Arab Affairs*, no.29 (Summer 1989): 65–74.

Loftus, P.J. *National Income of Palestine 1944*. Palestine: The Government Printer, 1945.

Lowdermilk, Walter C. *Palestine: Land of Promise*. New York: Harper Press, 1944.

Luxembourg, Rosa. *The Accumulation of Capital*. New York: Monthly Review Press, 1968.

MacDonald, Robert W. *The League of Arab States: A Study in the Dynamics of Regional Organization*. Princeton, NJ: Princeton University Press, 1965.

Mandel, Ernest. *Marxist Economic Theory*. New York: Monthly Review Press, 1962.

Mandell, Joan. "Gaza: Israel's Soweto." *MERIP Reports* (October–December 1985): 7–19.

Mansfield, Peter. *The Ottoman Empire and its Successors.* London: MacMillan Ltd., 1973.

Maoz, Moshe. *Palestinian Leadership on the West Bank: the Changing Role of the Arab Mayors under Jordan and Israel.* London: Frank Cass, 1984.

———. *Studies on Palestine During the Ottoman Period.* Jerusalem: Magnes Press, Hebrew University, 1975.

Marlowe, John. *Arab Nationalism and British Imperialism: A Study in Power Politics.* New York: Praeger, 1961.

Marlowe, J.A. *A History of Modern Egypt and Anglo–Egyptian Relations 1800–1953.* New York: Praeger, 1954.

Marx, Emanuel. "Changes in Arab Refugee Camps." *The Jerusalem Quarterly* 8 (Summer 1978): 43–52.

Maspero, Gaston. *The Struggle of Nations: Egypt, Syria and Assyria.* London: Society for Promoting Christian Knowledge, 1896.

Masri, Munther W. *The Gaza Technical Center.* Washington, DC: American Near East Refugee Aid Committee (ANERA), 1988.

Massey, W.T. *How Jerusalem Was Won.* New York: Charles Scribner's Sons, 1920.

Mattar, Philip. "The Mufti of Jerusalem and the Politics of Palestine." *Middle East Journal* 42, no.2 (Spring 1988): 227–40.

———. "Palestinian Trends and the U.S. Peace Initiative." *The World and I* 7, no.4 (April 1992): 485–99.

McGranahan, Donald. "Development Indicators and Development Models." *Journal of Development Studies* 8, no.3 (April 1972): 91–102.

Medebielle, Pierre. *Gaza et son histoire chretienne.* Jerusalem: Imprime du Patriarcat Latin, 1982.

Meron, Raphael. *Economic Development in Judea–Samaria and the Gaza District: Economic Growth and Structural Change 1970–1980.* Jerusalem: Bank of Israel Research Department, 1993.

Metzer, Jacob. "Fiscal Incidence and Resource Transfer Between Jews and Arabs in Mandatory Palestine." *Research in Economic History* 7 (1982): 87–132.

Metzger, Jan, Martin Orth, and Christian Sterzling. *This Land is Our Land: The West Bank under Israeli Occupation.* London: Zed Press, 1980.

Meyer, Martin A. *History of the City of Gaza from Earliest Times to the Present Day.* New York: Columbia University Press, 1907.

Mi'ari, Mahmoud. *Vocational Education in the Occupied Territories.* Bir Zeit, West Bank: Center of Documents and Research, Bir Zeit University, 1988. *Middle East Record.* London: Weidenfeld and Nicolson Ltd., 1960.

Middle East Record. Jerusalem: Israel Program for Scientific Translations, 1961

Middle East Contemporary Survey, 1976–1987.

Miller, Ylana N. *Government and Society in Rural Palestine 1920–1948.* Austin: University of Texas Press, 1985.

Minces, Juliette. *The House of Obedience: Women in Arab Society.* London: Zed Books, 1982.

Monroe, Elizabeth. *Britain's Moment in the Middle East 1914–1971.* Baltimore: Johns Hopkins University Press, 1981.

More, John. *With Allenby's Crusaders.* London: Health Cranton Ltd., 1923.

Morris, Benny. *The Birth of the Palestinian Refugee Problem 1947–1949.* Cambridge: Cambridge University Press, 1987.

―――. *1948 and After: Israel and the Palestinians.* New York: Oxford University Press, 1990.

Myint, H.L.A. *Economic Theory and the Underdeveloped Countries.* Oxford: Oxford University Press, 1971.

Nakhleh, Emile A. *The West Bank and Gaza: Toward the Making of a Palestinian State.* Washington, DC: American Enterprise Institute, 1979.

Nakleh, Khalil. *Indigenous Organizations in Palestine: Towards a Purposeful Societal Development.* Jerusalem: Arab Thought Forum, 1991.

Nammoura, Mahmoud Talab. *Palestinian Municipal Councils Under Israeli Occupation: 1967–1989.* Hebron, West Bank: American Near East Refugee Aid (ANERA), 1989.

Nathan, Robert R., Oscar Gass, and Daniel Creamer. *Palestine: Problem and Promise—An Economic Study.* Washington, DC: Public Affairs Press, 1946.

Nerfin, Marc. *Another Development: Approaches and Strategies.* Uppsala: The Dag

Hammarskjold Foundation, 1977.

Neu, Thomas Joseph. "Employment, Labor Migration and Economic Development in the Gaza Strip: A Case Study of Rafah." Ph.D diss., Fletcher School of Law and Diplomacy, Tufts University, 1987.

Nijim, Bashir K. *Toward the De-Arabization of Palestine/Israel 1945–1977*. Dubuque, Iowa: Kendal/Hunt, 1984.

Nijim, Monthor. *Assessment of the Availability and Demand for Credit Financing by the Palestinian Industrial Sector*. Vienna: United Nations Industrial Development Organization (UNIDO), 1989.

Nisan, Mordechai. *Israel and the Territories: A Study in Control 1967–77*. Ramat Gan, Israel: Turtledove Publishing, 1978.

Nixon, Anne Elizabeth. *The Status of Palestinian Children during the Uprising in the Occupied Territories*. Jerusalem: Radda Barnen/Swedish Save the Children, 1990.

Obeidat, Adnan. *Cooperatives in the Occupied West Bank of Jordan*. Washington, DC: American Near East Refugee Aid (ANERA), 1982.

Okasha, Mahmoud. *Population and Labour Force in the Gaza Strip: Statistical Survey*. Gaza City: Arab Thought Forum, 1990.

Orni, Efraim and Elisha Efrat. *Geography of Israel*. Fourth edition. Jerusalem: Israel Universities Press, 1980.

Owen, Roger. "Economic Development in Mandatory Palestine: 1918–1948." In *The Palestinian Economy: Studies in Development under Prolonged Occupation*, edited by George T. Abed. London: Routledge, 1988.

———. "Introduction." In *Studies in the Economic and Social History of Palestine in the Nineteenth and Twentieth Centuries*, edited by Roger Owen. Carbondale, IL: Southern Illinois University, 1982.

———. *The Middle East in the World Economy 1800–1914*. New York: Methuen, 1981.

Owen, Roger, and Bob Sutcliffe. *Studies in the Theory of Imperialism*. London: Longman, 1972.

Padilla, Carlos. "Report on Palestine Resistance." *Arab Palestinian Resistance* 2, no.4 (January 1970): 29–40.

Paige, Jeffrey. *Agrarian Revolution: Social Movements and Export Agriculture in the Underdeveloped World*. New York: Free Press, 1975.

The Palestine Economist, Annual—1948: A Review of Palestine's *Economy*. Jerusalem: Azriel Printing Works, 1948.

Palma, Gabriel. "Dependency: a formal theory of underdevelopment, or a methodology for the analysis of concrete situations of underdevelopment?" *World Development* 6 (1978): 881–924.

Peretz, Don. "Israel's Administration and Arab Refugees." *Foreign Affairs* 46, no.2 (January 1968): 336–46.

Petrie, Flinders. *Ancient Gaza*. London: British School of Archeology in Egypt, 1931.

Pinner, Walter. *How Many Arab Refugees? A Critical Study of UNRWA's Statistics and Reports*. London: Macgibbon & Kee, 1959.

Plascov, Avi. *A Palestinian State? Examining the Alternatives, Adelphi Papers #163*. London: Institute of Strategic Studies, 1981.

Pollock, Alex. "Society and Change in the Northern Jordan Valley." In *The Palestinian Economy—Studies in Development under Prolonged Occupation*, edited by George T. Abed, 245–258. London: Routledge, 1988.

Ponko Jr., Vincent. *Britain in the Middle East 1921–56: An Annotated Bibliography*. New York: Garland, 1990.

Porath, Yehoshua. *The Palestinian Arab National Movement: From Riots to Rebellion 1929–1939*. London: Frank Cass, 1977.

Prawer, Joshua. *The Latin Kingdom of Jerusalem: European Colonialism in the Middle Ages*. London: Weidenfeld and Nicolson, 1972.

Prescott, H.F.M. *Once to Sinai*. New York: Macmillan, 1958.

al-Qeeq, Hasan. *Vocational Education in the Occupied Territories*. Jerusalem: Arab Thought Forum, 1988.

Quandt, William B. 1988. "Introduction." In *The Middle East: Ten Years After Camp David*, edited by William B. Quandt. Washington, DC: The Brookings Institution, 1988.

Rabinow, Paul. *Reflections on Fieldwork in Morocco*. Berkeley, CA: University of California Press, 1977.

Raphaeli, Nimrod. "Gaza Under Four Administrations." *Public Administration in Israel and Abroad 1968* 9 (1969).

―――. "Military Government in The Occupied Territories: An Israeli View." *Middle East Journal* 23, no.2 (Spring 1969): 177–90.

————. "Problems of Military Administration in the Controlled Territories." *Public Administration in Israel and Abroad 1967* 8 (1968): 48–51.

Rappaport, Uriel. "Gaza and Ascalon in the Persian and Hellenistic Periods in Relation to their Coins." *Israel Exploration Journal* 20 (1970): 75–80.

Reifenberg, Adolf. *Report of an Expedition to Southern Palestine.* Jerusalem: L. Picard, 1926.

Rekhess, Elie. "The Employment of Arab Laborers from the Administered Areas." *Israel Yearbook on Human Rights* 5 (1975): 389–411.

"Republican Decree Announcing Constitutional System of Gaza Sector, arch 9, 1962." *Middle East Journal* 17, nos.1&2 (Winter and Spring 1963): 156–61.

Richards, Alan, and John Waterbury. *A Political Economy of the Middle East: State, Class, and Economic Development.* Boulder, CO: Westview Press, 1990.

Richardson, John P. "Tug-of-War: American Voluntary Organizations in the West Bank." *Journal of Palestine Studies* 14, no.2 (Winter 1985): 137–148.

Robinson, Edward. *Biblical Researches in Palestine, Mount Sinai and Arabia Petraea.* New York: Arno Press, 1977.

Robinson, Gregory. *Survey of Industries and of Assistance Available to Industries on the West Bank and in the Gaza Strip (First Draft).* United States Agency for International Development (USAID), 1988.

Rockwell, Susan. "Palestinian Women Workers in the Israeli–Occupied Gaza Strip." *Journal of Palestine Studies* 14, no.2 (Winter 1985): 119–30.

Rodney, Walter. *How Europe Underdeveloped Africa.* London: Bogle-L'Ouverture Publishers, 1972.

Rokach, Livia. *Israel's Sacred Terrorism: A Study Based on Moshe Sharett's Personal Diary and Other Documents.* Belmont, MA: Association of Arab–American University Graduates (AAUG), 1980.

Rolef, Susan H. *Political Dictionary of the State of Israel.* New York: Macmillan Publishing Co., 1987.

Rosenfeld, Henry. "From Peasantry to Wage Labor and Residual Peasantry: The Transformation of an Arab Village." In *Process and Pattern in Culture: Essays in Honor of Julian H. Steward,* edited by R.A. Manners, 211–34. Chicago: Aldine Publishing Co., 1964.

Rostovtzeff, M. *The Social and Economic History of the Hellenistic World.* Oxford: Clarendon, 1953.

Rostow, W.W. *The Stages of Economic Growth: A Non-Communist Manifesto.* Cambridge: Cambridge University Press, 1960.

Roxborough, Ian. *Theories of Underdevelopment.* London: Macmillan, 1979.

Roy, Sara. "Development Under Occupation?: The Political Economy of U.S. Aid to the West Bank and Gaza Strip." *Arab Studies Quarterly* 13, nos.3&4 (Summer and Fall 1991): 65–89.

———. "From Hardship to Hunger: The Economic Impact of the Intifada on the Gaza Strip." *American–Arab Affairs*, no.34 (Fall 1990): 1–24.

———. "Gaza: New Dynamics of Civic Disintegration." *Journal of Palestine Studies* 22, no.4 (Summer 1993): 20–31.

———. "The Gaza Strip: A Case of Economic De-Development." *Journal of Palestine Studies* 17, no.1 (Autumn 1987): 56–88.

———. "The Gaza Strip: Critical Effects of the Occupation." In *Occupation: Israel Over Palestine*, edited by N. Aruri. Belmont, MA: Association of Arab–American University Graduates (AAUG), 1989.

———. *The Gaza Strip Survey.* Boulder, CO: Westview Press, 1986.

———. *The Palestinian Industrial Sector: Structure, Institutional Framework and Future Requirements.* Vienna: United Nations Industrial Development Organization (UNIDO), 1989.

———. "The Political Economy of Despair: Changing Political and Economic Realities in the Gaza Strip." *Journal of Palestine Studies* 20, no.3 (Spring 1991): 58–69.

———. "Separation or Integration: Closure and the Economic Future of the Gaza Strip Revisited." *Middle East Journal* 48, no.1 (Winter 1994): 11–30.

Ruedy, John. "The Dynamics of Land Alienation." In *The Transformation of Palestine*, edited by I. Abu-Lughod. Evanston, IL: Northwestern University Press, 1971.

Ryan, Sheila. "Israeli Economic Policy in the Occupied Areas: Foundations of a New Imperialism." *MERIP Reports* 24 (January 1974).

Sadan, Ezra. *Durable Employment for the Refugee–Populated Region of Gaza.* N.p., 1993.

———. *A Policy for Immediate Economic–Industrial Development in the Gaza Strip: A Summary Report.* N.p.: Ben-Ezra Consultants, Ltd., 1991.

Sadler, Peter. *Brief Overview of the Investment Opportunities in the Occupied Territories and Possibilities For Future Development.* Vienna: United Nations Industrial Development Organization (UNIDO), 1989.

Sadler, P.G., U. Kazi, and E. Jabr. *Survey of the Manufacturing Industry in the West Bank and Gaza Strip*. Vienna: United Nations Industrial Development Organization (UNIDO), 1984.

Sagi, Eli, and Yacov Sheinin. *Israel, the West Bank and Gaza: the Case of Economic Cooperation*. Ramat Gan, Israel: Economic Models Ltd., 1989.

Sakkah, Salah S. *Survey of the Infrastructure Needs of the Outlying Communities in the Gaza Strip*. Jerusalem: Save the Children Federation, 1988.

Saleh, Samir Abdullah. *Urgent Priorities for the Development of Physical Infrastructure of the Occupied Palestinian Territory*. Paris: United Nations, 1993.

Salman, Hind Kattan. *Manufacturing in the Bethlehem Area*. Jerusalem: Arab Thought Forum, 1990.

Samara, Adel K. *The Political Economy of the West Bank 1967–1987*. London: Khamsin, 1988.

———. "The Political Economy of the West Bank 1967–1987: From peripheralization to development." In *Palestine: Profile of an Occupation*, edited by Khamsin, 7–31. London: Zed Books, 1989.

Sayigh, Yusif A. "Dispossession and Pauperisation: The Palestinian Economy Under Occupation." In *The Palestinian Economy: Studies in Development under Prolonged Occupation*, edited by George T. Abed, 259–85. London: Routledge, 1988.

———. *Elusive Development: From Dependence to Self-Reliance in the Arab Region*. London: Routledge, 1991.

Schölch, Alexander. "European Penetration and the Economic Development of Palestine 1856–1882." In *Studies in the Economic and Social History of Palestine in the Nineteenth and Twentieth Centuries*, edited by Roger Owen, 10–54. Carbondale, IL: Southern Illinois University, 1982.

Seers, Dudley. *Dependency Theory: A Critical Reassessment*. London: Frances Pinter, 1981.

Segev, Tom. *1949: The First Israelis*. New York: Free Press, 1986.

Semyonov, Moshe, and Noah Lewin-Epstein. *Hewers of Wood and Drawers of Water: Noncitizen Arabs in the Israeli Labour Market*. New York: New York School of Industrial and Labor Relations, Cornell University, 1987.

Shafir, Gershon. *Land, Labour and the Origins of the Israeli–Palestinian Conflict 1882–1914*. Cambridge: Cambridge University Press, 1989.

Shama, Avraham. "Administrative Aspects of Water Planning in Israel." *Public Administration in Israel and Abroad 1968* 9 (1969): 99–107.

Shamgar, Meir. "The Law in the Areas Held by the Israel Defense Forces." *Public Administration in Israel and Abroad 1967* 8 (1968): 40–57.

————. *Military Government in the Territories Administered by Israel 1967–1980: The Legal Aspects.* Jerusalem: Hebrew University, Faculty of Law, Harry Sacher Institute for Leigislature Research and Comparative Law, 1982.

Sharon, Ariel, and David Charnoff. *Warrior: An Autobiography.* NewYork: Simon and Schuster, 1989.

Shehadeh, Raja. *Legal and Institutional Constraints to Industrial Development in the Palestinian Occupied Territories.* Vienna: United Nations Industrial Development Organization (UNIDO), 1989.

————. *Occupier's Law: Israel and the West Bank.* Washington, DC: Institute for Palestine Studies, 1988.

Shiffer, Varda. "The 1949 Israeli Offer to Repatriate 100,000 Palestinian Refugees." *Middle East Focus* 9, no.2 (Fall 1986).

Shlaim, Avi. *Collusion Across the Jordan: King Abdullah, the Zionist Movement, and the Partition of Palestine.* New York: Columbia University Press, 1988.

————. *Conflicting Approaches to Israel's Relations With the Arabs: Ben-Gurion and Sharett, 1953–1956.* Working paper #27. Washington, DC: International Security Studies Program, The Wilson Center, 1981.

————. "The Rise and Fall of the All-Palestine Government in Gaza." *Journal of Palestine Studies* 20, no.1 (Autumn 1990): 37–53.

al-Shuaibi, Issa. "The Development of Palestinian Entity-Consciousness: Part I." *Journal of Palestine Studies* 9, no.1 (Autumn 1979): 67–84.

Smith, George Adam. *The Historical Geography of the Holy Land.* Jerusalem: Ariel Publishing House, 1974.

Stark, K.B. *Gaza und die philistaische Kuste: Eine Monographie.* Jena: Druck und Verlag von Friedrich Mauke, 1852.

Starr, Joyce. *Development Diplomacy: U.S. Economic Assistance to the West Bank and Gaza.* Washington, DC: The Washington Institute for Near East Policy, 1989.

Stein, Kenneth. *The Land Question in Palestine, 1917–1939.* Chapel Hill: University of North Carolina, 1984.

Stephens, Marc. *Taxation in the Occupied West Bank 1967–1989*. Ramallah, West Bank: Al-Haq, 1990.

Stork, Joe. "Water and Israel's Occupation Strategy." *MERIP Reports* 13, no.6 (July-August 1983): 19–24.

Stoyanovsky, J. *The Mandate for Palestine*. New York: Longmans, Green and Co., 1928.

Susser, A. "The Israeli–Administered Territories." In *Middle East Record 1969–1970*, edited by D. Dishon. Jerusalem: Israel Universities Press, 1977.

Sykes, Christopher. *Crossroads to Israel 1917–1948*. Bloomington: Indiana University Press, 1965.

Szereszewski, Robert. *Essays on the Structure of the Jewish Economy in Palestine and Israel*. Jerusalem: Maurice Falk Institute for Economic Research in Israel, 1968.

Szeskin, Arieh. "The Areas Administered by Israel: Their Economy and Foreign Trade." *Journal of World Trade Law* 3, no.5 (1969): 522–52.

Tamari, Salim. "Building Other People's Homes: The Palestinian Peasant's Household and Work in Israel." *Journal of Palestine Studies* 11, no.1 (Autumn 1981): 31–66.

———. "The Dislocation and Reconstitution of a Peasantry: The Social Economy of Agrarian Palestine in the Central Highlands and the Jordan Valley 1960–1980." Ph.D diss., University of Manchester, Manchester, England, 1983.

Tamari, Salim, and Rita Giacaman. *Zbeidat: The Social Impact of Drip Irrigation on a Palestinian Peasant Community in the Jordan Valley*. Bir Zeit, West Bank: Bir Zeit University Documentation and Research Centre, 1980.

Taqqu, Rachelle. "Peasants into Workmen: Internal Labor Migration and the Arab Village Community under the Mandate." In *Palestinian Society and Politics*, edited by J.S. Migdal. Princeton, NJ: Princeton University Press, 1980.

Tessier, Arlette. *Gaza*. Beirut: Research Center, Palestine Liberation Organization, 1971.

Teveth, Shabtai. *Ben-Gurion And The Palestinian Arabs: From Peace To War*. New York: Oxford University Press, 1985.

Thomson, W.M. *The Land and the Book*. London: T. Nelson & Sons, 1872.

Thorton, D.S. "Agriculture in Economic Development." *Journal of Agricultural Economics* 24, no.2 (1973): 225–87.

Tomeh, George J. "Legal Status of Arab Refugees." *Law and Contemporary Problems* 33 (Winter 1968): 110–24.

———. *United Nations Resolutions On Palestine And The Arab–Israeli Conflict 1947–1974*. Beirut: Institute for Palestine Studies, 1975.

Toynbee, Arnold. "Blood on All Hands." *Arab Palestinian Resistance* 2, no.5 (February 1970): 14–20.

Troen, Selwy Ilan, and Moshe Shemesh. *The Suez-Sinai Crisis 1956: Retrospective and Reappraisal*. New York: Columbia University Press, 1990.

Tuma, Elias, and Haim Darin-Drabkin. *The Economic Case for Palestine*. London: Croom-Helm, 1978.

Turki, Fawaz. *Soul in Exile: Lives of a Palestinian Revolutionary*. New York: Monthly Review Press, 1988.

Van Arkadie, Brian. *Benefits and Burdens: A Report on the West Bank and Gaza Strip Economies Since 1967*. New York: Carnegie Endowment for International Peace, 1977.

Vandergeest, Peter, and Frederick H. Buttel. "Marx, Weber, and Development Sociology: Beyond the Impasse." *World Development* 16, no.6 (1988): 683–95.

Volney, Constantin Francois. *Voyage en Egypt and en Syrie Pendent Les Annees 1783, 1784 & 1785, Tome Premier et Tome Second*. Paris: Desenne-Librairie au Palais Royal, 1787.

Ward, Richard. "The Economics of a Palestinian Entity. In *A Palestinian Entity*, edited by D. Peretz, E. Wilson, and R. Ward. Washington, DC: Middle East Institute, 1970.

Ward, Richard J., Don Peretz, and Evan Wilson. *The Palestine State: A Rational Approach*. Port Washington, NY: Kennikat Press, 1977.

Warren, Bill. *Imperialism: Pioneer of Capitalism*. London: Verso, 1980.

Warriner, Doreen. *Land Reform and Development in the Middle East: A Study of Egypt, Syria and Iraq*. London: Royal Institute of International Affairs, 1957.

———. "Land Tenure Problems in the Fertile Crescent." In *The Economic History of the Middle East 1800–1914: A Book of Readings*, edited by Charles Issawi, 71–78. Chicago: University of Chicago, 1966.

Water Planning in Israel, Ltd. *Closed Water System in the Gaza Strip: Interim Report No. 2*. Tel Aviv: Tahal, May 1987.

———. *Closed Water System in Gaza Strip Intermediate Stage (1990)*. Tel Aviv: Tahal, June 1987.

Wavell, Archibald P. *The Palestine Campaigns*. London: Constable and Co., 1929.

Wechsler, Marcello. "The Connection between the Question of Peace and the Question of Orientalism in Israel." In *Walking The Red Line: Israelis in Search of Justice for Palestine*, edited by D. Hurwitz, 56–65. Philadelphia: New Society Publishers, 1992.

Weigert, Gideon. "Gaza Farmers Look Forward." *Bulletin of the Jerusalem Chamber of Commerce* (April 1977): 33–36.

———. *Life Under Occupation*. Jerusalem: Jerusalem Post Press, 1971.

Weinstock, Nathan. "The Impact of Zionist Colonization on Palestinian Arab Society before 1948." *Journal of Palestine Studies* 2, no.2 (Winter 1973): 49–63.

Weiss, Dieter. *Industrial Development for Palestine—A Conceptual Framework with Special Reference to the Size Constraints*. Vienna: United Nations Industrial Development Organization (UNIDO), October 1989.

Wellesley, William Robert [Earl Peel]. *Palestine Royal Commission Report, Cmd. 5479*. London: His Majesty's Stationery Office, 1937.

Wilmington, Martin W. *The Middle East Supply Centre*. New York: State University of New York Press, 1971.

Wilson Harris, William. *Taking Root: Israeli Settlement in the West Bank, the Golan and Gaza–Sinai 1967–1980*. New York: Research Studies Press, 1980.

Wilson, Rodney. "The International Economic Relations of the Palestinian Economy." Paper presented at the University of Nijmegen, Nijmegen, The Netherlands, 18–20 April 1990.

———. "The Palestinian Problem." In *Economic Perspectives on Key Issues*, edited by P. Johnson and B. Thomas, 19–35. Deddington, Oxford: Philip Allan, 1985.

Wolpe, Harold. "The Theory of Internal Colonialism: The South African Case." In *Beyond the Sociology of Development: Economy and Society in Latin America and Africa*, edited by I. Oxaal, Tony Barnett, and David Booth, 229–52. London: Routledge and Kegan Paul, 1975.

The Workers' Hotline for the Protection of Workers' Rights, November 1991.

The World Bank. *World Development Report 1990*. New York: Oxford University Press, 1990.

"World Documents: Israeli–Egyptian Armistice: Text of Agreement." *Current History* 16, (April 1949): 232–36.

Zakai, Dan. *Economic Development in Judea–Samaria and the Gaza District 1983–84*. Jerusalem: Research Department, Bank of Israel, July 1986.

————. *Economic Development in Judea–Samaria and the Gaza District 1985–86.* Jerusalem: Research Department, Bank of Israel, December 1988.

Zeev, H., M. Gihon, and Z. Levkowich. *The Gaza Strip: Background Paper.* Jerusalem: Carta, 1974.

Zureik, Elia. "The Economics of Dispossession: The Palestinians." *Third World Quarterly* 5, no.4 (October 1983): 775–90.

————. *The Palestinians in Israel: A Study in Internal Colonialism.* London: Routledge & Kegan Paul, 1979.

Abasan, 49, 76–77, 166, 200 n12, 201 n14

Abasan el-Kabira, 16, 172

Abasan el-Saghira, 16, 172

Abd al-Nasir, Gamal, 69, 72

Abd al-Shafi, Haidar, 72, 287 n13

Abu Daher bedouin, 19

Abu Ghazaleh, Hatem, 283

Abu Hajaj bedouin, 19

Abu Middain, 19, 49, 62 n82, 76–77, 200 n12

Abu Rahme, Fayez, 109

Acre, 14

Agrexco, 329

Agriculture, 18, 36–37, 44, 48, 78, 82, 86–88, 89–91, 143, 166–67, 213–15, 219–34; citrus

production, 47, 71, 86–87, 89, 146, 163, 166–67, 220, 221, 225, 228, 229–31, 232, 233, 234, 295, 303–304, 312–13, 316–17; crop prices, 312–14, 316–17; cultivated land, 86–87, 223–24, 230–31; exports, 31, 71, 87, 143, 146, 221, 232–33, 245, 314; productivity, 36, 43, 47, 223, 224–30, 233–34, 303–304, 312, 329; supports, 232, 257 n74, 329; water and irrigation, 61 n72, 86, 143, 163, 165–67, 221, 223, 225, 229–30, 304

Agriculture Department of the Civil Administration, 224, 230

El-Alami, Ragheb, 105, 148

Algeria, 124

All-Palestine Government, 3, 67

Allenby Bridge, 316

Allon Plan, 103–104, 111 n3

Allon, Yigal, 149

American Friends Service Committee, 65, 79

American Near East Refugee Aid (ANERA), 280

Amman, 24, 72, 84

Apter, David, 127

Arab Development and Credit Company (ADCC), 275, 276–77

Arab Higher Committee, 34

Arab League, 67, 72

Arab Revolt of 1936–39, 33, 42–43

Arab riot of 1929, 44

Arab Socialist Union, 72

Arab summits, 72, 151

Arafat, Yasir, 294

Ard el-Ishra, 45

al-Arif, Arif, 48

el-Arish, 105, 154 n6, 173

"Armed struggle", 104, 106

Asad, Talal, 39

Ashdod, 233

Ashkelon, 65

Asia, 244

Association of Engineers (AE), 22, 272–73

Associations, 272–73

Assyrians, 14

Avodah ivrit, 41

Awartani, Hisham, 225

al-Azhar University, 280

B'tselem, 301

Babylonians, 14

Baghdad, 72. *See also* Iraq

Balfour, Arthur James, 33

Balfour Declaration, 33, 35, 70, 124

BaMahane, 140

Bani Suheila, 16, 49, 76–77, 172, 200 n12

Bank of Israel, 90, 143, 158 n59, 222, 304

Bank of Palestine, 107, 274

Banks, 268, 274–77, 303

Baram, Moshe, 214

Baron, Mordechai, 198, 206 n97

Barqa, 45

Basel, Switzerland, 33

Batani, 45

Beach camp, 16, 164, 172

Bedouin, 19-20, 78

Beer Tuvya, 45

Beersheba, 62 n82

Beersheba subdistrict, 45, 47, 75, 76–77

Begin, Menachem, 108, 109

Beirut, 47

Beit Hanoun, 16, 45, 49, 76–77, 163, 164, 172

Beit Jirja, 45
Beit Lahiya, 16, 49, 76–77, 163, 166, 172, 188, 201 n14, 271
Ben-Aharon, Yitzhak, 147
Ben-Gurion, David, 42, 67, 69–70
Benvenisti, Meron, 137, 141–42, 163, 175, 195, 234, 242
Bernadotte, Count Folke, 66
Bethlehem, 34
Bi'lin, 45
Black September, 107
Boers, 124
Britain. *See* Great Britain
British Mandate, 32–34, 46, 52, 73–74, 78, 110, 149, 325; economic policies during, 31–55, 216; political policies during, 136, 175, 268–69
el-Bureij camp, 16–17, 54, 69, 164, 166, 170, 172, 180, 200 n12, 201 n14
Bureir, 45

Cabinet Committee on the Territories, 142, 144
Cairo-Amman Bank, 274
Camp David Accords, 107–108, 176, 294
Central Bureau of Statistics, 9, 235–36
Chambers of Commerce, 272
China, 178
Christians, 15
Citrus Marketing Board, 232–33
Civil Administration, 109, 161, 164, 189, 190, 224, 251, 265, 268, 269, 270, 317; Agriculture Department of, 224, 230
Clapp Commission, 68, 79–80
Coastal Plain, 14, 34
College of Science and Technology, 280
Committee for Settlement of the Gaza Strip, 106
Communists, 21, 69
Construction, 18, 38, 83, 88, 214, 248, 270, 271
Crusaders, 14, 16
Cuba, 233
Culture, as deinstitutionalization force, 283–85
Curfews, 298–99

Damascus, 15

Daraj, 181
Dayan, Moshe, 69, 103, 106, 144, 145, 147–48, 149, 185, 293
de Boisanger, Claude, 66
De-development, 4–5, 110, 117, 128–32, 135, 153, 161, 198–99, 209, 243, 246, 249, 251, 267, 274, 286, 306, 327, 330–332
Declaration of Principles, 8, 22, 327
Deinstitutionalization, 131, 265–86
Deir el-Balah, 15, 16, 49, 76–77, 105, 148, 163, 172, 179, 180, 187, 268–69
Deir Suneid, 45
Democratic Front for the Liberation of Palestine (DFLP), 21
Demography, 15–17, 36, 49, 75–76, 86, 139, 154 n11, 175, 177–79, 181–82, 210–11
Department of Public Works, 37
Dependency theory, 119, 123–25
Development, 137; defined, 4; Jewish development in Palestine, 32; theories of, 117–32
Dimra, 62 n82, 76–77
Directly productive investment (DPI), 250
Dorot, 45
Dutch Calvinists, 124

East Bank, 278
East Jerusalem, 106, 109, 150, 276, 314. *See also* Jerusalem
Eban, Abba, 149
Economic Development Group (EDG), 275–77
Educational institutions, 277–81
Egypt, 14, 15, 24, 46, 47, 67, 117, 120, 173, 183; and Camp David, 107–108, 294; economic policies in Gaza Strip, 66, 73–91, 120, 162; military administration of Gaza Strip, 3, 13, 14, 65–92, 109–10; political policies in Gaza Strip, 24, 72, 165, 168, 179, 277
Egyptian-Israeli General Armistice Agreement, 65, 326
Egyptian Law No. 255, 72
Emergency Law of 1945, 175
Emir Abdullah, 33–34
Employment Service, 195

Eretz, 176

Erez, checkpoint, 105, 271, 300, 305, 316; industrial zone, 142–43

Eshkol, Levi, 103

Europe, 169, 243, 280, 329, 330, 331; interest in Palestine, 31; market for Gaza exports, 89, 146, 232–33, 244, 312

European Economic Community (EEC), 6, 242, 276, 281

Expulsions of Palestinians, 65–66, 104, 105

al-Faluja, 65

Fateh, 21

Federation of the Israeli Chambers of Commerce, 328

FIDA. *See* People's Democratic Union

Finance and credit institutions, 268, 274–77, 303

Flapan, Simha, 53

Foreign assistance, 281–83

France, 70, 124

Galilee, 34, 44, 61 n70

"Galili Document", 146

Galili, Israel, 106, 149–50

Galnoor, Itzhak, 166, 174

Gan Yavne, 45

Gat, 45

Gaza campaign of 1956, 325

Gaza City, 14, 76–77, 105, 148, 188, 189, 269, 274; demography, 15–16, 76; industry in, 235, 237; municipal council of, 268–69; water in, 163–64, 166, 168–69, 172

Gaza District, 34, 44–46, 75

"Gaza First", 108, 109

Gaza Islamic University, 280

Gaza Plan (1949) 67–68, 103, 161–62, 166, 170, 179, 181, 182, 186–88, 192, 235, 270, 278–79, 325

Gaza Strip, 3, 7, 9, 13–14, 19–26, 125, 272, agriculture, 18, 31, 36–37, 43–44, 47–48, 71, 78, 82, 86–91, 143, 146, 163, 165–67, 213–15, 219–34; 245, 295, 303–304, 312–14, 316–17, 329; budget, 190–91, 193–94, 196–97, 257 n73, 269; construction, 18, 38, 83, 88, 214,

248, 270, 271; demography, 15–17, 36, 49, 75–76, 86, 139, 154 n11, 175, 177–79, 181–82, 210–11; Egyptian administration of, 3, 13, 14, 24, 65–92, 109–10, 162, 165, 168, 179, 277; foreign assistance, 281–83; geography, 75–77; housing and resettlement, 181–88; income, 43, 60 n53, 81, 83, 192; industry, 18, 31, 39–40, 71, 83, 88–91, 142–43, 213–15, 234–43, 248, 269, 295, 304; integration and externalization, 209–52; Israeli policies in, 13, 23, 66, 71, 103–10, 118, 135–50, 161–99, 192, 195, 224, 231, 267–81, 298–99, 302, 305, 317–18, 327–31; labor, 37, 44, 139, 141, 143–45, 156 n41, 209–19, 235, 241, 296, 311–12; Palestinian policies in, 51–55, 150–52, 330–32; public finance, 189–98; resistance in, 104–106, 107, 109, 113, n30, 127–28; resources, 247–52; settlements, 17, 42, 105, 106, 150, 173, 174, 175–81, 187, 222, 241, 270; sewage system, 163–66, 188, 269, 270; social structure, 19–22, 120–21; taxation, 38–40, 192, 195, 231–32, 240–41, 244, 259 n105, 271, 299–302; trade, 31, 71, 82, 87, 90, 143, 146, 221, 232–33, 240, 242, 243–52, 304, 312, 314

Gaza subdistrict, 45, 46–48, 75, 76–77

Gaza town, 49

Gaza Weaver's Union, 83

Gaza-Jericho Agreement, 4, 7, 22, 26, 110, 123, 137, 162, 173, 181, 234, 240, 267, 268, 295, 318, 326–32

Gazit, Shlomo, 140, 145

General Federation of Trade Unions, 72

General Principles of a Fundamental Law, 72–73

Geneva Convention, 175

Gillerman, Danny, 328

Golan Heights, 109

"Good Gazan" sticker, 302

Great Britain, 70, as colonial power, 124; as invader of Gaza Strip, 14, 46; military bases in Gaza Strip, 54. *See also* British Mandate

Greek Orthodox, 15

Green line, 147, 244, 304, 328

Gross Domestic Product (GDP), 18, 83, 86, 88, 217, 223, 234, 236, 237, 238, 245, 247–52, 305, 311, 313

Gross National Disposable Income (GNDI), 251

Gross National Product (GNP), 18, 88, 91, 130, 147, 157 n58, 217, 219, 223, 247–52, 297, 305, 311, 313, 315

Gulf of Aqaba, 73

Gulf states, 74, 84, 233, 244, 251; remittances from, 297, 303, 313

Gulf war, 295, 296, 299, 305, 306, 311–14, 318, 327

Gur, Mordechai, 140

Gush Katif, 173

Haaretz, 109

Haifa, 34, 44, 47, 50, 61 n70; building permits in, 62 n87

Hakarat al-Muqawamah al-Islamiya. See Hamas

Halhoul, 108

al-Hallees, Walid, 333

Hamama, 45

Hamas, 21–22

Hanajreh bedouin, 19

Hebron, 108

Hiltermann, Joost, 265, 266

Hirbiya, 45

Histradrut, 147

Hitler, Adolf, 33

Hong Kong, 178

Huj, 45

ID cards, 298–99, 305, 317, 318

IDF. *See* Israeli Defense Forces

Immigration, 33–34, 38, 51, 74, 79. *See also* Settlements

India, 87, 178

Industry, 31, 71, 83, 89, 234–43, 270; imports, 90; labor, 91, 143, 213–15, 235; output, 89, 304; productivity, 142–43, 236, 239–42; service sector, 18, 88, 215, 248, 269, 295, 304; taxation, 39–40

Infant mortality rate, 49–50

Infiltrations, Palestinian refugees into Israel, 69

Institutions, mainstream, 266; private, 273–81; public, 268–73

Intifada, 3, 9, 20, 110, 126, 152, 176, 192, 228, 250, 272–73, 283, 293–306, 311; economic developments in, 295–305; political developments in, 293–95

Iran, 233

Iraq, 35, 48, 74, 80, 295, 296, 311, 312, 313. *See also* Gulf war

'Iraq el-Manshiya, 45

Isdud, 45

Islam, 128

Islamic Jihad, 21–22

Islamic movement, 22

Islamic Resistance Movement. *See* Hamas

Israel, 5–7, 71, 224, 232, deinstitutionalization policies, 267–81; economic policies, 103-10, 118, 135–38, 174, 298, 327–30; expropriation and dispossession policies, 161–99; integration policies, 147–50; "iron fist" policy, 108; land policies, 175–81; military orders and activity, 13, 23, 66, 69–70, 108, 165, 267, 268, 331; normalization policies, 140–47; pacification policies, 139; Palestinian employment in, 213–16; responses to March 1993 closure, 317–18; restrictions in Gaza Strip, 298-99, 302, 305; settlements, 17, 42, 105, 106, 150, 173, 174, 175–81, 187, 222, 241, 270; settlers, 17, 23, 124, 165, 167, 172, 181, 271 taxation, 38–40, 192, 195, 231–32, 240–41, 244, 259 n105, 271, 299–302

Israel Marketing Board, 71

Israel Water Law of 1959, 165

Israeli Defense Forces, 104–105, 140, 301, 303

Israeli Foreign Ministry, 66

Israeli Labor Employment offices, 211

al-Ittihad al-Qawmi al-Falastini, 72

Jabalya, 15–16, 17, 49, 76–77, 105, 164, 172, 180, 188, 294; municipality, 317

Jaffa, 34, 47, 50

Jericho, 4, 105

Jerusalem, 34, 50, 72, building permits in,

62 n87; district, 61 n70. *See also* East
    Jerusalem
Jerusalem Post, 293
Jewish immigrants, 33–34, 38, 51, 75, 79
Jewish labor, 41, 144
Jewish National Fund, 40, 44
Jewish National Home, 135
Jewish settlements. *See* Settlements
Jewish settlers. *See* Settlers
Johnson-Crosbie Report, 43
Jordan, 23–25, 80, 104, 105, 107, 120, 142,
    145, 146, 232, 233, 240–41, 244, 245,
    251, 272, 278, 281, 303, 316
Jordanian-Palestinian Joint Committee for
    the Support of the Steadfastness of the
    Palestinian
People in the Occupied Homeland, 151,
    281
June 1967 war, 141, 241, 294

Katif, 176
Kawasme, Fuad, 108
Kefar Bitsaron, 45
Kefar Warburg, 45
Keren hanikuyum, 192
Kfar Daron, 176
Khan Younis, 15–16, 76–77, 105, 148, 163,
    164, 168, 170, 172, 180, 268–69, 274,
    280; building permits in, 62, n87,
    demography, 48–49
Khirbet Ikhza'a, 49, 77
Khuza'a, 16, 49, 62 n82, 76–77
al-Kifah al-musallah. See "Armed
    struggle."
King Abdullah, 25, 67–68
King Hussein, 105, 107, 110, 145
Kuhn, Thomas, 121
Kuwait, 296, 312, 313
Kuza'ah, 172

Labor, 37, 44, 139, 141, 143–45, 156 n41,
    209–19, 235, 241, 296, 311–12
Land, 44–45, 175–81; confiscation, 180;
    use, 149, 161, 177
Laski, Harold J., 53
Latin America, 219
Lausanne, 67–68
Law for the Encouragement of Capital In-

vestments, 142
Law of Closed Areas (1949), 175
Law of Security Areas, 175
Law of Taking Action (1953), 175
League of Nations, 32
Lebanon, 74, 80, 87, 89, 150; PLO defeat
    in, 151
Lebanon war, 109
Legal system, 22
Levies and fines, 302–303
Lewin-Epstein, Noah, 215
Libya, 89
Likud party, 176, 222
Lydda district, 61 n70

el-Maghazi camp, 16–17, 172, 180, 200
    n12
Mahrru' Amer, 200 n12
Majdal, 65, 83
Mamelukes, 14
Mandate. *See* British Mandate
March 1993 closure of Gaza Strip, 314–
    18
Masmiya el-Kabira, 45
al-Masri, Zaafer, 109
Master Plan for the Gaza Strip (1981), 164
al-Mawasi, 167
Mawasi land, 86
Mediterranean Sea, 75
Meir, Golda, 139
Mekorot, 162, 167, 170, 172, 173
Mesopotamia, 15
Meyer, Martin A., 15
Milhelm, Mohammed, 108
Military Order #158, 165
Military Order #194, 268
Military Order #236, 268
Mining, 47
Ministry of Agriculture, 143
Ministry of Defense, 298–99, 301, 328
Ministry of Interior, 302
Ministry of Labour and Social Affairs, 217
Modernization theory, 118–19, 120, 123–
    25
Moneychanging, 275
Morag, 176
Mubarak, Hosni, 109–110
Mufti of Jerusalem, 67

Municipal Corporation Ordinance (1934), 268
Municipal Council, appointment of, 106–107, 109
Municipal councils, 268–72
Muslim Brotherhood, 69

Nablus, 109
Nahal Oz, 105
Najd, 45
National Insurance Institute, 195
"Natural poverty," 5, 8, 55
Nazareth, 106
Nazla, 16, 449, 76–77, 164
Negba, 45
Negev, 14, 34, 67, 68, 174
Netzarim, 176
Netzer Hazani, 176
New York Times, 104
Nile River, 173
Nir 'Am, 45
Nongovernmental organizations (NGOs), 10, 281–82
Nuseirat, 16–17, 49, 54, 62 n82, 76–77, 164, 172, 180, 200 n12; bedouin, 19

October 1973 war, 139, 146, 150
"Open bridges" policy, 145–46, 240, 260 n119
Oslo, agreement, 270; period, 281, 285, 314
Ottoman Empire, 14, 35, 54, 74, 120, 273

Pakistan, 87
Palestine Conciliation Commission, 66
Palestine, economic development of, 6–7
Palestine, importance to British, 36,
Palestine Liberation Army (PLA), 73, 83, 90–91, 104–105, 141
Palestine Liberation Organization (PLO), 6, 21, 104–108, 150, 273, 275, 281, 294, 331; agreements with Israel, 318, 326, 327; defeat in Lebanon, 151; dialogue with United States, 294, 295; economic department, 11 n2; establishment, 72–73; Gulf war and, 313
Palestine National Council, 73
Palestine National Union, 72

Palestine Students Organization, 72
Palestinian National Authority, 277, 330
Palestinian National Covenant, 72
Palestinian refugees. *See* Refugees
Palestinian Women's Union, 72
Pan-Arab movement, 72
Partition, 33, 43, 65
Peel Commission. *See* Royal Peel Commission
People's Democratic Union, 21
People's Party, 21
Peres, Shimon, 110
Persians, 14
Popular Front for the Liberation of Palestine (PFLP), 21
Philistian Plain, 14
Phoenicia, 15
Plain of Esdraelon, 14
Port Said, 89
Potash Company, 41
Private volunteer organizations (PVOs), 10, 273, 281, 301
Professional associations, 272–73
Public finance, 189–98

Qarara, 16
Qastina, 45
Qiryat Gat, 65

Rabin, Yitzak, 195, 198, 206 n97, 222, 298, 314
Rafaeli, Nimrod, 139
Rafah, 15, 16, 49, 54, 76–77, 105, 154 n6, 164, 166, 172, 180, 200 n12, 201 n14, 269–70, 271
Railway lines, 47
Rand Corporation, 148
Red Crescent Society, 287 n13
Refugees, 13, 16, 19, 23–24, 28 n18, 66, 67–69, 73–75, 78–80, 105, 152, 175, 183–84, 185–86
Replogle, Delbert, 65
Rimal, 15
Rishon Le Ziyyon, 295
Romans, 14
Royal Peel Commission, 33–34, 43
Ruhama, 45

Sadan, Ezra, 315, 328–30
Sadan Report, 328–29
Sadat, Anwar, 107
Sahara desert, 170
Sajaia, 181
Samaria district, 61 n70
Sapir, Pinhas, 147–48
Saudi Arabia, 312, 313
Save the Children Federation, 273
Sawafir esh-Shamaliya, 45
Sawafir esh-Sharqiya, 45
Scythians, 14
Semyonov, Moshe, 215
Sephardi, 215
Service sector. *See under* Industry
Settlements, 17, 42, 105, 106, 150, 173, 174, 175–81, 187, 222, 241, 270
Settler colonialism, 124
Settlers, 17, 23, 124, 165, 167, 172, 181, 271
Seven-Up bottling plant, 89
Sewage system, 163–66, 188, 269, 270
Shamir Plan, 295
Shamir, Yitzhak, 294
Sharett, Moshe, 69–70, 94 n16, 95 n20
Sharm el-Sheikh, 71
Sharon, Ariel, 69, 105–106, 108, 185, 293
Sharqi, 45
Shati camp, 15–16, 17, 105, 180
Shawa, Rashad, 29 n27, 106–109, 269
Sheikh Ajlein, 200 n12
Sheikh Radwan housing project, 188
Shiffer, Varda, 94 n16
Shin Bet, 302
Sinai, 70, 71, 103, 106, 154 n6, 173, 176; campaign, 84, 150, 325; desert, 75
Singapore, 89, 178, 232
Social overhead investment (SOI), 250
Society for the Care of the Handicapped, 283
South African Land Act, 124
Soviet Union, 71, 118
Straits of Tiran, 70
Structure of Scientific Revolutions, The, 121
Suez, 78
Suez Canal, 70
Suez war, 70–71

Sumeiri, 19, 49, 62 n82, 76–77
Summei Sumsum, 45
Sumud, 150–51, 153, 297
Sumud maqawim, 151
Sunni Muslims, 15
Syria, 35, 74, 80, 89

Tahal, 164–65, 173
Tamari, Salim, 216
Tarabin bedouin, 19–20
Taxation, 38–40, 192, 195, 231–32, 240–41, 244, 259 n105, 271, 299–302
Tel Aviv, 50, 239, 329; building permits in, 62 n87
Tel et-Turmos, 45
Tel Tsofim, 45
Trade, 31, 71, 82, 87, 90, 143, 146, 221, 232–33, 240, 242, 243–52, 304, 312, 314
Trade unions, 287 n14
Transjordan, 35
Turks, battle with British (1915-1917), 46

Ukraine, 233
Underdevelopment, 4–5, 32, 54, 117–32, 153
Unified National Leadership of the Uprising (UNLU), 297, 298, 311
United Arab Emirates, 312
United Arab Kingdom, 107
United Arab Republic, 72, 85
United Nations, 17, 65, 67, 68, 79, 82, 141, 184, 213, 295; Conference on Trade and Development (UNCTAD), 11 n2, 213; Development Programme, 281; Disaster Relief Project, 79; Emergency Force (UNEF), 71, 73, 90–91; General Assembly, 66, 185–86; Children's Fund (UNICEF), 79; Palestine Conciliation Commission, 66; Relief for Palestine Refugees, 79; Resolution 194, 66; Resolution 242, 103, 294; Special Commission on Palestine (UNSCOP), 34, 41. *See also* United Nations Relief and Works Agency for Palestine Refugees.
United States, 67–68, 71, 79, 169, 178, 243, 281, 294–95, 328, 330–31; State Department, 68

UNCTAD. *See under* United Nations

UNSCOP. *See under* United Nations

United Nations Relief and Works Agency
   for Palestine Refugees (UNRWA), 10,
   70, 77, 80–85, 88, 90, 165, 211, 251,
   313; as employer, 75, 91, 312; educational facilities, 278–79; established,
   79, 80; financial aid, 281–82; public
   works programs, 82–84, 314, 315–16,
   318; refugee camps, 17, 68, 182–86;
   staff, 20; transfer of payments, 81, 83;
   water department, 172

U.S.-PLO dialogue, 294

U.S. Save the Children Federation, 273

USAID, 287 n13

Value Added Tax (VAT), 232, 257 n72, 300,
   302

Vegetable Marketing Board, 233

Via Maris, 14–15, 17

Wadi Gaza, 14, 162, 165

Wages, 38, 84, 217, 315. *See also* Labor

Water, 87, 149, 161–75, 229, 269, 270. *See
   also under* Agriculture

Weber, 128

West Bank, 75, 106–108, 147, 151, 162,
   198, 316; agriculture, 86, 222, 242,
   303–304; budget, 301; compared with
   Gaza Strip, 23–26; curfew in, 312, 314;
   development planning, 123, 124, 277;
   economy, 32, 119, 218, 296–97, 311–
   15; education in, 279, 280; financial
   assistance, 276, 281, 282, 313; industry, 235–37, 242; intifada and, 294–97;
   labor, 144–45, 212, 215; refugees, 67,
   74, 103; trade, 146, 242, 244, 304

White Paper of 1939, 34

Women, 212, 238, 253 n10

World Bank, 198

World War I, 32, 35

World War II, 37, 47, 48, 118

Yasur, 45

Younis, Mameluke governor, 16

Zawaida, 16, 172

Zeitoun, 181

Zionism and Zionists, 35, 41–44, 53, 55,
   100, 117, 124, 130, 144

AGREEMENT ON THE GAZA STRIP
AND THE JERICHO AREA

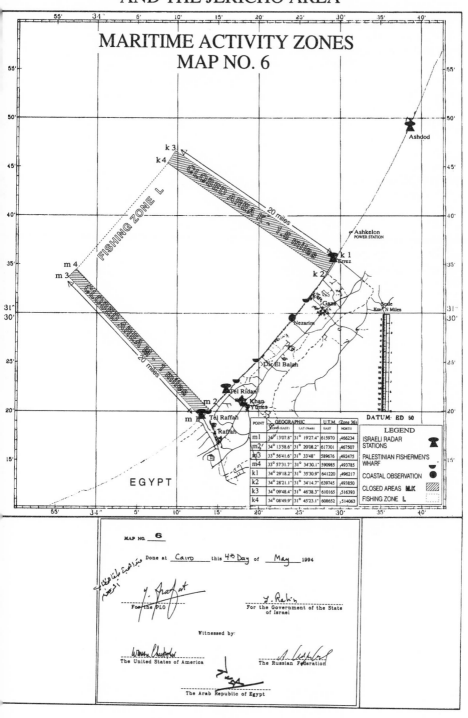

MARITIME ACTIVITY ZONES
MAP NO. 6

POINT	GEOGRAPHIC		U.T.M. (Zone 36)	
	LONG. (EAST)	LAT. (North)	EAST	NORTH
m1	34° 13'07.8"	31° 19'27.4"	615970	,466234
m2	34° 13'58.6"	31° 20'08.2"	617301	,467507
m3	33° 56'41.6"	31° 33'48"	589676	,492475
m4	33° 57'31.7"	31° 34'30.1"	590985	,493785
k1	34° 29'18.2"	31° 35'30.9"	641220	,496217
k2	34° 28'21.1"	31° 34'14.7"	639745	,493850
k3	34° 09'48.4"	31° 46'38.3"	610165	,516393
k4	34° 08'49.9"	31° 45'23.1"	608652	,514063

DATUM· ED 50

LEGEND

- ISRAELI RADAR STATIONS
- PALESTINIAN FISHERMEN'S WHARF
- COASTAL OBSERVATION
- CLOSED AREAS M.K
- FISHING ZONE L

Ashdod

Ashkelon POWER STATION

k1 Erez
k2

Gaza

Nezarim

Diz El Balah

Tel Ridan
Khan Yunes
m2
m1 Tel Raffah
Raffah

CLOSED AREA K. 1.5 miles
20 miles

CLOSED AREA M. 20 miles

FISHING ZONE L

EGYPT

Scale
Km· N Miles

MAP NO. 6

Done at Cairo this 4th Day of May 1994

For the PLO

Y. Rabin
For the Government of the State of Israel

Witnessed by:

The United States of America

The Russian Federation

The Arab Republic of Egypt

E G Y P T

Rafiah

Qatif

Khan Yunis

Kefar

Rafiah Terminal

Kissufim Cr

The Delimiting Line

DONE AT Cairo THIS

OR THE PLA

WITNESS

THE UNITED STATES OF AMERICA

THE ARAB REPUBLIC

Kerem Shalom
Crossing

Sufa Crossing

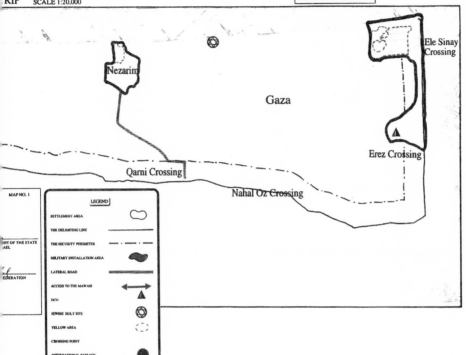

Nezarim

Gaza

Ele Sinay
Crossing

Erez Crossing

Qarni Crossing

Nahal Oz Crossing

MAP NO. 1

NT OF THE STATE
AEL

DERATION

LEGEND

SETTLEMENT AREA

THE DELIMITING LINE

THE SECURITY PERIMETER

MILITARY INSTALLATION AREA

LATERAL ROAD

ACCESS TO THE MAWASI

DCO

JEWISH HOLY SITE

YELLOW AREA

CROSSING POINT

INTERNATIONAL PASSAGE